Networking Lab Practice Kit
For Microsoft® and Cisco® Systems

Networking Lab
Practice Kit

For Microsoft® and Cisco® Systems

John Chirillo

Wiley Computer Publishing

John Wiley & Sons, Inc.

NEW YORK · CHICHESTER · WEINHEIM · BRISBANE · SINGAPORE · TORONTO

Publisher: Robert Ipsen

Editor: Carol A. Long

Assistant Editor: Adaobi Obi

Managing Editor: Micheline Frederick

New Media Editor: Brian Snapp

Text Design & Composition: Thomark Design

Published by John Wiley & Sons, Inc.

Published simultaneously in Canada.

This publication is designed to provide accurate and authoritative information in regard to the subject matter covered. It is sold with the understanding that the publisher is not engaged in professional services. If professional advice or other expert assistance is required, the services of a competent professional person should be sought.

Library of Congress Cataloging-in-Publication Data:

Chirillo, John, 1970–
     Networking lab practice kit / John Chirillo
         p. cm.
     Includes bibliographical references and index.
     ISBN 0-471-05570-0
         1. Computer networks. I. Title.
     TK5105.5. C4825 2002
     004.6–dc21

                                   2001006295

Printed in the United States of America.

10 9 8 7 6 5 4 3 2 1

Contents

Acknowledgments

Foremost I would like to thank my wife, Kristi. Next in line would be my family and friends, for their encouragement and confidence. I'm also grateful to several people at Microsoft and Cisco Systems; and to Scott Blaul for contributing ideas, Cliffton Fischbach, from Thomark Design; David Fugate from Waterside Productions; and Bob Ipsen, Carol Long, Janice Borzendowski, Adaobi Obi, Micheline Frederick, Brian Snapp, and anyone else I forgot to mention from John Wiley & Sons.

Introduction

The *Networking Lab Practice Kit* represents something unique on the technical market: It is the *workbook* for the accompanying CD-ROM. Together, the pair can be regarded as a training tour de force. To quote my editor, Carol Long, "It's like Learning Tree in a book!"

That means by following the *Networking Lab Practice Kit*, you'll cover Windows NT and 2000 Server operating systems, Cisco fundamentals, plus LAN and WAN internetworking—encompassing much of the required MCP, MCSE, CCDA, CCDP, CCNA, and CCNP subject matter. More, you'll also get "real-world" experience using the interactive simulation CD-ROM. Using this training pair, you'll be spared becoming what is known in the field today as a *paper-MCSE* or *newbie-CCNA*. These terms refer to those individuals who study for weeks, pass the exams, and earn the certifications, but regrettably lack the necessary experience to apply their knowledge in the real world.

If you seek this knowledge, and/or need the hands-on experience, look no further. *Networking Lab Practice Kit* addresses all the major topics, most of it partnered by a hand's-on interactive simulation. In this way, your learning experience will be as if you were sitting in front of a server, or directly connected to the console of a Cisco router. Lists of comprehensive exam questions at the end of each chapter facilitate the certification process.

This workbook and CD-ROM set have been designed to reach a wide range of engineering professionals, from the introductory, to the intermediate and advanced. Additionally, the material in this book will be of extreme interest to any consultant and/or Windows, networking and internetworking aficionados. With a better understanding of the topics in this book, all these groups will be better equipped to provide sound advice and services in these areas. Finally, Webmasters, network administrators, chief information officers (CIOs), and IT directors will also find this material easy to navigate and extremely valuable.

Should you require support or product upgrades for the software accompanying this book, please visit http://www.TigerTools.net on the Internet. Should you require basic installation assistance, or if your media is defective, please call Wiley's product support number at (212) 850-6194 weekdays between 9AM and 4PM Eastern Standard Time. Or, contact product support via e-mail at: techhelp@wiley.com. To place additional orders or to request information about other Wiley products, please call (800) 879-4539.

About the Author

Now a renowned superhacker who works on award-winning projects, assisting security managersin a wide variety of venues, John Chirillo began his computer career at 12, when after a one-year self-taught study program in computers, he wrote a game called Dragon's Tomb. Following its publication, thousands of copies were sold to the Color Computer System market. During the next five years, John wrote several other software packages, including The Lost Treasure (a game-writing tutorial), Multimanager (an accounting, inventory, and financial management software suite), Sorcery (an RPG adventure), PC Notes (a GUI used to teach math, from algebra to calculus), Falcon's Quest I and II (a graphical text adventure), and Genius (a complete Windows-based point-and-click operating system), among others.

John went on to become certified in numerous programming languages, including QuickBasic, VB, C++, Pascal, Assembler, and Java. He later developed the PC Optimization Kit (increasing speeds up to 200 percent of standard Intel 486 chips).

John has been equally successful as a student and businessman. He received a scholarship to Benedictine University, and headed two businesses, Software Now and Geniusware. Subsequently, John became a consultant to prestigious companies, specializing in security and analysis. For these companies, he performed security and sniffer analyses, and undertook LAN/WAN design, implementation, and troubleshooting. During this period, John acquired numerous internetworking certifications, among others: Cisco's CCNA, CCDA, CCNP, pending CCIE; Intel's Certified Solutions Consultant; Compaq's ASE Enterprise Storage; and Master UNIX.

Networking Lab Practice Kit
For Microsoft® and Cisco® Systems

How to Use the Networking Lab Practice Kit

The *Networking Lab Practice Kit* was written as a workbook to supplement the interactive CD-ROM. You can use this book simultaneously with the CD simulations, or as a tool for review, by following the figures throughout the text. This "mini" chapter introduces the concepts addressed throughout the book and explains how to use it with the CD-ROM simulations.

Requirements

All you need to fully experience the potential of this kit is a modern Internet Web browser—either Microsoft Internet Explorer or Netscape Communicator will suffice—and at least a screen resolution of 800 × 600 (but 1024 × 768 is better), with at least a 256-color palette.

If you need a current version of one of these Web browsers, you can download it from www.microsoft.com or www.netscape.com. You'll also want to install the current Macromedia Flash plug-in, which is available from www.macromedia.com. Or, for your convenience, go to my Web site, at www.TigerTools.net, to find direct links to these packages and more. This will save you having to fill out many of those annoying registration forms (see Figure 1.1). If you're using a UNIX operating system, the default X-Window settings are typically preconfigured to match these requirements. If you're

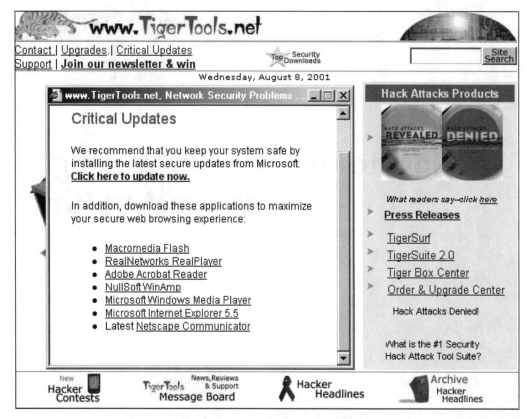

Figure 1.1   Using TigerTools.net to link directly to browser updates and more.

using a Microsoft Windows operating system, you can modify your screen resolution and color palette from Start/Settings/Control Panel/Display, as shown in Figure 1.2.

Be aware that certain system property utilities may vary, but the concept is the same. From the Display Properties utility, advance to the Setting window by clicking the Settings tab, which is displayed in Figure 1.3. To modify your properties, follow these simple steps:

1. In the Screen area, drag the slider to read 800×600 or higher.

2. In the Colors area, select 256 or higher.

3. Click OK. When prompted about resizing your desktop, click OK again.

A higher screen resolution reduces the size of items on your screen and increases the size of your desktop. Your monitor and display adapter determine whether you can change your screen resolution. And note, on some

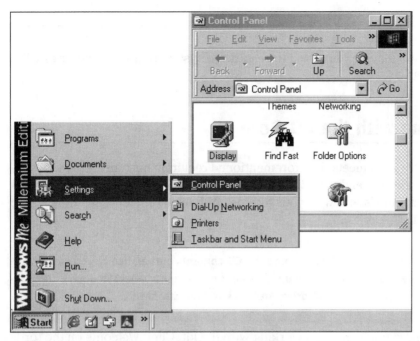

Figure 1.2   Modifying your screen settings in Windows.

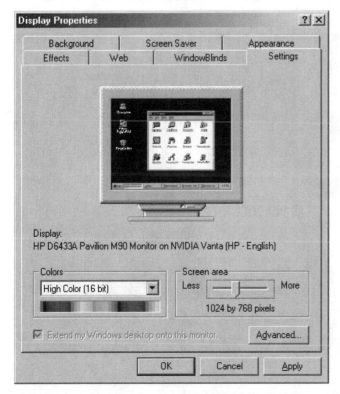

Figure 1.3   Changing the display properties in Settings.

systems, you may be prompted to restart the system before the settings will take effect.

Working with the CD-Rom

Once your system meets the aforementioned requirements, insert the CD-ROM into your system's CD-ROM drive; wait a moment while the interactive CD automatically starts with your Internet Web browser. You'll see the graphic displayed in Figure 1.4.

 If your browser fails to open the CD contents automatically, you can open your browser manually. From the File menu, select to open a URL, browse the CD-ROM drive, and click to load Start.html.

Now you're ready to begin working with the kit. Click Welcome on the top left of the page to advance to the main menu. With the textbook handy, from the main menu, click a topic. Follow along with either the CD or textbook

COMPLETE NETWORKING
LAB PRACTICE KIT
●●●

Figure 1.4   Launching the Networking Lab Practice Kit CD-ROM.

until you reach an interactive lab, at which point you'll continue with the CD simulation.

The following guidelines will help you get the most from the CD:

To reduce scrolling. If you are viewing a topic in a low resolution, consider increasing the resolution to 800 × 600 or larger. Another way to reduce scrolling is to simply disable your browser's toolbar and location displays. A third way is to reduce the size and/or selection of the fonts your browser displays.

To change the background. You can change the background of the interactive CD-ROM screens by clicking your color choice from the top-left menu bar. Upon selecting a new background, the simulator will automatically apply the new color to all screens.

To search for a topic. There is an interactive search engine included on the interactive CD-ROM. Simple click the Search button on the top-left menu bar, and enter a keyword or keywords that pertain to a specific topic. Within seconds the search engine will automatically produce links from which you may navigate directly to a specific topic throughout the entire book.

To use the simulated exercises. Some topics contain exercises that give you the opportunity to practice a procedure in a virtual environment. To

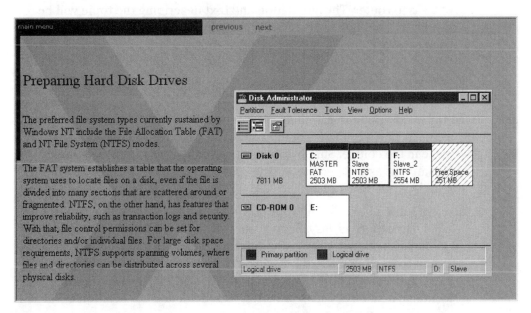

Figure 1.5   Simulations and topic text can be viewed simultaneously.

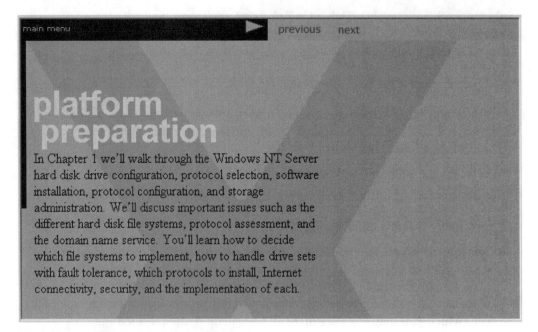

Figure 1.6   Navigating the CD-ROM topics.

take this opportunity, simply work along in the browser window as if you were sitting in front of a server or directly connected to the console of a Cisco router. The simulation and text describing the topic will be displayed simultaneously (see Figure 1.5 for an example). Move from page to page by clicking Next and Previous on your browser's top window or jump to a particular topic (including the interactive chapter exams) by clicking Main Menu found on the top left corner of the window (see Figure 1.6).

To take examinations. Taking the interactive CD-ROM examinations is easy. Each test is a new pop-up application, so you will not lose your place in the course. Simply select the best answer to each question by clicking the associated circle. The score is automatically calculated in real time (see Figure 1.7).

To save your place. Saving your current position in the interactive CD-ROM simulations is easy. Simply use your Web browser's Favorites or Bookmark option to mark your current position. Each page view is tantamount to a self-contained Internet Web page. And if you've lost your place in the workbook, don't worry; the book and CD-ROM headings are identical, making it a snap to match your book and CD positions.

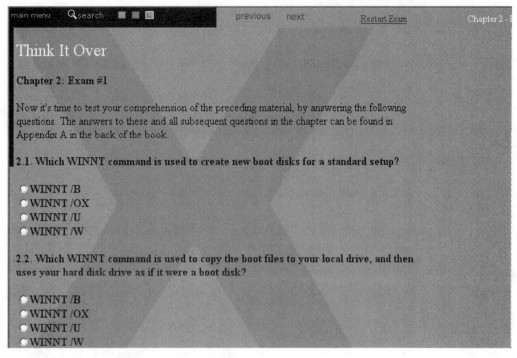

Figure 1.7   Taking the interactive exams.

Moving Forward

You're now ready to turn the page and start your interactive journey, exploring the Windows NT and 2000 Server operating systems, networking, and local area and wide area network (LAN/WAN) internetworking with Cisco routers.

Windows NT Server

In Part 1 we'll explore the mechanical details of the conventional Windows NT Server suite. We'll then examine configuration details, from both a nontechnical standpoint and a certified engineer's perspective. All this will be accompanied with step-by-step procedures including a typical standard Windows NT Server installation and configuration, using the recommended setup procedure from the Windows NT CD-ROM. These steps will be given as a continuous sequence throughout the various aspects of the many required procedures.

Installation and Basic Configuration

In this chapter you'll learn to install the Windows NT Server, configure domains, bind protocols, and connect to the Internet. But first it's essential that you understand the Windows NT architecture, so we'll begin with an overview of that.

Windows NT Architecture

The Windows NT architecture is composed of three primary mechanisms that interact to formulate the operating system functionality: the NT Executive, environment subsystems, and the Hardware Abstraction Layer (HAL). We'll take them one at a time, in that order.

The NT Executive

The NT Executive coordinates control of important tasks to the system, including object, virtual memory, input/output (I/O), and process management. Object management involves creating, modifying, and deleting conceptual data objects for all subsystems that work together as the kernel of the NT Executive. I/O management is the synchronization of all input and output processes, whereas process management involves creating, modifying, and deleting all threads and system processes. The components involved in meeting these responsibilities include:

Kernel. The heart of the system, responsible for scheduling processes alongside system interrupts and processor functions.

Object Manager. Used to construct/deconstruct objects used by the NT Executive, ranging from a port to a process thread.

Process Manager. Used to construct/deconstruct and monitor the active states of processes and threads.

Virtual Memory Manager (VMM). Manages the system's virtual memory.

Local Procedure Call Facility (LPC). Communicates message exchanges to and from different threads.

Security Reference Monitor (SRM). Enforces the security policies that are applied administratively to the system.

I/O Manager. Handles all system input and output.

Environment Subsystems

The environment subsystems coordinate between applications and the NT Executive. With Windows NT, there are three environment subsystems: Win32, the portable operating system interface (POSIX), and OS/2:

- Win32 is the native subsystem.
- POSIX was developed as a standard for UNIX systems—when a POSIX application runs on Windows NT, the subsystem translates (with language support) the program code for Win32.
- OS/2 is not extensively supported and works only on Intel-based systems.

Hardware Abstraction Layer

HAL is a software interface implemented to make Windows NT more reliable and portable by mediating hardware specifics. Basically, all hardware access calls are supposed to be ported through the HAL; however, some drivers (i.e., I/O drivers) circumvent it to communicate with system hardware directly—this may lead to a loss of portability.

Laying the Foundation

Installing the Windows NT Server/Workstation is a relatively simple process, but before we step through it, we must lay the groundwork, which means familiarizing ourselves with hardware requirements, installation methods, server licensing, and server types.

Minimum Hardware Requirements

Like most 32-bit operating systems, Windows NT is very hardware-aware, meaning that drivers are written to and polled even when their use is not required for I/O instructions. This may accommodate plug-n-play conceptually, but for this reason it's common to experience hardware problems that are uncommon to other operating systems. To avoid these problems, you must take two steps:

1. Be sure your system complies with the Windows NT Hardware Compatibility List.

2. Adhere to the following Microsoft NT standard requirements before installing the system:

    *   *Computer/Processor.* For Intel and compatible systems: 486/33 MHz or higher. For Pentium or Pentium PRO processor reduced instruction set computing- (RISC) based systems: RISC processor compatible with the Microsoft Windows NT Server version 4.0 operating system.

    *   *Memory.* At least 16 megabytes (MB) of random access memory (RAM).

    *   *Hard Disk.* For Intel and compatible systems: a minimum of 125 MB of available hard disk space. For RISC-based systems: 160 MB of available hard disk space.

    *   *Drive.* CD-ROM drive, floppy disk drive, or active network connection.

    *   *Display.* VGA, super VGA, or video graphics adapter compatible with Windows NT Server 4.0.

Installation Methods

There are three ways to install Windows NT: directly from the CD-ROM or floppy disks, using direct local/network installation, and using various other unsupported installation methods.

From the CD-ROM or Floppies

Microsoft recommends installing Windows NT directly from the CD-ROM (Figure 2.1) or from Windows NT boot floppy disks and CD-ROM together. For the most part, you'll find many necessary third-party drivers on the CD-ROM, though some may require a separate manufacturer's installation disk.

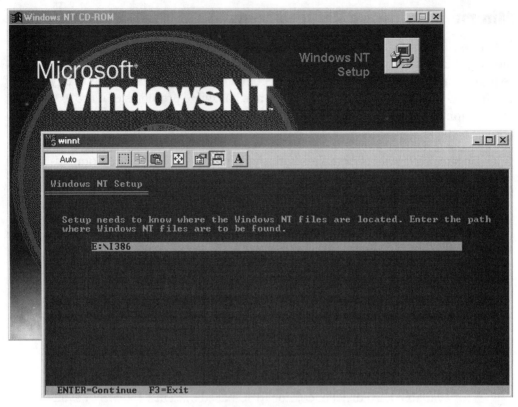

Figure 2.1 Installing NT from the CD-ROM is easy.

 If you cannot boot from the CD-ROM and you misplaced the boot floppy disks, don't worry; they can be created from the Windows NT CD-ROM. Just run either WINNT /OX or WINNT32 /OX to create new boot disks for a standard setup (see Figure 2.2).

Via Direct Local/Network Installation

Another method of deploying Windows NT is the direct local/network installation. This method is used especially for systems with unsupported CD-ROM drives. By copying the entire /I386 folder from Windows NT CD-ROM to a shared network drive, or directly from a shared CD-ROM drive to your system's hard drive, you can then execute WINNT.EXE.

For floppyless installs, type WINNT /B or WINNT32 /B from the command prompt. This copies the boot files to your local C drive and then uses your hard disk drive as if it were a boot disk.

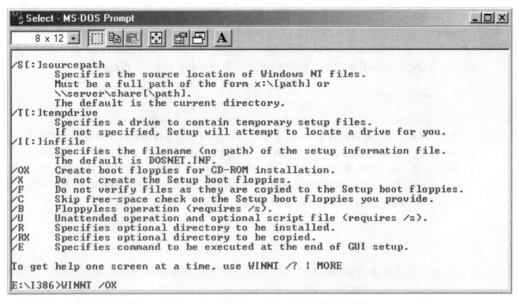

Figure 2.2 NT uses option /OX to create bootable floppies.

Via Other Unsupported Installation Methods

Unsupported installation methods described by Microsoft, and therefore only briefly covered in this text, include the Within-Windows and Unattended Setup procedures. By typing WINNT /W from a command prompt, you can set up Windows NT from within a current Windows session, bypassing conflicting issues involved with a standard setup. Alternatively, with the command WINNT /U, you can set up Windows NT in unattended mode. Note, however, that this method should be attempted only on computers that only have standard hardware and where user input is not required for supplying third-party drivers, etc. You must specify the following complete syntax:

```
winnt /u:<answer file> /s:<install source>
```

where <answer file> is a file containing information to automate the installation process and <install source> is the location of the Windows NT installation files.

Server Licensing

During the setup installation process, you will be asked the inevitable licensing question: Per Seat or Per Server? Regardless of your selection, you don't have to notify Microsoft. For either option, however, a server license is required, giving you the right to run the server software on a particular system. For an explanation of each method, and its recommended uses, read through the following Microsoft's official licensing option clauses:

Per-Seat Licensing

A per-seat license associates a Client Access License with a specific computer or "seat." Client computers are allowed access to any Windows NT Server or Windows NT Server, Enterprise Edition on the network, as long as each client machine is licensed with the appropriate Client Access License. The per-seat mode is most economical in distributed computing environments where multiple servers within an organization provide services to clients, such as a company that uses Windows NT Server for file and print services.

Per-Server Licensing

A per-server license associates a Client Access License with a particular server. This alternative allows concurrent-use licensing: If customers decide to use the server in per-server mode, they must have at least as many Client Access Licenses dedicated to that server to accommodate the maximum number of clients that will connect to that server at any one point in time. The server assigns Client Access Licenses temporarily to client computers; there is no permanent Client Access License association with a specific client machine. If a network environment has multiple servers, then each server in per server mode must have at least as many Client Access Licenses dedicated to it as the maximum number of clients that will connect to it at any one point in time. Under this option, the customer designates the number of Client Access Licenses that apply to the server during setup. The per-server mode is most economical in single-server, occasional, or specialty-use server solutions (with multiple concurrent connections). Some examples include, Remote Access Service solutions, CD ROM servers, or the initial server of a planned larger deployment.

Server Types

During the installation, you'll be given an option in regard to the overall server configuration type. From this option, you must choose one of three standard configuration types: Primary Domain Controller (PDC), Backup Domain Controller (BDC), or Stand-alone Server. Let's break down and investigate each of these types briefly.

Primary Domain Controller

A *domain* is a unique administration group within which members can easily collaborate. This structure simplifies administration when, for example, changing user privileges or adding resources. The changes can be applied to the domain as a whole and also affect each individual user. When a system acts as a PDC, it manages the master domain group database from where user authentication derives—the first server in a domain must act as the PDC. When a user logs in and is verified from the database, this user will have access to predefined resources on many different servers, all controlled by the domain that is managed by the PDC.

 A PDC cannot be configured for an existing domain. Rather, a PDC creates the domain.

During the domain setup process, you'll be required to specify a unique name for the domain. After you do, NT will check to determine whether the name is currently in use. Assuming your name has been accepted, and the domain has been created, the server will assign a Security ID (SID) that is used to identify the server and everyone else on the domain. For this reason, it's important not to overwrite a PDC (or BDC—covered next) by creating a new one in its place because existing users will not be able to communicate via the newly created SID.

By default, the system Administrator account will be used to govern the domain. A utility that is installed with the PDC, aptly named *User Manager for Domains*, can be used for further domain administration (see Figure 2.3). Only users with administrative privileges (such as the Administrator account) can use the utility to govern the domain.

Username	Full Name	Description
admin		
Administrator		Built-in account for administering the computer/domain
Guest	Gina E Guest	Built-in account for guest access to the computer/domain

Groups	Description
Administrators	Members can fully administer the computer/domain
Backup Operators	Members can bypass file security to back up files
Guests	Users granted guest access to the computer/domain
NAIEvents	Members of this group are allowed to use the NAIEvents on this computer.
Power Users	Members can share directories and printers
Replicator	Supports file replication in a domain
Users	Ordinary users

Figure 2.3 Configuring domains with User Manager for Domains.

Both PDCs and BDCs (or stand-alones mentioned in a following section) can be created from the Windows NT setup process.

Back Domain Controller

In Windows network domains, NT servers can be set up as BDCs for the PDC. BDCs can provide redundancy if a PDC fails and can also share the load if the network gets too busy for the PDC. In a nutshell, a BDC will retain a copy of the domain group database from the PDC. If the PDC fails or requires extensive maintenance, a BDC may be promoted to the PDC level. Therefore, the BDC must have administrative access to the domain via PDC. Microsoft recommends that every PDC have a BDC to provide some fault tolerance for a domain.

As mentioned previously, to share the load on a busy network, a BDC can provide direct user authentication to spread out the logon process load— BDCs can be strategically placed to provide authentication for different user subgroups (see Figure 2.4).

 A BDC can be configured only when a PDC is active in the domain. And when moving a BDC to a new domain, Windows NT will have to be reinstalled.

Stand-alone Server

On some networks, Windows NT servers may be configured as stand-alones. That means that they participate in the domain but do not act as a PDC or a BDC. That said, a stand-alone server might be used to administer the domain group on a domain controller, unless it maintains its own user list for local server access.

Stand-alone servers have two primary advantages over domain controllers. One, they can be easily moved from domain to domain, without reinstalling the operating system. Two, stand-alone servers are typically integrated in networks and/or domains to focus on application services (see Figure 2.4). With this design, stand-alone servers can focus on application loads, whereas domain controllers manage the domain. This model provides better resource management communication efficiency.

World Wide Web Services

During the installation process, you will be given the opportunity to choose to install World Wide Web services such as Microsoft's Internet Information

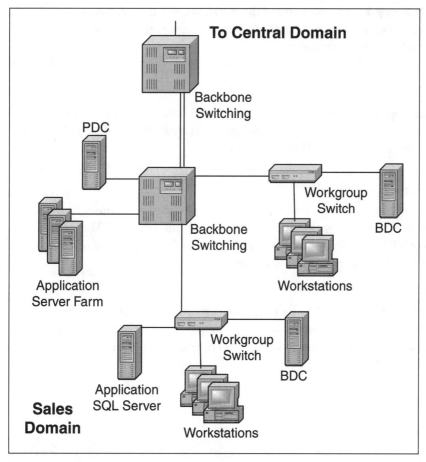

Figure 2.4   A typical network domain with all three server types (PDC, BDC, and stand-alone).

Server (IIS). If you're planning on serving Web pages, providing file transfer with the file transfer protocol (FTP) and/or Gopher services, be sure to check this option during the setup procedure. Be aware that once you do, you'll also trigger the configuration of the Transmission Control Protocol/Internet Protocol (TCP/IP) protocol suite. We'll investigate protocol configurations such as TCP/IP in the next few sections.

Step-by-Step Installation

Now we're ready to step through a typical standard installation, using the recommended setup procedure from the Windows NT CD-ROM. The steps are given as a continuous sequence throughout the various aspects of the procedure.

This step-by-step overview of the install process assumes your system complies with the Microsoft Windows NT hardware compatibility list and system requirements.

BOOT DISK

1. Power up the system up by inserting the Microsoft Windows NT Server Setup Boot Disk in your primary floppy drive. At this point the Windows NT Executive and the HAL will load.

2. Insert Setup Disk 2 and press Enter to continue. This will load critical drivers and system files.

3. At this point, you'll be given two options: proceed with the installation by pressing Enter or repair a previously installed copy of Microsoft Windows NT Server that may have been damaged. Because we're doing a new installation, press Enter to continue.

I/O CONTROLLERS

4. You have two choices here: to have Setup auto-detect the devices in your system, or to install manually by pressing S. By choosing the auto-detect method, Setup will prompt you to insert Setup Disk 3; do so and then press Enter to continue.

5. After Setup works through the driver installation/identification process, press Enter to continue the installation.

LICENSE AGREEMENT

6. Next, the product license agreement will load. It's a good idea to read the entire Windows NT End User License Agreement. To do so, press Page Down. At the end of the agreement, press F8 to accept its terms— assuming that you do—and continue.

WINDOWS NT SERVER

7. Again, assuming this is a fresh installation, at this point Setup will ask you to identify your computer type, video display, keyboard, and mouse. In this scenario, Windows NT will have detected (and will support) suitable choices. Proceed by pressing Enter.

8. In this step, you select an installation location for Windows NT. You may create/delete active hard drive partitions in File Allocation Table (FAT) or NT File System (NTFS) format, if they do not already exist. The FAT and NTFS file systems are explained in Chapter 4.

    In this step select the partition to which to install the operating system and press Enter. You may now choose to format the partition using FAT or NTFS. Then, be sure to use default directory, \WINNT, by pressing Enter.

9. In this step, Setup offers to check for hard disk corruption. For our scenario, let's go with "exhaustive" examination by pressing Enter. The alternative is to press Esc, which activates only a simple examination. Either way, following the examination, Setup will begin copying files to the hard drive.

10. When the file copy procedure is complete, remove the floppy disk and press Enter to reboot the system.

SETUP WIZARD

11. After the reboot, a graphical user interface (GUI), controlled by the NT Setup wizard, will display. Click the Next button with your mouse to continue. At this stage, Setup will gather information about the system.

SITE INFORMATION AND LICENSE

12. When Setup has all the information it needs about your system, it will display a screen requesting site and licensing information. Enter your name and company name (optional) and then click Next. You'll be instructed to enter the CD-ROM License Key, which, typically, you can find on the back of the jewel case. Click Next.

13. As described earlier in this chapter, choose either the Per Seat or Per Server licensing type. Click Next.

SERVER TYPE

14. After you've chosen a server type, you'll be asked to enter a unique name for the server (up to 15 characters). Once you've done that, click Next. Now, keeping in mind what you learned earlier in the chapter, select the server type: Primary Domain Controller, Backup Domain Controller, or stand-alone server.

ADMINISTRATIVE PASSWORD

15. Choose the administrative password (up to 14 characters); click Next.

EMERGENCY REPAIR DISK AND OPTIONAL COMPONENTS

16. This step allows you to create an Emergency Repair Disk (ERD), which is used to recover from system failures. Be sure to direct Setup to do this. It's recommended that you accept the default components during Setup. Click Next to accept and continue.

NETWORKING

17. After setting up the ERD, click Next twice to confirm the network setup process and that the system is (and will be) connected to a network.

WEB SERVICES AND THE INTERNET INFORMATION SERVER

18. At this point you can choose to install the Web services with IIS, described earlier. Remember, you can always choose to install these later, if you don't want to now.

NETWORK INTERFACE CARD (NIC)

19. Click Start Search to direct Setup to detect your NIC. Upon completion, click Next to move on.

PROTOCOLS AND SERVICES

20. Select the network protocol(s) to install—in this case TCP/IP; click Next. The recommended choice is to allow Setup to install the default network services. Here, too, you can opt to add additional protocols and services later. Click Next to continue.

PROTOCOL SETTINGS

21. At this time, you'll be asked to configure the IP settings that will be bound to your NIC(s). These include IP address, hostname, gateway, and/or Domain Name Service (DNS) server. Click Continue to register your input, and then click Next twice to accept and start the network service.

WORKGROUP OR DOMAIN

22. As described earlier, enter the domain (if the system is a domain controller) or workgroup name and click Next.

DATE AND TIME

23. Configure the correct date, time, and time zone. Click Close to confirm and accept.

VIDEO

24. Confirm the video adapter and click OK. Remember to click Test to verify these settings.

FINISH SETUP

25. That's it! Now click Restart Computer to complete the installation process.

Logging In

The next time you restart the system, you'll be asked to log in using the administrative password you chose during the Setup process (see

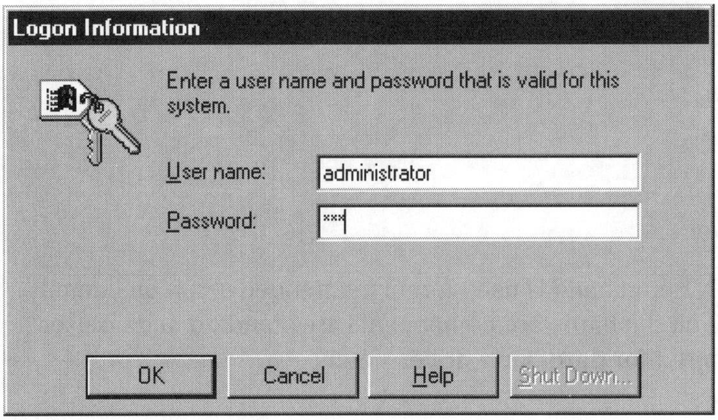

Figure 2.5 Logging in as the administrator.

Figure 2.5). For security purposes, when you type, the letters will appear only as asterisks.

Think It Over

Now it's time to test your comprehension of the preceding material by answering the following questions. The answers to these and all subsequent questions in the chapter can be found in Appendix A in the back of this book.

2.1. Which Windows NT (WINNT) command is used to create new boot disks for a standard setup?

○ WINNT /B

○ WINNT /OX

○ WINNT /U

○ WINNT /W

2.2. Which WINNT command is used to copy the boot files to your local drive and then uses your hard disk drive as if it were a boot disk?

○ WINNT /B

○ WINNT /OX

○ WINNT /U

○ WINNT /W

2.3. Which WINNT command is used to set up Windows NT from within Windows?

○ WINNT /B

○ WINNT /OX

○ WINNT /U

○ WINNT /W

2.4. Which WINNT command is used for an unattended setup on computers in which all the hardware components are standard and no user input is required for third party drivers, etc?

○ WINNT /B

○ WINNT /OX

○ WINNT /U

○ WINNT /W

2.5. If you were to install a single Windows NT server on a network with 50 concurrent connections, which licensing method would typically be most economical?

○ Per Seat

○ Per Server

2.6. If you were to install a Windows NT server on a network with multiple NT servers, which licensing method would typically be most economical?

○ Per Seat

○ Per Server

2.7. A PDC will retain a copy of the domain group database from the BDC.

○ True

○ False

2.8. Why is it important not to overwrite a PDC?

○ Existing BDCs and/or users will not be able to communicate via the new SID.

○ The BDC will have to be promoted to the PDC level.

○ The first server in a domain must act as the PDC.

2.9. A PDC can be configured for an existing domain.

○ True

○ False

2.10. Which NT server type is easy to move from domain to domain without reinstalling the operating system?

○ PDC

○ BDC

○ Stand-alone

Basic Windows NT Configurations

This section describes next-step configurations to our new Windows NT server. We'll:

1. Bind protocols on preliminary steps for connecting to the Internet.
2. Perform important administrative functions.
3. Create a TCP/IP lab network and IP address scheme with subnetting.

 Hands-on simulations of the material in this section can be found on the book's CD-ROM.

Binding Protocols

The process of configuring network protocols and services with interfaces for network communications is called *binding*. Microsoft's official definition states that binding is the connection made between a network card, protocol(s), and the service(s) installed.

To view the current protocol(s), services, and bindings and to add new configurations, proceed to the Control Panel in Start/Settings/Control Panel and double-click the Network icon to start the network administration program, as shown in Figure 2.6.

To view the protocol bindings of the current network interface card, click the Protocols tab of the network administration program. There you'll see the protocol(s) bound to the network adapter as configured during the setup process. From here you can add, remove, view, change, or update protocols and their settings (see Figure 2.7).

Adding a Protocol

TCP/IP is a protocol designed to interconnect networks forming an internet to pass data back and forth. Its popularity is due primarily to its worldwide acceptance as the protocol of the Internet.

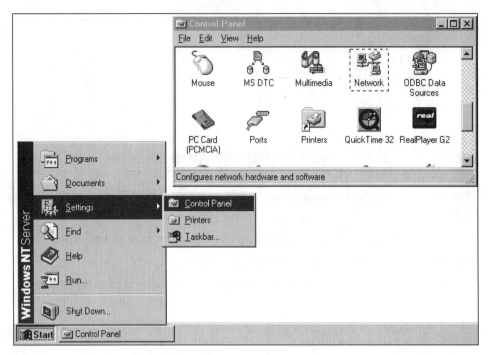

Figure 2.6 The Network icon in the NT Server Control Panel.

TCP/IP is a high-maintenance protocol suite that contains advanced routing properties. Therefore, it works best in large routed networks, with or without Internet access, where reliability is necessary. The IP portion contains unique addressing and control information that enables *packets* to be routed through the Internet. (A packet is defined as a logical grouping of information that includes a header containing control information and, most times, user data.) The equipment—that is, routers—that encounter these packets, strip off and examine the headers that contain the sensitive routing information. These headers are then modified and reformulated as a packet to be passed along.

IP's primary functions include providing a permanently established connection (called somewhat ironically, *connectionless*) that offers unreliable (no guarantee), best-effort delivery of *datagrams* through an internetwork. Datagrams can be described as a logical grouping of information sent as a network layer unit over a communication medium. As such, they are the primary information units in the Internet. Also among IP's principal responsibilities are the fragmentation and reassembly of datagrams to support links with different transmission sizes.

As the fundamental transfer unit of the Internet, an IP datagram is the unit of data commuted between IP modules. That said, be aware that the data in a packet is not really a concern for the IP. Rather, IP is concerned with the control information as it pertains to the upper-layer protocol. This information is

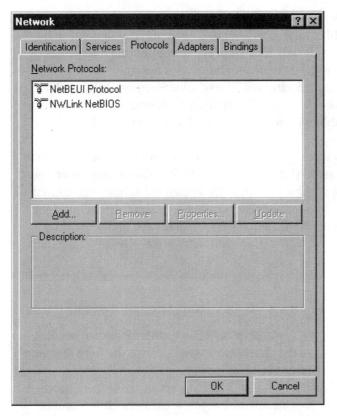

Figure 2.7 Current protocols bound to our network interface card.

stored in the IP header, whose objective it is to deliver the datagram to its destination on the local network or over the Internet. Think of it this way: IP is the method; the datagram is the means.

With that last statement in mind, it is important to understand the methods a datagram uses to travel across networks. To successfully travel across the Internet over physical media, we want some guarantee that each datagram travels in a frame. The process of a datagram traveling across media in a frame is called *encapsulation*. An ideal situation is when an entire IP datagram fits into a frame and the network it is traveling across supports that particular transfer size. Of course, in the real world, ideal situations rarely occur. One problem our traveling datagram will encounter is that networks enforce a maximum transfer unit (MTU) size, or limit on the size of transfer. To further confuse the issue, different types of networks enforce their own MTU; for example, Ethernet has an MTU of 1500, FDDI uses 4470 MTU, and so on. When datagrams traveling in frames cross network types with different specified size limits, routers must sometimes divide the datagram to accommodate a smaller MTU. This process is called *fragmentation*.

An IP address is an identifier for a device on a TCP/IP network. The format of an IP address is a 32-bit number written in four groupings separated by periods. Each number can be 0 to 255. To prevent duplicating address assignments, routing between nodes is based on addresses assigned from a pool of *classes*, or range of available addresses. These addresses typically derive from one of three classes—A, B, and C—again, which consist of 32-bit numbers. By default, the usable bits, for Classes A, B, and C are 8, 16, and 24 respectively.

An example of an IP address is 207.0.135.1. Let's break it down. The first octet, 207, indicates a Class C (Internet-assigned) IP address range with the format *Network.Network.Network.Host*, with a standard subnet mask binary indicating 255.255.255.0. This means that we have 8 bits in the last octet for hosts. The 8 bits that make up the last, or fourth, octet are understood by infrastructure equipment such as routers and software in the following manner:

Bit: 1   2   3   4   5   6   7   8

Value: 128 + 64 + 32 + 16 + 8 + 4 + 2 + 1 = 255 (254 usable hosts)

In this example of a full Class C, we have only 254 usable IP addresses for hosts (0 and 255 cannot be used as host addresses because the network number is 0 and the broadcast address is 255).

With the abundant utilization of Class B address space by large corporations, and the lack of available Class C addresses, a Classless Interdomain Routing (CIR) system was introduced in the early 1990s. Basically, a route is no longer an IP address; it is now an IP address and mask that allow us to break a network into subnets and supernets. This increases Internet routers by drastically reducing the size of Internet routing tables. The process of dividing an assigned or derived IP address class into smaller individual but related physical networks is called *subnetting*. A subnet mask is a 32-bit number that determines the network split of IP addresses on the bit level. We'll cover subnetting in detail later on.

IP Address Management

Windows NT contains two IP address management protocols: the Dynamic Host Configuration Protocol (DHCP), which is primarily used to dynamically assign addresses to network computers, and the Windows Internet Naming Service (WINS), which is used as a naming service to Windows NT networks using TCP/IP.

Because DHCP uses dynamic addressing, a device may have a different IP address every time it powers up and/or connects to the network. Dynamic addressing helps simplify network administration because it assigns IP addresses automatically and keeps track of them.

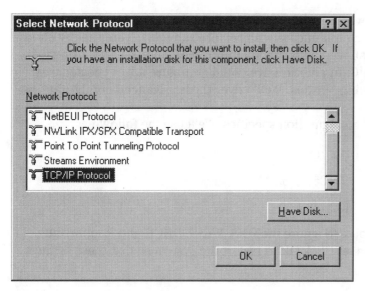

Figure 2.8 Adding protocols to bind to an interface.

WINS provides *name resolution* for computers on a network. For example, when DHCP assigns IP addresses dynamically, WINS uses a distributed database that is automatically updated with the names of computers currently available and the IP address assigned to each one. This way, computers can be tracked via unique names rather than IP addresses, which may change dynamically if using DHCP. We'll explore DHCP and WINS in greater depth later in this book.

In this step, adding protocols to bind to an interface is a relatively simple process. Start by clicking the Add button in the Protocols tab in the Network administration module (see Figure 2.8). In this scenario we're going to add the TCP/IP protocol as a preliminary step to connecting with the Internet in the next section.

Select TCP/IP by clicking on it; then click OK. At this point, the protocol setup module will need to copy some files from the Windows NT CD-ROM. If, however, you've copied the server CD files to a network drive for easy accessibility, you may manually specify an alternate location. Furthermore, if the protocol you wish to install is proprietary and/or not listed, you may manually load it by clicking Have Disk… in the previous step. After Setup copies files, it will ask if you prefer to use DHCP. For this exercise, we'll elect not to use it. We'll cover DHCP in Chapter 6.

After Setup loads the TCP/IP protocol files, click Close at the bottom of the Network administration module. Subsequently, the Microsoft TCP/IP Properties configuration window will appear (see Figure 2.9). With the detected network adapter selected, we'll be asked to specify the following for our current network: an IP Address, Subnet Mask, and Default Gateway (the router used to communicate with remote subnets). Note that by choosing the Advanced tab we could specify multiple IP addresses and/or gateways for a single NIC. In addition, we could configure advanced security and protocol tunneling options. We'll cover these advanced configurations later on.

Enter our TCP/IP configuration specifics. We'll use the following:

IP Address   192.168.1.34

Subnet Mask   255.255.255.224

Default Gateway   192.168.1.33

For now, we're going to ignore the DNS, WINS, DHCP, and Routing tabs; we'll discuss them later. Click OK to restart the system so that these settings take affect.

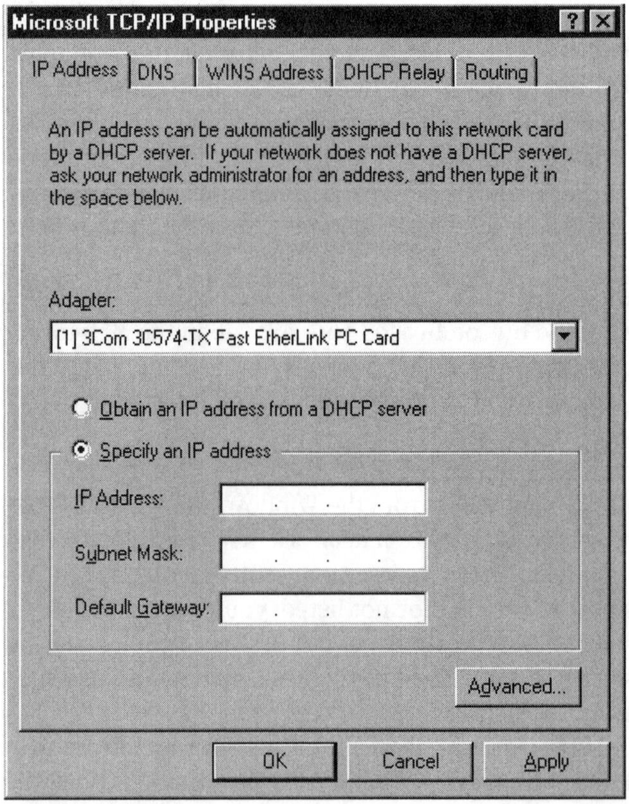

Figure 2.9   Configuring TCP/IP network properties.

The following section explains how these TCP/IP configuration specifics were established.

Subnetting

Subnetting is the process of dividing an assigned or derived address class into smaller, individual, but related, physical networks. Keep in mind that IP addresses are uniquely assigned network addresses. For this scenario, we're going to build a lab network (see Figure 2.10), break it down into five mini-networks, or *subnets* (three active, two to accommodate future growth), and assign IP addresses (25 per subnet).

For our scenario, the subnet mask is a 32-bit number that determines the network split of IP addresses on the bit level. Given our network block number of 192.168.1.0, we need to divide our network address block to accommodate three usable subnets, which we'll identify as 1-Admin, 2-Marketing, and 3-Sales, and the two subnets reserved for future growth. Each subnet or network must have at least 25 available network addresses for workstations.

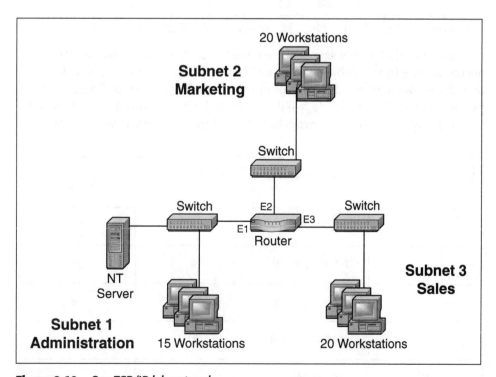

Figure 2.10 Our TCP/IP lab network.

This division process requires taking five steps. The first step in this virtual exercise requires establishing three host addresses for each network's router interfaces [Ethernet 1 (E1), Ethernet 2 (E2), and Ethernet 3 (E3) interfaces]. In the second step, we are given only one option (shown in bold in Figure 2.11) to support our scenario of five subnets with at least 25 IP addresses per network.

Let's further explore the subnet mask bit breakdown for our chosen mask of 255.255.255.224. When a bit is used, we indicate this with a 1, as shown here:

3 Bits:	1	1	1					
Value:	128	64	32	16	8	4	2	1

When a bit is not used, we indicate this with a 0:

3 Bits:				0	0	0	0	0
Value:	128	64	32	16	8	4	2	1

3 Bits:	1	1	1	0	0	0	0	0
Value:	128	64	32	16	8	4	2	1

Value: 128 + 64 + 32 = 224 (mask = 255.255.255.224)

Remember that in this scenario we need to divide our address block to accommodate three usable subnets and two future-growth subnets with at least 25 available node addresses per each of the five networks. To make this process as simple as possible, we'll start with the five required subnets or networks, as opposed to the 25 available node addresses needed per network. To

Bits in Subnet Mask	Subnet Mask	# of Subnets	# of Hosts Per Subnet
2	255.255.255.192	2	62
3	**255.255.255.224**	**6**	**30**
4	255.255.255.240	14	14
5	255.255.255.248	30	6
6	255.255.255.252	62	2

Figure 2.11   Subnet chart by number of subnets versus number of hosts per subnet.

understand the values in the subnet chart, look at the following equation, where we'll solve for n in $2^n - 2$, being sure to cover the required five subnets or networks.

Let's start with the power of 2 and work our way up:

$$2^2 - 2 = 2 \quad 2^3 - 2 = 6 \quad 2^4 - 2 = 14$$

The third power in the equation indicates the number of bits in the subnet mask. Here we see that $23 - 2 = 6$ subnets if we use these 3 bits. This will cover the required five subnets, with an additional subnet (or network) left over.

Now let's determine the number of bits left over for available addresses. In this scenario, we will be using 3 bits in the mask for subnetting. How many are left over? Out of the given 32 bits that make up IP addresses, the default host availability (for networks versus hosts on the network), as previously explained, for Classes A, B, and C blocks are as follows:

Class A (first octet between 0–127): 8 bits

Class B (first octet between 128–191): 16 bits

Class C (first octet between 192–223): 24 bits

For all practical purposes, our scenario involves a given Class C-type network block. If we subtract our default bit availability for Class C of 24 bits from the standard 32 bits that make up IP addresses, we have 8 bits remaining for networks versus hosts for Class C blocks.

Next, we subtract the 3 bits used for subnetting from the total 8 bits remaining for network versus hosts, which gives us 5 bits left for actual host addressing:

3 Bits:	1	1	1	0	0	0	0	0
Value:	128	64	32	(16	8	4	2	1)

5 bits left

Let's solve an equation to see if 5 bits are enough to cover the required available node addresses of at least 25 per subnet or network:

$$2^5 - 2 = 30$$

Placing the remaining 5 bits back into our equation gives us the available node addresses per subnet or network, $2^5 - 2 = 30$ host addresses per six subnets or networks (remember, we have an additional subnet left over).

Now we can divide our Class C block using 3 bits to give us six subnets with 30 host addresses each. This takes us to step 3. Now that we have determined the subnet mask, in this case 255.255.255.224 (3 bits), we need to calculate the actual network numbers or range of IP addresses in each network.

An easy way to accomplish this is by setting the host bits to 0. Remember, we have 5 bits left for hosts:

3 Bits:	1	1	1	0	0	0	0	0
Value:	128	64	32	(16	8	4	2	1)

5 host bits left

With the 5 host bits set to 0, we set the first 3 bits to 1 *in every variation* and then calculate the value (for a shortcut, take the first subnet value that is equal to 32 and add it in succession to reveal all six subnets):

3 Bits:	0	0	1	0	0	0	0	0
Value:	128	64	32	(16	8	4	2	1)

               32   **= 32**

3 Bits:	0	1	0	0	0	0	0	0
Value:	128	64	32	(16	8	4	2	1)

       64   **= 64**

3 Bits:	0	1	1	0	0	0	0	0
Value:	128	64	32	(16	8	4	2	1)

      64 + 32   **= 96**

3 Bits:	1	0	0	0	0	0	0	0
Value:	128	64	32	(16	8	4	2	1)

  128   **= 128**

3 Bits:	1	0	1	0	0	0	0	0
Value:	128	64	32	(16	8	4	2	1)

  128 + 32   **= 160**

3 Bits:	1	1	0	0	0	0	0	0
Value:	128	64	32	(16	8	4	2	1)

  128 + 64   **= 192**

Now let's take a look at the network numbers of our subnetted Class C block with mask 255.255.255.224:

192.168.1.32	192.168.1.64	192.168.1.96
192.168.1.128	192.168.1.160	192.168.1.192

Now that we have solved the network numbers, we can proceed to step 4, where we'll resolve each network's *broadcast address* by setting host bits to all 1s. (The broadcast address is defined as the system that copies and delivers a single packet to all addresses on the network.) All hosts attached to a network can be notified by sending a packet to the broadcast address:

3 Bits:	0	0	1	1	1	1	1	1	
Value:	128	64	32	(16	8	4	2	1)	
			32 +	16 +	8 +	4 +	2 +	1	**= 63**

3 Bits:	0	1	0	1	1	1	1	1	
Value:	128	64	32	(16	8	4	2	1)	
		64 +		16 +	8 +	4 +	2 +	1	**= 95**

3 Bits:	0	1	1	1	1	1	1	1	
Value:	128	64	32	(16	8	4	2	1)	
		64 +	32 +	16 +	8 +	4 +	2 +	1	**= 127**

3 Bits:	1	0	0	1	1	1	1	1	
Value:	128	64	32	(16	8	4	2	1)	
	128 +			16 +	8 +	4 +	2 +	1	**= 159**

3 Bits:	1	0	1	1	1	1	1	1	
Value:	128	64	32	(16	8	4	2	1)	
	128 +		32 +	16 +	8 +	4 +	2 +	1	**= 191**

3 Bits:	1	1	0	1	1	1	1	1	
Value:	128	64	32	(16	8	4	2	1)	
	128 +	64 +		16 +	8 +	4 +	2 +	1	**= 223**

Let's take a look at the network broadcast addresses of our subnetted Class C block with mask 255.255.255.224:

192.168.1.63	192.168.1.95	192.168.1.127
192.168.1.159	192.168.1.191	192.168.1.223

If you're wondering what the available IP addresses are for each of our six networks, you're ready for step 5. They are the addresses between the network and broadcast addresses for each subnet or network (see Figure 2.12):

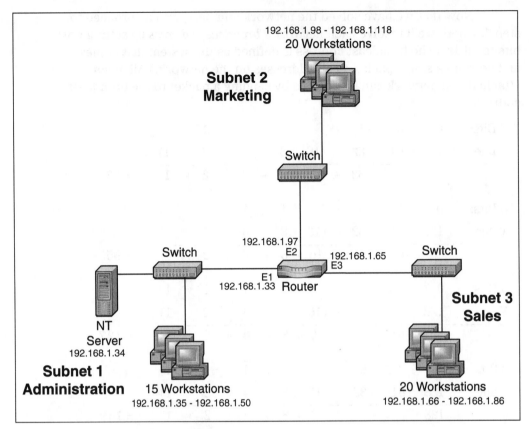

Figure 2.12   Our TCP/IP lab network with IP addresses.

NETWORK ADDRESS	BROADCAST ADDRESS	AVAILABLE IP ADDRESSES
192.168.1.32	192.168.1.63	192.168.1.33–192.168.33.62
192.168.1.64	192.168.1.95	192.168.1.65–192.168.33.94
192.168.1.96	192.168.1.127	192.168.1.97–192.168.33.126
192.168.1.128	192.168.1.159	192.168.1.129–192.168.33.158
192.168.1.160	192.168.1.191	192.168.1.161–192.168.33.190
192.168.1.192	192.168.1.223	192.168.1.193–192.168.33.222

Connecting to the Internet

Recall that we indicated during Setup that we plan to connect our NT server to the Internet. In preparation for configuring Internet services on our server, which we do later on, this section serves as a brief review of the history of the Internet and how it works.

The Internet started during the 1960s with the U.S. Department of Defense's Advanced Research Projects Agency (ARPA, later called DARPA). ARPA launched an experimental wide area network (WAN) called ARPANET that spanned the United States. Its original goal was to enable government affiliations, educational institutions, and research laboratories to share computing resources and to collaborate via file sharing and electronic mail. It didn't take long, however, for DARPA to realize the more far-reaching implications of ARPANET and the possibilities of providing these network links publicly around the world.

Into the 1970s, DARPA continued aggressively funding and conducting research on ARPANET, to motivate the development of the framework for a community of networking technologies. The result of this framework was the TCP/IP suite. (A protocol is a set of rules for communication over a computer network.) To increase acceptance of the use of protocols, DARPA released a less expensive implementation of this project to the computing community— that is, the public. A primary target for this experiment was the Berkeley Software Distribution (BSD) UNIX system at the University of California at Berkeley. DARPA funded a company called Bolt Beranek and Newman, Inc. (BBN) to help develop the TCP/IP suite on BSD UNIX.

This new TCP/IP technology emerged during a time when many establishments were in the process of developing local area network (LAN) technologies to connect two or more computers at a common site. By January 1983, all of the computers connected on ARPANET were running the new TCP/IP suite for communications. In 1989, Tim Berners-Lee, then at the Conseil Europeén pour la Recherche Nucléaire (CERN), Europe's high-energy physics laboratory, invented the World Wide Web. CERN's primary objective for this development was to give physicists around the globe the means to communicate more efficiently using what was called *hypertext* (text linked together in a complex, nonsequential web of associations in which users can browse through related topics). This soon developed into the Hypertext Markup Language (HTML), a language with which programmers could generate viewable pages of information. In February 1993, the National Center for Supercomputing Applications at the University of Illinois (NCSA) released a browser named Mosaic. With this browser, users could view graphical pages of information produced in HTML.

At the time of Mosaic's release, there were approximately 50 Web servers providing archives for viewable HTML. Nine months later, the number had grown to more than 500. Approximately 1 year later, there were more than 10,000 Web servers in 84 countries comprising the World Wide Web, all running on ARPANET's backbone, called the Internet.

Today, the Internet provides a means of collaboration for millions of hosts across the world. The current backbone infrastructure of the Internet can carry a volume well over 45 megabits per second (Mbps), about 1000 times the *bandwidth* of the original ARPANET. (Bandwidth is a measure of the amount of traffic a media can handle at one time. In digital communication, this describes the amount of data that can be transmitted over a communication line at bits per second, commonly abbreviated as bps.)

Managing Addresses

As you know, the Internet could not function without a system of unique addressing. To prevent the use of duplicate addresses, routing between nodes is based on addresses assigned from a pool of classes, or range of available addresses, assigned by the InterNetwork Information Center (InterNIC). InterNIC controls all network addresses used over the Internet by assigning them in three classes (A, B, and C). Then InterNIC allocates these blocks to Internet service providers (ISPs), who then allocate addresses to their clients.

Address Translation

To conserve available address space, ISPs may not allocate a block of Internet-routable IP addresses to cover every node in an organization. For this reason, gateways and/or routers and firewalls use network and port address translation (NAT and PAT, respectively). Address translation enables a LAN to use one block of IP addresses for internal traffic and a second block of addresses for external traffic. Having NAT/PAT enabled on an Internet router or firewall provides some protection by hiding internal IP addresses. Another benefit is that all internal addresses can share an external pool of addresses or even a single external address when communicating with the Internet. Later in the book, we'll configure address translation on our router.

Internet Domain Names

An Internet domain name is the address of a device connected to the Internet or any other TCP/IP network in a system that uses words to identify servers (organizations and types of) in this form: www.companyname.com. Humans establish domain names as alphabetic characters for mnemonic reasons—the domain name is a character-based handle that identifies one or more IP addresses. The DNS is a server-side program that implements the *Domain Name System* by translating these domain names back into their respective IP addresses, by hosts on the Internet. These hosts maintain both domain name addresses (the human-readable version) and the numerical IP address. Datagrams that travel through the Internet use these addresses;

every time a domain name is specified, a DNS daemon must translate the name into the corresponding IP address. When you enter a domain name into a browser, say, TigerTools.net, a DNS server maps the alphabetic domain name into an IP address, which is where the user is forwarded to view the Web site.

Registering for an available Internet domain name is easy—here's a list of some popular service organizations:

www.networksolutions.com

www.internic.net/alpha.html

www.domainnameregistration.com

www.DomainNameRegistrationCenter.net

www.longdomainnamesregistration.com

www.bulk-domain-name-registration.com

www.123-domain-name-registration.com

www.0-domain-name-registration-stuff.com

www.dot-com-domain-name-registration.com

www.007s-1st-domain-name-registration-service.com

www.siteleader.com/domain-registration

www.1domain-name-registration.com

http://exclaimationpointdomainnamesregistrationandhostingservices.com

www.dotdnr.com

www.domaindingo.com

www.speedyregistration.com

www.0-free-domain-name-registration.com

www.1step-domain-names-registration.com

www.1-domain-names-registrations.com

www.1-dnr.com

Though the process is simple, before you attempt to register an Internet domain name, you should use Whois to be sure your name choice is not already being used on the Internet. For Internet domain name discovery, Whois acts as a tool for looking up records in the Network Solutions Inc. (NSI) Registrar database. Each record within the NSI Registrar database has a unique identifier assigned to it: a name, a record type, and various other fields. To use Whois for a domain search, using a previously mentioned Whois service provider, simply type in the domain name you seek.

The Whois service is also used to obtain information about a universal resource locator (URL) for a given company or even, a user who has an account at that domain. The following is a list of URLs for domains that provide the Whois service:

> **In North America: www.networksolutions.com/cgi-bin/whois/whois**
> **In Europe: www.ripe.net**
> **In Asia-Pacific: www.apnic.net**

Information required for domain name registration includes address, administrative contact, technical contact, billing contact, and DNS addresses. For extra security, it is advisable to use an ISP for domain name services. ISPs offer domain hosting for a minimal fee. And be sure to do some research to identify a first-tier vendor before you sign up with an ISP. Ensure that the ISP provides the necessary security and includes an uptime policy in accordance with your internal policy. Some ISPs guarantee 99 percent uptime with state-of-the-art fault tolerance and automatic failover infrastructure designs.

First-tier also means minimal "hops" from the Internet. Fewer hops from the Internet to these services mean less equipment to be concerned about, fewer hack attacks, fewer equipment failures, scheduled downtime, and more. Be aware that some providers are actually middlemen; that is, they resell the services of larger providers, which adds hops to the actual Internet backbone. To learn this information, of course, ask the provider; but then use *trace routing* to find out the hop distance. Tracing a route displays the path for data traveling from a sending node to a destination node, returning the time in milliseconds and each hop count in between (e.g., router and/or server). Tracing a route is typically a vital mechanism for troubleshooting connectivity problems. An example of using trace routing on an NT server would begin at the Start/Programs/Command Prompt. Enter `tracert domainname.com`, as illustrated in Figure 2.13.

Summary

In this chapter we covered the Windows NT architecture, including the NT Executive, environment subsystems, and the Hardware Abstraction Layer (HAL). We reviewed the Windows NT Server installation process, domain configuration, protocol bindings, and Internet specifics. We also performed next-step configurations, including binding protocols on our new Windows NT server, and created a network address scheme. In the next few chapters we will perform administration functions such as creating a user account, converting a file system, examining the System Registry, and performing some general system optimization techniques.

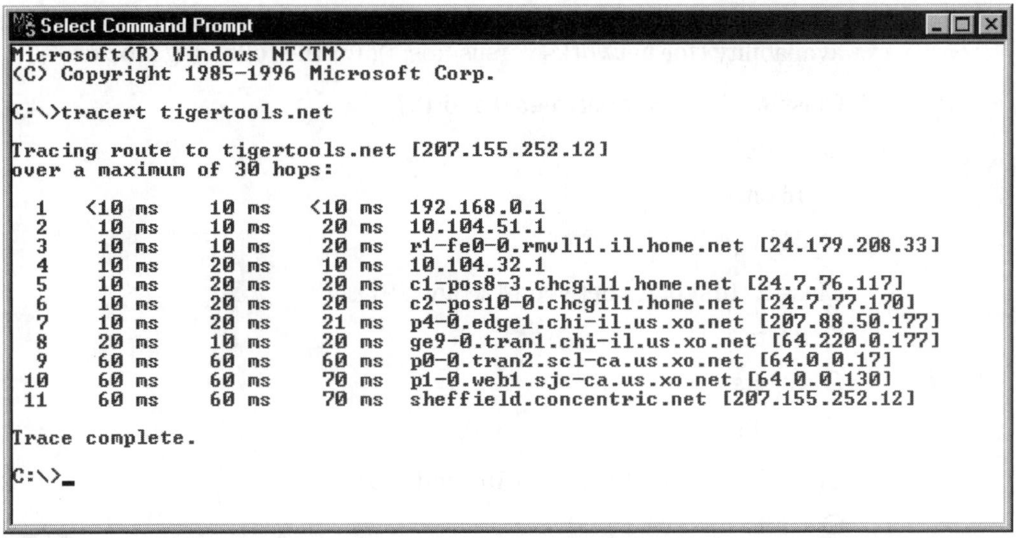

```
Select Command Prompt                                              _ □ X
Microsoft(R) Windows NT(TM)
(C) Copyright 1985-1996 Microsoft Corp.

C:\>tracert tigertools.net

Tracing route to tigertools.net [207.155.252.12]
over a maximum of 30 hops:

   1   <10 ms     10 ms    <10 ms   192.168.0.1
   2    10 ms     10 ms     20 ms   10.104.51.1
   3    10 ms     10 ms     20 ms   r1-fe0-0.rmvll1.il.home.net [24.179.208.33]
   4    10 ms     20 ms     10 ms   10.104.32.1
   5    10 ms     20 ms     20 ms   c1-pos8-3.chcgil1.home.net [24.7.76.117]
   6    10 ms     20 ms     20 ms   c2-pos10-0.chcgil1.home.net [24.7.77.170]
   7    10 ms     20 ms     21 ms   p4-0.edge1.chi-il.us.xo.net [207.88.50.177]
   8    20 ms     10 ms     20 ms   ge9-0.tran1.chi-il.us.xo.net [64.220.0.177]
   9    60 ms     60 ms     60 ms   p0-0.tran2.scl-ca.us.xo.net [64.0.0.17]
  10    60 ms     60 ms     70 ms   p1-0.web1.sjc-ca.us.xo.net [64.0.0.130]
  11    60 ms     60 ms     70 ms   sheffield.concentric.net [207.155.252.12]

Trace complete.

C:\>_
```

Figure 2.13   Tracing a route on an NT server.

Think It Over

Take the time to test your comprehension of the previous section by answering the following questions:

2.11. What is the connection called that is made between a network card, protocol(s), and the service(s) installed?

   ○ WINS

   ○ Binding

   ○ DNS

   ○ DHCP

2.12. Subnetting is the process of obtaining an IP address class and expanding it to create a larger physical network.

   ○ True

   ○ False

2.13. Adding a protocol to be bound to an interface is a relatively simple process that you launch from the Protocols tab in the Network administration module found in the Control Panel.

   ○ True

   ○ False

2.14. Out of the given 32 bits that make up IP addresses, match the default availability (for networks versus hosts), for the following blocks:

Class A (first octet between 0 and 127):

○ 8 bits

○ 16 bits

○ 24 bits

Class B (first octet between 128 and 191):

○ 8 bits

○ 16 bits

○ 24 bits

Class C (first octet between 192 and 223):

○ 8 bits

○ 16 bits

○ 24 bits

2.15. When a bit in a subnet mask octet is set to 1, it is an indication that it is being used.

○ True

○ False

2.16. Which subnet mask would most likely be used to accommodate 12 subnets with 10 workstations each?

○ 255.255.255.192

○ 255.255.255.224

○ 255.255.255.240

○ 255.255.255.248

○ 255.255.255.252

2.17. Which subnet mask would most likely be used to accommodate 3 subnets with 25 workstations each?

○ 255.255.255.192

○ 255.255.255.224

○ 255.255.255.240

○ 255.255.255.248

○ 255.255.255.252

2.18. Which subnet mask would most likely be used to accommodate 20 subnets with 5 workstations each?

  ○ 255.255.255.192

  ○ 255.255.255.224

  ○ 255.255.255.240

  ○ 255.255.255.248

  ○ 255.255.255.252

2.19. Which of the following represents 6 bits in the subnet mask?

  ○ 255.255.255.192

  ○ 255.255.255.224

  ○ 255.255.255.240

  ○ 255.255.255.248

  ○ 255.255.255.252

2.20. Which of the following represents 3 bits in the subnet mask?

  ○ 255.255.255.192

  ○ 255.255.255.224

  ○ 255.255.255.240

  ○ 255.255.255.248

  ○ 255.255.255.252

Subsequent Configuration and Administration

This chapter will provide you with a novice-level knowledge base in the areas of configuration and administration of Windows NT. The information you learn here will enable you to perform advanced service configurations in upcoming chapters. To that end, in this chapter we'll briefly examine the Windows NT desktop interface, including files and folders; we'll also look at Control Panel utilities and administrative modules.

 Hands-on simulations of the material presented in this chapter can be found on the book's companion CD-ROM.

Desktop Interface

The Windows NT desktop interface, shown in Figure 3.1, is very similar to that of Windows 95, 98, and Millennium Edition. You can left- and right-click on it to manipulate icons, create new folders and icons, and modify the display properties, such as background, screen saver, and overall appearance. By pressing Alt-Tab in Windows NT, you can jump between different open programs in forward sequence; by pressing Shift-Alt-Tab, you can jump between programs in reverse order.

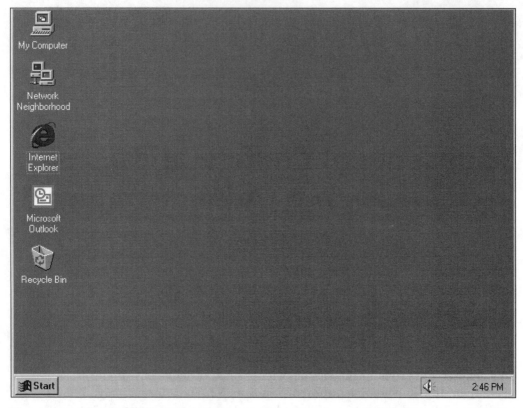

Figure 3.1   Windows NT desktop interface.

Another useful feature in Windows NT is the Task Manager, (see Figure 3.2) which is called up on the desktop by pressing Ctrl-Alt-Del; in all previous Windows editions, that key combination was used to reboot the system, in particular after it had frozen. From the utility front end, you can lock the system, log off, shut down, change your password, and invoke the new Task Manager active monitoring.

Active monitoring enables you to use the Task Manager to view or end active system processes and applications; monitor current CPU usage; review CPU usage history, memory usage, and memory usage history; and get real-time statistics on physical and kernel memory usage.

Taskbar

Next, from the desktop, we'll begin our detailed exploration of the Windows NT interface at the taskbar. From the right side on the taskbar, you can view the current time and change speaker volume settings. On the left side is the familiar Start button, from which you can open programs, access utilities, search for and/or run files, and explore help topics (shown in Figure 3.3).

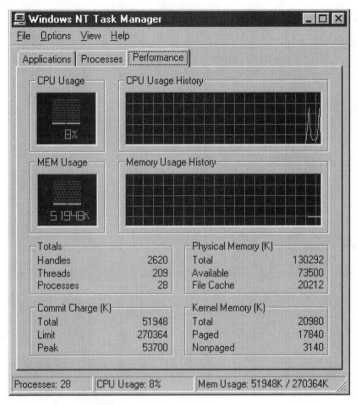

Figure 3.2   Windows NT Task Manager.

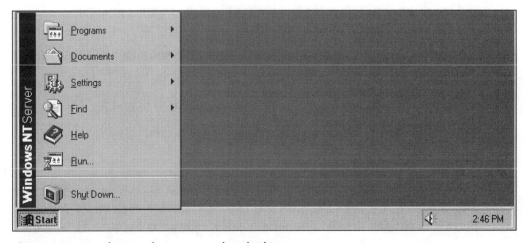

Figure 3.3   Use the Start button to explore further.

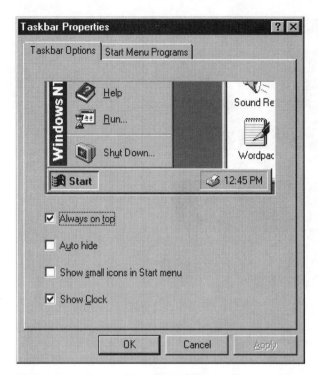

Figure 3.4 Customizing the taskbar.

As on your Win 9x/ME desktop interface, the Windows NT taskbar can be positioned on either side of the screen and either horizontally or vertically (the default alignment). To customize the taskbar settings, click, in this sequence, on Start/Settings/Taskbar. You will see the screen shown in Figure 3.4. Here you're given these options for taskbar settings:

Always on top. Makes the taskbar visible when running programs.

Auto hide. Hides the taskbar.

Show small icons in Start menu. Shortens the Start menu.

Show Clock. Enables or disables the clock in the taskbar.

When you're through customizing the taskbar, click OK and we'll begin managing files and folders.

Files and Folders

Working with files and folders in Windows NT is just as easy as with your current version of Windows. At the desktop screen, double-click on the My Computer icon to open the My Computer window (shown in Figure 3.5), which

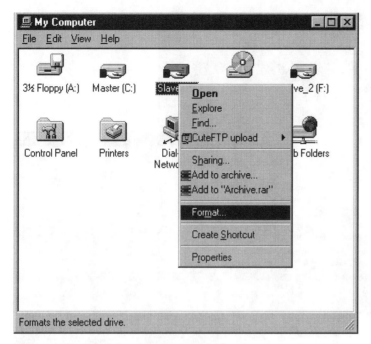

Figure 3.5 Administering files and folders.

displays all available drives: floppy, CD-ROM, and hard disk drive mappings; you'll also see a link to the Control Panel and Printers, among others. By positioning your mouse over an icon and pressing the right button, you can access administrative options (which options you are offered depends on your computer type and the third-party software installed on it); typically these options include sharing, formatting, deleting, and creating shortcuts, as you can see in the figure. If you select Open, or double-click a partition in the My Computer window, you'll directly access a directory of files and/or folders within its hierarchy.

When you're through exploring the My Computer screen, close it to go back to the desktop, and look for the Recycle Bin icon.

Recycle Bin

The Recycle Bin is called that to more clearly identify its capabilities and to distinguish it from the terms *trash* and *trash can*, with which you may be familiar. *Recycle* means that if you delete a file or folder and then realize you shouldn't have, you will be able to recover it—*if* you haven't emptied the Recycle Bin since you deleted the file or folder. Until you empty the Recycle Bin, all files and folders you've sent there by the delete action remain there for

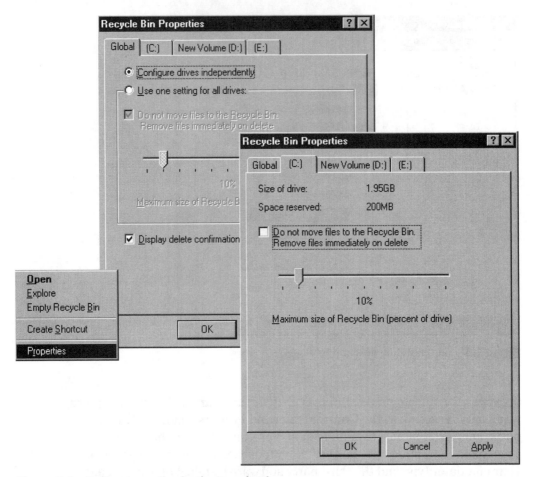

Figure 3.6 Setting properties for the Recycle Bin.

easy retrieval. (But keep in mind that files and folders in the Recycle Bin are also still taking up space.)

By right-mouse clicking on the Recycle Bin icon, you can permanently delete its contents and free up the space. This action also enables you to customize the bin, for example, by allocating available space using the Properties option (see Figure 3.6). Toggle the sliding bar to increase/decrease the size that should be allocated for Recycle Bin use. You can conserve disk space by reducing its size.

Now, close out of the Recycle Bin and return to the desktop.

NT Explorer

Back at the desktop, select, in this sequence, Start/Programs/Windows NT Explorer. The Windows NT Explorer (shown in Figure 3.7) is a global

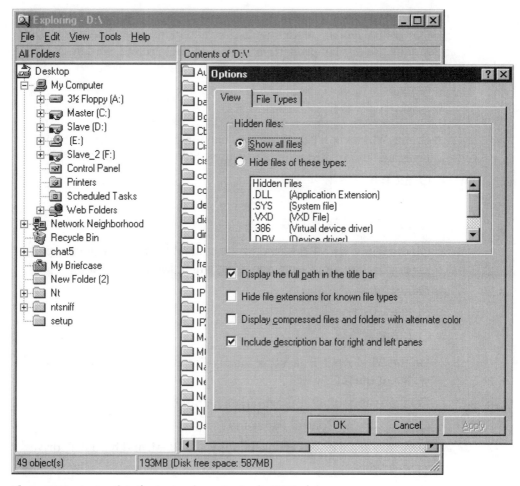

Figure 3.7   Inspecting the system's contents via NT Explorer.

file/folder management utility. This feature enables you to quickly review the system's entire contents, as well as to move, copy, rename, and delete files. Furthermore, you can customize views and map drives directly from the Explorer window.

Think It Over

Take a couple of minutes before moving on to the next section to test your comprehension of the preceding material by answering these questions. The answers to these and subsequent questions in this chapter can be found in Appendix A in the back of this book.

3.1. On the Windows NT desktop, you can left- and right-mouse click to manipulate icons, create new folders and icons, install software, and modify the display properties, including background, screen saver, and overall appearance.

    ○ True

    ○ False

3.2. On the Windows NT desktop, you can jump between different open programs in forward sequence using which key combination?

    ○ Alt-Tab

    ○ Shift-Alt-Tab

    ○ Ctrl-Esc

3.3. On the Windows NT desktop, you can jump between different open programs in reverse sequence using which key combination?

    ○ Alt-Tab

    ○ Shift-Alt-Tab

    ○ Ctrl-Esc

3.4. On the Windows NT desktop, the My Computer window displays which of the following?

    ○ A directory of all files within its hierarchy

    ○ A link to the Control Panel and Printers

    ○ All available drives such as floppy, CD-ROM, and hard disk drive mappings

3.5. Pertaining to the Windows NT Explorer, which of the following are true statements?

    ○ The Windows NT Explorer is a global file/folder management utility.

    ○ Using this feature, you can quickly explore the system's entire contents and move, copy, view, rename, and delete files.

    ○ You can customize views and map drives directly within the Explorer window.

Basic Administration

By now it should be apparent that, given the collection of utilities and administrative modules, working in Windows NT is very easy. The next sections will

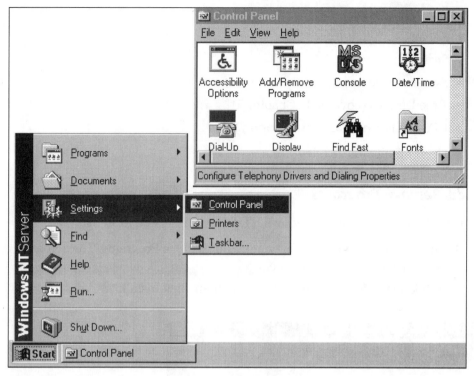

Figure 3.8   Displaying the Control Panel's many useful utilities.

demonstrate just how easy it is by stepping through a number of the more useful techniques as we work our way through the Start menu.

Control Panel Step by Step

To begin, access the Control Panel by clicking, in this sequence, Start/Settings/Control Panel, as illustrated in Figure 3.8. The Control Panel houses programs used to configure many of the computer's settings. Among the most useful modules are the following:

- Add/Remove Programs
- Devices
- Licensing
- Modems
- Network (covered in in Chapter 5)
- Ports
- Printers (covered in Chapter 5)

- SCSI Adapters
- Server
- Services
- System (covered later in this chapter)
- Tape Devices (covered in Chapter 5)
- UPS (uninterruptible power supply)

We'll go through these one by one.

Add/Remove Programs

To install new software to Windows NT, follow these simple steps:

1. In the Control Panel, double-click Add/Remove Programs. The screen shown in Figure 3.9 will appear.
2. Click on the Install/Uninstall tab and then click Install.

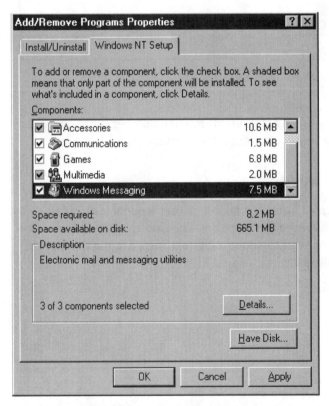

Figure 3.9   Adding/removing software to/from Windows.

3. Follow the Windows prompt to insert the appropriate medium, CD-ROM or floppy disk, or to identify the hard disk drive location of the program.

To remove software from Windows, follow these simple steps:

1. In the Control Panel, double-click Add/Remove Programs.
2. Click on the Install/Uninstall tab and select the component you want to remove.
3. Click Add/Remove.

To add or remove a Windows NT Setup component, follow these simple steps:

1. In the Control Panel, double-click Add/Remove Programs.
2. Click on the Windows NT Setup tab and select the component you want to add or remove.
3. To add all parts of a component, click its check box. To remove all parts of a component, clear its check box. To add or remove some parts of a component, highlight the component, then click Details. Check or clear the parts as needed, then click OK.

 During the Add/Remove Programs process, depending on the Windows NT Setup component, at the conclusion of step 3, you may be prompted to insert your Windows NT Server CD-ROM into your computer.

Devices

To enable and disable device configurations when you boot the system using specific hardware profiles, follow these simple steps:

1. In the Control Panel, double-click Devices (see Figure 3.10).
2. Under Devices, click a device to highlight it.
3. Click the HW Profiles button.
4. Click the profile to change.
5. Click Enable or Disable.

To set the device's startup type or to select how to start the device, follow these simple steps:

1. In the Control Panel, double-click Devices.
2. Under Devices, click the device whose startup type you want to change.

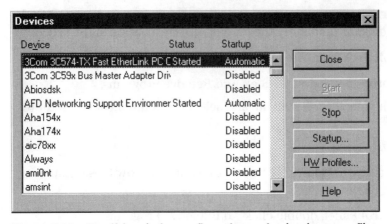

Figure 3.10   Specifying device configurations using hardware profiles.

3. Click Startup.

4. Under Startup Type, click, as appropriate, Boot, System, Automatic, Manual, or Disabled.

 Be careful when changing the startup type of a Boot or System device, such as for critical system devices, because doing so can crash the system.

To start or deactivate a device, follow these simple steps:

1. In the Control Panel, double-click Devices.

2. Under Devices, click the device you want to start or deactivate.

3. Click Start or Stop.

 If "Started" appears in the status column, this indicates the device driver is already loaded. If the status column is blank, the device driver is not loaded. Also note: If a device is essential to system operation, the Stop button will be unavailable.

Licensing

You use the Licensing utility, shown in Figure 3.11, for the following three actions:

- To specify the appropriate licensing mode (Per Server or Per Seat) for each server product installed on your computer (explained in Chapter 2)

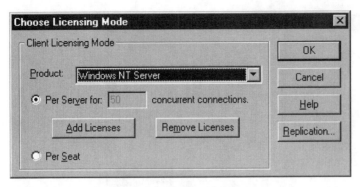

Figure 3.11   Specifying the Windows NT license mode.

- To add or remove Per Server mode licenses
- To configure licensing replication

If you are unsure which licensing mode to choose, click Per Server. The license agreement allows you a one-time, one-way option to change to Per Seat licensing mode later.

Modems

To install or remove a modem, you use the NT Modem Wizard, which takes you through a three-step process:

1. In the Control Panel, double-click Modems.
2. In the Modems Properties window, click Add. To remove a currently installed modem, click Remove.
3. Follow the Modem Wizard's (Figure 3.12) instructions: If you want to select the modem manually from the supplied list, check the appropriate box and then click Next; otherwise, the wizard will query the available ports on your system as it searches for the new modem.

Depending on the modem type, you may be prompted to insert your Windows NT Server CD-ROM or manufacturer disk into your computer.

To modify the current modem's properties, follow these simple steps:

1. In the Control Panel, double-click Modems.
2. In the Modems Properties window, click Properties (Figure 3.13).

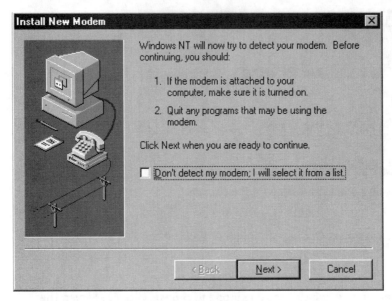

Figure 3.12   Adding a new modem using the Modem Wizard.

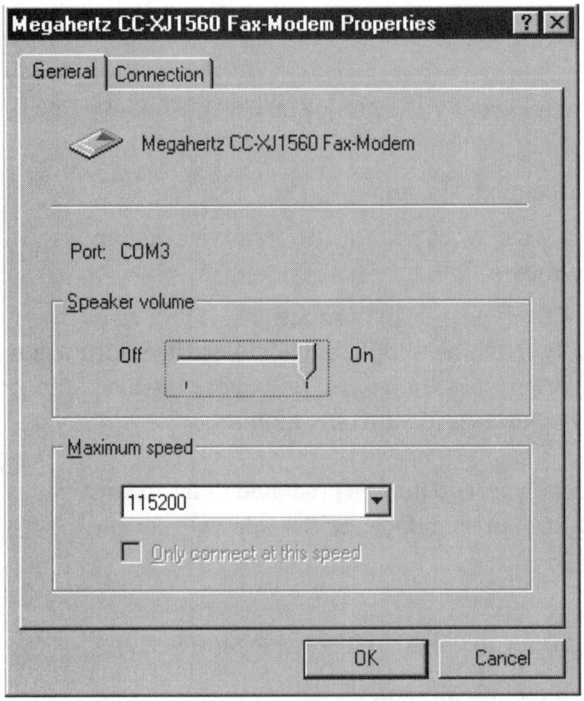

Figure 3.13   Changing modem settings.

3. Here you can toggle the speaker; change the connection speed; specify data bits, parity, and stop bits; modify call preferences, including dial tone acceptance, hang-up, disconnection timeout, error and flow control, and modulation type; and specify whether or not to keep a call log.

Ports

Windows NT lets you specify the communications settings for a selected serial (COM) port, as shown in Figure 3.14. Adding and deleting a port couldn't be simpler: To add a new serial port to your system, click Add; to delete a port, click the particular port in the Ports box, then click Delete. Specifying basic serial port settings is easy, too: Here are the steps:

1. In the Control Panel, double-click Ports.
2. Click the port, then click Settings. To display the options for each setting, click the arrow to the right of each box.
3. Set the options to match the device connected to the port.
4. Click OK.
5. Click Close.

To specify advanced serial port settings, follow these simple steps:

1. Double-click Ports in the Control Panel.
2. Click the port, then click Settings.
3. Click Advanced.
4. If your serial port hardware uses address values other than those detected by Windows NT, change the base I/O address to one available in

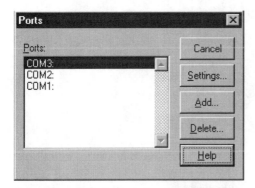

Figure 3.14   Changing serial port settings.

the I/O address drop-down list. If you are using a computer that cannot access COM1 and COM3 or COM2 and COM4 simultaneously, and you want to use these ports, specify a unique interrupt request (IRQ) number for each port to one available in the IRQ drop-down list. You may also change the port number of a port (e.g., from COM3 to COM33).

5. To enable buffering for incoming data, along with additional functionality on newer COM ports, select the FIFO (first in-first out) Enabled check box.

6. Click OK.

7. Click Restart Now to make the changes take effect.

SCSI Adapters

To view information about an attached SCSI adapter, follow these steps:

1. In the Control Panel, double-click SCSI Adapters.

2. Click the SCSI adapter or connected device.

3. Click Properties.

4. Click the Card Info (shown in Figure 3.15) to view information about the device and its current status; click the Driver tab to view information about the device driver; click the Resources tab to view the resource settings for the adapter.

Figure 3.15   Viewing information about an SCSI adapter.

To install a new SCSI device driver, follow this procedure:

1. In the Control Panel, double-click SCSI Adapters.

2. Click the Drivers tab in the SCSI Adapters window.

3. Click Add.

4. Click the driver you want to add. If the driver you want to install is not listed, click Have Disk, then follow the instructions on the screen.

To remove an SCSI device, log on as Administrator, and follow these steps:

1. In the Control Panel, double-click SCSI Adapters.

2. Click the Drivers tab in the SCSI Adapters window.

3. Click the driver to be removed.

4. Click Remove.

Server

The Server program (shown in Figure 3.16) enables you to manage server properties on the system. Invoke the utility to view a list of the computer's open shared resources, shared resources, and users connected to the computer. Or use the Server program to view a list of, and manage locks for, imported subdirectories. In addition, you can use this program to manage locks, stabilization, and subtree replication for the subdirectories exported from this computer; manage the list of administrative alert recipients; set the logon script path for a server; and set up an export server and import computer. We'll step through this program's numerous capabilities one at a time.

To view a list of the computer's open shared resources, follow these steps:

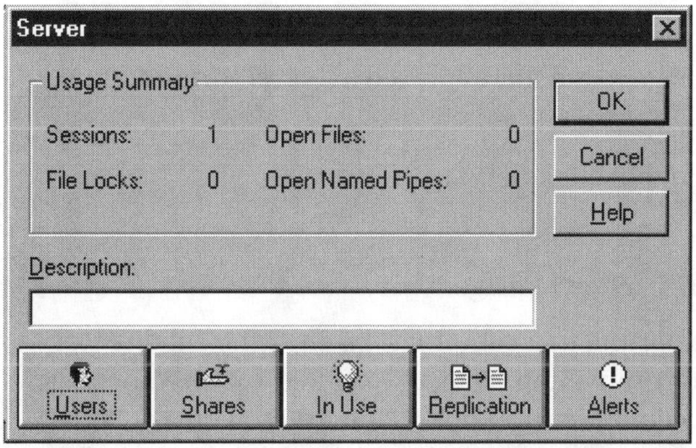

Figure 3.16   Managing server properties on the system.

1. In the Control Panel, double-click Server.

2. Click In Use.

3. To close an open resource, click the resource in the list, then click Close Resource. To close all open resources, click Close All Resources.

4. If necessary, click Refresh to update the list.

 Closing resources may result in loss of data, so before you do this, always warn connected users. Also be aware that when you are administering another computer remotely, your connection appears as an open named pipe; therefore your connection cannot be closed.

Here's the process to access a list of the computer's shared resources:

1. In the Control Panel, double-click Server.

2. Click Shares.

3. To view the users connected to a shared resource, click a sharename in the Sharename box. To disconnect one user from all shared resources, click the username in the Connected Users box, and then click Disconnect. To disconnect all users from all shared resources, click Disconnect All.

To view a list of users connected to the computer, follow these simple steps:

1. In the Control Panel, double-click Server.

2. Click Users.

3. To view the resources opened by one user, click a username in the Connected Users box. To disconnect one user, click the username in the Connected Users box, then click Disconnect. To disconnect all users, click Disconnect All.

To view a list of, or to manage locks for, imported subdirectories, follow this procedure:

1. In the Control Panel, double-click Server.

2. Click Replication.

3. Under Import Directories, click Manage.

4. To temporarily stop importing to a subdirectory, click the subdirectory and click Add Lock. To resume importing to a locked subdirectory, click the subdirectory, then click Remove Lock. Click Add to add a subdirectory to the list. Click Remove to remove the selected subdirectory from the list.

In general, you should remove only those locks that you have applied. Moreover, you should import resources only when the Locks column shows a value of 0 for the subdirectory, indicating it has zero locks.

To manage locks, stabilization, and subtree replication for the subdirectories exported from the computer, follow these simple steps:

1. In the Control Panel, double-click Server.

2. Click Replication.

3. Under Import Directories, click Manage.

4. To temporarily stop exporting a subdirectory, click the subdirectory; then click Add Lock. To resume exporting a locked subdirectory, click the subdirectory, then click Remove Lock. To export a subdirectory and all the subdirectories in its tree, click the subdirectory; then select the Entire Subtree check box. To export only the highest subdirectory in a tree, click the subdirectory; then click to clear this check box.

5. To specify a 2-minute or longer delay during which no changes can be made before files are exported, click a subdirectory, then select the Wait Until Stabilized check box. To export files immediately after they are changed and saved, click a subdirectory, then click to clear this check box.

Follow these steps to manage server properties:

1. In the Control Panel, double-click Server.

2. To change the computer description, type appropriate new text in the Description box.

3. To change server properties, click, as appropriate, Users, Shares, In Use, Replication, or Alerts.

 The computer description will appear in the Comment field of the computer's properties and in the Network Neighborhood. This can be used to identify a specific computer in large networks that have numerous server systems.

To manage the list of people who are to receive administrative alerts, take these steps:

1. In the Control Panel, double-click Server.

2. Click Alerts.

3. To add a user or computer to the list of alert recipients, type the user- or computer name in the New Computer or Username box, then click Add.

To remove a user or computer from the list of alert recipients, click the user- or computer name in the Send Administrative Alerts To box, then click Remove.

 Administrative alerts related to server and resource use are generated by the system; they inform recipients about security, access, user session, server shutdown, and printer problems.

Setting the logon script path for a server is a three-step process:

1. In the Control Panel, double-click Server.
2. Click Replication.
3. In the Logon Script Path box, type a local path. Typically, you will enter a path to a \Scripts subdirectory of the replication To Path.

 For Windows NT Workstation computers, you cannot change the logon script path from the default (usually, systemroot\System32 \Repl\Import\Scripts).

In regard to the procedure for setting the logon script, make note of the following points:

- When a server authenticates a logon request for a user account that has a logon script assigned, Windows NT locates the logon script by combining a local logon script path specified using the Server option in Control Panel with a filename (and optionally a relative path) as indicated in User Manager.

- Make sure to store master copies of every logon script for a domain under the same replication export directory of a given Windows NT Server computer. (This makes it possible to replicate copies of these scripts to the other servers in the domain.) Then, for each Windows NT Server computer, enter the path to the imported logon scripts in the Logon Script Path of the Directory Replication dialog box.

To set up a replication export server, follow these steps:

 Only Windows NT Server computers can be set up as replication export servers; Windows NT Workstation computers cannot. And before performing this procedure, make sure an appropriate logon account has been assigned to the Directory Replicator service.

1. In the Control Panel, double-click Server.

2. Click Replication.

3. Click Export Directories.

4. To change the path from which subdirectories will be exported, type a local path in the From Path box.

5. Under Export Directories, click Add; specify to which domain or computer to export subdirectories. To stop exporting subdirectories to a domain or computer, click the domain or computer in the To List, then click Remove. To manage locks, stabilization, and subtree replication for the subdirectories exported from this computer, click Manage; make the appropriate entries in the dialog box that appears.

6. In the Directory Replication dialog box, click OK.

Regarding this procedure, note the following:

- The directories to be exported must be subdirectories of the replication From Path. Optionally, you can add the files to be exported to these subdirectories. Once you set up replication, any files added later to these subdirectories will be exported automatically. You can also later add other subdirectories to the From Path.

- By default, the To List contains no entries, and the computer automatically exports to the local domain. If you add entries to the To List, the computer will no longer automatically export to the local domain; if you want to export to the local domain, you must explicitly add the domain name to the To List.

To set up a replication import computer, follow these simple steps:

 Make sure an appropriate logon account has been assigned to the Directory Replicator service before performing this procedure. And note, both Windows NT Server computers and Windows NT Workstation computers can be set up as import computers.

1. In the Control Panel, double-click Server.

2. Click Replication.

3. Click Import Directories.

4. To change the path in which imported subdirectories will be stored, type a local path in the To Path box.

5. Click Add, then specify from which domain or export server to import subdirectories. To stop importing subdirectories from an export server or domain, click the domain or computer name in the From List, then click Remove. To view a list of the subdirectories that have been

imported to the computer or to manage locks on those imported subdi-rectories, click Manage.

Two additional points complete the discussion of this procedure:

- When you finish setting up a replication import server, the system starts the Directory Replicator service if it's not running already.
- By default, the From List contains no entries, and the computer automati-cally imports from the local domain. If you add any entries to the From List, the computer will no longer automatically import from the local domain; if you want to import from the local domain, you must explicitly add the domain name to the From List.

Services

The Services program, shown in Figure 3.17, is where you'll start, stop, pause, or continue each of the services available on the computer and pass startup parameters to the services. Among the default services provided with Win-dows NT are the following (some of which will be added later in this book and not all of which are visible in the figure; use the scroll bar on the right to view them all):

- Alerter
- ClipBook Server
- Computer Browser
- Directory Replicator
- EventLog
- Messenger
- Net Logon
- Network DDE
- Network DDE DSDM
- NT LM Security Support Provider
- Remote Procedure Call (RPC) Locator
- Remote Procedure Call (RPC) Service
- Schedule
- Server
- Spooler
- UPS
- Workstation

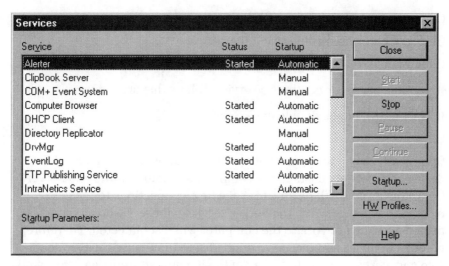

Figure 3.17   Managing services on the system.

In addition to these default offerings, others may be listed in the Services dialog box, indicating that third-party services that have been installed.

To configure startup for a service, follow these simple steps:

 To configure service startup, you must be logged on to a user account that has membership in the Administrators local group.

1. In the Control Panel, double-click Services.

2. Click the service you want to start.

3. Click Startup.

4. Under Startup Type, select either Automatic or Manual (the Disabled option can be used to stop a service and prohibit it from starting again). To specify the user account the service will use to log on, click System Account or This Account. If you choose This Account, click the browse button (…), specify a user account, and then type the password for the user account in both the Password and Confirm Password boxes. To provide a user interface on a desktop that can be used by whomever is logged in when the service is started, select the Allow Service to Interact with Desktop check box. (Note that Allow Service to Interact with Desktop is available only if the service is running as a Local System account.)

Take these steps to enable or disable a service for a hardware profile:

1. In the Control Panel, double-click Services.

2. Click the service, then click HW Profiles.

3. Click the hardware profile to configure.

4. Click Enable or Disable.

To start, stop, pause, or continue a service, follow this procedure:

1. In the Control Panel, double-click Services.

2. Click the service.

3. Click Start, Stop, Pause, or Continue. Note that when you pause the Server service, only users in the computer's Administrators and Server Operators groups will be able to make new connections to the computer; and when you stop the Server service, all users who are connected over the network to the computer will disconnected. Therefore, before stopping a service, it is a good idea to first pause the Server service and alert all connected users of the impending stoppage. Once you stop a Server service, the affected computer can no longer be administered remotely, meaning that the Server service can only be restarted locally.

4. Optionally, to pass startup parameters to a service, type the parameters in the Startup Parameters box before clicking Start. Note that a backslash (\) is treated as an escape character.

UPS

Windows NT give you the option to use the UPS program, shown in Figure 3.18, to configure an uninterruptible power supply. The UPS program enables you to set various options—which depend on the specific UPS hardware installed on your system—for controlling how UPS services work on a computer. With the UPS tool you can determine:

- The serial port to which the UPS device is connected

- Whether the UPS device sends a signal if the regular power supply fails, if battery power is low, or if the UPS device allows remote shutdown

- The time intervals for maintaining battery power, recharging the battery, or sending warning messages after power failure

To install an uninterruptible power supply for a computer, follow these simple steps:

1. In the Control Panel, double-click UPS.

2. In the UPS dialog box, select the Uninterruptible Power Supply Is Installed On check box, then specify the serial port to which you want the UPS battery connected.

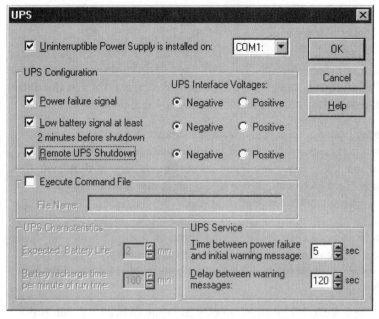

Figure 3.18   Managing UPS services on the system.

To turn off UPS for a computer:

1. In the Control Panel, double-click UPS.

2. In the UPS dialog box, click to clear the Uninterruptible Power Supply Is Installed On check box.

To start the UPS services:

1. In the Control Panel, double-click Services.

2. Click UPS.

3. Click Start.

To configure UPS options:

1. In the Control Panel, double-click UPS.

2. In the UPS dialog box, select the Uninterruptible Power Supply Is Installed On check box, then specify the serial port to which you want the UPS battery connected.

3. If the UPS device on your system makes it possible to send a message when the power supply fails, select the Power Failure Signal check box. This setting corresponds to the clear-to-send (CTS) cable signal for the UPS serial port connection. If the UPS device on your system makes it possible to send a warning when battery power is low, select the Low

Battery Signal check box. This setting corresponds to the data-carrier-detect (DCD) cable signal for the UPS serial port connection.

4. Next to the Remote UPS Shutdown check box, click Positive or Negative to specify the interface voltage. To enable remote shutdown, select the Remote UPS Shutdown check box. This setting corresponds to the data-terminal-ready (DTR) cable signal for the UPS serial port connection.

 If the battery can accept a signal from the UPS service telling it to shut down, you must specify the correct interface voltage in the UPS configuration dialog box, even if you do not enable remote shutdown. If the voltage is set incorrectly, some UPS devices may shut down your computer immediately upon loss of power.

5. For *each item* selected in the UPS Configuration group, under UPS Interface Voltages, click Positive or Negative. This setting defines how your UPS device communicates with the UPS service based on pin settings for the COM port.

6. In the Expected Battery Life box, specify the time in minutes that the system can run on battery power. The range is 2 to 720 minutes; the default is 2 minutes. Be sure to input the expected time found in the specification guide packaged with your battery.

7. In the Battery Recharge Time box, specify the time in minutes that the battery must be recharged for every minute of run time. The range is 1 to 250 minutes; the default is 100 minutes for each minute of battery run time. Be sure to input the recharge time found in the specification guide packaged with your battery.

8. In the Time Between Power Failure box, specify how much time, in seconds, you want to elapse between the occurrence of a power failure and when the first message is sent to notify users. The range is 0 to 120 seconds; the default is 5 seconds.

9. In the Delay Between Warning Messages box, specify the interval, in seconds, that you want to elapse between a message being sent notifying users of a power failure and one sent to advise them to stop using the computer. The range is 5 to 300 seconds; the default is 120 seconds.

10. When you're satisfied that you have all these time factors as you want them, click OK.

 You can also configure the UPS option to execute a command file immediately before system shutdown; for example, such a file might run a command to close remote connections. Be aware, however, that this command file must execute within 30 seconds; if it does not, it will jeopardize the safe shutdown of your Windows NT computer.

Windows NT also makes it possible for you to test your UPS configuration:

1. Simulate a power failure by disconnecting the power to the UPS device. The computer and peripherals connected to the UPS device should remain operational, and a warning message and/or alert should appear on screen.

2. Wait until the UPS battery reaches a low level, at which point system shutdown should occur.

3. Restore power to the UPS device.

4. Check the system login Event Viewer to ensure that all actions were logged and that there were no errors.

Summary

This chapter introduced you to the Windows NT desktop interface. You learned about file and folder management, and gained an understanding of the most useful control panel utilities and administrative modules, including Add/Remove Programs, Devices, Licensing, Modems, Ports, SCSI Adapters, Server, Services, and UPS. To expand on this knowledge, as we move forward, we'll perform a number of server optimization and system administration tasks using Administrative Tools.

Think It Over

3.6. Which of the following best describes the Windows NT Control Panel?

O The Control Panel houses programs used to change many of the computer's settings.

O The Control Panel lists a directory of all files within its hierarchy.

O The Control Panel is used to enable and disable device configurations.

3.7. Which of the following sequences best describes using the Add/Remove Programs module from the Control Panel to remove a Windows NT Setup component?

O Double-click Add/Remove Programs in the Control Panel. From the Windows NT Setup tab, select the component you want to remove. To remove all parts of a component, clear its check box. To remove some parts of a component, highlight the component, then click Details. Clear the parts as needed, then click OK.

○ Double-click Add/Remove Programs in the Control Panel. From the Windows NT Setup tab, select the component you want to remove. To remove all parts of a component, clear its check box. To remove some parts of a component, highlight the component, then click Details. Check the parts as needed, then click OK.

○ Double-click Add/Remove Programs in the Control Panel (refer to Figure 3.9). From the Install/Uninstall tab, click Uninstall. Follow the Windows prompt to insert a CD-ROM or floppy disk or to identify a hard disk drive.

3.8. Changing the startup type of a Boot or System device may potentially do what?

○ Nothing

○ Reboot the system

○ Crash the system

3.9. In the Device module from the Control Panel, if a device is essential to system operation, the Stop button will be unavailable.

○ True

○ False

3.10. In the Licensing module from the Control Panel, the Per Seat license agreement allows you a one-time, one-way option to change to Per Server licensing mode later.

○ True

○ False

3.11. Closing open shared resources from the Server module in the Control Panel may result in loss of data.

○ True

○ False

3.12. Using the Server module under managing locks, stabilization, and subtree replication for the subdirectories, which best describes the process to temporarily stop exporting a subdirectory?

○ Click the subdirectory, then click Add Lock.

○ Click the subdirectory, then click Remove Lock.

○ Click the subdirectory, then select the Entire Subtree check box.

3.13. As related to server and resource use, which of the following administrative alerts are generated by the system?

  ○ Security problems

  ○ Access problems

  ○ Drive mapping problems

  ○ User session problems

  ○ Licensing problems

  ○ Server shutdown problems

  ○ Printer problems

3.14. When a server authenticates a logon request, and that user account
has a logon script assigned, Windows NT locates the logon script by
combining a local logon script path specified using the Server option
in Control Panel with a filename as specified in User Manager.

  ○ True

  ○ False

3.15. Any Windows computer can be set up as a replication export server.

  ○ True

  ○ False

3.16. To configure service startup, you do not have to be logged on to a
user account that has membership in the Administrators local group.

  ○ True

  ○ False

Administration Tools

This chapter will provide information that will enable you to perform server administration and user configurations using the NT Administrative Tools. Step-by-step, we'll examine the functionalities and also make configurations from the Disk Administrator, Event Viewer, License Manager, Network Client Administrator, Server Manager, System Policy Editor, and finally User Manager for Domains.

 Hands-on simulations of the material contained in this chapter can be found on the book's companion CD-ROM.

Using the Administration Tools Step by Step

By default during the installation process, the Windows NT Setup program creates and populates a file folder named Administrative Tools. To examine the folder's contents click on Start/Programs/Administrative Tools (see Figure 4.1). The programs that can be executed from this folder enable you to perform a variety of useful administrative functions, from managing hard disk drives and troubleshooting event files to creating groups of users. In this chapter, we'll be working with the following utilities:

Figure 4.1   Windows NT administrative tools.

Disk Administrator

Event Viewer

License Manager

Network Client Administrator

Server Manager

System Policy Editor

User Manager for Domains

Later chapters will cover Backup, DNS Manager, Migration Tool for Net-Ware, Performance Monitor, Remote Access Admin, and NT Diagnostics.

Disk Administrator

According to Microsoft, Disk Administrator (shown in Figure 4.2) is a graphical tool for managing hard disks—the magnetic disk used to store files and data. This tool encompasses and extends the functionality of character-based disk management tools into one graphical interface. Examples are MS-DOS fdisk, which is used to create and format DOS partition (space divided on a hard drive that behaves like a separate disk drive), and the fault tolerance character applications, which are used to create backup or mirror drives (so

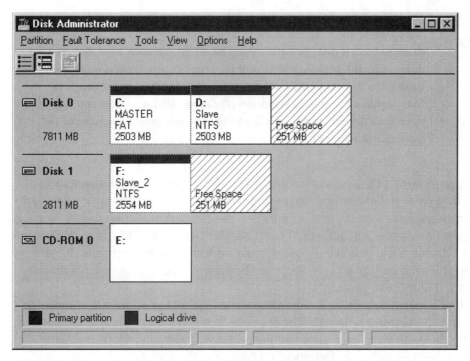

Figure 4.2   Using the Disk Administrator to manage partitions.

that if one fails, the other can take over). The following list provides an overview of some of the things you can do with this graphical tool:

- Create and delete partitions on a hard disk and logical drives within an extended partition
- Format and label volumes
- Read status information about disks, such as the partition sizes and the amount of free space that is available for creating additional partitions
- Read status information about Windows NT volumes, such as the drive-letter assignment, volume label, file system type, and size
- Make and change drive-letter assignments for hard disk volumes and CD-ROM devices
- Create and delete volume sets
- Extend volumes and volume sets
- Create and delete stripe sets with or without parity
- Regenerate a missing or failed member of a stripe set with parity
- Establish or break disk-mirror sets

The internal hard disk on a new computer is partitioned during initial
setup when you load the Windows NT operating software. Making
changes to that disk, or partitioning an additional new hard disk, is
done using the Disk Administrator program. Disk Administrator cannot
be used to further partition the system partition because it contains
files required to operate Windows NT Server. Also note that you can
open Disk Administrator only if you are logged on as a member of the
Administrators group.

Upon starting Disk Administrator, a scrollable, graphical representation of
all the physical disks connected to your computer appears, along with their
partitions. For example, in the figure, we see the two most popular file system
types: File Allocation Table (FAT) and NT File System (NTFS). A status bar at
the bottom of the window provides basic information on partitions. A color-
coded legend on top of the status bar shows what the different partition colors and patterns represent.

If you make changes and commit to them by clicking on the OK button,
Disk Administrator will make the requested changes and display a message
after the disks have been successfully updated. To expand on file system
types, we'll examine the details of FAT and NTFS.

  Sometimes after you click OK, another message will advise you that
changes have been made that require you to restart the computer. This
happens when, for example, you extend a volume set, lock a volume, or
search for or restore disk configuration information. When you click OK,
Disk Administrator initiates a complete system shutdown, closes all
open applications, and restarts the computer.

File Allocation Table System

The two file system types currently sustained and supported by Windows NT
include the FAT and NTFS modes. The FAT is a system that establishes a table
used by the operating system to locate files on a disk, even if the file is divided
into many sections that are scattered around, or fragmented. This table makes
it possible for the FAT to find and monitor them all.

The FAT is the most uncomplicated type of file system supported by Windows NT. And because it begins with very little overhead, it is most applicable
to drives and/or partitions that are smaller than 400 MB. It resides at the top of
the fixed quantity of allocated storage space on the hard disk, referred to as
the *volume*. Two copies of the FAT are maintained for security purposes, in
case one becomes corrupt.

A FAT table and the root directory must be stored in a predetermined location for successful booting, each preset by the system during the initial setup.

FAT partition formats are allocated in groups called *clusters*, and cluster sizes are determined by the correlating volume size—fixed amounts of storage space. For example, when a file is created, an entry is automatically made in the directory and the first cluster number containing data is recognized. This entry in the FAT table either indicates that this is the last cluster of the given file or points to the next one.

 If the FAT table is not updated regularly, it can lead to data loss.

Because the disk read heads must be repositioned to the drive's logical track zero each time the FAT table is updated, updating FAT tables is time-consuming. And because, typically, there is no organization to the FAT directory structure, files are given the first open location on the drive.

The FAT supports only read-only, hidden, system, and archive file attributes, and it uses the traditional 8.3 file-naming convention—that is, all filenames must be created with the ASCII character set. All FAT names must start with either a letter or number, and they may contain any characters except the following:

period (.)

quotation mark (")

slashes in either direction (/ \ )

square brackets ([ ])

colon (:)

semicolon (;)

pipe symbol (|)

equal sign (=)

comma (,)

A file- or directory name may be up to eight characters long, followed by a period (.), plus an extension of up to three characters.

Advantages and Disadvantages of the FAT

The FAT has two primary advantages:

- In the case of hard disk failures, even on today's machines a bootable DOS floppy can be used to access the partition for problem troubleshooting.

- Under Windows NT, it is not possible to perform an undelete. However, if the file was located on a FAT partition and the system is restarted under MS-DOS, the file can be undeleted.

The disadvantages of FAT are as follows:

- As the size of the volume increases, FAT performance decreases; therefore, when working with drives or partitions over 400 MB in size, the FAT file system is not recommended.

- It is not possible to set security permissions on files located in FAT partitions. Also, FAT partitions are limited in size to 4 gigabytes (GB) maximum under Windows NT.

NT File System

The NTFS has features that improve reliability; these include transaction logs that help resolve disk failures. In addition, security features, such as access control permissions, can be set for directories and/or individual files. For large disk space requirements, NTFS supports *spanning volumes,* which makes it possible to distribute files and directories across several physical disks (see Figure 4.3). Because NTFS performance does not degrade, it is best used on volumes of 400 MB or more.

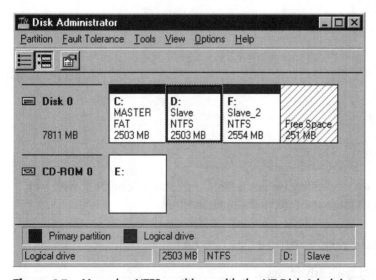

Figure 4.3   Managing NTFS partitions with the NT Disk Administrator.

NTFS file and directory names may be up to 255 characters long (which includes file extensions, separated by a period). Although these names preserve the case of the letters as they were typed in, they are not case-sensitive. NTFS names must start with either a letter or number and may contain any characters except the following:

question mark (?)

quotation mark (")

slashes in either direction (/ \)

ampersand (&)

asterisk (*)

pipe symbol (|)

colon (:)

Advantages and Disadvantages of the NTFS

There are several advantages to using the NTFS:

- Its recoverability functions preclude the need for disk repair utilities.
- It enables setting file and directory control permissions.
- Activity logging makes troubleshooting failures easier.
- It enables large-disk space management and long filename support (up to mixed-case 255 characters).

The disadvantages of NTFS are the following:

- Because of the amount of space overhead, NTFS should not be used on volumes smaller than 400 MB.
- It does not have integrated file encryption. Therefore, it is possible to boot under MS-DOS or another operating system and use a low-level disk-editing utility to view data stored on an NTFS volume.
- The NTFS overhead would not fit on a floppy disk; therefore, it is not possible to format a floppy with the NTFS file system; Windows NT always uses the FAT during the formatting procedure.

Permission Control

Permission control, whether on a FAT or NTFS partition, is a simple process, as long as you remember the limitations of each type of file system. Basically, the NTFS supports both local and remote user permissions on both local and

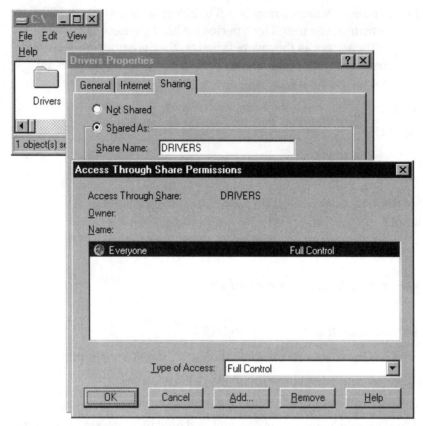

Figure 4.4   Applying permissions to a shared folder on a FAT partition.

shared files and/or folders, whereas the FAT supports only network shares. For example, by setting control access to a shared folder on a FAT partition (see Figure 4.4), all of its files and subfolders inherit the same permissions.

Creating Primary Partitions

When creating primary partitions, the system assigns space to a partition starting from the beginning of the available space. Therefore, in the beginning, there are no gaps between partitions. Gaps happen only when you delete a partition later on. For example, if you delete the second of three partitions and create a new smaller-sized second partition, that leaves a gap of free space between the second and third partitions. A disk can have up to four primary partitions, including the extended partition.

Creating a primary partition is easy with Disk Administrator—follow these simple steps:

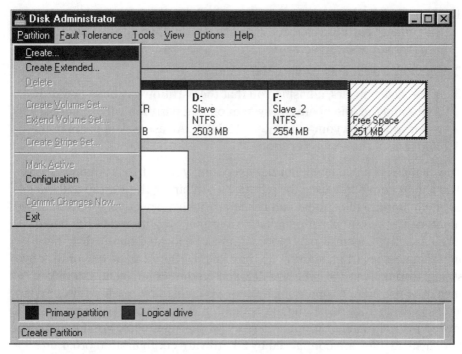

Figure 4.5   Creating a partition using the Disk Administrator.

1. From Start/Programs/Administrative Tools/Disk Administrator, select an area of free space on a disk.

2. On the Partition menu, click Create, as shown in Figure 4.5.

3. If the space you select is not the first primary partition created on the disk, the partition will not be recognized by MS-DOS and you'll receive a message prompting you to confirm the creation of another primary partition. Click Yes. Disk Administrator displays the minimum and maximum allowable sizes for the primary partition.

4. In the Create Partition of Size box, type the size of the primary partition that you want to create, then click OK. For a primary FAT partition, be sure to limit its size to under 2 gigabytes (GB). The new unformatted primary partition is assigned a drive letter.

The changes you make here will not be saved until you click Commit Changes Now or you quit Disk Administrator.

Marking Partitions as Active

To mark a partition as active, follow these simple steps:

1. From Start/Programs/Administrative Tools/Disk Administrator, select the primary partition that contains the startup files for the operating system that you want to activate.

2. On the Partition menu, click Mark Active.

3. A message appears, advising you that the partition has been marked active and that the operating system on that partition will be started when you restart your computer. Click OK. An asterisk appears in the color bar of the active partition.

The changes you make will not be saved until you quit Disk Administrator.

The names commonly used for partitions containing the startup and operating system files are the system and boot partitions, respectively. On x86-based computers, the system partition must be a primary partition that has been marked as active for startup purposes. It must be located on the disk that the computer accesses when starting up the system. There can be one only active system partition at a time, which is denoted on the screen by an asterisk. If you want to use another operating system, you must first mark its system partition as active before restarting the computer. But note that partitions on a Reduced Instruction Set Computing- (RISC) based computer are not marked active. Instead, they are configured by a hardware configuration program supplied by the manufacturer. On RISC-based computers, the system partition must be formatted for the FAT file system. The system partition can never be part of a stripe or volume set on either an x86- or RISC-based computer.

To secure the system partition on a RISC-based computer, follow these steps:

1. From Start/Programs/Administrative Tools/Disk Administrator, click on the Partition menu, then click Secure System Partition. When the command is in effect, a check mark appears next to it.

2. Click OK when a message appears asking you to confirm this request. Disk Administrator initiates a restart of your computer, which activates security on the system partition.

3. If you want to remove security from the system partition on a RISC-based computer, click Secure System Partition on the Partition menu to clear the check mark. Because security on the system partition is not removed until after you restart your computer, Disk Administrator initiates a restart.

 Because the system partition on a RISC-based computer must be formatted for the FAT file system, you cannot secure information in individual directories and files on that partition. The only way to secure the system partition is to allow access only to members of the Administrators group.

Creating Extended Partitions

Only one extended partition can be created per disk. You can use the free space in the extended partition to create multiple logical drives or use all or part of it when creating volume sets or other kinds of volumes for fault-tolerance purposes.

To create an extended partition, follow these steps:

1. From Start/Programs/Administrative Tools/Disk Administrator, select an area of free space on a disk.

2. On the Partition menu, click Create Extended. Disk Administrator displays the minimum and maximum sizes for the extended partition.

3. Type the size of the extended partition that you want to create, then click OK.

The changes you have made will not be saved until you click Commit Changes Now or you quit Disk Administrator.

Creating Logical Drives

To create a logical drive (see Figure 4.6) in an extended partition, follow these simple steps:

1. From Start/Programs/Administrative Tools/Disk Administrator, select an area of free space in an extended partition.

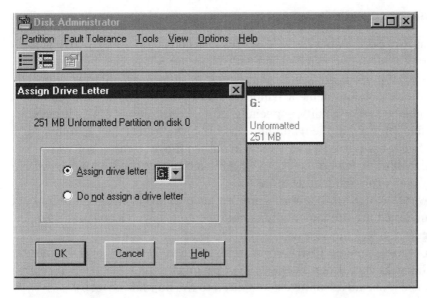

Figure 4.6   Assigning a logical drive letter.

2. On the Partition menu, click Create. Disk Administrator displays the minimum and maximum sizes for the logical drive.

3. Type the size of the logical drive that you want to create, then click OK.

Deleting Partitions, Volumes, or Logical Drives

Windows NT places certain restrictions on your ability to delete partitions, volumes, or logical drives, as follows:

- It will not let you delete the volume that contains the system files.

- You cannot delete individual partitions that are part of a set without deleting the entire set.

- You must delete all the logical drives or other volumes in an extended partition before you can delete the extended partition.

To delete a partition, volume, or logical drive, follow these simple steps:

1. From Start/Programs/Administrative Tools/Disk Administrator, select the partition, volume, or logical drive you want to delete.

2. On the Partition menu, click Delete.

3. When a message appears advising you that all data will be lost and asking you to confirm your action, click Yes. The partition, volume, or logical drive and any data are deleted, and the space becomes free again.

Fault Tolerance with Drive Sets

Redundant Array of Independent (formerly, Inexpensive) Disks (RAID) is a fault-tolerant system that can be used with Windows NT. It uses a combination of drive sets for performance and redundancy. In some cases, hardware-based RAID solutions that complement Windows NT are implemented for even better performance and reliability, especially with a fault-tolerant RAID subsystem (i.e., dual power supplies) and hard disk hot-swapping (the capability to replace a faulty hard drive without shutting down the system). A software-based RAID solution cannot compete with the latter because it struggles with current system processing utilization.

Windows NT RAID configurations are broken into levels based on redundant features that are fundamentally uncomplicated, as you'll see in the sample configuration techniques described in the next few chapters.

The four most common RAID levels are 0, 1, 3, and 5 (RAID Level 4 looks very much like Level 3, but now the stripes are much larger. Level 4 is rarely used because it has no advantages compared to the popular Level 5).

Level 0: Data Striping. Blocks of each file are spread across multiple disks. This level delivers no redundancy, but it does improve performance.

Level 1: Disk Mirroring. A technique whereby data is written to two identical disks simultaneously. If one of the disk drives goes down, the system can instantly switch to the other disk without any loss of data or interruption in service.

Level 3: Same as Level 0. In addition, one dedicated disk is reserved for error correction data. Level 3 provides good performance and some level of fault tolerance.

Level 5: Byte-Level Data Striping and Error Correction. Delivers excellent performance and good fault tolerance.

Hardware-based fault-tolerant mechanisms under Windows NT offer much better RAID performance and reliability. The most critical advantages include less downtime, fully redundant subsystems, and hot-swappable disk drives—upon drive failure.

There are three types of drive sets: *volume*, *stripe*, and *mirror*. But before we delve into those, we need to address how hardware reliability is measured. At the granular level, the reliability of hardware can be rated in the factor known as *mean time between failure* (MTBF), which is defined as average equipment uptime (in hours) without failure. Basically, when volume sets (fixed amounts of storage space on hard disk drives) of two or more drives are created, the MTBF will be significantly less than that of the individual drives. The formula for calculating the MTBF is:

$$MTBF_{set} = MTBF_{disk}/ N$$

where:

- $MTBF_{set}$ is the MTBF for the volume set.
- $MTBF_{disk}$ is the average MTBF for an individual disk.
- N is the number of disks in the set.

Volume Drive Sets

In Windows NT, volume sets can be made from free space segments (as available space) on hard disk drives (see Figure 4.7). (In subsequent chapters, you'll become more familiar with volumes as we practice configuring sets.) In a volume set, files are stored sequentially—meaning that after the first segment is filled, the second segment is filled, then the third, and so on. Volume sets can be composed of up to 32 hard disk drives, and a single hard-disk drive can contain more than one volume (via partitions); it's also possible for a single volume to contain or span multiple hard-disk drives.

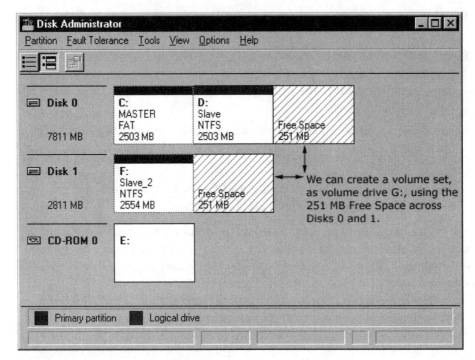

Figure 4.7   Creating a volume set across dual hard disk drives

 In our discussions, I'll often use the term *volume* as a synonym for the storage medium itself.

As just stated, in a volume set, files are stored sequentially. In contrast, in a stripe drive set, data is distributed and written equally in *stripes*, or layers, to all segments in the set. This results in an increase in performance. To achieve this, however, the segments—the available free space—must be sized equally; otherwise the larger segment's extra space would be wasted. On the other hand, based on these *striping properties*, there's no need for the system to store redundant information, which keeps overhead to a minimum.

 If a physical hard drive that participates in a stripe set becomes corrupt or fails, all data in the stripe set will be lost.

Adding Parity

Stripe sets with parity defeat the fault limitation by using error-checking in a fault-tolerant array. Consequently, if a physical hard drive that participates in a stripe set becomes corrupt or fails, not all data in the stripe set will be lost.

Here's how this works: For each layer or stripe of data in the set, a *parity record* is prepared. If a drive fails, the system can automatically rebuild the data that was in the now-missing segment using the information from parity records. You can think of the parity record as a kind of backup, or image, of the particular stripe or layer. Parity records, however, do come with an overhead space requirement, which, generally speaking, is as follows: an additional 30 percent for a three-disk set, 25 percent for a four-disk set, and 20 percent for a five-disk set. Still, overhead is less (by 50 percent or more) than that of RAID Level 1 using two mirrored hard disk drives.

 Microsoft recommends implementing striping with parity only on read-intensive sets—that is, primarily for data retrieval scenarios. Microsoft also recommends an additional 25 percent memory be added to accommodate the additional processes.

The disadvantages of adding parity to stripe sets include the additional required memory, a slight decrease in write performance as compared to striping alone, and the fact that neither the system nor boot hard disk drive partitions can be stored on a stripe set with parity.

Mirror Drive Sets

As you might guess from the name, in a mirror set, files are stored equally on two identical segments (two separate hard disk drives or equal-sized partitions on each). If one drive should fail, its mirror set will remain functional, thus providing fault tolerance. In fact, mirror drive sets provide the best performance and fastest recovery from failure. However, because of its duplicate setup, it should come as no surprise that there is a 50 percent overhead space requirement for mirror drive sets—two 500-MB mirrored segments equaling 1000 MB, or 1 GB, total space, allowing for 500 MB of actual data storage and retrieval (because both drives are identical, you're only using half the total size space).

Two methods are typically used with mirror drive sets: *data* and *disk duplexing*. In data duplexing, one hard disk drive controller is used for the two-disk drive mirror set. The disadvantage of this method is that although fault tolerance is active when one drive fails, if the single hard disk drive controller fails, both mirrored drives will become inoperative. But, when you add fault tolerance at the hard disk drive controller level, with a single controller for each hard disk drive, you achieve disk duplexing—which is recommended over simple data duplexing (see Figure 4.8).

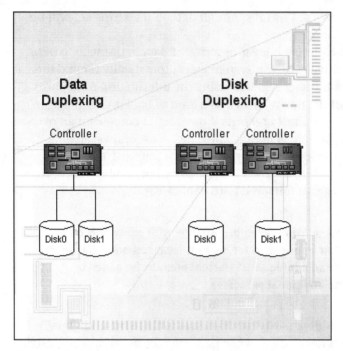

Figure 4.8   Using single versus dual hard disk drive controllers.

Creating Volume Sets

To create a volume set, follow these simple steps:

1. From Start/Programs/Administrative Tools/Disk Administrator, select two or more areas of free space (on from 1 to 32 disks) by selecting the first area of free space; then press Ctrl and click each of the other areas.

2. On the Partition menu, click Create Volume Set (see Figure 4.9). Disk Administrator displays the minimum and maximum sizes for the volume set.

3. Type the size of the volume set that you want to create, then click OK.

The changes you make will not be saved until you either click Commit Changes Now or quit Disk Administrator. If you choose to use less than the total available space, Disk Administrator uses an equal percentage of the free space on each disk to create a partition of the size you specified. A single drive letter is assigned to the collection of partitions that make up the volume set. Operating systems, such as MS-DOS, that do not have volume-set functionality cannot recognize any volume sets that are created by Windows NT. Therefore, if you create a volume set on a dual-boot computer, those partitions become unusable by MS-DOS.

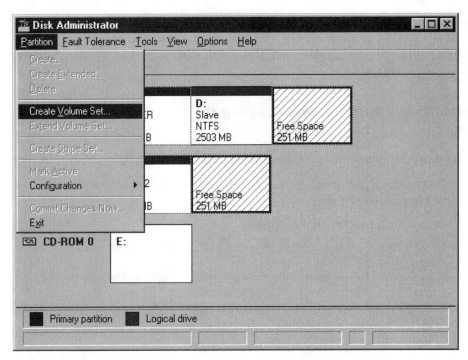

Figure 4.9   Creating volume sets with Disk Administrator.

Extending Volumes and Volume Sets

To extend a volume or volume set, follow these simple steps:

1. From Start/Programs/Administrative Tools/Disk Administrator, select an existing NTFS volume (that is not part of a stripe set or mirror set) or an NTFS volume set. Press Ctrl while selecting one or more areas of free space.

2. On the Partition menu, click Extend Volume Set. Disk Administrator displays the minimum and maximum sizes allowed for the volume set.

3. Type the size of the volume set that you want to create, and click OK. Disk Administrator determines how much of the free space to use for the size that you specified and then initiates a restart of your computer.

 The changes you make will not be saved until you click Commit Changes Now or quit Disk Administrator.

Existing NTFS volumes and volume sets can also be extended by adding free space. Disk Administrator forces the system to restart after you quit; it saves your changes and then formats the new area without affecting any existing files on the original volume or volume set. Be aware, however, that once a volume set has been extended, no portion of it can be deleted without deleting the entire volume set.

Formatting a Partition and Labeling the Volume

To format a partition and label the volume, follow these simple steps:

1. From Start/Programs/Administrative Tools/Disk Administrator, select the newly created partition.

2. On the Tools menu, click Format.

3. In the Format dialog box (see Figure 4.10), select a file system. Optionally, to:

   • Name the partition, type a name in Volume Label.

   • Skip scanning for bad sectors in the partition during formatting, click Quick Format. (*Note*: This option is not available when formatting mirror sets and stripe sets with parity.)

   • Compress the folders and files that are added to the volume, click Enable Compression. (*Note*: This option is available if the partition is being formatted with NTFS.)

4. Click Start to initiate the format request.

5. When the message appears warning you that all data on the disk will be erased, click OK.

6. When the Format Complete message appears, click OK; click Close to return to the Disk Administrator window.

 You can cancel the formatting at any time during the process. However, clicking Cancel will not necessarily restore a volume to its previous state. Before files and directories can be stored on the partitions that you have created, you must first commit the changes to disk and then individually format each partition with a file system.

Reassigning Drive Letters to Partitions

Before explaining how to reassign drive letters to partitions, a word of caution: Be careful when making drive-letter assignments because many MS-DOS and Windows programs make references to a specific drive letter. For example, the Path environment variable shows specific drive letters in conjunction

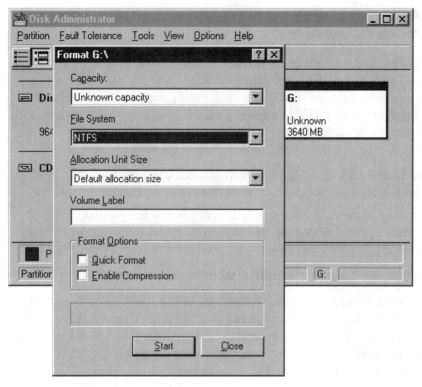

Figure 4.10 Partition format options.

with program names. Also, when you are attempting to assign a letter to a CD-ROM drive, an error message could appear, possibly because it is being used by some application in the system. You must then close the application that is accessing the CD-ROM drive and click the command again.

Windows NT allows the static assignment of drive letters on volumes, partitions, and CD-ROM drives. This means that a drive letter can be permanently assigned to a specific hard disk, partition or volume, and CD-ROM drive. When a new hard disk is added to an existing computer system, it will not affect statically assigned drive letters.

To reassign or change a drive letter to a partition, follow these steps:

1. From Start/Programs/Administrative Tools/Disk Administrator, select the partition or logical drive whose drive letter you want to assign.

2. On the Tools menu, click Assign Drive Letter.

3. In the Assign Drive Letter dialog box, click Assign drive letter and select the appropriate letter (as illustrated in Figure 4.6).

4. Click OK.

Saving, Restoring, and Searching for Disk Configuration Information

This procedure can be used for saving the following disk-configuration information: assigned drive letters, volume sets, stripe sets, stripe sets with parity, and mirror sets. Be sure to save the disk configuration information before upgrading the operating system to ensure that you do not lose your current configuration information.

To save disk configuration information, follow these simple steps:

1. From Start/Programs/Administrative Tools/Disk Administrator, click on the Partition menu, point to Configuration, and then click Save.

2. A message appears, asking you to insert a blank floppy disk, a floppy disk with a previous version of the configuration information, or the Emergency Repair Disk. Insert a blank floppy disk and then click OK.

To restore disk configuration information, follow these steps:

1. From Start/Programs/Administrative Tools/Disk Administrator, on the Partition menu, point to Configuration, then click Restore. A message warns you that this operation will overwrite your current disk configuration information with what was previously saved on the floppy disk and that any changes made during this session will be lost.

2. Insert the floppy disk (or the Emergency Repair Disk containing the saved configuration information) and click OK.

3. Click OK to restart your computer. When Disk Administrator is restarted, a message informs you that the disk configuration has changed and that the changes will be saved the next time you quit Disk Administrator.

This procedure can be used for restoring the following disk-configuration information: assigned drive letters, volume sets, stripe sets, stripe sets with parity, and mirror sets.

To search for disk configuration information, follow these simple steps:

1. From Start/Programs/Administrative Tools/Disk Administrator, on the Partition menu, point to Configuration, then click Search.

2. When a warning message appears reminding you that this operation will overwrite your current disk configuration information, click OK to proceed with the operation. Disk Administrator scans your disk for other Windows NT installations and then displays a list of the installations.

3. Select an installation and click OK. Disk Administrator initiates a restart of your computer.

This procedure can be used to search for any currently defined disk-configuration information for different installed versions of Windows NT. You can select a specific version to replace another, but be careful to update this version information every time you change your disk configuration. To do this, first make your changes, quit Disk Administrator, and restart your computer and Disk Administrator; then save the configuration information and quit Disk Administrator again.

Event Viewer

The Event Viewer is the tool supplied by Microsoft to monitor events in your system. You can use it to view and manage System, Security, and Application event logs. You can also archive event logs. The event-logging service starts automatically when you run Windows NT. To stop event logging, use the Services tool from Control Panel, as explained in Chapter 3.

In addition to Date and Time columns, the Event Viewer (shown in Figure 4.11) contains the following information:

Source. The software that logged the event.

Category. Classification of the event indicated by the source.

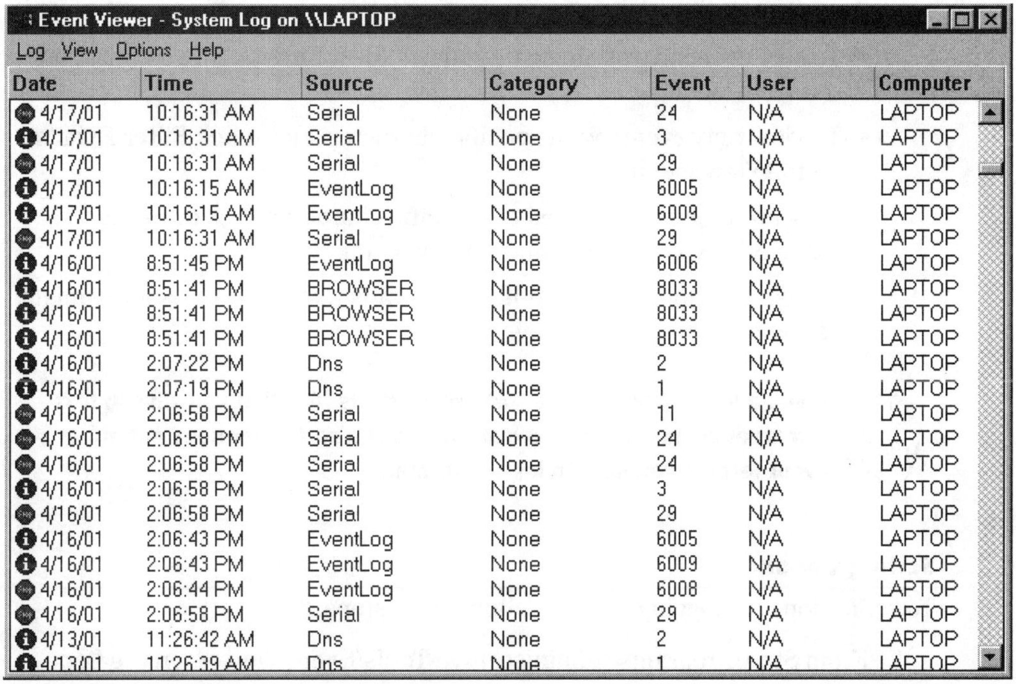

Figure 4.11   Contents of the Windows NT Event Viewer.

Event. Product support event number.

User. The text from the user name field.

Computer. Computer name of the system from which the event occurred.

Type. (not shown for brevity) Classification of the event indicated by Windows NT.

Viewing Event Logs

To view an event log for a particular system, follow these simple steps:

1. From Start/Programs/Administrative Tools/Event Viewer, on the Log menu, click Select Computer.

2. Enter the name of a computer in the Computer field.

3. If your computer is connected to the selected computer by a low-speed device, such as a modem, select the Low Speed Connection check box.

To view a specific event log, follow these steps:

1. From Start/Programs/Administrative Tools/Event Viewer, on the Log menu, click System, Security, or Application.

2. If you want to view specific event records in that log, you can do one of the following:

    *   To sort events chronologically, click Oldest First or Newest First on the View menu.

    *   To view only events with specific characteristics, click Filter Events on the View menu.

    *   To search for events based on specific characteristics or event descriptions, click Find on the View menu.

    *   To see descriptions and additional details that the event source might see, click Detail on the View menu.

 When a log is archived, the sort order affects files that you save in text format or comma-delimited text format. The sort order does not affect event records you save in log-file format.

Setting Options

To set options for logging events, follow these steps:

1. From Start/Programs/Administrative Tools/Event Viewer, on the Log menu, click Log Settings.

2. In the Event Settings dialog box, select the type of log to which the settings will apply under Change Settings For.

3. In Maximum Log Size, specify the log size in kilobytes.

4. Under Event Log Wrapping, select an option that defines how the events are retained for the selected log. These include the following:

   Overwrite Events As Needed. (Default option) Ensures that all new events are written to the log. Even when the log is full, the oldest event(s) will be replaced.

   Overwrite Events Older Than [ ] Days. (Default is 7 days) Retains a log for a specified number of days before overwriting it.

   Do Not Overwrite Events. Retains all existing events when the log is full.

 If you want to restore all default settings, click Default.

Refreshing Event Logs

Refreshing an event log requires only one step:

1. From Start/Programs/Administrative Tools/Event Viewer, on the View menu, click Refresh to update the events currently shown in Event Viewer.

 Refresh is not available for archived logs because those files are never updated. When you first open a log, Event Viewer displays the current information for that log. That information is not updated while you are viewing the list unless you refresh it. The log is automatically updated only when it is no longer the current log displayed in Event Viewer.

Filtering Event Logs

Use the Filter dialog box, shown in Figure 4.12, to define the date range, type of events, source, and category of events displayed for the current log. The filtering choices you make will be used throughout the current Event Viewer session. When filtering is on, a check mark appears next to Filter on the View menu, and "(Filtered)" appears in the title bar. The filter settings include the following:

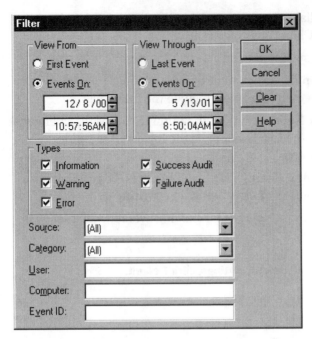

Figure 4.12   Filtering Windows NT Event Viewer logs.

View From. Events that occurred after a specific date and time.

View Through. Events that occurred up to and including a specific date and time.

Information. Events logged as successful operations of server services.

Warning. Events that indicate a potential future problem that may occur.

Error. Events that indicate that a problem has occurred.

Success Audit. Successful user security access attempts.

Failure Audit. Failed user security access attempts.

Source. The software that logged the event.

Category. A classification of the event as defined by the source.

User. The text from the username field.

Computer. The name of the computer where the log event occurred.

Event ID. Product support event number.

To filter events, follow these steps:

1. From Start/Programs/Administrative Tools/Event Viewer, on the View menu, click Filter Events.

2. In the Filter dialog box, specify the characteristics of the filter settings for displayed events.

To return to the default criteria, click Clear. To turn off event filtering, click All Events on the View menu.

Archiving and Viewing Archived Event Logs

When you archive a log file, the entire log is saved, regardless of filtering options. Logs saved as text files or comma-delimited text files retain the current sort order but not the binary data for each event record.

To archive an event log, follow these steps:

1. From Start/Programs/Administrative Tools/Event Viewer, on the Log menu, click Save As.

2. In Save as type, click a file format (Event Log Format (*.EVT), Text File Format (*.TXT), or Comma-Delimited Text File Format (*.TXT).

3. In File Name, enter a filename for the archived log file. By default, Event Viewer adds the .EVT filename extension for log files.

To open and display an archived log in Event Viewer, follow these steps:

1. From Start/Programs/Administrative Tools/Event Viewer, on the Log menu, click Open.

2. In the Open dialog box, enter the filename in File Name, and click OK.

3. The Open File Type dialog box appears. Click System, Security, or Application to match the type of log you want to see.

If you do not specify the correct log type, the Description displayed log in the Event Detail dialog box will be incorrect. You can view an archived file in Event Viewer only if the log is saved in log file format. And note, you cannot click Refresh or Clear All Events to update the display or to clear an archived log.

License Manager

Microsoft highly recommends the use of License Manager (shown in Figure 4.13), noting that tracking licenses manually on local computers or within a small domain is possible but time-consuming. Moreover, tracking licenses without the assistance of automated tools across an entire organization or enterprise that has multiple domains can be unreasonably difficult, costly, as well as time-consuming.

License Manager helps to contain these costs by managing and tracking licenses and usage throughout an organization. It makes it easier for a com-

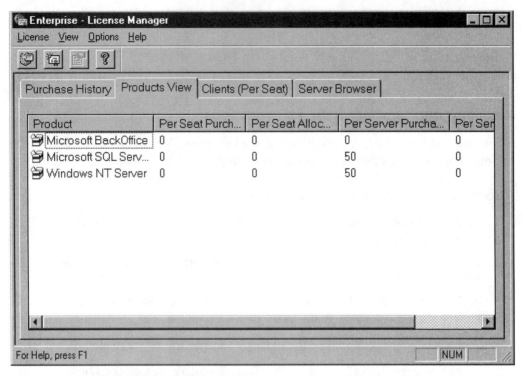

Figure 4.13   Tracking licenses with the Windows NT License Manager.

pany to comply with legal requirements by automatically replicating licensing data from all primary domain controllers (PDCs) in the organization to a centralized database on a specified master server.

Administrators (those who certify that the company has purchased licenses) can use License Manager to:

- See a centralized view of Per Seat and Per Server licenses across the organization

- Manage the purchase or deletion of licenses for products on network servers over which they have administrative rights

- Review usage statistics for each user

- Balance the licensing replication load across the network

As you know, a server license is required for the right to run Windows NT Server software on any particular system. Microsoft's official licensing option clauses, shown in Chapter 2 on page 16 under *Server Licensing*, explain Per Seat and Per Server licensing and give their recommended uses.

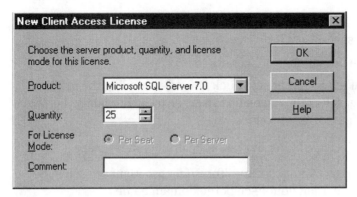

Figure 4.14 Adding new client access licenses.

Adding/Removing Client Access Licenses

When you add Client Access Licenses in Per Seat mode, you are adding these licenses to a pool of licenses rather than to specific users. As users access the product, they are assigned a license. When the pool of available licenses is depleted, license violations will occur if new users access the product.

To add a new Client Access License in Per Seat mode (see Figure 4.14), follow these steps:

1. From Start/Programs/Administrative Tools/License Manager, on the License menu, click New License.

2. In Product, select the appropriate server product.

3. In Quantity, enter the number of licenses purchased.

4. In Comment, type a brief comment to aid in identifying the purchase.

To delete a Client Access License in Per Seat mode, follow these steps:

1. From Start/Programs/Administrative Tools/License Manager, on the Products View tab, select the product for which one or more licenses are to be deleted.

2. On the License menu, click Delete.

3. In Quantity, enter the number of licenses to be deleted.

4. In Comment, type a brief comment to aid in identifying the deletion.

To add a Client Access License in Per Server mode, follow these steps:

1. From Start/Programs/Administrative Tools/License Manager, click the Server Browser tab, then double-click the domain name.

2. Double-click the appropriate server name.

3. Double-click the appropriate product.

4. Click Add Licenses.

5. In Quantity, type the number of licenses to add.

6. Type a comment in Comment, and click OK. After reading the information in Licensing, select the check box to agree to be bound by the license agreements for this product.

To remove a Client License in Per Server mode, follow these steps:

1. From Start/Programs/Administrative Tools/License Manager, click the Server Browser tab, then double-click the domain name.

2. Double-click the appropriate server name.

3. Double-click the appropriate product.

4. Click Remove Licenses.

5. Click the serial number of the licenses you want to remove and type a number in the Number of Licenses to remove box. Click Remove.

6. Click OK.

Managing Users and Servers with License Manager

To view the properties of a particular user, go to Start/Programs/Administrative Tools/License Manager, click the Clients (Per Seat) tab, then double-click the user's name. If the usage statistics show that a user does not access it often enough to warrant a Client Access License in Per Seat mode, you may wish to revoke a user's Client Access License for a product by taking the following steps:

1. From Start/Programs/Administrative Tools/License Manager, click the Products View tab.

2. Double-click the product for which you are revoking a license. If necessary, click the Clients (Per Seat) tab or the Products View tab and click the user whose license to the product is being revoked; click Revoke.

3. Click Yes.

To create a new license group that relates users to specific computers, follow these steps:

1. From Start/Programs/Administrative Tools/License Manager, on the Options Advanced menu, click New License Group (see Figure 4.15).

2. In Group Name, type a short descriptive name.

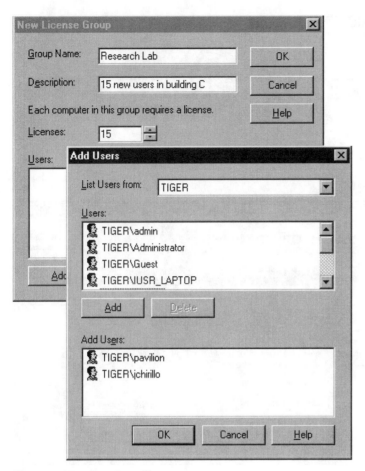

Figure 4.15 Creating a license group.

3. In the Description box, type any additional details that will help you identify the group.

4. In Licenses, enter the number of licenses needed in the Per Seat licensing mode.

5. In Users, click Add.

6. In List Users From, click the appropriate domain.

7. Select the individual users, then click Add.

To change the current server-licensing mode from Per Server to Per Seat, follow these steps:

1. From Start/Programs/Administrative Tools/License Manager, click the Server Browser tab (see Figure 4.16).

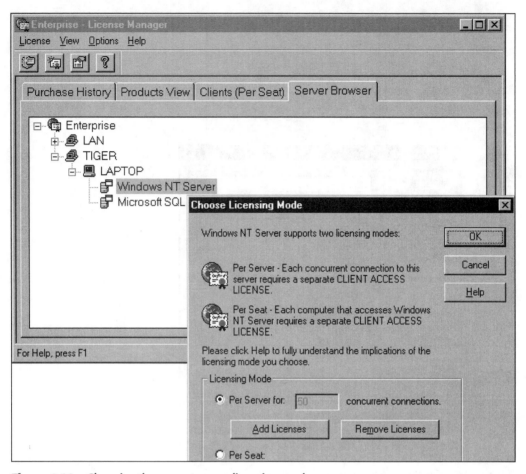

Figure 4.16   Changing the current server-licensing mode.

2. Double-click the domain name.

3. Double-click the appropriate server name.

4. Double-click the appropriate product.

5. In Licensing Mode, click Per Seat, then click OK.

6. After reading the information in Licensing, select the check box to agree to be bound by the license agreements for this product.

Network Client Administrator

The Network Client Administrator enables you to quickly install the client programs and tools contained on the Windows NT Server CD. These include:

- Microsoft Windows 9x
- Microsoft Network Client for MS-DOS
- Microsoft LAN Manager for MS-DOS
- Microsoft LAN Manager for OS/2
- Client-based network administration tools
- Microsoft Remote Access Service (RAS) for MS-DOS
- Microsoft TCP/IP-32 for Windows for Workgroups and Microsoft's 32-bit implementation of the industry-standard TCP/IP internet-working protocols

 You can use Network Client Administrator to share the installation files contained on the Windows NT Server CD or to copy the directories and files contained on the CD to a network server (recommended). If you use the second method, you can use the CD as a backup copy.

Using the Network Client Administrator, you can quickly install network client software by creating a network installation startup disk or an installation disk set. The type of installation disk you need to create depends on the type of software you intend to install. After you have installed the network client software on the target computer, you can install RAS for MS-DOS, TCP/IP-32 for Windows for Workgroups, or client-based network administration tools.

Creating Installation Disks

To create a network installation startup disk, follow these steps:

1. From Start/Programs/Administrative Tools/Network Client Administrator, in the Network Client Administrator dialog box, click Make Network Installation Startup Disk, then click Continue.

2. In the Share Network Client Installation Files dialog box (shown in Figure 4.17), specify where the files are located by clicking Use Existing Path or Use Existing Shared Directory; specify the path, then click OK.

3. In the Target Workstation Configuration dialog box, set options for the computer on which you want to install the network client software, then click OK.

4. In the Network Startup Disk Configuration dialog box, configure the network installation startup disk so that a connection can be made to the server containing the installation files; click OK.

5. In the Confirm Network Startup Disk Configuration dialog box, confirm that the information you entered is correct; click OK.

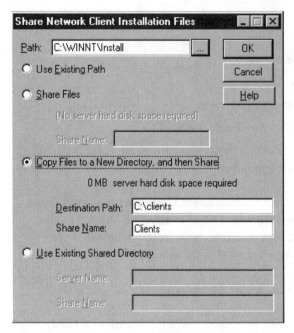

Figure 4.17   Creating installation disks with Network Client Administrator.

If you have not copied and shared the source files on your network from the Windows NT Server CD, click Share Files or Copy Files to a New Directory and then Share in the Share Network Client Installation Files dialog box. Follow these guidelines for creating a network installation startup disk:

- Format the disk using the operating system version that is resident on the target computer.

- Use a high-density system disk that fits the target computer drive A. If the computer you are using to create the disk does not have a floppy drive that is compatible with the target computer, follow the instructions in the Help topic "To copy the installation files to a new directory and then share the files."

- Use a disk that contains the system files necessary to start the target computer; otherwise, the computer cannot be started during the installation process. If you do not have a system disk to use when creating a network installation startup disk, follow the instructions in the Help topic "If you do not have a system disk."

Server Manager

Server Manager is a tool you can use to manage domains and computers. With Server Manager you can:

- **Select a domain, workgroup, or computer to administer.**

- **Manage a computer.** For a selected computer you can view a list of connected users, view shared and open resources, manage directory replication, manage the list of administrative alert recipients, manage services and shared directories, and send messages to connected users.

- **Manage a domain.** When administering a domain you can promote a backup domain controller to the primary domain controller, synchronize servers with the primary domain controller, and add computers to and remove computers from the domain.

Some of the capabilities offered by Server Manager are also offered by the Services and Server tools found on the Control Panel of every Windows NT computer. However, Server Manager can manage both local and remote computers, whereas these Control Panel tools can only be applied to the local computer.

In most cases, when Server Manager is first started, it displays your logon domain. The Server Manager title bar shows the domain name, and the body of the Server Manager window lists the computers of that domain. You can select a computer from this list and then use commands on the Computer menu to manage it.

To administer a domain and its servers using Server Manager, you must be logged on to a user account that is a member of the Administrators, Domain Admins, or Server Operators group for that domain. Members of the Account Operators group can also use Server Manager, but only to add computers to the domain. To use Server Manager to administer a workstation computer or server running Windows NT that is not a domain controller, you must be logged on to a user account that is a member of the Administrators or Power Users group for that computer.

Managing Server Properties

To manage properties of an NT server, follow these steps:

1. From Start/Programs/Administrative Tools/Server Manager, in the Server Manager window, double-click on a computer name. The Properties dialog box appears (see Figure 4.18), displaying usage statistics for the following:

   Sessions. The number of connected users.

   Open Files. The number of open files.

   File Locks. The number of file locks by connected users.

   Open Named Pipes. The number of opened named pipes (communication mechanism that allows a process to communicate with another process).

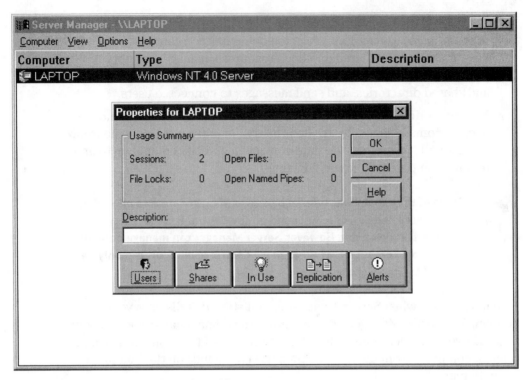

Figure 4.18 Managing an NT server with Server Manager.

2. To change the computer description, type the appropriate text in the Description box.

3. To administer a property associated with a button at the bottom of the Properties dialog box, click the button and complete the dialog box for that property. There are five buttons:

   Users. Click to see a list of all connected users and the open resources for each.

   Shares. Click to see a list of all shared resources and a list of all connected users for each.

   In Use. Click to see a list of all open shared resources.

   Replication. Click to manage directory replication and to specify the path of user logon scripts. Directory replication exports selected directories and files for storage on another system and vice versa.

   Alerts. Click to manage a list of users and computers that will be notified when administrative alerts occur.

4. When you finish managing properties, click OK in the Properties dialog box.

Viewing User Sessions and Resources

To view a list of users connected to the computer, follow these steps:

1. From Start/Programs/Administrative Tools/Server Manager, in the Server Manager window, double-click a computer name.

2. In the Properties dialog box, click Users (Figure 4.19).

3. To disconnect one user, select the username from Connected Users and then click Disconnect. Or, to disconnect all users, click Disconnect All. *Note*: While you are remotely administering another computer, your user account will be listed as a user connected to the IPC$ resource, and it cannot be disconnected.

4. To view the resources opened by one user, select a username in Connected Users. This opens the display showing the shared resource to which that user connects, how many are open (Opens), and the duration (Time).

5. To exit, click Close, then click OK in the Properties dialog box.

Managing Domain Properties

To promote a Backup Domain Controller to Primary Domain Controller, follow these steps:

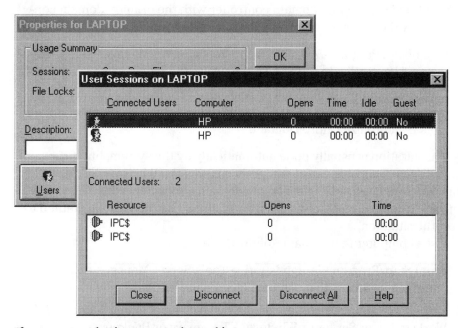

Figure 4.19   Viewing user sessions with Server Manager.

1. From Start/Programs/Administrative Tools/Server Manager, select a backup domain controller from the list of computers in the Server Manager window. Be sure to choose a computer that is capable of reliably handling high network traffic loads.

2. On the Computer menu, click Promote To Primary Domain Controller. If it is available, the former primary domain controller is demoted to backup domain controller status.

To demote a primary domain controller to backup domain controller, follow these steps:

1. From Start/Programs/Administrative Tools/Server Manager, select the former primary domain controller from the list of computers in the Server Manager window. Promote To Primary Domain Controller on the Computer menu changes to Demote To Backup Domain Controller.

2. On the Computer menu, click Demote to Backup Domain Controller.

Usually, when a server is promoted to primary domain controller, no special action needs to be taken to demote the former primary domain controller to backup domain controller status because the system does this automatically. However, if a server is promoted to primary domain controller while the existing primary domain controller is unavailable (for example, if it is being repaired) and the former primary domain controller later returns to service, you must demote it.

To synchronize a backup domain controller with the primary domain controller, follow these steps:

1. From Start/Programs/Administrative Tools/Server Manager, select the server from the list in the Server Manager window.

2. On the Computer menu, click Synchronize with Primary Domain Controller. To synchronize all BDCs in the domain, on the Computer menu, click Synchronize Entire Domain.

Synchronization is usually done automatically by the system, but if the domain directory database on a computer running the Windows NT Server becomes unsynchronized or if a backup domain controller is unable to establish network connections due to password failure, use this manual method to correct the situation.

To add a computer to a domain, follow these steps:

1. From Start/Programs/Administrative Tools/Server Manager, on the Computer menu, click Add to Domain (see Figure 4.20).

2. In the Add Computer to Domain dialog box, select either Windows NT Workstation or Server or Windows NT Primary or Backup.

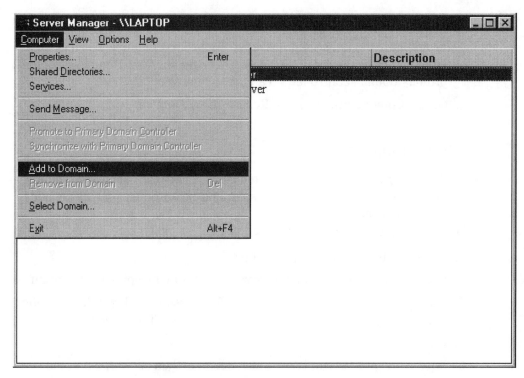

Figure 4.20 Adding a computer to the domain.

3. Type the computer name in the Computer Name box, and click Add. An account for that computer name is added to the domain directory database.

4. Click Close. The computer is added to Server Managers list.

For workstations and servers, this can be done either while installing Windows NT on the computer or after installation using the Network tool in the Control Panel of that computer. For domain controllers, this can only be done during installation.

To add a computer to a domain, you must be logged on to a user account that is a member of the Administrators, Domain Admins, or Account Operators group of that domain. After adding the computer to the domain, the computer's icon appears dimmed, and its version number and description are absent in Server Manager's list until the computer joins the domain.

An added computer name should be treated as a security element. For example, until the intended computer joins the domain, it is possible for a user to give a different computer that computer name and then have it join the domain using the computer account you have just created. If the added computer is a server, when it joins, it receives a copy of the domain directory database.

To remove a computer from the domain, follow these simple steps:

1. From Start/Programs/Administrative Tools/Server Manager, select a computer from the list in the Server Manager window. Do not select the primary domain controller; it cannot be removed.

2. On the Computer menu, click Remove from Domain.

System Policy Editor

Software vendors can develop policy templates to enable policies to be implemented for their applications. With System Policy Editor, you can easily add, remove, and manage system policies.

To add policy templates, follow these steps:

1. Close all currently active policy files.

2. Copy any .adm files to the Windows NT Inf folder (typically \\winnt\inf).

3. From Start/Programs/Administrative Tools/System Policy Editor, on the System Policy Editor Options menu, click Policy Template.

4. Click Add.

5. Specify the policy template (.adm) filename, then click Open.

To remove policy templates:

1. Close all currently active policy files.

2. From Start/Programs/Administrative Tools/System Policy Editor on the System Policy Editor Options menu, click Policy Template.

3. Click the policy template you wish to remove, then click Remove.

Managing System Policies

To create a new policy for a domain, follow these steps:

1. From Start/Programs/Administrative Tools/System Policy Editor, on the File menu, click New Policy.

2. To specify the computers to which your Registry setting changes will apply, you can do the following:

   • Double-click Default User to change HKEY_CURRENT_USER Registry settings for all computers on the domain.

   • Double-click Default Computer to change HKEY_LOCAL_MACHINE Registry settings for all computers on the domain (Figure 4.21).

3. To add to the Registry settings, click Commands on the Edit menu to do the following:

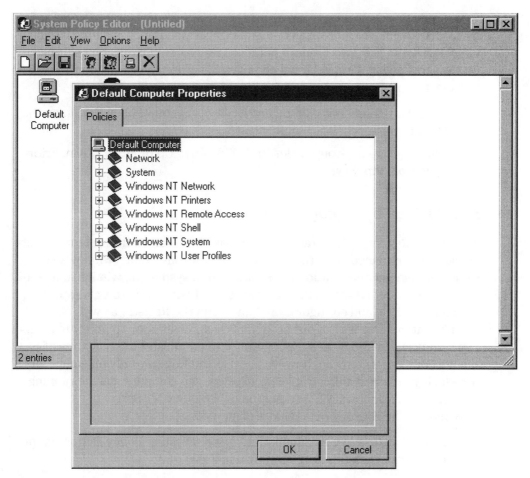

Figure 4.21   Changing Registry settings for all computers on the domain.

- To change HKEY_CURRENT_USER for specific users, click Add User.
- To change HKEY_LOCAL_MACHINE for specific computers, click Add Computer.
- To change HKEY_CURRENT_USER for specific groups, click Add Group.

4. If necessary, finish configuring policy settings for any other policy files you have added, then click Save As on the File menu.

5. In Save in, specify the Netlogon folder on the PDC, such as \\PDCServer-Name\netlogon.

6. In File Name, type NTconfig.pol, and click Save. The policy is enforced on each computer running Windows NT Workstation or Windows NT Server when users log on.

The order in which groups are evaluated may be important; examples are if some users belong to more than one group for which policy is defined and if the policy settings in two or more of these groups contain different settings for the same policy. To specify which policy has priority, use Group Order to sort the groups. To set group priority:

1. From Start/Programs/Administrative Tools/System Policy Editor, on the Options menu, click Group Priority.

2. Click a group in Group Order, and click Move Up or Move Down. Priority is from top down.

Remote Registry Management

The system Registry is a hierarchical database in which all the system settings are stored. It replaced all of the .ini files that controlled older Windows versions. All system configuration information from system.ini, win.ini, and control.ini are contained within the Registry, and all Windows programs store their initialization and configuration data within the Registry as well.

With that in mind, it's important to know that, in addition to policy management, you can use the System Policy Editor to administer the registries of remote computers. You can, however, access the Registry only on computers for which you have administrative permission (the computer can be running any version of Windows NT Workstation or Windows NT Server).

To modify the Registry on a remote computer:

1. From Start/Programs/Administrative Tools/System Policy Editor, on the File menu, click Connect, as shown in Figure 4.22.

2. Type the name of the remote computer.

3. In the Users on Remote Computer dialog box, click the user who is interactively logged on; typically, there is only one user logged on. Click OK.

4. Double-click Local User to change HKEY_CURRENT_USER Registry settings.

5. Double-click Local Computer to change HKEY_LOCAL_MACHINE Registry settings.

6. On the File menu, click Save.

7. On the File menu, click Disconnect.

User Manager for Domains

Simply stated, User Manager for Domains is a utility for managing users, security, member servers, and workstations. With it you can select and administer

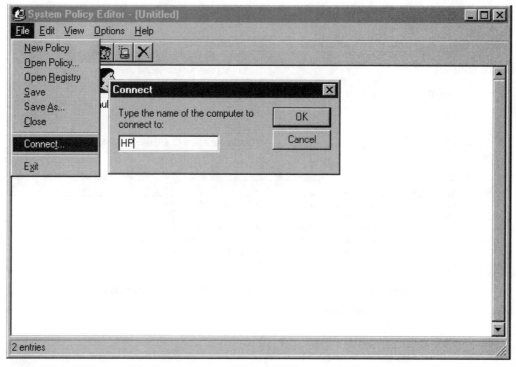

Figure 4.22   Accessing the Registry on a remote computer.

a domain or computer and create and manage user accounts, groups, and security policies.

In most cases, User Manager for Domains displays your logon domain when it first starts. The title bar shows the domain name; the body of the User Manager for Domains window displays two lists. The upper list contains user accounts; the lower list contains group accounts. You can select one or more user accounts or one group account and manage them using commands on the User menu (see Figure 4.23).

Managing New User Accounts

Follow these steps to create a new user account:

1. From Start/Programs/Administrative Tools/User Manager for Domains, on the User menu, click New User (see Figure 4.24).

2. Type the appropriate information in the dialog box:

   - *In Username, type a username.* A username cannot be the same as any other user- or group name of the domain or computer being administered. It may contain up to 20 upper- or lowercase characters and may not consist of the following characters:

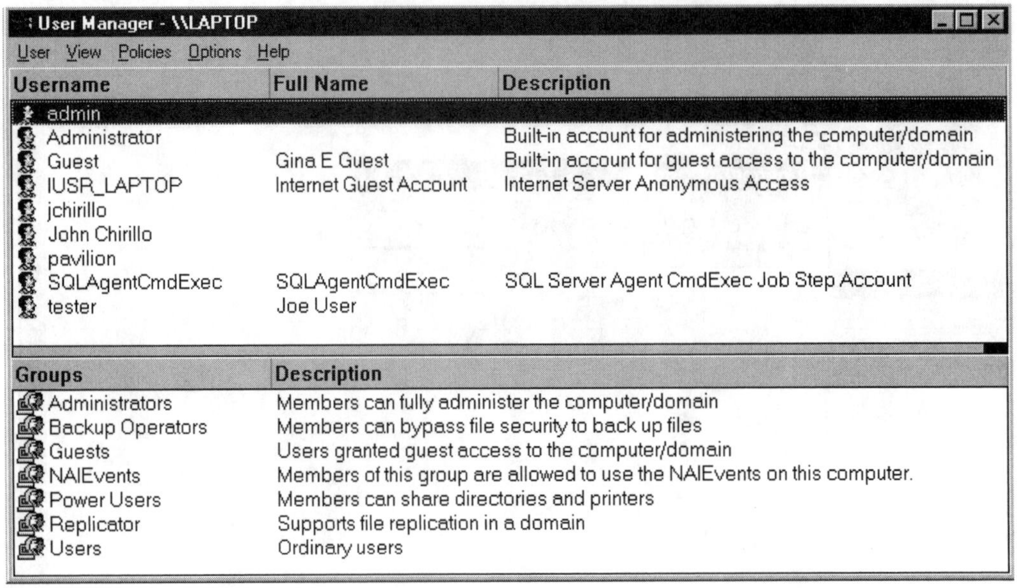

Figure 4.23 The User Manager main window.

question mark (?)

quotation mark (")

slashes in either direction (/ \ )

square brackets ([ ])

ampersand (&)

asterisk (*)

pipe symbol (|)

colon (:)

semicolon (;)

equal sign (=)

comma (,)

various equation signs (+ < >)

- In Full Name, type the user's complete name.

- In Description, type a description of the user or the user account.

- In both Password and Confirm Password, type a password of up to 14 characters in length. For security, the existing password is represented by a row of asterisks; the number of asterisks displayed differs from the actual number of characters used in the password.

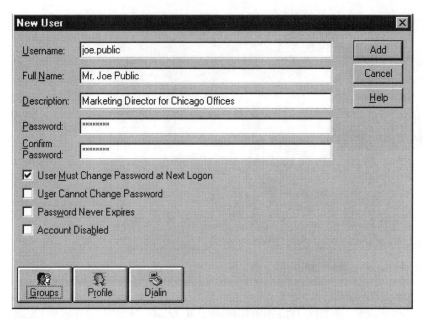

Figure 4.24 Creating a user with User Manager for Domains.

3. Click to select or deselect the check boxes for User Must Change Password at Next Logon, User Cannot Change Password, Password Never Expires, and Account Disabled.

4. To administer a property associated with a button in the New User dialog box, click the button and complete the dialog box that appears; click OK.

5. Click Groups.

6. To add the user account to one or more groups, select one or more groups in Not Member Of, then click Add (e.g., if the account is a new Admin user, add to the Administrators group; see Figure 4.25). To remove the user account from one or more groups, select one or more groups in Member Of, then click Remove. To change the user account primary group, select one global group from Member Of, then click Set.

7. Click OK

8. Click Profile to add a User Profile Path, Logon Script Name, or Home Directory path to this user account (see Figure 4.26). *Note*: These settings are optional; if you choose not to set them, you may jump to step 13.

9. To enable the user profile as roaming or mandatory, type the full path in User Profile Path, for example, \\profiles\joepublic.

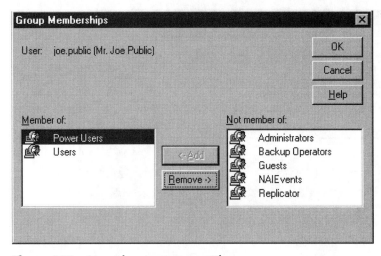

Figure 4.25   Managing user group settings.

10. To assign a logon script, type the filename in Logon Script Name, such as marketing.cmd. If the logon script is stored in a subdirectory of the logon script path, precede the filename with that relative path, such as marketing\joepublic.cmd.

11. To specify a home directory, click Connect, specify a drive letter, click To, then type a network path, such as \\users\joepublic. If the directory does not exist, User Manager for Domains creates it.

12. Click OK.

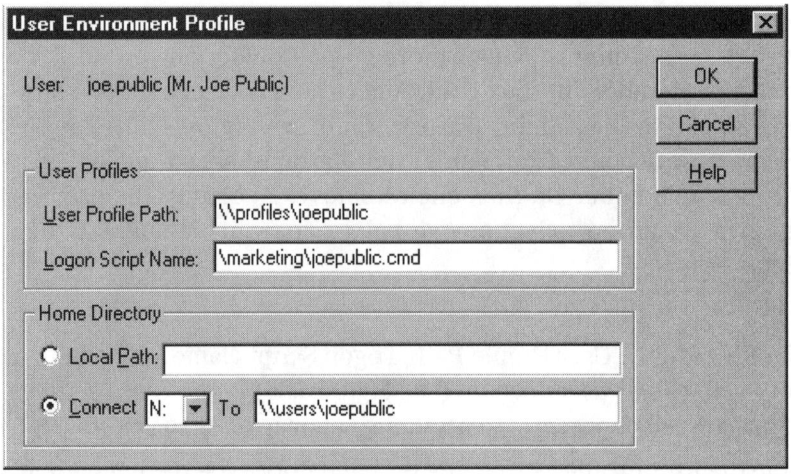

Figure 4.26   Managing user profile settings.

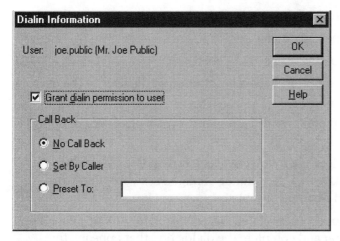

Figure 4.27   Managing user dialin settings.

13. In the User Properties dialog box, click Dialin. These settings are optional; if you choose not to set them, you may jump to step 16.

14. In the Dialin Information dialog box (see Figure 4.27), click Grant dialin permission to user to grant the permission to the selected user. You can revoke the selected user's permission by clicking to clear the check box.

15. Under Call Back, select only one of the following:

    • To disable callback for a user account, click No Call Back (the default setting).

    • To cause the server to prompt the user for a telephone number, click Set By Caller.

    • To cause the server to call the user at a fixed telephone number, click Preset To, then type in the fixed phone number. The server will call the user back at this number only.

16. Click Add.

17. Repeat the previous steps to add another user or click Close to finish.

Copying a User Account

When you copy a user account, group memberships of the original account are copied to the new account. Which buttons appear in the Copy Of dialog box depends on whether you are administering domains or workstations. To copy user account settings for quick replication:

1. From Start/Programs/Administrative Tools/User Manager for Domains, on the User menu, click Copy.

2. Type appropriate information in the dialog box:

- In Username, type a username.

- In Full Name, type the user's complete name.

- (Optional) In Description, type a description of the user or the user account.

- In both Password and Confirm Password, type a password of up to 14 characters.

3. Click to select or clear the following check boxes: User Must Change Password at Next Logon, User Cannot Change Password, Password Never Expires, and Account Disabled.

4. To administer a property associated with a button in the Copy Of dialog box, click the button and complete the dialog box that appears, then click OK.

5. Click Add. To add another user account, repeat steps 2 through 5.

Managing Logon Hours

The default settings allow users to connect at any time, but you can restrict individual users to certain days and hours. These settings affect only connections to the server; they do not affect a user's ability to use a workstation.

To alter logon hours:

1. From Start/Programs/Administrative Tools/User Manager for Domains, click Hours in the New User, Copy Of, or User Properties dialog box.

2. In the Logon Hours dialog box, select the hours to be administered:

- To select 1 hour, click that hour.

- To select a block of time, click the beginning hour and drag through the rows and columns to the ending hour.

- To select an entire day, click that day in the left column.

- To select one hour for all 7 days, click the top of that column.

- To select the entire week, click the upper left box (above Sunday).

3. To allow connections during the selected hours, click Allow. Or, to deny connections during the selected hours, click Disallow.

4. Repeat steps 2 and 3 as necessary.

Managing User Account Policy Information

The Account Policy window is used to configure how all user accounts must use passwords on the workstation or member server. Before you start changing Account Policy settings, be aware that if you select Allow Changes Immediately under Minimum Password Age, you should also click Do Not Keep Password History under Password Uniqueness. If you enter a value under Password Uniqueness, you should also enter a value for Allow Changes in _ Days under Minimum Password. Maximum values for the various options are as follows:

1 to 999 days for Maximum Password Age and Minimum Password Age

1 to 14 characters for Minimum Password Length

1 to 24 passwords for Remember _ Passwords under Password Uniqueness

Follow these steps to manage the Account policy:

1. From Start/Programs/Administrative Tools/User Manager for Domains, on the Policies menu, click Account (see Figure 4.28).

2. Enter the values you want under any of these groups: Maximum Password Age, Minimum Password Age, Minimum Password Length, and

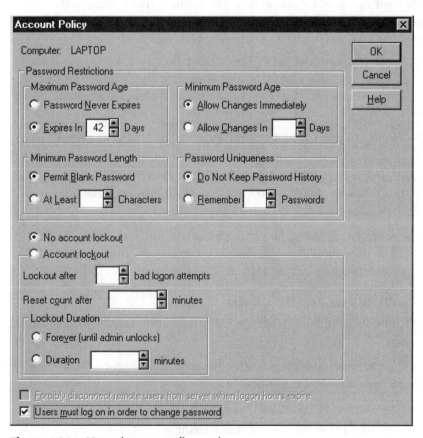

Figure 4.28   Managing user policy settings.

Password Uniqueness. Or, click Password Never Expires, Allow Changes Immediately, Permit Blank Password, or Do Not Keep Password History.

3. Click Account lockout, and then enter values in Lockout after, Reset count after, and Lockout Duration. Or, click No account lockout.

4. If necessary, select or click to clear the Forcibly disconnect remote users from server when logon hours expire check box.

5. If necessary, select or click to clear the Users must log on in order to change password check box.

Managing Multiple User Account Properties

To make the same modification to two or more user accounts, follow these steps:

1. From Start/Programs/Administrative Tools/User Manager for Domains, select two or more user accounts.

2. On the User menu, click Properties. The buttons that appear in the User Properties dialog box depend on whether you are administering domains or workstations.

3. Type the appropriate text in the Description box as it applies to all the selected user accounts. Note that text appears only if all the selected user accounts have identical descriptions. Otherwise, Description appears blank.

4. Click check boxes to change any settings for Password or Account Disabled.

5. To administer a property associated with a button in the User Properties dialog box, click the button and complete the dialog box that appears; then click OK.

If all the accounts have the same setting for an option, the setting for that check box will be displayed. If any of the accounts has a different setting for an option, that check box is grayed out.

Managing Multiple User Account Groups

To manage common group memberships for two or more user accounts, follow these steps:

1. From Start/Programs/Administrative Tools/User Manager for Domains, select two or more user accounts.

2. On the User menu, click Properties.

3. In the User Properties dialog box, click Groups.

4. Use the following methods as required to make the changes you want:

- To add all the user accounts to one or more groups, select one or more groups in Not All Are Members Of, then click Add.

- To remove all the user accounts from one or more groups, select one or more groups in All Are Members Of, then click Remove.

- To change the primary group for all the selected user accounts, select one global group from All Are Members Of, then click Set.

Note that you cannot remove a primary group. If even one of the selected user accounts is not a member of a particular group, that group is listed in Not All Are Members Of.

Managing Groups

Groups can be a local or global assemblage of user accounts with common rights and custom permissions. For example, an organization may create an accounting group whose members have privileges specific to tax and book-keeping files. All users granted membership to the accounting group would inherit the designated privileges.

Global groups can be used anywhere in the domain, whereas a local group can be used only on the system from which it was created, unless it was created on a domain controller from which it would be propagated. Furthermore, global groups typically organize users by department, job, and/or security level. Similarly, local groups are typically organized to access local resources.

From the Command Prompt

When starting User Manager for Domains from the MS-DOS command prompt, you can append two parameters for connection speed:

[/l]   For low-speed connection (i.e., modem)

[/h]   For normal (high-speed) connection (i.e., 10/100 Mbps)

For example, to start User Manager for Domains and administer a domain named Admin using Low-Speed Connection, type: `usrmgr admin /l` (see Figure 4.29). This will cause the following changes to User Manager for Domains:

- The list of user accounts will not appear in the User Manager for Domains window, and on the User menu, Select Users will be unavailable. To manage user accounts, you can use commands on the User menu.

- The list of groups will not appear in the User Manager for Domains window. To manage local groups, you can use commands on the User menu.

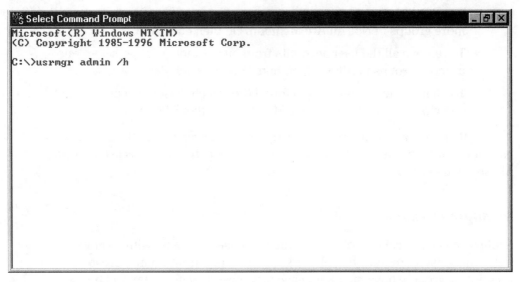

Figure 4.29 Appending parameters for connection speed to the User Manager for Domains from the command prompt.

- Global groups cannot be created or copied, properties of existing global groups cannot be managed, and New Global Group on the User menu will be unavailable. You can indirectly manage global group memberships by managing the group memberships of individual user accounts.

- The View menu commands are unavailable.

To select or clear Low-Speed Connection, from Start/Programs/Administrative Tools/User Manager for Domains, on the User menu, click Select Domain. Next, select a domain or computer to administer, in the Select Domain dialog box, click to select or clear Low-Speed Connection.

Global Groups

A global group name cannot be identical to any other user- or group name of the domain or computer being administered. A global group name may contain up to 20 upper- or lowercase characters, except for the following:

question mark (?)

quotation mark (")

slashes in either direction (/ \)

square bracket ([ ])

asterisk (*)

pipe symbol (|)

colon (:)

semicolon (;)

equal sign (=)

comma (,)

various equation signs (+ < >)

And note, a global group name may not consist solely of periods (.) and spaces.

New Global Group is unavailable when Low-Speed Connection is selected or when you administer a computer running Windows NT Workstation or Windows NT Server that is not a domain controller.

To create a new global group, follow these steps:

1. From Start/Programs/Administrative Tools/User Manager for Domains, do one of the following:

   • Select the user accounts you want to include as the members of the new group.

   • Select any group to ensure no user accounts are initially selected.

2. On the User menu, click New Global Group.

3. In Group Name, type a group name.

4. In Description, type a description of the group.

5. To add members, select one or more user accounts in Not Members, then click Add. To remove members from the new group, select one or more user accounts in Members, then click Remove.

To make a copy of an existing global group, follow these steps:

1. From Start/Programs/Administrative Tools/User Manager for Domains, select one global group.

2. On the User menu, click Copy.

3. In Group Name, type a new group name.

4. You can make changes, as follows:

   • To change the description of the group, type new text in Description.

   • To add members to the group, select one or more user accounts in Not Members, then click Add.

   • To remove members from the global group, select one or more user accounts in Members, then click Remove.

The main advantage of copying a global group is that the new group will have the same members as the original group. Note, however, that the permissions and rights of the original group will not be copied to the new group. Also, global groups cannot be managed when Low-Speed Connection is selected or when you are administering a computer running Windows NT Workstation or Windows NT Server that is not a domain controller.

Local Groups

A local group name may not be identical to any other group or username of the domain or computer being administered. It may contain up to 256 upper- or lowercase characters, except for the backslash character (\). You can add user accounts and global groups from this domain and from trusted domains.

To create a new local group, follow these steps:

1. From Start/Programs/Administrative Tools/User Manager for Domains, do one of the following:

   - Select the user accounts you want as the initial members of the new group (see Figure 4.30).

   - Select any group to ensure no user accounts are initially selected.

2. On the User menu, click New Local Group.

3. In Group Name, type a name for the new group.

4. If necessary, click Show Full Names. This can be a lengthy operation if the group is large.

5. In Description, type a description of the new group.

6. To add members, click Add, then complete the Add Users and Groups dialog box. To remove members from the new group, select one or more names in Members, then click Remove.

As for global groups, the main advantage of copying a local group is that the new group will have the same members as the original group. However, the permissions, rights, and built-in capabilities of the original group will not be copied to the new group.

To make a copy of an existing local group, follow these steps:

1. From Start/Programs/Administrative Tools/User Manager for Domains, select a local group.

2. On the User menu, click Copy.

3. In Group Name, type a new group name.

4. You can make changes, as follows:

   - To change the description, type new text in Description.

   - To add members, click Add, and complete the Add Users and Groups dialog box.

   - To remove members from the local group, select one or more names in Members, then click Remove.

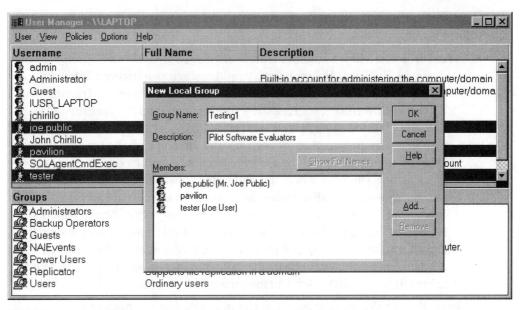

Figure 4.30 Creating a new local group in User Manager for Domains.

Managing Security Policies

In most situations, rather than manipulating the User Rights policy, the easiest way to provide rights to a user is to add that user's account to one of the built-in groups that already possesses the needed rights. Advanced rights are primarily used by programmers who are writing applications for computers running Windows NT Workstation and Windows NT Server.

There are four types of policies: Account Policy, Audit Policy, Trust Relationships, and User Rights Policy.

Account Policy. Controls how passwords must be used by all user accounts. Account Policy defines things such as maximum password age, minimum password age, whether a password history is maintained, and whether users must log on before changing their passwords. It also determines lockouts. If locking out is enabled, a user account cannot log on after a number of failed attempts to do so within a specified time limit between failed attempts. Finally, the Account Policy also determines whether a remote user is forcibly disconnected from a domain when that user's logon hours expire.

Audit Policy. Used to track selected user activities by auditing security events and storing the data in a security log. You can use Event Viewer to review this log, as described earlier in this chapter. But because the security log is limited in size, you should carefully select events to be logged.

The maximum size of the computer's security log is defined in Event Viewer.

Trust Relationship. Describes a link between two Windows NT Server domains. Use Trust Relationships to add and remove trusting domains (resource domains) and trusted domains (account domains). Trusting domains allow their resources to be used by accounts in other trusted domains. Trusted-domain users and global groups can hold user rights, resource permissions, and local group memberships on the trusting domain. Trust relationships can allow a user to access resources on the entire network using a single user account and a single password. This expands the convenience of centralized administration from the domain level to the network level. Trust relationships can be established only between Windows NT Server domains. Establishing a trust relationship requires both domain administrators to take action in their respective domains. Note that the domain name will always be displayed in uppercase, whether you type it in using either or both upper- and lowercase characters.

User Rights Policy. Manages the rights granted to groups and user accounts. A right authorizes a user to perform certain actions on the system. A user who logs on to an account to which the appropriate rights have been granted can carry out the corresponding actions. User rights apply to the system as a whole and are different from permissions, which apply to specific objects. The rights granted to a group are provided to the members of that group. Members of a group have all the rights granted to that group. In most situations, the easiest way to provide rights to a user is to add that user's account to one of the built-in groups that already possesses the needed rights, rather than by administering the User Rights policy.

To alter the User Rights policy, shown in Figure 4.31, follow these steps:

1. From Start/Programs/Administrative Tools/User Manager for Domains, on the Policies menu, click User Rights.

2. Select a user right from those listed in the drop-down list labeled Right. The users and groups who currently have that right appear under Grant To.

3. To grant the selected right to additional groups or user accounts, click Add and complete the Add Users and Groups dialog box.

4. To remove a group or user account from the list, select a name in the Grant To box, then click Remove.

5. Repeat steps 2 and 3, as necessary. To administer advanced user rights, select the Show Advanced User Rights check box and repeat steps 2 and 3, as necessary.

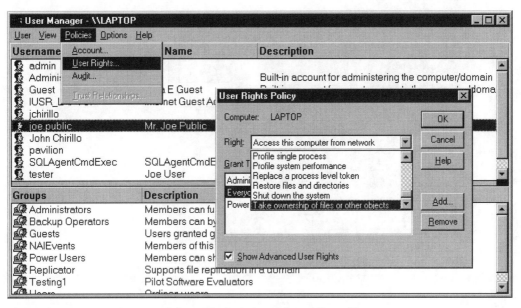

Figure 4.31   Managing user rights with the User Rights policy utility.

To manage the Audit Policy, follow these steps:

1. From Start/Programs/Administrative Tools/User Manager for Domains, on the Policies menu, click Audit.

2. To record events in the security log, click Audit These Events. Or click Do Not Audit to not record any events in the security log,.

3. If you selected Audit These Events, click to select or clear the Success and Failure check boxes for each type of event (see Figure 4.32):

   Logon and Logoff. Indicates a user logged on or off or made a network connection.

   File and Object Access. Indicates a user accessed a directory, file, or printer that is being audited.

   Use of User Rights. Indicates a user exercised his or her rights.

   User and Group Management. Indicates a user account or group was created, changed, or deleted; a user account was renamed, disabled, enabled; or a password was set or changed.

   Security Policy Changes. Indicates that a change was made to user rights, audit, or trust relationships.

   Restart, Shutdown, and System. Indicates that a user restarted or shut down the computer.

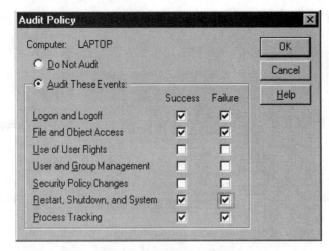

Figure 4.32 Managing tracked, or audited, security events.

Process Tracking. Gives detailed tracking of events, such as program activation.

When administering domains, the Audit Policy utility affects the security logs of all domain controllers in the domain because they share the same audit policy. When administering a computer running Windows NT Workstation or Windows NT Server that is not a domain, the audit policy affects only the security log of that computer.

To add a trusted domain, follow these steps:

1. Obtain a password from the administrator of the domain that will be trusted.

2. If necessary, from Start/Programs/Administrative Tools/User Manager for Domains, click Select Domain on the User menu and complete the Select Domain dialog box, specifying the name of your domain that will be configured to trust the other domain. On the Policies menu, click Trust Relationships.

3. Click Add, and in Trusted Domains type the name of the Windows NT Server domain that is to be trusted.

4. In Password, type the case-sensitive password required by that domain.

To add a trusting domain, follow these steps:

1. If necessary, from Start/Programs/Administrative Tools/User Manager for Domains, click Select Domain on the User menu and complete the Select Domain dialog box, specifying the name of the domain that will

be added to its list of trusting domains. On the Policies menu, click Trust Relationships.

2. Click Add, then in Trusting Domain type the name of the Windows NT Server domain that will trust your domain.

3. Type a case-sensitive password in both the Password and Confirm Password boxes.

4. Provide the password to the administrator of the domain that you have added to the Trusting Domains list. That administrator must complete the trust relationship by adding your domain to the list of trusted domains as explained in this procedure.

Think It Over

To review the material in this chapter, see if you can correctly answer the following questions. (The answers can be found within Appendix A in the back of this book.)

4.1 Which Windows NT file system supports permission security?

○ FAT

○ NTFS

4.2. Two copies of the FAT are kept in case one is damaged.

○ True

○ False

4.3. The NTFS is best used on partitions of less than 400 MB.

○ True

○ False

4.4. Under Windows NT, hardware-based fault-tolerant mechanisms offer the same performance as the software-based ones in regard to RAID performance and reliability.

○ True

○ False

4.5. Which RAID technique is being used when data is written to two identical disks simultaneously?

○ Level 0

○ Level 1

○ Level 5

4.6.   Which best describes RAID level 5?

   ○ Reserves one dedicated disk for error correction data, with good performance and some level of fault tolerance

   ○ Provides data striping, which means blocks of each file are spread across multiple disks

   ○ Provides byte-level data striping and error correction

4.7.   A single hard disk drive always contains more than one volume.

   ○ True

   ○ False

4.8.   In a volume set, a file is stored equally on each segment simultaneously.

   ○ True

   ○ False

4.9.   In a stripe set, data is written equally to all segments in the set.

   ○ True

   ○ False

4.10.   In a stripe set with parity, if a physical hard drive becomes corrupt or fails, not all data in the stripe set will be lost.

   ○ True

   ○ False

4.11.   What is the overhead space requirement for a mirror drive set?

   ○ 20 percent

   ○ 25 percent

   ○ 30 percent

   ○ 50 percent

4.12.   Using Event Viewer, when a log is archived, the sort order affects files that you save in text format or comma-delimited text format. The sort order does not affect event records you save in log-file format.

   ○ True

   ○ False

4.13.   Which utility enables you to quickly install network client software by creating a network installation startup disk or an installation disk set?

   ○ Disk Administrator

○ Event Viewer

○ License Manager

○ Network Client Administrator

○ Server Manager

○ System Policy Editor

○ User Manager for Domains

4.14. To administer a domain and its servers using Server Manager, it is not necessary to be logged on to a user account that is a member of the Administrators, Domain Admins, or Server Operators group for that domain.

○ True

○ False

4.15. Which of the following is a true statement about domain management?

○ Global groups typically organize users by department, job, and/or security level, and can be used only on the local system.

○ A local group is used only on the system from which it was created, unless it was created on a domain controller from which it would be propagated.

○ Local groups are typically organized to access all domain resources and therefore are created by service.

4.16. In regard to managing security policies, the Account Policy controls how passwords must be used by all user accounts.

○ True

○ False

4.17. In regard to managing security policies, the Audit Policy utility manages the rights granted to groups and user accounts.

○ True

○ False

4.18. In regard to managing security policies, which policy is used to track selected user activities?

○ Account Policy

○ Audit Policy

○ User Rights Policy

4.19   In regard to managing security policies, which policy defines maximum password age, minimum password age, whether a password history is maintained, and whether users must log on before changing their passwords?

○ Account Policy

○ Audit Policy

○ User Rights Policy

Advanced System Configurations: Networking and Optimization

In this chapter we'll investigate a number of advanced system configurations and networking and optimization techniques. You'll learn to manage the Network Neighborhood; set up printers, print schedules, and jobs; conduct storage backup; and institute general operating system customizations for tuning performance. Most, if not all, of the procedures described in this chapter are essential to accommodating many standard-operating policies.

 Hands-on simulations of the material given in this chapter can be found on the book's companion CD.

Network Neighborhood

The Network Neighborhood was designed primarily to replace the manual drive-mapping processes found in earlier versions of NT and in other operating systems. By double-clicking the Network Neighborhood icon on the desktop, as shown in Figure 5.1, you can browse through and use the computers and printers connected to the network or those in multiple remote networks.

Browsing the Network

To connect to another computer on your network just double-click the computer in the Network Neighborhood window; or, if you don't see the computer

Figure 5.1   Browsing the network via Network Neighborhood.

or remote network, double-click Entire Network to perform a comprehensive network search (see Figure 5.2). To connect to the same computer but with Windows NT Explorer, simply right-click on the computer in the Network Neighborhood window and select Explore (Figure 5.3).

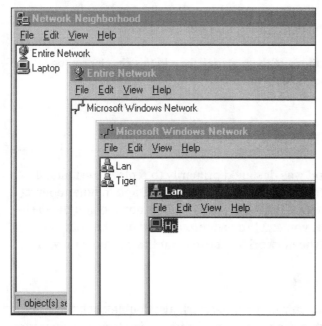

Figure 5.2   Searching for a computer via Entire Network.

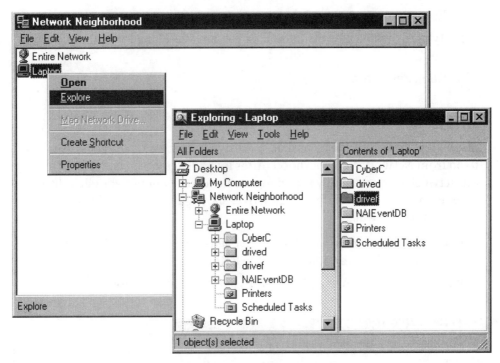

Figure 5.3   Connecting to a computer with Windows NT Explorer.

You can also manually search for a computer on your network by following these steps, illustrated in Figure 5.4:

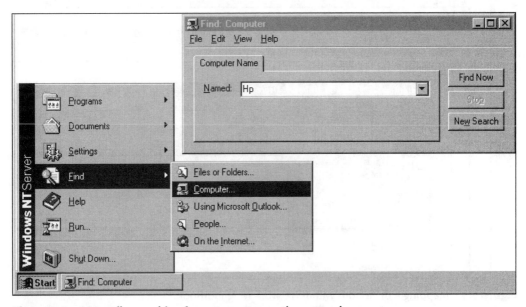

Figure 5.4   Manually searching for a computer on the network.

1. From Start/Find, click Computer.
2. Type in the name of the computer you are searching for in the Named field.
3. Click Find Now.

Mapping Network Drives

Mapping a network drive by assigning a drive letter to a resource is also easy to do from Network Neighborhood. After locating a target system by browsing the network or by manually searching for its name, simply right-click the computer icon and select Map Network Drive, shown in Figure 5.5. This window includes the following:

Drive. Displays the first available drive letter of your system. You may advance to select another available letter.

Path. Specifies the network path for your mapped selection.

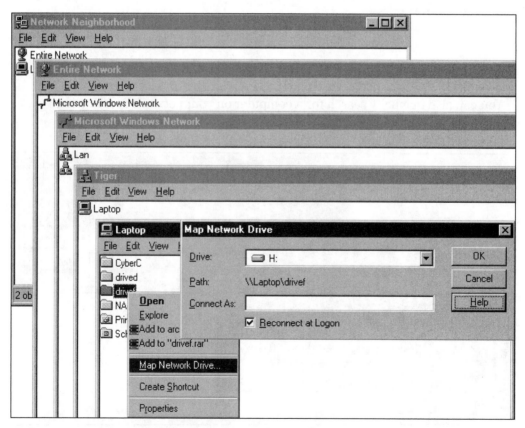

Figure 5.5 Mapping a drive from within Network Neighborhood.

Connect As. Enables you to connect using a different user account. For example, you may have an account on the target system, but as a different account than the one you're currently using. To connect using a different user account on a different domain, preceding the intended user account name, simply add the domain name, followed by a backslash (e.g., domain\user).

Reconnect at Logon. Selecting this box automatically maps this drive every time you log in.

To map a network drive by assigning a drive letter to a resource from your desktop or NT Explorer, follow these steps:

1. In the Windows NT Explorer or on the desktop, right-click My Computer or Network Neighborhood, then click Map Network Drive (see Figure 5.6).

2. Click the Path box, then type the path to the intended resource. For example: \\computername\foldername (shared directory). Or, in Shared Directories, double-click to expand a network, domain/workgroup, or computer; then select a shared directory.

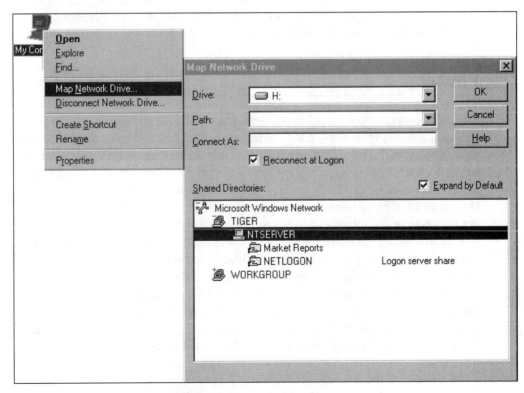

Figure 5.6 Mapping a drive directly from your desktop.

3. To connect under a different username, type the name in Connect As. If the user account is in a different domain, use the format domain\username.

4. If you do not want to connect to the shared directory each time you log on, click to clear Reconnect at Logon.

To map to a resource you have used recently, click the arrow to access the drop-down list in Path; the previous 10 paths are displayed. Click the resource you want. In the NT Explorer, you can also click Map Network Drive on the Tools menu. If you know the name of a computer but want to view its shared directories, in Path, type the computer name, preceded by two backslashes (\\), then click OK. The name of the computer's first shared directory is added to Path, and the computer's shared directories are displayed in Shared Directories. To connect to a different directory, select it in Shared Directories.

If you've finished with a resource mapping and want to remove a drive-letter assignment, follow these steps:

1. In the Windows NT Explorer or on the desktop, right-click My Computer or Network Neighborhood, then click Disconnect Network Drive.

2. In Network Drive, click the resource whose drive-letter assignment you intend to remove. Alternatively in the NT Explorer, click Disconnect Network Drive on the Tools menu.

Printing

Depending on network printing requirements, a Windows NT Server can also function as a *print server*—a logical interface that governs user print jobs and schedules with physical printers. This process is illustrated in Figure 5.7. For example, a user could send a print job to the print server, where it would be stored for *spooling* (simultaneous peripheral operations online), which places the job in a buffer or temporary storage area. The buffer is essentially a waiting area where the job sits until the specified printer is ready to print it.

Fundamentally each print server can operate as a logical printer interface to output from several physical printers. Though some of these logical printers might be configured differently, they would print from the same physical printer. For example, one logical printer might be configured to print from the top tray (letter-size paper) of a physical printer, whereas another might be set to print from the bottom tray (legal-size paper) of the same physical printer. Moreover, a single logical printer might also be set up to print to two physical printers.

That brings us to the next configuration type: the *printer pool*. A printer pool is where a single logical printer sends the same job to many physical

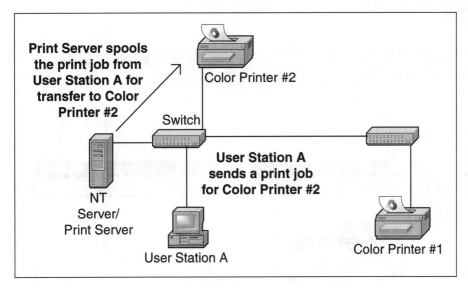

Figure 5.7   Managing print jobs with a print server.

printers. Obviously, the printers must be connected to the same print server with matching condition specifications. We'll go through printer pool configurations step by step later on.

Installing a Printer

Installing a printer on a Windows NT server is a straightforward process. If you want to use a shared network printer, you can set it up quickly by browsing in Network Neighborhood for the computer that shares the printer, double-clicking the Printers folder, clicking (or right-clicking) the Printer icon, and then selecting Install on the File menu (see Figure 5.8)—it's that easy.

Adding a Local Printer

Adding a local printer to Windows NT Server can be accomplished effortlessly with the Add Printer Wizard. From Start/Settings/Printers simply double-click the Add Printer icon to start the wizard, shown in Figure 5.9. At this point you can choose either to manage the printer on the NT server, by selecting My Computer, or connect to a printer on another machine with Network printer server. After choosing, click Next to continue.

For our purposes here, let's select My Computer and continue with the wizard. The next screen to appear contains available ports, from which we'll select the appropriate local port with an attached printer (see Figure 5.10). After selecting the correct port, click Next to continue.

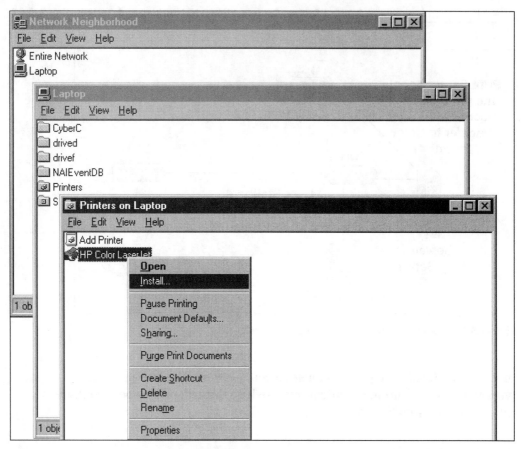

Figure 5.8 Sharing a network printer.

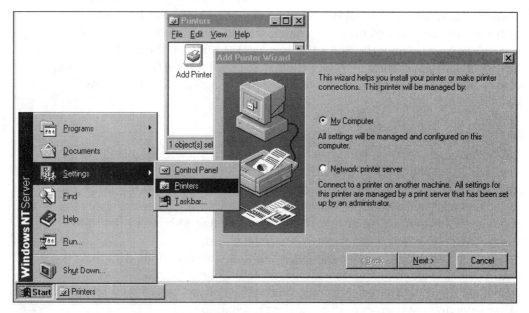

Figure 5.9 Using the Add Printer Wizard.

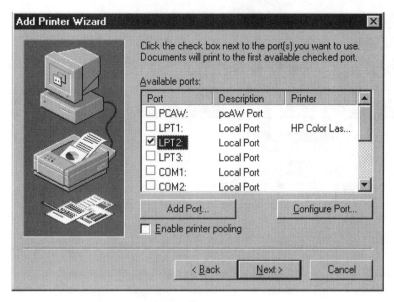

Figure 5.10 Selecting a local port.

 If a port for a printing device is not listed, use Add Port to specify a new port that supports the printing device. Configure Port lets you specify the amount of time you want to elapse before you are notified that the printing device is not responding. The setting affects the printer you've selected and any other local printers that use the same driver. If you use a plotter-printing device, you may need a longer timeout.

On the next screen to appear (Figure 5.11), look to see if your printer is listed. If it is, click the manufacturer and model of the printer and then Next to continue. If your printer is not listed and if it came with an installation disk, click Have Disk to browse the media (CD-ROM or floppy) for the necessary printer drivers.

Next the wizard will request that you type in a printer name for the device. Be sure to select a unique name for each printer, making sure it's no more than 31 characters long. (Exceeding that character maximum may cause incompatibilities with some programs.) You'll also be asked to specify whether the printer should be used as the default printer. After making your selections, click Next to continue.

The next screen asks you to indicate whether this printer should be available to share with other network users. If you select Shared, you must enter a name for the device in the Share Name: text box—this is the name that will be displayed when browsing the network for available printers. Or you may select from a list of the operating system names that would be printing from

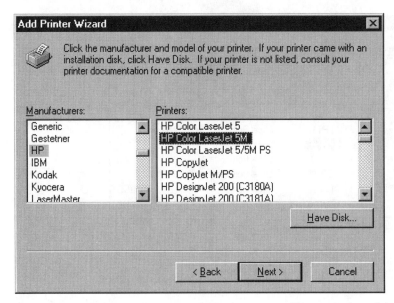

Figure 5.11 Selecting the compatible printer manufacturer and model.

this printer via network share. Click Next to continue. If the required printer drivers have not been previously installed, you'll be required to insert the Windows NT Server CD-ROM for specific driver installation. Finally, you'll be asked if you want to print a test page from the device. The last step is to click Finish to complete the Add Printer Wizard configuration.

Printer Management

Changing printer settings with Windows NT is not difficult. But to do so, you must have full control access permissions. By default, members of the following groups have these permissions: Administrators, Server Operators, Print Operators, and Power Users.

To change printer settings, follow these steps:

1. From Start/Settings/Printers, right-click the printer you are using, then click Properties (see Figure 5.12).

2. You will see a number of tab options, typically labeled General, Ports, Scheduling, Sharing, Security, and Device Settings. These differ based on the printer model and configuration. Click each tab to see each of the available options, and make your changes. In addition to the choices shown on the General page shown in Figure 5.12, the following settings may be modified:

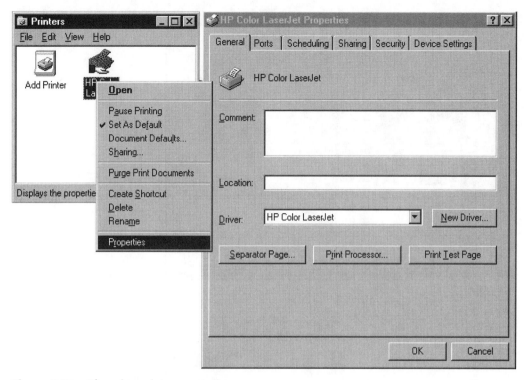

Figure 5.12 Changing printer properties.

Ports. Lists the available ports (see Figure 5.13). From here you can add, delete, and configure ports for new devices. Additionally, you can select Enable bidirectional support, if your printer driver supports two-way dialogs, or reports setting and status information. Finally, you can configure printer pooling from this window—we'll talk more about this later.

Scheduling. Includes settings for printer availability—the default is 24 hours (use this, for example, to delay specific print jobs until after busy hours); lets you determine whether to spool documents before printing; and lets you set document priority—high-priority documents can be set to print before low-priority documents regardless of order (see Figure 5.14).

The printer spooling options under the Scheduling tab also give you control over printing speed. For example, by selecting Start printing after last page is spooled, you will delay output until the entire project has been spooled. You can disable spooling altogether by selecting Start printing immediately.

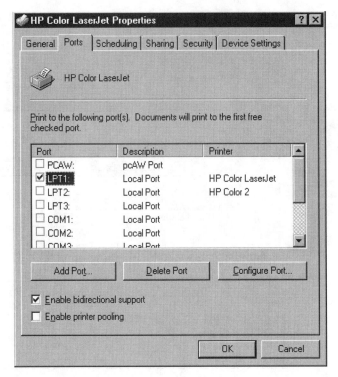

Figure 5.13 Managing printer ports.

If you select Hold mismatched documents, the printer will not print documents that do not conform to the current form or paper size. This can be handy to minimize manual form changes during print sessions.

When Print spooled documents first is selected, an already spooled job will print before a currently spooling job, even if the new job has priority.

When Keep documents after they have printed is selected, a copy of the job will be retained, in case you lose the original document and it cannot be re-created. (*Note*: Enabling this option means that all print jobs will have to be manually deleted.)

Sharing. Includes settings that let you indicate whether this printer should be available to share with other network users. If you select Shared, you must enter a name for the device in the Share Name text box—this is the name that will be displayed when browsing the network for available printers. You may also optionally select from a list of the operating system names of computers that would be printing from this printer via network share (see Figure 5.15).

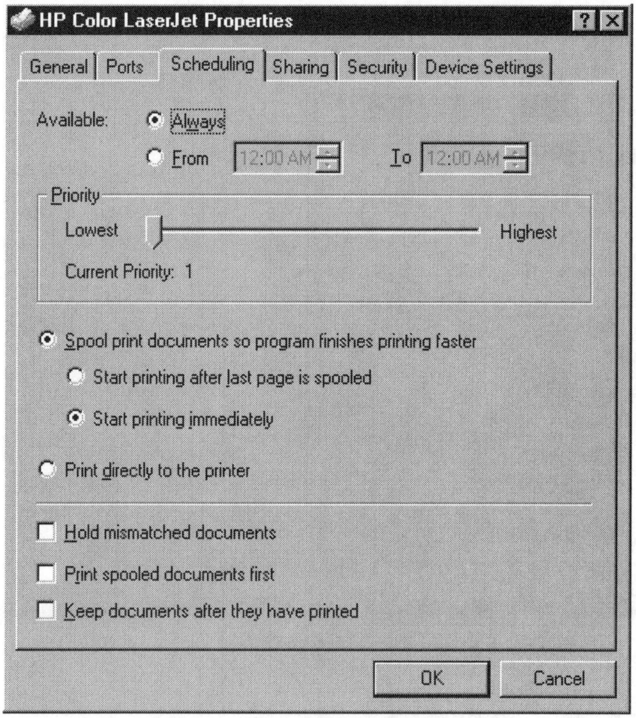

Figure 5.14   Managing printer scheduling.

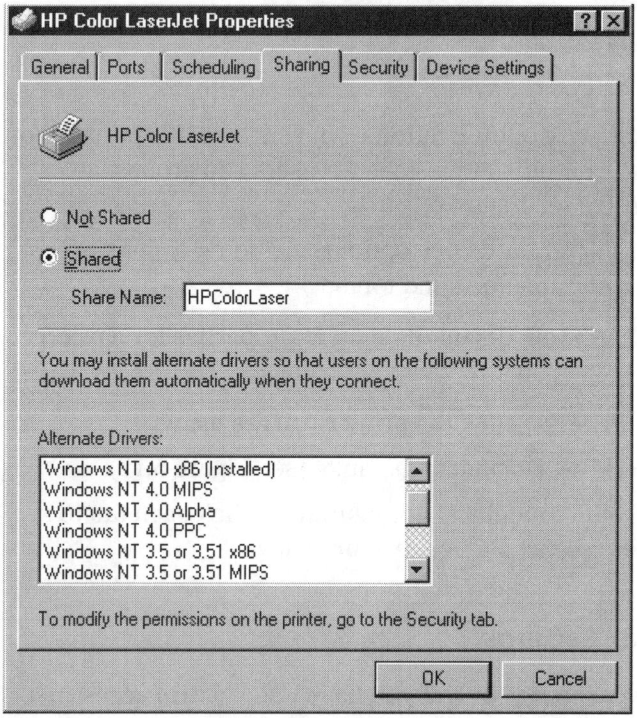

Figure 5.15   Managing printer shares.

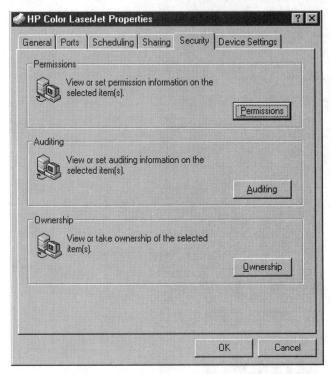

Figure 5.16   Managing printer security.

Security. Specifies sharing authorization—who can use this printer. You use these settings to assign permissions for users and groups, as described previously (see Figure 5.16).

Device Settings. Lists printer device options, including paper tray source settings, printer memory, and fonts.

Additionally, you can change the default document properties for a printer with these simple steps:

1. From Start/Settings/Printers, click the printer you are using.

2. On the Printer menu, click Document Defaults (see Figure 5.17).

3. Depending on the printer model and configuration, click each tab to see each of the available options, and make your changes.

Managing Print Server Settings

You can change print server settings only if you have Full Control access permissions (that is, you must be a member of the Administrators, Server Opera-

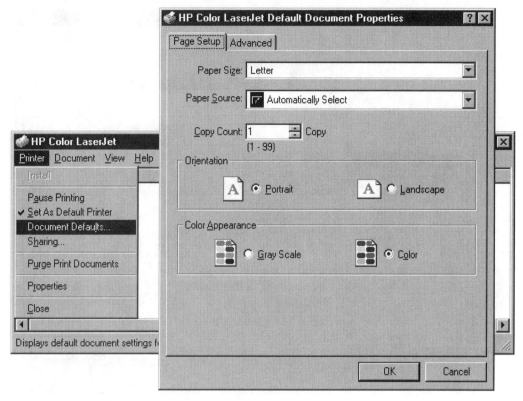

Figure 5.17   Changing document default settings.

tors, Print Operators, or Power Users group). Be aware that changing the server properties affects *all* printers on the print server.

To change the server properties, follow these steps:

1. From Start/Settings/Printers, on the File menu, click Server Properties (see Figure 5.18).

2. Click each tab to evaluate all of the options before making your changes. They include:

   Forms. Lists forms (e.g., paper, envelopes) available to this system.

   Ports. Lists the available ports.

   Advanced. Specifies the spooler folder; click to set the following options:

   Log spooler error events

   Log spooler warning events

   Log spooler information events

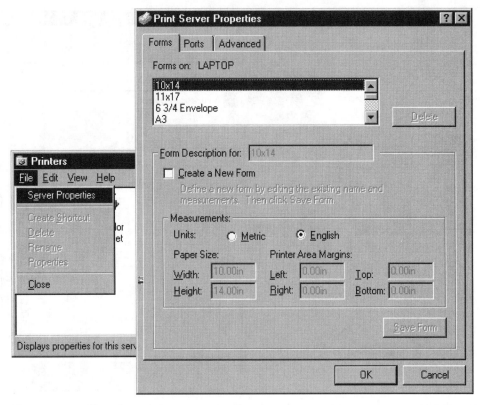

Figure 5.18 Changing print server properties.

Beep on errors of remote documents

Notify when remote documents are finished

Managing a Printer Pool

Setting up a printer pool (a single logical printer that sends the same job to several different physical printers) can be accomplished easily by modifying printer settings. From Start/Settings/Printers, right-click one of the printers you'll be pooling, and click Properties. To enable print pooling, click on the Ports tab, then select the Enable printer pooling check box at the bottom of the screen, as shown in Figure 5.19.

The final step requires you to simply click to enable each of the ports to add to the pool (the identical printing devices through the logical printer). If a pool port hasn't been added yet, simply click New Port to configure a new one (see Figure 5.20) and follow the configuration steps that we explored previously.

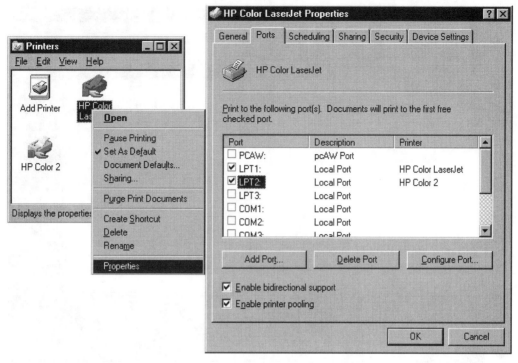

Figure 5.19   Enabling a printer pool.

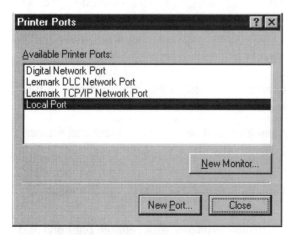

Figure 5.20   Configuring a new printer pool port.

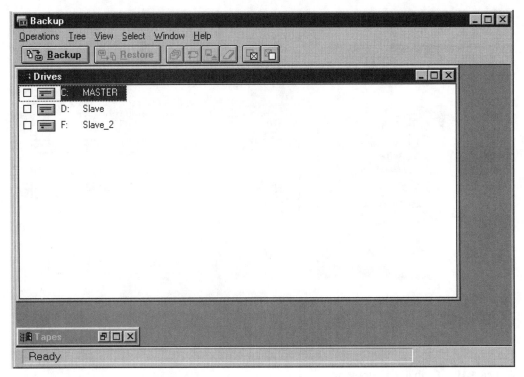

Figure 5.21   Managing storage with Windows NT Backup.

Storage Backup

Windows NT Backup, shown in Figure 5.21, is a graphical tool used to protect data from accidental loss or hardware and media failures. Backup makes it easy for you to use a tape drive to back up and restore your important files on either the Windows NT file system (NTFS) or file allocation table (FAT) file system.

The following list provides an overview of some of the actions you can take with this graphical tool to protect your data:

- Using an attached tape drive, back up and restore both local and remote files on the NTFS or FAT volumes from your own computer.

- Select files for backing up or restoring by volume, directory, or individual filename; view detailed file information, such as size or modification date.

- Select the optional verification procedure to ensure reliable backups and restorations.

- Perform any of the following common backup operations: Normal, Copy, Incremental, Differential, and Daily Copy.

- Place multiple backup sets on a tape, and either append new backup sets or overwrite the whole tape with the new ones.

- Span multiple tapes with both backup sets and files; there is no file-size restriction.

- Create a batch file to automate repeated backups of drives.

- Review a full catalog of backup sets and individual file and directory information so you can select files to be restored.

- Control the destination drive and directory for a restore operation, and receive appropriate options for action you can take when a restore would overwrite a more recently created file.

- Save log information on tape operations to a file. Also view tape-operation information in the Windows NT Event Viewer.

Selecting Hardware

If you are using Backup for the first time, or if you have just installed a new or additional tape drive, you can load the appropriate tape device driver by having Backup detect the tape drive for you. To do this, however, the tape drive must be listed in the Hardware Compatibility List that came with your copy of Windows NT Server. If the tape drive is not listed, you must add its driver from the manufacturer's disk because Backup does not detect most unlisted drives.

To load a tape driver, follow these steps:

1. From Start/Settings/Control Panel, double-click Tape Devices (see Figure 5.22).

2. Click Detect.

3. When prompted, click OK to install the driver detected by Tape Devices. The driver files are located on the Windows NT CD-ROM, so be sure to have the compact disc ready to insert.

Adding a Tape Driver

As an alternative to using Backup to detect a newly installed tape drive, you can add a tape driver manually with the following steps:

1. From Start/Settings/Control Panel, double-click Tape Devices.

2. Click the Drivers tab.

3. Click Add.

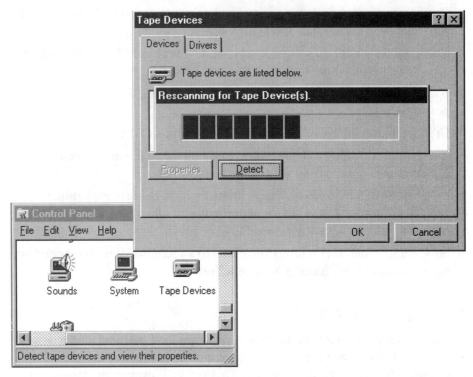

Figure 5.22 Detecting a tape drive.

4. Choose from the list of compatible drivers, or click Have Disk and load the driver from the Manufacturer's disk; then follow the instructions in the Install Driver dialog box (see Figure 5.23). Click OK when you're finished. In some cases, you will be prompted to restart your computer. Again, the driver files are located on the Windows NT CD-ROM, so be sure to have the compact disc handy.

Shuffling Tape Backup Drives

When you start Windows NT, the system automatically checks for a tape drive. The tape drive is initialized each time you start Backup. However, for the drivers to be loaded properly, the tape drive must be turned on before you start Windows NT. If you have more than one tape backup drive, you can use Hardware Setup on the Operations menu to select a different drive.

To change to a different tape backup drive, follow these steps:

1. From Start/Programs/Administrative Tools/Backup, on the Operations menu, click Hardware Setup (shown in Figure 5.24).

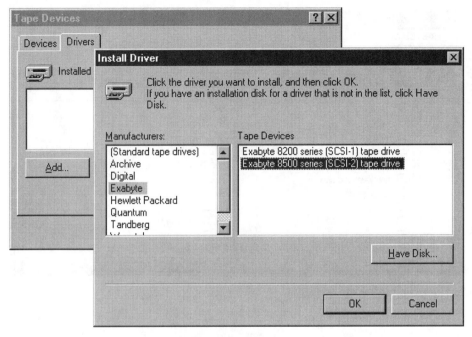

Figure 5.23   Manually adding a tape driver.

2. In the Hardware Setup dialog box, select the new tape backup drive.

3. Click OK.

Backing Up Files

You can back up all the files on a drive shown in the Drives window. However, the program will not back up any files (including hidden files) and directories that you do not own or whose access has been restricted, even when such a drive is selected. (Hidden files are identified by an exclamation point in the file icon.) All file attributes are preserved, including permissions.

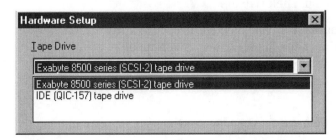

Figure 5.24   Changing to a different tape backup drive.

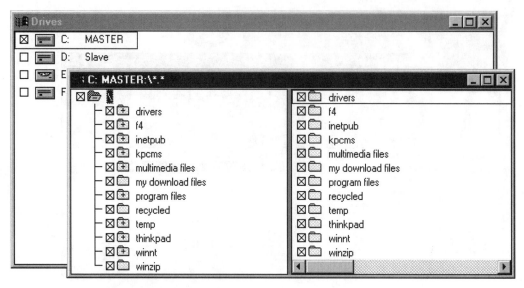

Figure 5.25 Selecting to backup all files.

To back up all the files on a disk, follow these steps:

1. From Start/Programs/Administrative Tools/Backup, in the Drives window, select the drive that you want to back up.

2. On the Select menu, click to check the main folder (see Figure 5.25). To back up individual files, select all the individual files you want to back up, using the appropriate method:

   - To select contiguous files, click the first filename, hold down the Shift key, and click the last contiguous filename.

   - To select noncontiguous files, click a filename, hold down the Ctrl key and click each filename.

3. On the Select menu, click Check to specify the selected files for backing up. A check mark appears in the check box beside each selected file.

4. On the Operations menu, click Backup.

To remove the check marks from all selected files, click Uncheck on the Select menu. To remove the check mark from an individual file, clear the check box. When only some files are selected, the corresponding drive and directory check boxes appear grayed out.

Setting Tape, Backup Set, and Log Options

Use these steps to set these tape options: Registry backup, compression, and security:

1. From Start/Programs/Administrative Tools/Backup, click Backup on the Operations menu to open the Backup Information dialog box. The upper section provides information on the tape that you loaded.

2. In Tape Name, type a name of fewer than 32 characters for the new tape.

3. In Operation, click Append to place the new backup set after the last backup set. Or click Replace to overwrite all the information on the tape.

4. Click the settings you want, as follows:

   - To confirm that the tape was backed up accurately, select the Verify After Backup check box.

   - To add a copy of your Registry to the backup set, select the Backup Local Registry check box. Make note of the following: Backup Local Registry is available only if the local drive is selected, and Backup cannot be used to back up registries on remote computers.

   - To limit access to the files on the tape, select the Restrict Access To Owner Or Administrator check box.

   - To have the tape drive compress the data onto the tape media, select the Hardware Compression check box.

 Moving tapes between different brands of tape drives can cause problems if one brand supports compression and the other one does not. Depending on the tape drive, the program might display a message such as "Tape Drive Error Detected," Tape Drive Not Responding," or "Bad Tape." To erase a tape that is causing one of the problems, type `ntbackup /nopoll` **at the command prompt. Be careful not to use Backup with the /nopoll parameter to perform anything other than erasing the tape.**

To set the backup set options, follow these steps:

1. From Start/Programs/Administrative Tools/Backup, click Backup on the Operations menu to open the Backup Information dialog box. The second section shows how many backup sets have been selected, each set being a collection of related files on one drive that is backed up during a single backup operation.

2. In Backup Set Information, type a description for the backup set.

3. In Backup Type, enter the type of backup operation you want.

If you select more than one drive, Backup provides a scrollbar for moving between backup sets so you can enter separate descriptions, up to a length of 32 characters, and select different backup types for each of the selected drives.

To set the backup log options, follow these steps:

1. From Start/Programs/Administrative Tools/Backup, click Backup on the Operations menu to open the Backup Information dialog box.

2. Click Full Detail, Summary Only, or Don't Log. When you select Full Detail, Backup logs all operation information; when you select Summary Only, Backup logs only major operations.

3. In Log File, enter the name of the text file to use for logging completed tape operations. You can click Browse (signified by the ellipsis) to locate the correct filename for a log.

4. Click OK to display the Backup Status dialog box and start the backup process.

Checking Backup Status

To check the status of Backup, as well as the names of the drive, directory, and files that are currently being backed up, or to view a log of major operations, including whether the operation completed successfully, go to Start/Programs/Administrative Tools/Backup. In the Backup Information dialog box, click OK. The Backup Status dialog box appears, and Backup begins.

The Backup Status dialog box displays the following information:

- An active status area

- The names of the drive, directory, and files that are being backed up

- A Summary area, showing a log of major operations, including whether operation completed successfully

If a large backup operation reaches the end of a tape before finishing, the Insert New Tape dialog box appears and prompts you to insert a new tape. *Note*: A collection of related tapes containing several backup sets is called a *family set*.

If you need to stop a backup job before it is completed, click Abort. A Backup Abort message appears, asking whether you want to continue the backup of the current file. Click Yes to stop now, which will cause it to display as a corrupted file.

Performing Backup Operations from the Command Prompt

During a remote console or command prompt session, backup operations can also be performed at the command prompt by typing `ntbackup` (see Figure 5.26). Most of the command parameters do not require user input and

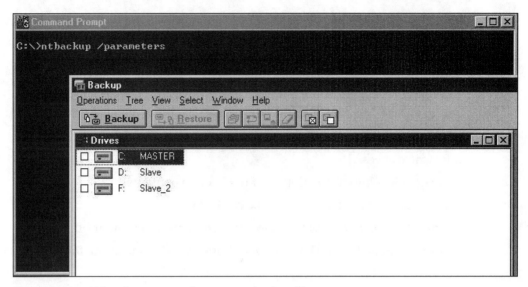

Figure 5.26   Using the command prompt to backup files.

can, therefore, be implemented in batch files. A few of the parameters do, however, require user input. The syntax is as follows:

```
ntbackup [/nopoll] [/missingtape]
```

The parameters that require input include:

/nopoll. Specifies that the tape should be erased. Do not use /nopoll with any other parameters.

/missingtape. Specifies that a tape is missing from the backup set when the set spans several tapes. Each tape becomes a single unit, as opposed to being part of the set.

You can create a batch file to back up one or more drives regularly. But be aware that using batch files enables you to back up directories *only*, not individual files. Wildcard characters cannot be used in the batch files.

In this syntax:

```
ntbackup (operation) (path) [/a] [/v] [/r] [/d "text"] [/b] [/hc:{on | off}]
    [/t {option}] [/l "filename"] [/e] [/tape:{n}]
```

the parameters are as follows:

Operation. Specifies the operation, backup, or eject. Each of the following parameters (except /tape) must be used only with the backup operation parameter:

Path. Specifies one or more paths of the directories to be backed up.

/a. Causes backup sets to be added or appended after the last backup set on the tape. When /a is not specified, the program overwrites previous data. When more than one drive is specified but /a is not, the program overwrites the contents of the tape with the information from the first drive selected and then appends the backup sets for the remaining drives.

/v. Verifies the operation.

/r. Restricts access.

/d "text". Specifies a description of the backup contents.

/b. Specifies that the local registry be backed up.

/hc:{on | hc:off}. Specifies that hardware compression is on or off.

/t {option}. Specifies the backup type. Option can be one of the following:

normal

copy

incremental

differential

daily

/l "filename". Specifies the filename for the backup log.

/e. Specifies that the backup log include exceptions only.

/tape:{n}. Specifies the tape drive to which the files should be backed up; n is a number from 0 to 9 that corresponds to the number the drive was assigned when the tape drive was installed.

Restoring Files

All the files on a drive that have been backed up can be restored. Among the easiest ways to restore files is from the Tapes window. Because this window is not normally open when you start the Backup program, you will have to open it. Once there, you can choose to restore either the current tape, one or more backup sets, or individual files. All catalog information (backup set) is maintained on the corresponding tape for that backup. Family sets have the information on the last tape.

To access the Tapes window, from Start/Programs/Administrative Tools /Backup, on the main Window menu, click to maximize the Tapes window. The tape name appears in the left panel of the Tapes window to the right of each tape icon. The following information is shown in the right panel:

- Drive backed up

- Backup set number
- Tape number and what number it is in a sequential group of tapes for a backup set
- Backup type
- Date and time of backup
- Backup description

To load catalogs for tapes and backup sets, follow these steps:

1. In the Tapes window, select the tape or backup set for which you want a catalog loaded.

2. On the Operations menu, click Catalog to load the catalog of backup sets for a tape. The Catalog Status dialog box appears, indicating the ongoing search for backup sets. It continues until a complete list of backup sets on the tape appears in the Tapes window.

3. To load a backup-set catalog of directories and files, double-click the icon for that backup set. The Catalog Status dialog box appears. In the list in the Tapes window, a plus sign in the backup-set icon indicates that it has been cataloged. Corrupt files (files that contain errors) and their corresponding directories are marked by an icon with a red X.

 The Catalog Status dialog box offers you the option of stopping the operation. To do so, simply click Abort.

When you insert a tape to be restored, only information on the first backup set is displayed in the right panel. If you want to restore the entire tape, you need to load the tape catalog to display a list of any other backup sets. If you want to know which files are in each backup set, you need to load the individual catalogs for each backup set.

To restore a tape or individual backup sets, follow these steps:

1. On the Operations menu, click Catalog to load the tape catalog of backup sets.

2. In the Tapes window, select the files, sets, or tape you want to restore using the appropriate method:

   - To select contiguous sets, click the first set, hold down the Shift key and click the last contiguous set.

   - To select noncontiguous files, click a set, hold down the Ctrl key, and click each set.

3. On the Select menu, click Check.

4. Select the backup sets you want in the right panel of the Tapes window. When only some backup sets are selected, the corresponding tape check box is gray.

5. On the Select menu, click Check to select the check boxes for the selected backup sets. To remove the check marks from all selected sets, click Uncheck on the Select menu. To remove the check mark from an individual set, clear the check box.

6. On the Operations menu, click Restore.

The procedures for selecting files to restore are similar to those for selecting files to back up. When you load a tape, only the first backup set on the tape is displayed until you load the tape catalog. Therefore, when you select an entire tape, you are really only selecting those sets that are already displayed, so you must load the tape catalog first to get the complete list of backup sets.

To restore individual files in a backup set on a tape, follow these steps:

1. In the Tapes window, load the catalog of the backup set from which you want to restore certain files.

2. Select all the files you want to restore using the appropriate method:

   • To select contiguous files, click the first filename, hold down the Shift key and click the last contiguous filename.

   • To select noncontiguous files, click a filename, hold down the Ctrl key, and click each filename.

3. On the Select menu, click Check. A check mark appears in the check box for each selected file. To remove the check marks from all selected files, click Uncheck. To remove the check mark from an individual file, clear the check box. When only some files are selected, the corresponding disk drive and directory check boxes are gray.

4. On the Operations menu, click Restore.

Again, when you load a tape, only the first backup set on the tape is displayed until you load the tape catalog. Therefore, when you select an entire tape, you are really selecting only those sets that are already displayed; you must load the tape catalog first to access the complete list of backup sets. If you want to know which files are in each backup set, you need to load the individual catalogs for each backup set.

Setting Restore and Log options

To set the restore options for the Registry and file permission control, and to restore verification, follow these steps:

1. From Start/Programs/Administrative Tools/Backup, select the tapes, backup sets, or files, then click Restore on the Operations menu.

2. In the Restore Information dialog box, specify the drive to which you want your selections restored.

3. If you want to place backup-set files into a directory other than the original one on the default drive, enter the path in Alternate Path.

4. Click the settings you want, as follows:

   - To restore the Registry files, select the Restore Local Registry check box.

   - To restore the permissions information along with the file, select the Restore File Permissions check box. *Note*: If you do not make this selection, the restored files inherit the permissions of the directory into which they are restored.

   - To verify the contents of the restored files against the files on tape, and to log any exceptions, select the Verify After Restore check box.

To set the log options, follow these steps:

1. In the Restore Information dialog box, click Full Detail, Summary Only, or Don't Log. When selected, Full Detail sets Backup to log all operations information; Summary Only sets logging for only major operations.

2. In Log File, enter the name of the text file to use for logging completed tape operations. You can click Browse (...) to search for a filename.

3. Click OK to open the Restore Status dialog box and start the restore operation.

Checking Restore Status

To check the status of Restore, in the Restore Information dialog box, click OK. The Restore Status dialog box appears and the restore operation begins. If you need to stop a restore operation before it is completed, click Abort. Then click Yes when the Restore Abort message appears, asking whether to continue the restoration of the current file or to stop now and show it as a corrupted file.

   If the restore operation reaches the end of a tape before finishing, the Insert New Tape dialog box will prompt you to insert a new tape.

Tape Maintenance

There are three major types of tape maintenance with the Windows NT Backup utility: formatting, erasing, and retensioning. These can be executed

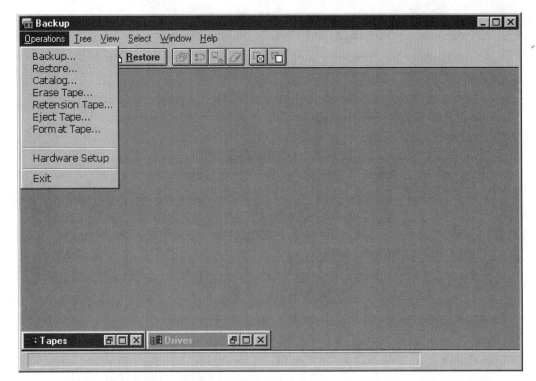

Figure 5.27   Selecting tape maintenance options.

from the Start/Programs/Administrative Tools/Backup, Operations menu, shown in Figure 5.27. They function as follows:

Format Tape. Formats an unformatted minicartridge tape. This type of tape is treated like a floppy disk and must be formatted before it can be used. If you do not have a minicartridge drive installed and activated, Format Tape is unavailable.

Erase Tape. Always erases the whole tape. You should categorize the information on the backup tapes by the method of erasing to be used, then create and maintain a list for easy reference. To erase a tape, on the Operations menu, click Erase Tape. In the Erase Tape dialog box, click Quick Erase to simply rewrite the tape header. To overwrite the entire tape, click Secure Erase (Secure Erase can take several hours, depending on the drive technology and tape length).

Retension Tape. Removes loose spots on the tape by fast-forwarding to the end of the tape and then rewinding. This procedure winds the tape evenly, so it will run more smoothly past the tape drive heads. To reduce tape slippage, manufacturers of tape-backup drives recommend that you retension quarter-inch tapes once every 20 uses. Because 4- and 8-mm tapes do not require retensioning, Retension Tape is unavailable for such tapes. The device and drive technology determines how much time is spent forwarding and rewinding the media. See the manufacturer's documentation for specific retensioning requirements.

System Optimization

You should consider the optimization of Windows NT Server a critical aspect of any standard operations policy, especially if you are running more than one communication protocol or service (e.g., Web server, remote access, database). Unfortunately, the default Windows NT installation does not incorporate specific optimization configurations, including those of system properties and performance and protocol binding preferences. Therefore, you must do these optimization procedures manually, which is what you'll learn to do in this section.

System Properties

We'll begin by configuring system properties. From Start/Settings/Control Panel/, double-click the System icon to load the System Properties utility (see Figure 5.28). From this window, we can perform a number of system optimization actions: We can change the application response time, the size of virtual memory, and even what NT does upon crashing or encountering a fatal system error during operation.

Startup/Shutdown Tab

Click first on the Startup/Shutdown tab in the System Properties window to display the default startup operating system (the one that starts automatically if more than one operating system is installed) and to set the time allowed before it starts automatically. This window also lists the actions Windows NT performs when a STOP error occurs (the fatal system error that requires a system reboot).

To specify the default operating system for startup, follow these steps:

1. From Start/Settings/Control Panel/System, under System Startup on the Startup/Shutdown tab (Figure 5.29), click the new default operating system in the Startup list.

2. In the Show list for box, type the number of seconds you want the list of choices to be displayed before the default operating system starts automatically. If the system is running only Windows NT, it is advisable to

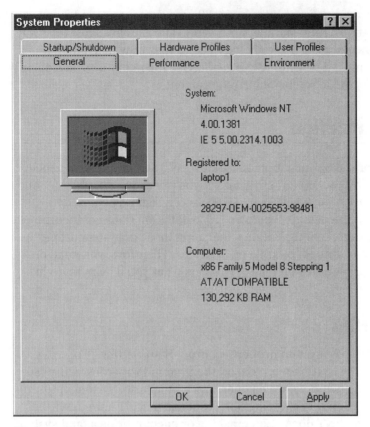

Figure 5.28 Windows NT System Properties utility.

select a minimum delay so that the system will start more quickly if and when a reboot is issued. This will reduce service downtime.

To change how Windows NT behaves when a STOP error occurs, from Start/Settings/Control Panel/System, under Recovery on the Startup/Shutdown tab, select the actions Windows NT should perform when a STOP error occurs. After you change the system recovery options, a message may appear instructing you to restart the server.

 You must be logged on as an Administrator to change Recovery options.

In regard to these options, make note of the following:

- Write an event to the system log, Send an administrative alert, and Automatically reboot require at least a 2-MB paging file on the system drive.

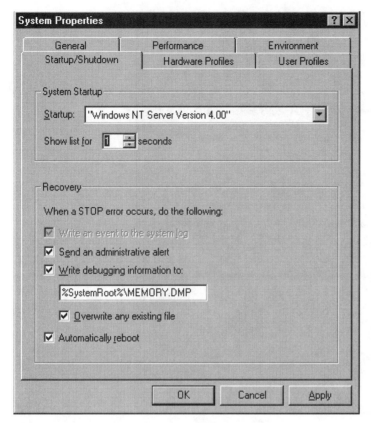

Figure 5.29   Startup/Shutdown property options.

- Write debugging information to requires a paging file on the system drive large enough to hold all of physical RAM, plus 1 MB. If you contact product support about the error, they may ask for the system-memory dump file generated by the Write debugging information to option. Notice that Windows NT always writes the dump file to the same filename. To keep dump files, copy them to a new filename after each STOP error.

- You can save some memory if you clear the Write debugging information to, Write an event to the system log, and Send an administrative alert. How much memory you save depends on the computer, but typically it ranges from 60 to 70 kilobytes (KB) on the drivers that enable these features.

Performance Tab

The Performance window is where you specify foreground-running application response priority and the sizes and locations of the paging files (virtual

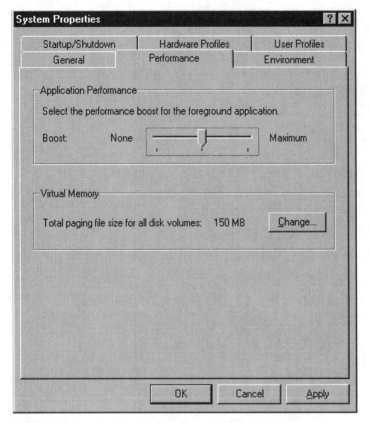

Figure 5.30 Changing the application response time.

memory). In regard to virtual memory under Windows NT, some of the program code and other information is kept in RAM, whereas other information is temporarily swapped to a virtual-memory paging file. When that information is required again, Windows NT pulls it back into RAM and, if necessary, swaps other information to virtual memory. As a result, you can run more programs at one time than the system RAM would typically allow.

To change application response time (see Figure 5.30), from Start/Settings/Control Panel/System, under Application Performance on the Performance tab, position the Boost slider. By default, Windows NT gives priority to the foreground application, so it receives more processor time than programs in the background. Set the slider as follows:

- To maximum for the best response time for the foreground application

- To the middle to give background programs a better response while continuing to give more processor time to the foreground application

- To None to give all programs equal amounts of processor time

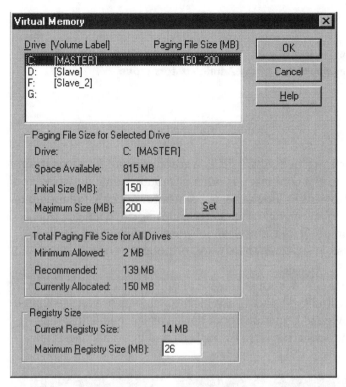

Figure 5.31   Changing the size of the virtual memory page file.

The virtual memory paging file, named pagefile.sys is typically located in the system partition. While running Windows NT, this file cannot be deleted. If while running another operating system (i.e., dual-boot O/S configuration) the paging file is deleted, a new one will be generated upon Windows NT startup.

The size of the virtual memory paging file can, however, be changed. To do so, follow these steps:

1. From Start/Settings/Control Panel/System, under Virtual Memory on the Performance tab, click Change.

2. In the Drive list (see Figure 5.31), click the drive where the file is located.

3. Under Paging File Size for Selected Drive, type a new size in megabytes in the Initial Size (MB) or Maximum Size (MB) box. For best performance, do not set the initial size to less than the Recommended size under Total Paging File Size for All Drives. Usually, you should leave the paging file at its recommended size for each drive, although you might increase it to routinely use programs that require a lot of memory.

4. Click Set.

You may have to restart your computer to see the effects of the changes.

 You can change the size of your computer's paging file only when you are logged on as a member of the Administrators group.

Performance Monitor

Performance Monitor, shown in Figure 5.32, is a graphical tool for measuring the performance of your own computer or other computers on a network. You can use Performance Monitor to look at resource use for specific components and program processes. You can also use charts and reports to gauge your computer's efficiency, identify and troubleshoot possible problems (such as unbalanced resource use, insufficient hardware, or poor program design), and plan for additional hardware needs.

On each computer, you can view the behavior of objects, such as processors, memory, cache, threads, and processes. Each of these objects has an associated set of counters that provide information about device usage, queue lengths, delays, and information used to measure throughput and internal congestion.

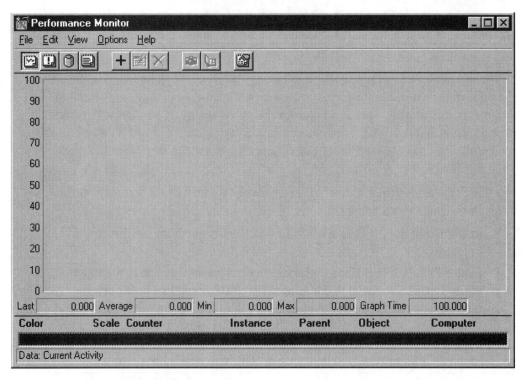

Figure 5.32   Windows NT Performance Monitor.

Performance Monitor provides charting, alerting, and reporting capabilities that reflect both current activity and ongoing logging. You can open, browse, and chart log files later as if they reflected current activity. The following overview lists how you use Performance Monitor to view the performance of objects:

- Simultaneously view data from any number of computers.

- View and dynamically change charts reflecting current activity and showing counter values that are updated at a user-defined frequency.

- Export data from charts, logs, alert logs, and reports to spreadsheet or database programs for further manipulation and printing.

- Add system alerts that list events in the Alert Log and notify you either by reverting to Alert view, logging the event in Event Viewer's Application log, or issuing a network alert.

- Run a predefined program every time or only the first time a counter value goes over or under a user-defined value.

- Create log files containing data about objects on different computers.

- Append selected sections of existing log files to a single file to form a long-term archive.

- View current-activity reports or create reports from existing log files.

- Save individual chart, alert, log, and report settings, or save the entire workspace setup to reuse when needed.

Understanding Objects

When monitoring a system, you are actually monitoring the behavior of its *objects*. In the Windows NT operating system, an object is a standard mechanism for identifying and using a system resource. Objects are created to represent individual processes, sections of shared memory, and physical devices. Performance Monitor groups the counters by object type. A unique set of counters exists for the processor, memory, cache, hard disk, processes, and other object types that produce statistical information. Certain object types and their respective counters are present on all systems. However, others, such as application-specific counters (e.g., Exchange), appear only if the computer is running the associated software.

Each object type can have several instances. For example, the Processor object type will have multiple instances if a system has multiple processors. The PhysicalDisk object type has two instances if a system has two disks. Some object types, such as Memory and Server, do not have instances at all. If an object type has multiple instances, each instance may be used with the same set of counters. The data is then tracked for each instance.

Two object types, Process and Thread, have a particularly close relationship. A Windows NT process is created when a program runs. A process may be an application (such as Microsoft Word or Corel Draw), a service (such as Event Log or Computer Browser), or a subsystem (such as the print spooler or portable operating system interface, or POSIX). In addition to an executable program, every process consists of a set of virtual-memory addresses and at least one thread.

Threads are objects within processes that execute program instructions. They allow concurrent operations within a process and enable one process to simultaneously execute different parts of its program on different processors. Each thread running on a system shows up as an instance for the Thread object type and is identified by association with its parent process. For example, if Print Manager has two active threads, Performance Monitor identifies them as Thread object instances *Printman ==> 0* and *Printman ==> 1*.

 Instances of the Process object type appear as numbers if they are internal system processes. Other types of processes are identified by the name of the executable file. Only 32-bit processes appear in the Instances box; 16-bit applications running in a Virtual DOS Machine (VDM) do not appear unless they are started in a separate memory space.

Performance Monitor consists of four main windows, which you display by clicking Chart, Alert, Log, or Report on the View menu (see Figure 5.33). These windows contain different information and have only the menu bar, status bar, and toolbar in common. You can press the F1 key to see Help about any Performance Monitor command.

On the Options menu, Data From is available in any of the four windows. Use this command to switch from working with current values for current activity (real-time data) to viewing and manipulating existing log files. The default is current activity.

To quit Performance Monitor, click Exit on the File menu. Be sure to save your individual chart, alert, log, or report settings or the entire workspace to a file before quitting, unless you are sure you will not need that exact combination of settings again.

As just stated, you can view any of four Performance Monitor windows: Chart, Alert, Log, or Report. The only consistent elements in the four windows are the display options: Menu and Title, Toolbar, Status Bar, and Always On Top. By showing or hiding any of these options, you can vary the amount of screen space available for display. Always On Top ensures that Performance Monitor, even when no longer the active window, stays visible over any other window on the display. To organize your screen, from Start/Programs/Administrative Tools/Performance Monitor, do the following:

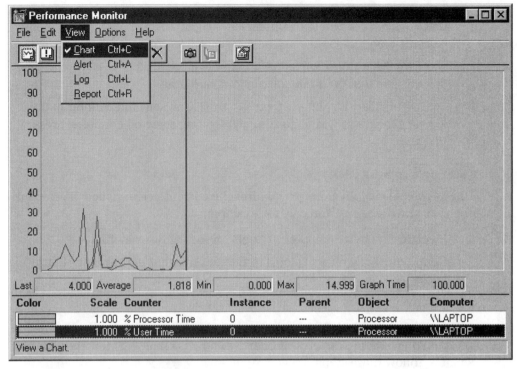

Figure 5.33 Performance Monitor display types.

- To show or hide a display option, on the Options menu, click the display options you want: Menu and Title, Toolbar, Status Bar, and Always On Top. A check mark appears alongside selected commands, as shown in Figure 5.34.

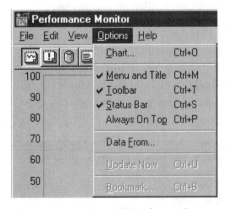

Figure 5.34 Organizing the Performance Monitor window.

- To hide the menu and title bars, double-click anywhere in the display area that does not contain text. Double-click again to again display the menu and title bars.

- To move the window while the title bar is hidden, click anywhere in the display area that does not contain text, and drag.

- To turn on chart highlighting, press Ctrl-H. The selected counter in the legend changes to white. To stop highlighting selected counters, press Ctrl-H again.

Charting Current Activity

You can create custom charts to monitor the current performance of selected counters and instances. You can, for example:

- Investigate why a computer or application is slow or inefficient

- Continuously monitor systems to find intermittent performance bottle-necks

- Discover why you need to increase capacity

If you switch to Chart from another view, and have not created or opened a chart in your current session, the Chart window is blank. To view the Chart window, follow these steps:

1. From Start/Programs/Administrative Tools/Performance Monitor, on the View menu, click Chart (shown previously in Figure 5.33).

2. To open an existing chart settings file, on the File menu, click Open. In the Performance Monitor-File Open dialog box, enter the pathname for the .pmc file that contains the selections you want to reuse, and click Open. Or, to create a new blank chart, on the File menu, click New Chart.

To add objects, counters, and instances to a chart, follow these steps:

1. On the Edit menu, click Add To Chart. The Add To Chart dialog box appears with the default settings and your server listed in the Computer box (see Figure 5.35). To make the graphs more readable, you can vary the scale of the displayed information and the color, width, and style of the line for each counter as you add it to the chart. You can also modify these properties after you add a selection.

2. In the Object box, select an available object to monitor. The Counter and Instance boxes change to display the available items for that object on the chosen computer.

3. In Counter, select one or more counters.

4. In Instance, select one or more instances, if appropriate.

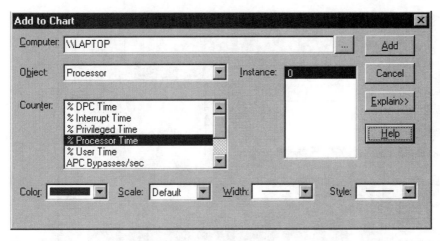

Figure 5.35 Adding objects, counters, and instances to a chart in the Performance Monitor window.

5. If you want different color, scale, line width, and style settings from the default, make those selections now, then click Add.

6. Repeat the steps 2 through 5 for any additional objects or computers that you want to monitor, then click Done.

If you want to save your chart selections in a settings file, click Save Chart Settings As on the File menu. The scale factor you select is applied to all the currently selected counters. The factor displayed is multiplied by the counter value, and the product is charted. Notice, however, that the value bar continues to show the actual value, *not* the scaled value.

A list of your selections appears in the legend at the bottom of the window, and Performance Monitor displays the changing values of your selections on the chart (refer to Figure 5.33). Notice that each displayed value is usually an average over the last two data reads, which are separated by the length of the time interval.

To change the way a selected counter appears on the chart, follow these steps:

1. In the legend, select the counter that you want to change.

2. On the Edit menu, click Edit Chart Line. The Edit Chart Line dialog box appears (see Figure 5.36).

3. Change any of the available options, as you prefer:
    - In Color, select a different line color.
    - In Scale, select the scale of the vertical display of the line.
    - In Width, select the width of the line.
    - In Style, select a solid line or dashed-line pattern.

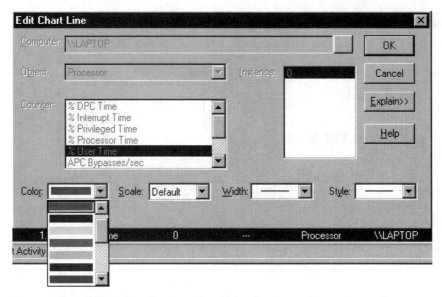

Figure 5.36 Using the Edit Chart Line dialog box in Performance Monitor.

4. When you have finished making selections, click OK. If you want to update chart selections that have been saved in a settings file, click Save Chart Settings on the File menu.

To turn the chart-highlighting mode on and change the color of the selected counter to white, press Ctrl-H. To stop highlighting selected counters, press Ctrl-H again.

To change chart options, follow these steps:

1. On the Options menu, click Chart to access the Chart Options screen shown in Figure 5.37.

2. In the Chart Options dialog box, select the options that you want to display:

   • In Vertical Maximum, type the maximum value to which the vertical axis should extend.

   • In Update Time, select either Manual Update or Periodic Update, then type a number in the Interval box to determine the time (in seconds) between chart updates.

   • In Gallery, click Graph or Histogram as the format. The Graph Time value displayed in the value bar shows the time (in seconds) that it takes to create a complete chart across the window. The Histogram view is useful for viewing simultaneous behavior of many instances of the same object.

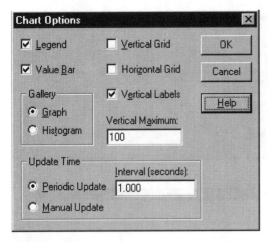

Figure 5.37 Changing chart options in Performance Monitor.

Logging Current Activity

You can collect data from multiple systems into a single log file. For capacity planning, you need to view trends over a longer period, which requires the capability to create a log file and to produce reports from that file. Note that if you switch to Log from another view and have not created or opened a log in your current session, the Log window will be blank. To view the Log window, follow these steps:

1. On the View menu, click Log (see Figure 5.38). If you are switching from another view, the Log window will be blank unless you already created or opened a log file during that session or from the command prompt.

2. To open an existing log settings file, on the File menu, click Open. In the Performance Monitor-File Open dialog box, enter the pathname for the .pml file that contains the selections you want to reuse. If there is a log filename associated with that log settings file, be aware that Performance Monitor will start logging data to that log upon opening that settings file. Click Open.

3. To create a new blank log file, on the File menu, click New Log Settings.

Performance Monitor saves the log filename with the log-settings file and will start logging data to that file upon reopening that settings file.

To add objects to a log, follow these steps:

1. On the Edit menu, click Add To Log (see Figure 5.39). The Add To Log dialog box appears with the default settings and your workstation or server listed in the Computer box. This information is used to create a log file that enables you to review at a later time the performance of

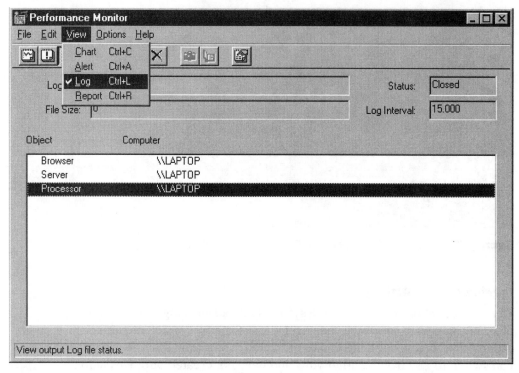

Figure 5.38 Viewing the log window in Performance Monitor.

counters and instances for objects. You can also collect data from multiple systems into a single log file. Log files contain detailed data for bottleneck detection or other detailed analysis. For capacity planning, you need to view trends over a longer period, which requires the capability to create a log file and to produce reports from that file.

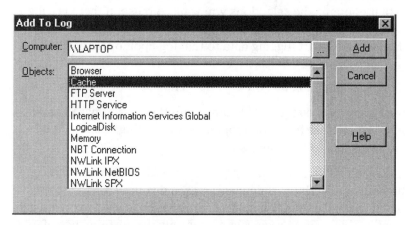

Figure 5.39 Adding objects to a log in Performance Monitor.

2. In Objects, select an available object or set of objects to monitor, then click Add.

3. Repeat the process for any additional computers that you want to monitor, then click Done.

To save log selections in a settings file, on the File menu, click Save Log Settings As. In the Performance Monitor-Save As dialog box, enter a pathname for the file that will contain the selections that you want to reuse; click OK.

To change the log options, follow these steps:

1. On the Options menu, click Log.

2. In Log File, type a name for the log file that you are creating.

3. In Update Time, click either Manual Update or Periodic Update, then enter a number in the Interval box for the time (in seconds) between log updates. If you do not want to start logging yet, click Save.

To start or stop logging, on the Options menu, click Log. In the Log Options dialog box, click Start Log. If Start Log is not enabled, you must first enter a log filename and add objects to log. After you start logging, a log symbol with the changing total file size appears on the right side of the status bar and remains there in all four views. To stop logging, click Stop Log.

If you enter the name of an existing log file when you change log options, new data will be appended to the old data. To replace the old data, you must first delete the file and then create a new one with the old name.

When a remote computer from which you are logging data shuts down, a bookmark comment is added to the log file. Another bookmark comment is added when that computer reconnects and logging starts again. To add a bookmark, on the Options menu, click Bookmark. Next, in Bookmark Comment, type a comment and click Add.

Setting Alerts on Current Activity

You can simultaneously monitor several counters. When a counter exceeds a given value, the date and time of the event are recorded in the Alert window. An alert file can hold a total of 1,000 events, after which the oldest event is discarded when the next new one is added. If you switch to Alert from another view and have not created or opened an alert log file in your current session, the Alert window will be blank.

To view the Alert window, follow these steps:

1. On the View menu, click Alert (see Figure 5.40).

2. To open an existing alert log settings file, on the File menu, click Open. In the Performance Monitor-File Open dialog box, enter the pathname for the .pma file containing the selections you want to reuse. Click Open.

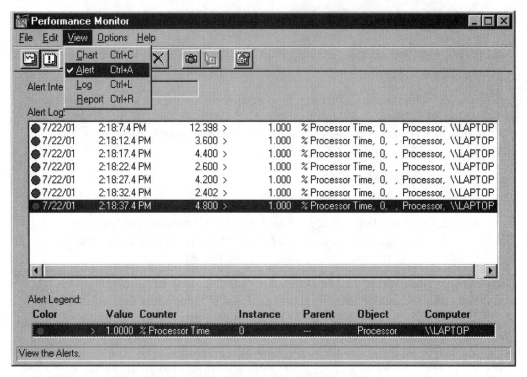

Figure 5.40 Viewing the Alert window in Performance Monitor.

3. To create a new blank alert log file, on the File menu, click New Alert Settings.

When an alert occurs while you are not in the Alert view, an alert icon appears in the status bar showing the number of alerts that have occurred since you were last in the Alert view. You can set the color assigned to a counter from within the Add to Alert dialog box if you do not want the default color selection. Each alert value is usually an average over the last two data reads, which are separated by the length of the time interval.

To add objects, counters, and instances to an alert log, follow these steps:

1. On the Edit menu, click Add to Alert (see Figure 5.41). The Add to Alert dialog box appears with the default settings and your workstation or server listed in the Computer box.

2. In Object, select an available object to monitor.

3. In Counter, select one or more counters.

4. In Instance, select one or more instances, if appropriate.

5. In Alert If, click Over or Under, and add a value.

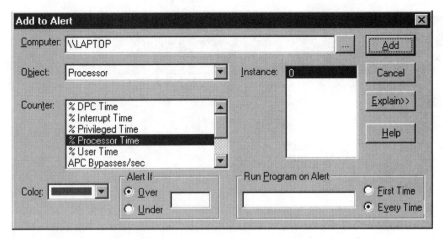

Figure 5.41   Adding objects, counters, and instances to an alert log in Performance Monitor.

6. In Run Program On Alert, click First Time or Every Time, and enter the complete pathname for the program or macro that you want to run whenever the specified alert occurs; then click Add.

7. Repeat the process for any additional objects or computers that you want to add, then click Done.

To save alert log selections in a settings file, on the File menu, click Save Alert Settings As. In the Performance Monitor-Save As dialog box, enter a pathname for the new file, and click Save.

Reporting Current Activity

The Report window remains blank until you add information to it by selecting objects, counters, and instances to be monitored with the Add To Report command on the Edit menu. The Options menu enables you to update manually the information on the screen. You can use the Update Now command between automatic data updates to get a current snapshot of the situation. Choosing the Report command on the Options menu enables you to select either an automatic updating frequency or only manual updates.

To view the Report window, on the View menu, click Report (see Figure 5.42). To begin, open an existing report or create a new one:

- In the Performance Monitor-File Open dialog box, enter the pathname for the .pmr file containing the selections you want to reuse. Click Open.

- To create a new blank report file, on the File menu, click New Report Settings. If you switch to Report from another view and have not created or

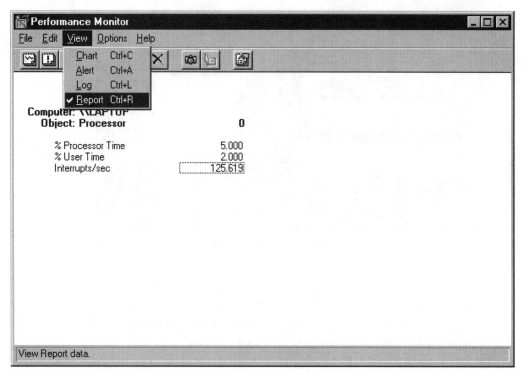

Figure 5.42 Viewing the Report window in Performance Monitor.

opened a report file in your current session, the Report window will be blank.

To add objects, counters, and instances to a report, follow these steps:

1. On the Edit menu, click Add to Report. The Add to Report dialog box appears (see Figure 5.43) with the default settings and your workstation or server listed in the Computer box.

2. In Object, select an available object to monitor from the list.

3. In Counter, select one or more available counters.

4. In Instance box, select one or more instances, if appropriate.

5. Click Add.

6. Repeat the process for any additional objects or computers that you want to monitor, then click Done.

To save report selections in a settings file, on the File menu, click Save Report Settings As. In the Performance Monitor-Save As dialog box, enter a pathname for the file that will contain the selections you want to reuse. Click Save.

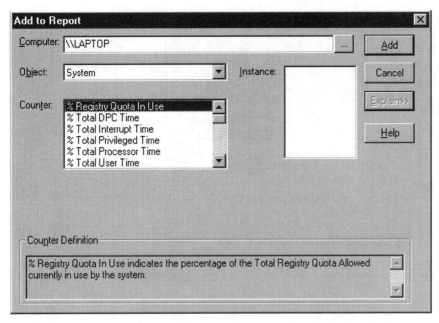

Figure 5.43   Adding objects, counters, and instances to a report in Performance Monitor.

Protocol Binding Preference

In Chapter 2 you learned how to bind protocols to network interfaces. Remember, bindings are connections between network cards and services installed on the computer. Keeping that in mind, here we'll address another server optimization technique that involves selecting protocol communication priority from the protocol bindings list.

To view the current protocol binding list, double-click the Network icon from Start/Settings/Control Panel/, then click Bindings to display the screen shown in Figure 5.44. In the Show Bindings for box, click the component whose bindings you want to view, then click the plus (+) or minus (–) sign next to a component to expand or collapse its path. Depending on the primary network protocol(s), you can optimize the server's communication process by changing the order of bindings for each selected network components. For example, you may wish to have the server communicate via TCP/IP first and Internetwork Packet Exchange and Sequenced Packet Exchange (IPX/SPX) second, if the former is not successful. To change the order of bindings for selected network components, follow these steps:

1. In Show Bindings for, click the component whose bindings you want to reorder.

2. Click the binding you want to move up or down.

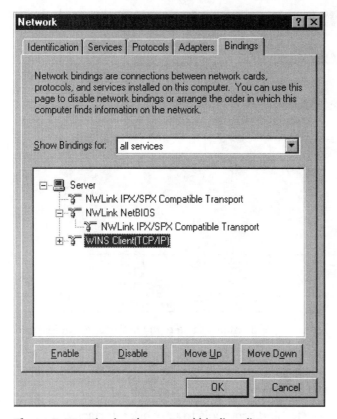

Figure 5.44 Viewing the protocol bindings list.

3. Click Move Up or Move Down to move the binding up or down in the list (see Figure 5.45).

Additionally, to enable or disable binding paths for selected network components, follow these steps:

1. In Show Bindings for, click the component whose bindings you want to view (see Figure 5.46).

2. Click the binding you want to enable or disable.

3. To enable a binding path, click Enable; to disable a binding path, click Disable.

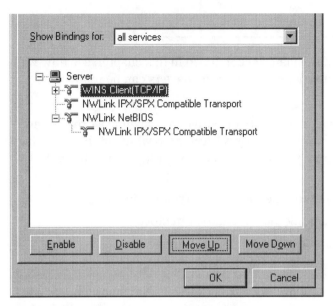

Figure 5.45   Changing the order of bindings for selected network components.

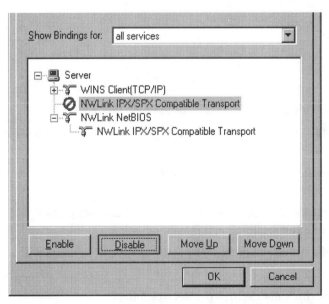

Figure 5.46   Disabling binding paths for selected network components.

Think It Over

To test your knowledge of the material contained in this chapter, see how well you do answering these questions. The correct answers can be found in Appendix A.

5.1. When manually mapping a network drive by assigning a drive letter to a resource from your desktop or NT Explorer, which of the following would most accurately be an example of your input into the Path field?

    ○ //domain/computername/foldername (shared directory)

    ○ \computername\foldername (shared directory)

    ○ \\computername\foldername (shared directory)

    ○ //computername\foldername (shared directory)

5.2. When mapping a network drive from Network Neighborhood, to connect using a different user account on a different domain, which of the following would most accurately be an example of your input to the Connect as field?

    ○ /domain/user

    ○ //domain/user

    ○ domain\user

    ○ \domain\user

5.3. Which of the following best defines a print server?

    ○ A logical interface that governs user print jobs and schedules with physical printers

    ○ A physical interface that governs user print jobs and schedules with logical printers

    ○ A physical interface that governs user print jobs and schedules with physical printers

    ○ A logical interface that governs user print jobs and schedules with logical printers

5.4. Which of the following best defines printer spooling?

    ○ A logical interface that governs user print jobs and schedules with physical printers

    ○ A single logical printer that sends the same job to many physical printers

    ○ The buffer that provides a waiting area until the specified printer is ready to print

5.6. Which of the following best defines printer pooling?

    ○ A logical interface that governs user print jobs and schedules with physical printers

    ○ A single logical printer that sends the same job to many physical printers

    ○ The buffer that provides a waiting area until the specified printer is ready to print

5.7. With the Add Printer Wizard you can install only a local printer to an NT server

    ○ True

    ○ False

5.8. When configuring a printing device, from which of the following configuration modules can you specify the amount of time to elapse before being notified that the printing device is not responding?

    ○ Add Port

    ○ Configure Port

    ○ Port Properties

5.9. Which of the following user groups has full-control permission to modify printer settings by default?

    ○ Administrators

    ○ Server Operators

    ○ Print Operators

    ○ Power Users

5.10. Which of the following is used if your printer driver provides two-way dialog or reports setting and status information?

    ○ Bidirectional Support

    ○ Printer Pooling

    ○ Printer Spooling

5.11. Which of the following list provides an overview of some of the things you can do with Windows NT Backup to protect data?

    ○ Back up and restore both local and remote files on the NTFS or FAT volumes from your own computer using an attached tape drive

○ Select files for backing up or restoring by volume, directory, or individual filename, and view detailed file information, such as size or modification date

○ Place multiple backup sets on a tape, and either append new backup sets or overwrite the whole tape with the new ones

○ Span multiple tapes with both backup sets and files, because there is no file-size restriction

○ Create a batch file to automate repeated backups of drives

○ Control the destination drive and directory for a restore operation, and receive appropriate options for action you can take when a restore would overwrite a more recently created file

5.12. To erase a tape that is causing a problem, which of the following would you type at the command prompt?

○ ntbackup /missingtape

○ ntbackup /nopoll

○ ntbackup /erase

5.13. To specify that a tape is omitted from the backup set when the set spans several tapes, which of the following would you type at the command prompt?

○ ntbackup /missingtape

○ ntbackup /nopoll

○ ntbackup /erase

5.14. Which of the following tape maintenance utilities will remove loose spots on the tape by fast-forwarding to the end of the tape and then rewinding?

○ Format Tape

○ Retension Tape

○ Erase Tape

5.15. Under Windows NT, some of the program code and other information is kept in RAM, whereas other information is temporarily swapped to a file named what?

○ Paging File

○ Virtual memory File

○ Pagefile.sys

5.16. Performance Monitor is a graphical tool for measuring the performance of your own computer or other computers on a network. On each computer, you can view which of the following behavior objects?

○ Processors

○ Memory

○ Logs

○ Cache

○ Threads

○ Alerts

○ Processes

5.17. In regard to Performance Monitor, which of the following describes an object?

○ A standard mechanism for identifying and using a system resource

○ Representations of individual processes, sections of shared memory, and physical devices

○ A set of counters that provide information about network usage

Advanced Service Configurations

In the previous chapter we investigated advanced system configurations, networking, and optimization techniques. You learned how to manage the Network Neighborhood; set up printers, print schedules, and jobs; do storage backup; and customize the general operating system to fine-tune performance. In this chapter we'll take a look at a number of common Windows NT services; specifically, you'll learn to install and administer the Dynamic Host Configuration Protocol (DHCP), the Windows Internet Naming Service (WINS), and the Remote Access Service (RAS).

 Hands-on simulations of the procedures detailed in this chapter can be found on the CD that comes bundled with this book.

Dynamic Host Configuration Protocol Step by Step

DHCP is used for assigning dynamic Internet Protocol (IP) addresses to devices on a network, such as workstations and diskless systems. Dynamic addressing makes it possible to assign a device a different IP address each time it connects to the network. DHCP also supports static IP address assignment for easier manageability of large networks.

Dynamic addressing with DHCP simplifies network administration because the server keeps a real-time tally of assigned IP addresses, and new computers can be added without the hassle of manually assigning a unique address. A good example of dynamic addressing is when users dial up to an Internet service provider (ISP) such as America Online for Internet access: They are assigned a unique IP address every time they dial up.

DHCP uses a client/server model. The network administrator establishes one or more DHCP servers that maintain Transmission Control Protocol/Internet Protocol (TCP/IP) configuration information (see Chapter 2) and provide it to clients. A DHCP server is a computer running Windows NT Server, Microsoft TCP/IP, and DHCP server software. The server database includes the following:

- Valid configuration parameters for all clients on the internetwork.

- Valid IP addresses maintained in a pool for assignment to clients, plus reserved addresses for manual assignment.

- Duration of leases offered by the server. The lease defines the length of time for which the assigned IP address can be used.

A computer running Windows NT becomes a DHCP client when Obtain an IP address from a DHCP server is selected in Windows NT TCP/IP. When a DHCP client computer is started, it communicates with a DHCP server to receive the required TCP/IP configuration information. This configuration information includes at least an IP address and submask, plus the lease associated with the configuration.

 You can read more about DHCP in Requests for Comments (RFCs), numbers 1533, 1534, 1541, and 1542. You'll find these at www.faqs .org/rfcs.

Configuring DHCP servers for a network provides the following benefits:

- The administrator can specify global and subnet-specific TCP/IP parameters centrally for the entire internetwork.

- Client computers do not require manual TCP/IP configuration.

- When a client computer moves between subnets, the old IP address is freed for reuse, and the client is reconfigured for TCP/IP automatically when the computer is started.

- Most routers can forward DHCP configuration requests, so DHCP servers are not required on every subnet in the internetwork.

DHCP Installation

Windows NT includes a DHCP server, but it is not installed by default. Therefore, you'll have to add the service. The easiest method is carried out from the Network utility, by following these steps:

1. From Start/Settings/Control Panel, double-click the Network icon.

2. From within the Services tab, click Add.

3. Select Microsoft DHCP Server from the Network Service list (see Figure 6.1) and click OK to continue.

4. When prompted, insert the Microsoft Windows NT Server CD and click Continue—the driver files are located on the Windows NT CD-ROM, so be sure to have it handy. If you want Setup to look in a different place, type in the location.

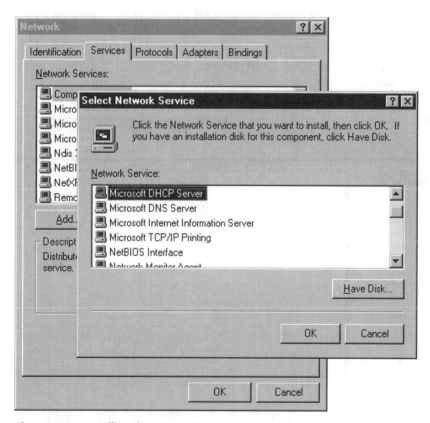

Figure 6.1   Installing the Microsoft DHCP Server.

5. After Setup copies the appropriate files, click Close to continue. If your server is using the DHCP client to acquire an IP address from another DHCP server, you'll be required to assign a static address before restarting the system.

6. Click Yes to complete the installation and restart the system.

DHCP Configuration

Upon installation of the DHCP server, Setup will install a new configuration manager in the Administrative Tools, aptly named DHCP Manager. To start DHCP Manager, from Start/Programs/Administrative Tools, click DHCP Manager. This automatically connects you to the servers and scopes to which you were last connected (see Figure 6.2). The DHCP Manager window shows a list of the scopes for the current server. You can connect to additional servers as well.

To connect to an additional DHCP server on the network:

1. On the Server menu, click Add.

2. Type the DHCP Server name or IP address, and click OK. To disconnect from a selected DHCP server, on the Server menu, click Remove.

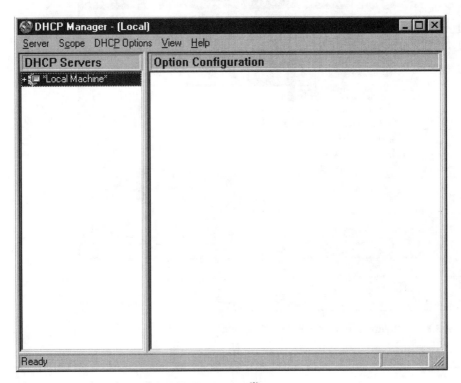

Figure 6.2 The Microsoft DHCP Manager utility.

Starting or stopping the DHCP Server service is easy from the Services utility in the Control Panel:

1. From Start/Settings/Control Panel, double-click the Services icon.

2. In the Services list, click Microsoft DHCP Server, then click Start, Stop, Pause, or Continue.

Alternatively, you can also start and stop the DHCP Server service at the command prompt using the commands: `net start dhcpserver`, `net stop dhcpserver`, `net pause dhcpserver`, or `net continue dhcpserver`. This is useful if you're accessing the server remotely via telnet. By default, the Microsoft DHCP Server service starts automatically when the computer is started.

Managing DHCP Scopes

A DHCP *scope* is a grouping of computers running the DHCP client service in a subnet. The scope is used to define parameters for each subnet. Each scope has the following properties:

- A unique subnet mask used to determine the subnet related to a given IP address

- A scope name assigned by the administrator when the scope is created

- Lease duration values to be assigned to DHCP clients with dynamic addresses

Creating a DHCP Scope

To create a new DHCP scope from the Microsoft DHCP Manager, follow these steps:

1. In the DHCP Servers list in the DHCP Manager window, select the server for which you want to create a scope.

2. On the Scope menu, click Create to access the Create Scope screen shown in Figure 6.3.

3. To define the available range of IP addresses for the scope, in the Start Address and End Address boxes type the beginning and ending IP addresses for the range. You must supply this information to activate the scope on the primary server.

4. In the Subnet Mask box, DHCP Manager proposes a subnet mask, based on the values of the Start Address and End Address. Accept the proposed value unless you know that a different value is required.

5. To define excluded addresses within the IP address pool range, use the Exclusion Range controls, as follows:

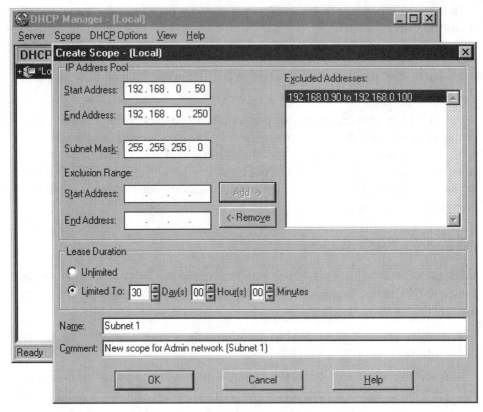

Figure 6.3 Creating a DHCP scope with the DHCP Manager utility.

- Type the first IP address of the excluded range in the Start Address box, type the last IP address of the excluded range in the End Address box, then click Add. Continue to define any other excluded ranges in the same way.

- To exclude a single IP address, type the number in the Start Address box. Leave the End Address box empty.

- To remove an IP address or a range from the excluded range, click it in the Excluded Addresses box, then click Remove. The excluded ranges should include all IP addresses that you assigned manually to other DHCP servers, non-DHCP clients, diskless workstations, or RAS and PPP clients.

6. To specify the lease duration for IP addresses in the scope, click Limited To and then type values defining the number of Days, Hours, and Minutes for the length of the address lease. If you do not want IP address leases in the scope to expire, click Unlimited.

7. In the Name box, type a scope name of up to 128 characters. This can be any name you want to use to describe the subnet and may include any combination of letters, numbers, and hyphens.

8. Optionally, in the Comment box, type any string of text to describe the scope. When you finish creating a scope, a message reminds you that the scope has not been activated and allows you to click Yes to activate the scope immediately. Please note that you should not activate a new scope until you have specified the DHCP options for this scope. The IP address range includes the Start and End values. This range should not include addresses of existing statically configured computers. These static addresses should either be outside the range for the scope or they should be immediately excluded from the range. The DHCP server itself is statically configured, so be sure that its IP address is outside of, or excluded from, the range of the scope.

9. To activate a DHCP scope, on the Scope menu, click Activate. The menu command name changes to Deactivate when the selected scope is currently activated.

Changing Scope Properties

The *subnet identifiers* and *address pool* make up the properties of scopes. You can change the properties of an existing scope, but you cannot exclude a range of addresses that includes an active lease. You must first delete the active lease and then retry the exclusion. Also, you can extend the address range of the scope, but you cannot reduce it. You can, however, exclude any unwanted addresses from the range.

To define the properties of a DHCP scope, follow these steps:

1. In the DHCP Servers list in the DHCP Manager window, select the scope for which you want to change properties.

2. On the Scope menu, click Properties (see Figure 6.4).

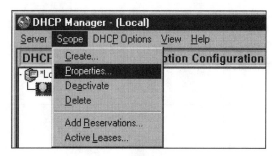

Figure 6.4 Changing the properties of a DHCP scope with the DHCP Manager utility.

3. Make any modifications (refer to the steps in *Creating a DHCP Scope*) and click OK.

Removing a Scope

When a subnet is no longer in use or when you want to remove an existing scope, you can remove it using DHCP Manager. If any IP address in the scope is still leased or in use, manually remove the client's lease, allow the client's lease to expire, or wait for the client's lease extension request to be denied.

When a scope is deactivated, it does not acknowledge lease or renewal requests, so existing clients lose their leases at renewal time and reconfigure with another available DHCP server. To ensure that all clients migrate smoothly to a new scope, you should deactivate the old scope for at least half of the lease time or until all clients have been moved off the scope manually. To move a client manually, type `ipconfig /renew` at the command prompt of the client computer and, if necessary, restart the computer.

To remove a scope from the DHCP Manager, follow these steps:

1. In the Scopes list in the DHCP Manager window, select the scope you want to remove. The scope should be deactivated until you are sure the scope is not in use.

2. On the Scope menu, click Deactivate. The command name changes to Activate when the scope is deactivated.

3. On the Scope menu, click Delete (see Figure 6.5).

Administering DHCP Clients

After you have established the scope and defined the range of available and excluded IP addresses, DHCP-enabled clients can begin using the service for automatic TCP/IP configuration. You can use DHCP Manager to manage individual client leases, which encompasses adding and managing reservations for clients.

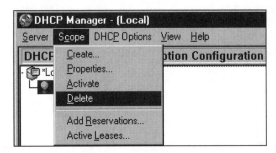

Figure 6.5   Deleting a DHCP scope with the DHCP Manager utility.

Managing Client Leases

The lease for the IP address assigned by a DHCP server has an expiration date, which the client must renew if it is going to continue to use that address. You can view the lease duration and other information for specific DHCP clients and add and change configuration settings for reserved DHCP clients.

Information about active leases in the currently selected scope appears in the Active Leases dialog box, shown in Figure 6.6. In addition to information on individual leases and reservations, the Active Leases dialog box also shows the total number of addresses in the scope, the number and percentage of addresses that are currently unavailable because they are active or excluded, and the number and percentage of addresses that are currently available.

Because the number of active leases and excluded addresses is an aggregate, it may not tell you what you want to know about only the active leases. The Active/Excluded count when a scope is deactivated reflects only excluded addresses. To determine the number of active leases and reservations, compare the Active/Excluded count before and after the scope is activated.

Leases are retained in the DHCP server database approximately 1 day after expiration. This grace period protects a client's lease in case the client and server are in different time zones, the two computers' clocks are not synchronized, or the client computer is off the network when the lease expires.

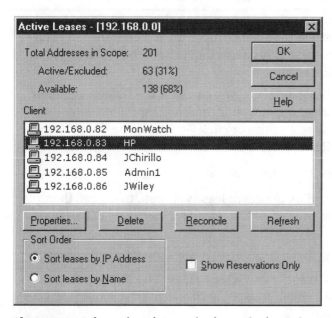

Figure 6.6 Information about active leases in the Active Leases dialog box.

These expired leases, which are distinguished by a dimmed icon, are included in the aggregate Active/Excluded count and in the list of active clients in the Active Leases dialog box.

You can delete the lease of any DHCP client in the scope. The main reason for doing so is to remove a lease that conflicts with an IP address exclusion or a client reservation that you want to add. Deleting a lease has the same effect as if the client's lease had expired: The next time that client computer starts, it must enter the initialization state and obtain new TCP/IP configuration information from a DHCP server. There is nothing, however, to prevent the client from obtaining a new lease for the same IP address. You must make the address unavailable before the client requests another lease.

Delete entries only for clients that are no longer using the assigned DHCP lease or that are to be moved immediately to a new address. Deleting an active client could result in duplicate IP addresses on the network because deleted addresses will be assigned to new active clients. After you delete a client's lease and set a reservation or exclusion, you should always use `ipconfig /release` from the command prompt on the client computer to force the client to free its IP address.

To view client lease information from the DHCP Manager, follow these steps:

1. In the DHCP Servers list in the DHCP Manager window, click the scope for which you want to view or change client information.

2. On the Scope menu, click Active Leases (refer to Figure 6.6).

3. Select the computer whose lease you want to view in the Client list, then click Properties to access the Client Properties screen shown in Figure 6.7. Or, if you want to view only clients that use reserved IP addresses, click Show Reservations Only.

4. In the Client Properties dialog box, you can view the Unique Identifier and other client information, including the lease expiration date. But note that you can only edit values or click Options in the Client Properties dialog box for clients with reserved IP addresses.

To delete a client's lease, follow these steps:

1. In the IP Address list, click the client lease you want to cancel, then click Delete; or if you want to cancel leases for all clients in the scope, click Delete All.

2. Make a reservation with the IP address, or exclude it from the range.

3. Force the client with the existing lease to give it up. At the command prompt on the client computer, type `ipconfig /release` (see command list in Figure 6.8).

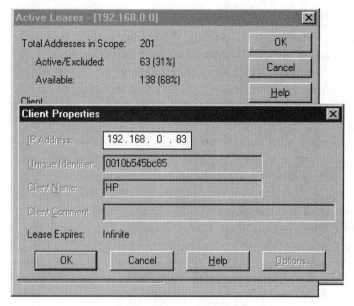

Figure 6.7   Viewing client lease information.

4. If you want, give this client a new IP address. At the command prompt
   on the client computer, type `ipconfig /renew`.

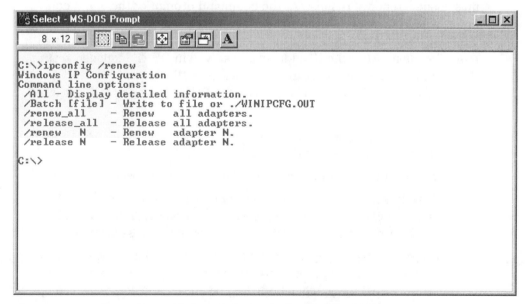

Figure 6.8   Forcing a client with the existing DHCP lease to give it up.

Managing Client Reservations

You can reserve a specific IP address for a client. Typically, you will need to do this if the client uses an IP address that was assigned using another method for TCP/IP configuration. If multiple DHCP servers are distributing addresses in the same scope, the client reservations on each DHCP server should be identical. Otherwise, the DHCP reserved client will receive different IP addresses, depending on the responding server. If you want to change a reserved IP address for a client, you have to remove the old reserved address and then add a new reservation. You can change any other information about a reserved client while keeping the reserved IP address.

Reserving an address does not automatically force a client who is currently using the address to move elsewhere. If you are reserving a new address for a client, or an address that is different from the client's current one, you should verify that the address has not already been leased by the DHCP server. If the address is already in use, the client that is using it must release the address by issuing a release request. To make this happen, at the command prompt of the client computer, type `ipconfig /release`. Clients using MS-DOS, and possibly clients using third-party operating systems, will have to restart their computers for the change to take effect. Because the client's current address is now reserved, the client is moved to a different address.

Also, reserving an address does not force the client for whom the reservation is made to move to the reserved address. In this case, too, the client must issue a renewal request. At the command prompt of the client computer, type `ipconfig /renew` and then restart the computer if necessary. The DHCP server will note that the client has a reserved address and will move the client. After the IP address is reserved in DHCP Manager, restart the client computer to configure it with the new IP address.

To add a reservation for a client using the DHCP Manager, follow these steps:

1. On the Scope menu, click Add Reservations to access the Add Reserved Clients screen shown in Figure 6.9.

2. Type the following information to identify the first reserved client:

   IP Address. Specifies an address from the reserved address pool. You can specify any reserved, unused IP address. DHCP Manager checks and warns you if a duplicate or nonreserved address is entered.

   Unique Identifier. Specifies the Media Access Control (MAC) address for the client computer's network adapter card. You can determine this address by typing net `config wksta` at the command prompt on the client computer.

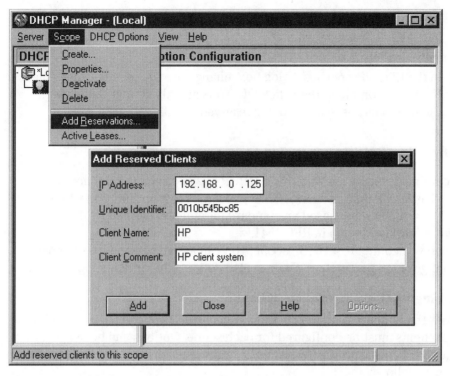

Figure 6.9 Adding a reservation for a client using the DHCP Manager.

> **Client Name**. Specifies the computer name for the client. This is used for identification purposes only and does not affect the actual computer name for the client.

> **Client Comment.** Is any optional text that you enter to describe the client.

3. Click Add to include the reservation in the DHCP database. You can continue to add reservations without closing this dialog box.

To change the reserved IP address using the DHCP Manager, follow these steps:

1. In the Active Leases dialog box, click the reserved IP address, click Delete, then OK.

2. On the Scope menu, click Add Reservations, then enter information for a new reservation as described earlier in this section.

To change basic information for a reserved client using the DHCP Manager, follow these steps:

1. On the Scope menu, click Active Leases.

2. In the IP Address list, click the address of the reserved client that you want to change, then click Properties.

3. In the Client Properties dialog box, change the Unique Identifier, Client Name, or Comment, then click OK. You can only change values in the Client Properties dialog box for reserved clients.

Configuring DHCP Option Types

The configuration parameters that a DHCP server assigns to a client are defined as DHCP options using DHCP Manager. Most options you will want to specify are predefined, based on standard parameters defined by the Internet Network Working Group in RFC 1541.

When you configure a DHCP scope, you can assign option types to govern all configuration parameters. You can also define, edit, or delete option types.

Assigning DHCP Configuration Options

Besides the IP addressing information, other DHCP options to be passed to DHCP clients must be configured for each scope. Options can be defined globally for all scopes, specifically for a selected scope, or for individual DHCP clients, as follows:

- Active global option types always apply, unless overridden by scope or DHCP client settings. Active option types for a scope apply to all computers in that scope, unless overridden for an individual DHCP client.

- The Microsoft DHCP network packet allocates 312 bytes for DHCP options. That is more than enough for most option configurations. With some DHCP servers and clients, you can allocate unused space in the DHCP packet to additional options. This feature, called *option overlay*, is not supported by Microsoft DHCP Server. If you attempt to use more than 312 bytes, some options settings will be lost. In that case, you should delete any unused or low-priority options.

- If you are using a third-party DHCP server, be aware that Microsoft DHCP clients do not support options overlays, either. If your option set is larger than 312 bytes, be sure that the settings used by Microsoft DHCP clients are included at the beginning of the option list. Settings beyond the first 312 bytes are not read by Microsoft DHCP clients.

To assign DHCP configuration options using the DHCP Manager, follow these steps:

1. In the DHCP Servers list in the DHCP Manager window, select the scope you want to configure.

2. On the DHCP Options menu, click Global or Scope, depending on whether you want to define option settings for all scopes on the currently selected server or the scope currently selected in the DHCP Manager window.

3. In the Unused Options list (see Figure 6.10), select the name of the DHCP option that you want to apply, then click Add to move the name to the Active Options list. This list shows both predefined options and any custom options that you created. For example, if you want to specify DNS servers for computers, click DNS Servers in the Unused Options list, then click Add. Or if you want to specify a gateway router for computers, click Router, then Add, and then click Edit Array and enter the IP address in the New IP Address field. When you're through, click Add and then OK (shown in the figure).

   If you want to remove a DHCP option that has been assigned for this class, click its name in the Active Options box, then click Remove.

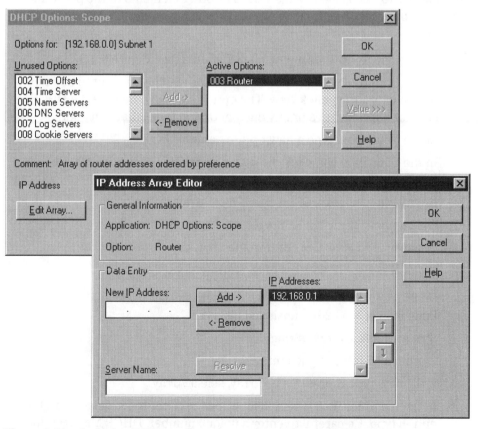

Figure 6.10   Assigning DHCP configuration options using the DHCP Manager.

4. To define the value for an active option, click its name in the Active Options box, click Values, then edit the information in the Current Value box, depending on the data type for the option, as follows:

- For an IP address, type the assigned address for the selected option.

- For a number, type an appropriate decimal or hexadecimal value for the option.

- For a string, type an appropriate ASCII string containing letters and numbers for the option.

For example, to specify the DNS name servers to be used by DHCP clients, click DNS Servers in the Active Options list, then type a list of IP addresses for DNS servers in the Current Value box. The list should be in the order of preference so that the first server in the list is the first server to be consulted.

Adding New Option Types

You can add custom parameters to include with DHCP client configuration information. You can also change values or other elements of the predefined DHCP option types. To add new option types using the DHCP Manager, follow these steps:

1. On the DHCP Options menu, click Defaults (see Figure 6.11).

2. In the Option Class list, click the class for which you want to add new option types, then click New. The option class can include the DHCP standard option types or any custom option types that you add.

3. In the Name box, type a new option name.

4. In the Data Type list, click the data type for this option as described in the following list:

   Binary = a value expressed as a binary array

   Byte = an 8-bit, unsigned integer

   Encapsulated = an array of unsigned bytes

   IP address = an IP address of the form w.x.y.z

   Long = a 32-bit, signed integer

   Long integer = a 32-bit, unsigned integer

   String = an ASCII text string

   Word = a 16-bit, unsigned integer

5. If the data type represents an array, select Array.

6. In the Identifier box, type a unique code number to associate with the option type. Be careful to enter a unique number. DHCP Manager does not check for duplicate entries.

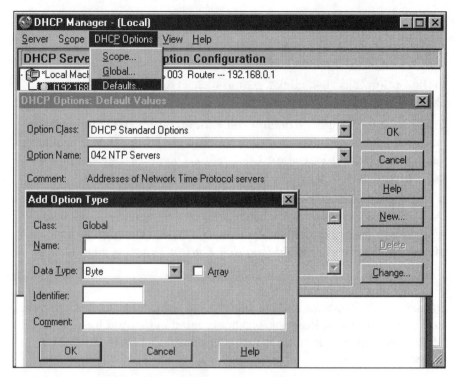

Figure 6.11 Adding new option types using the DHCP Manager.

7. In the Comment box, type a description of the option type, then click OK.

8. In the Value box of the DHCP Options: Default Values dialog box, type the value to be configured by default for this option type.

Follow these steps to delete an option type using the DHCP Manager:

1. On the DHCP Options menu, click Defaults.

2. In the Option Class list, click the related option class.

3. In the Option Name list, click the option you want to delete, then click Delete.

Changing Option Values

You can change the values for the predefined and custom DHCP option types. Options that take an array of IP addresses have a default value of 0.0.0.0. You should reset the default value of any such options you intend to use, or be sure to set a different value when you assign the option either globally or for a selected scope, as described in the previous section *Assigning DHCP Configuration Options*.

To change an option type value using the DHCP Manager, follow these steps:

1. On the DHCP Options menu, click Defaults.

2. In the Option Class list, click the option class for which you want to change values (see Figure 6.12).

3. If you want to change the default value for an option, click the option you want to change in the Option Name list, click Edit, then type a new value in the Default Value box. Clicking Edit displays a special dialog box for editing strings, arrays of IP addresses, or binary values.

4. If you want to change basic elements of a custom option, click it in the Option Name list, then click Change. You can change the name, data type, identifier, and comment for an option type, following the procedures described earlier in *Adding New Option Types*.

Defining Options for Reservations

You can assign DHCP options and specify custom values for DHCP clients that use reserved IP addresses. Reservations are created in the Add Reserved Client dialog box. To change options for reservations using the DHCP Manager, follow these steps:

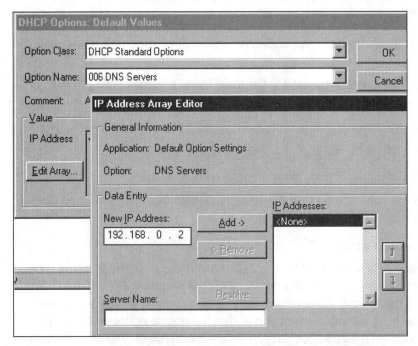

Figure 6.12 Changing an option type value using the DHCP Manager.

1. On the Scope menu, click Active Leases.

2. In the IP Address list, click the reservation address that you want to change, click Properties, then click Options. The Options button is available only for reserved addresses; it is not available for DHCP clients with dynamic addresses.

3. In the DHCP Options: Reservation dialog box, click an option name in the Unused Options list, then click Add to move the name to the Active Options list (see Figure 6.13). If you want to remove an option type that has been assigned to the scope, click its name in the Active Options box, then click Remove.

4. To change a value for an option selected in the Active Options list, click Value, then enter a value in the Current Value box.

Windows Internet Naming Service Step by Step

WINS is a name resolution service that resolves an IP address with an associated node on a network. WINS uses a distributed database that contains this information for each node currently available. According to Microsoft, a WINS server is a Windows NT Server computer running Microsoft TCP/IP and the WINS server software. WINS servers maintain a database that maps computer

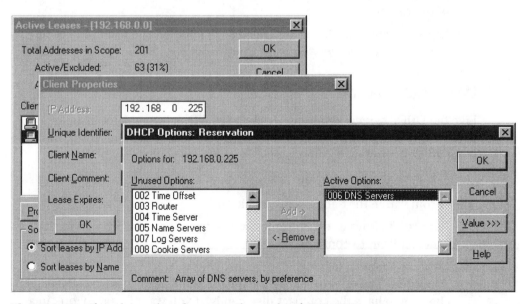

Figure 6.13 Changing options for reservations using the DHCP Manager.

names to TCP/IP addresses, allowing users to easily communicate with other computers while gaining all the benefits of TCP/IP.

A computer running the WINS server should be assigned a fixed IP address. The WINS server computer should not be a DHCP client. If the WINS server computer has more than one network adapter card, make sure the binding order of IP addresses is not changed. You must be logged on as a member of the Administrator's group to install or run the WINS Manager tool. To use or configure a WINS server, you must have full administrative rights for that server.

Using WINS servers can offer these benefits on your internetwork:

- Dynamic database maintenance to support computer name registration and name resolution. Although WINS provides dynamic name services, it offers a NetBIOS namespace, making it much more flexible than DNS for name resolution.

- Centralized management of the computer name database and the database replication policies, alleviating the need for managing LMHOSTS files.

- Dramatic reduction of IP broadcast traffic in LAN Manager internetworks, while allowing client computers to easily locate remote systems across local or wide area networks.

- Enables clients running Windows NT and Windows for Workgroups on a Windows NT Server network to browse domains on the far side of a router without a local domain controller being present on the other side of the router.

- Its extremely scaleable design makes it a good choice for name resolution on medium to very large internetworks.

WINS Installation

Like the DHCP server, Windows NT includes WINS, but it is not installed by default. The easiest method of adding this service is carried out from the Network utility, by following these steps:

1. From Start/Settings/Control Panel, double-click the Network icon.

2. From within the Services tab, click Add.

3. Select Windows Internet Name Service from the Network Service list and click OK to continue.

4. When prompted, insert the Microsoft Windows NT Server disc and click Continue. The driver files are located on the Windows NT CD-ROM, so be sure to have the compact disc handy. If you want Setup to look in a different place, type in the location.

5. After Setup copies the appropriate files, click Close to continue.

6. Click Yes to complete the installation and restart the system.

WINS Configuration

Once WINS has been installed, Setup will install a new configuration manager in the Administrative Tools utility, aptly named WINS Manager. The WINS service is a Windows NT service running on a Windows NT server. The supporting WINS client software is automatically installed for Windows NT Server and for Windows NT computers when the basic operating system is installed. To start the WINS service manager, from Start/Programs/Administrative Tools, click WINS Manager (see Figure 6.14), or, at the command prompt, type `start winsadmn`. You can include a WINS server name or IP address with the command (for example, `start winsadmn 192.168.0.2` or `start winsadmn mywinsserver`).

To start and stop the actual WINS service, use the Services utility from the Control panel, as described in Chapter 3. You can also start and stop the WINS Server service at the command prompt using the commands `net start wins`, `net stop wins`, `net pause wins`, and `net continue wins`. When paused, WINS will not accept a WINS name registration packet (as a point-to-point directed IP message) from a client. This enables a WINS admin-

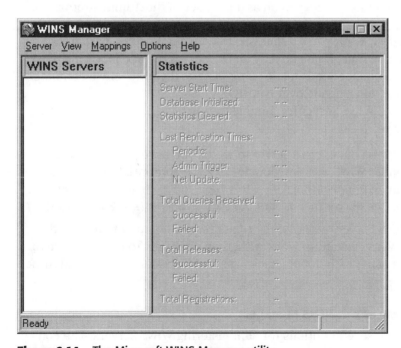

Figure 6.14 The Microsoft WINS Manager utility.

istrator to prevent clients from using WINS while continuing to administer, replicate, and scavenge old records.

Configuring WINS Servers and Replication Partners

When you install a WINS server, the WINS Manager icon is added to Program Manager. You can use this tool to view and change parameters for any WINS server on the internetwork, but you must be logged on as a member of the Administrators group for a WINS server to configure that server.

If the Windows Internet Name Service is running on the local computer, that WINS server is opened automatically for administration. If the Windows Internet Name Service is not running when you start WINS, the Add WINS Server dialog box appears.

The WINS Manager window appears when you start WINS Manager. The title bar in the WINS Manager window shows the IP address or computer name for the currently selected server, depending on whether you used the address or name to connect to the server. WINS Manager also shows some basic statistics for the selected server. To display additional statistics, on the Server menu, click Detailed Information.

Connecting to a WINS Server

As just stated, you must be logged on as a member of the Administrators group for a WINS server to configure the WINS server to which you are connecting. Furthermore, only one administrator can administer a particular WINS server at any time. If you specify an IP address when connecting to a WINS server, the connection is made using TCP/IP. If you specify a computer name, the connection is made over NetBIOS.

To connect to a WINS server for administration using the WINS Manager, follow these steps:

1. If you want to connect to a server to which you have previously connected, under WINS Servers, double-click the appropriate server icon; or, if you want to connect to a server to which you have not previously connected, on the Server menu, click Add WINS Server (see Figure 6.15).

2. In the WINS Server box, type the IP address or computer name of the WINS server you want to work with, then click OK. You do not have to prefix the name with double backslashes; WINS Manager will add these for you.

Setting Preferences for WINS Manager

You can configure several options for administering WINS servers. The commands for controlling preferences are on the Options menu. To display the

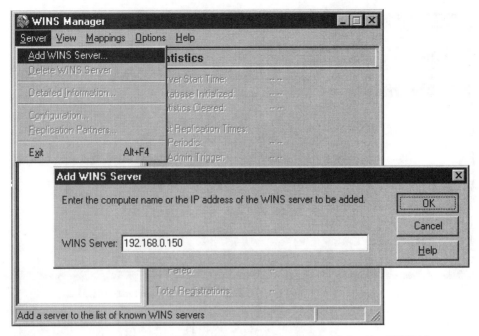

Figure 6.15 Connecting to a WINS server for administration using the WINS Manager.

status bar for help on commands, click Status Bar on the Options menu. When this command is active, its name is checked on the menu, and the status bar at the bottom of the WINS Manager window displays descriptions of commands as they are highlighted in the menu bar.

To set preferences for the WINS Manager, using the WINS Manager, follow these steps:

1. On the Options menu, click Preferences (see Figure 6.16).

2. To see all the available preferences, click Partners.

3. Click an Address Display option to indicate how you want address information to be displayed throughout WINS Manager: as computer name, IP address, or an ordered combination of both.

4. Click Auto Refresh if you want the statistics in the WINS Manager window to be refreshed automatically. Then type a number in the Interval box to specify the number of seconds between refresh actions. WINS Manager also refreshes the statistical display automatically each time an action is initiated while you are working in WINS Manager.

5. Click LAN Manager-Compatible if you want computer names to adhere to the LAN Manager naming convention. Windows NT follows the LAN Manager convention, so unless your network accepts NetBIOS names from other sources, this box should be selected.

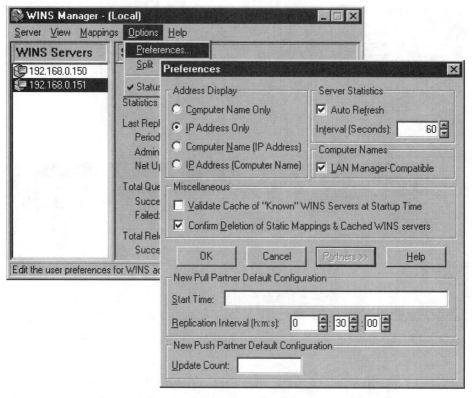

Figure 6.16   Setting preferences for the WINS Manager.

6. If you want the system to query the list of servers for available servers each time the system starts, click Validate Cache of "Known" WINS Servers at Startup Time.

7. If you want a warning message to appear each time you delete a static mapping or the cached name of a WINS server, click Confirm Deletion of Static Mappings & Cached WINS servers.

8. In the Start Time box, specify the default for replication start time for new pull partners. Then specify values for the Replication Interval to indicate how often data replicas will be exchanged between the partners. The minimum value for the Replication Interval is 5 hours.

9. In the Update Count box, type the number of registrations and changes that can occur locally before a replication trigger is sent by this server when it is a push partner. The minimum value is 20.

Configuring a WINS Server

You will want to configure multiple WINS servers to increase availability and to balance the load among servers. Each WINS server must be configured with at least one other WINS server as its replication partner. For each WINS server, you must configure threshold intervals for triggering database replication, based on a specific time, a time period, or a certain number of new records. If you designate a specific time for replication, the replication occurs only once. If a time period is specified, replication repeats at that interval.

To configure a WINS server using the WINS Manager, follow these steps:

1. On the Server menu, click Configuration (see Figure 6.17). This command is available only if you are logged on as a member of the Administrators group for the WINS server you want to configure.

2. For the WINS Server Configuration options, specify time intervals by typing a time or clicking the spin buttons, as described in this list:

   Renewal Interval. Specifies how often a client reregisters its name

   Extinction Interval. Specifies the interval between when an entry is marked as *released* and when it's marked *extinct*

   Extinction Timeout. Specifies the interval between when an entry is marked *extinct* and when the entry is finally scavenged from the database

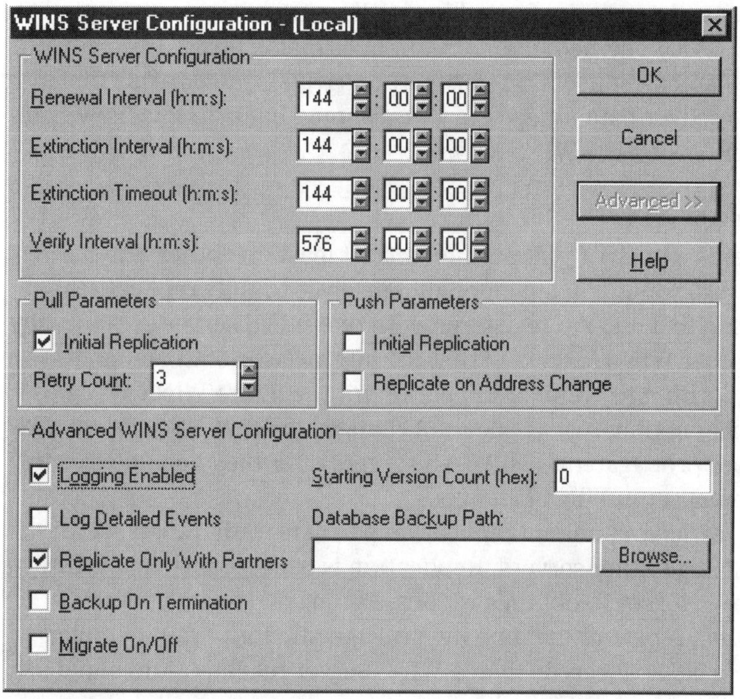

Figure 6.17 Configuring a WINS server using the WINS Manager.

Verify Interval. Specifies the interval after which the WINS server must verify that old names it does not own are still active

3. If you want this WINS server to pull replicas of new WINS database entries from its partners when the system is initialized or when a replication-related parameter changes, click Initial Replication in the Pull Parameters options, then type a value for Retry Count. In a push/pull relationship, data is passed from Primary to Secondary WINS server if the Secondary (pull partner) requests that the Primary (push partner) send an update or if the Primary asks the pull partner to start requesting updates.

4. To inform partners of the database status when the system is initialized, click Initial Replication in the Push Parameters group.

5. To inform partners of the database status when an address changes in a mapping record, click Replicate on Address Change.

6. Set any Advanced WINS Server Configuration options.

The replication interval for this WINS server's pull partner is defined in the Preferences dialog box. The extinction interval, extinction timeout, and verify interval are derived from the renewal interval and the replication interval specified. The WINS server adjusts the values specified by the administrator to minimize the inconsistency between a WINS server and its partners.

The retry count is the number of times the server should attempt to connect (in case of failure) with a partner for pulling replicas. Retries are attempted at the replication interval specified in the Preferences dialog box.

The file where database update operations are saved is *jet.log*. This file is used by WINS to recover data if necessary. You should back up this file when you back up other files on the WINS server.

Configuring Replication Partners

Each WINS server is a push or pull partner with at least one other WINS server. WINS servers communicate among themselves to fully replicate their databases, ensuring that a name registered with one WINS server is eventually replicated to all other WINS servers within the internetwork. All mapping changes converge within the replication period for the entire WINS system, which is the maximum time for propagating changes to all WINS servers. All released names are propagated to all WINS servers after they become extinct, based on the interval set in WINS Manager.

Replication is carried out among replication partners, rather than each server replicating to all other servers. Replication is triggered when a WINS server polls another server to obtain a replica. Polling can begin at system startup and can then repeat at the time interval specific for periodic replication. Replication is also triggered when a WINS server reaches a threshold set by the administrator, which is an update count for registrations and changes.

In this case, the server notifies its partners that it has reached this threshold, and the other servers then decide to pull replicas. Additionally, the administrator can cause a replication immediately or at a specified time. Replication at a specified time is a one-time-only event. If the time specified has already passed, replication does not occur.

When you designate replication partners, you need to specify parameters for push and pull partners that govern when replication will begin. To configure replication partners for a WINS server, using the WINS Manager, follow these steps:

1. In the WINS Server list of the Replication Partners dialog box, click the server you want to configure (see Figure 6.18).

2. Click either Push Partner or Pull Partner to indicate the replication option you want, then click Configure.

3. Complete the entries in the Properties dialog box, as follows:

    *   To define push partner properties, in the Update Count box of the Push Partner Properties dialog box, type a number to indicate how many additions and updates can be made to records in the database

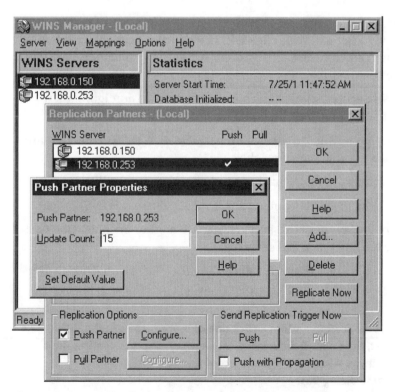

Figure 6.18   Configuring replication partners for a WINS server.

before the changes result in replication. Replications that have been pulled in from partners do not count as insertions or updates in this context. The minimum is 20. To return to the value specified in the Preferences dialog box, click Set Default Values.

- To define pull partner properties, in the Start Time box of the Pull Partner Properties dialog box, type a time to indicate when replication should begin. You can use any separator for hours, minutes, and seconds. Any A.M. or P.M. designations will work, but only if these are configured for your system's time setting options. Next, in the Replication Interval box, type a time in hours, minutes, and seconds to indicate how often replications will occur, or click the spin buttons to set the time you want. If you want to return to the values specified in the Preferences dialog box, click Set Default Values.

To add a replication partner for a WINS server, using the WINS Manager, follow these steps:

1. On the Server menu, click Replication Partners. This command is available only if you are logged on as a member of the Administrators group for the local server.

2. Click Add, type the name or IP address of the WINS server that you want to add to the list, then click OK. If WINS Manager can find this server, it will add it to the WINS Server list in the Replication Partners dialog box.

3. In the WINS Server list, click the server you want to configure, then complete the actions described in the previous section.

4. If you want to view only push or pull partners or WINS servers that are neither push nor pull partners, click:

   - Push Partners to display push partners for the current WINS server.

   - Pull Partners to display pull partners for the current WINS server.

   - Other to display the WINS servers that are neither push nor pull partners for the current WINS server.

5. To specify replication triggers, follow the procedures described in *Triggering Replication between Partners*, the next section.

 To delete replication partners, click one or more servers in the WINS Server list, then click Delete. WINS Manager asks you to confirm the deletion if you selected the related confirmation option in the Preferences dialog box.

Triggering Replication between Partners

You can replicate the database between the push or pull partners immediately, rather than waiting for the start time or replication interval specified in the Preferences dialog box as described previously. You will probably want to begin replication immediately after you make a series of changes, such as entering a range of static address mappings.

To send a replication trigger, using the WINS Manager, follow these steps:

1. On the Server menu, click Replication Partners.

2. In WINS Servers list box (see Figure 6.19), click the WINS servers to which you want to send a replication trigger, then click Push or Pull, depending on whether you want to send the trigger to push partners or pull partners.

3. Optionally, you can select the Push with Propagation check box if you want the specified WINS server to propagate the trigger to all its pull partners after it has pulled in the latest information from the source WINS server. If it does not need to pull in any replicas because it has the same or more up-to-date replicas than the source WINS server, it does not propagate the trigger to its pull partners. Otherwise, if the Push with Propagation check box is cleared, the specified WINS server will not propagate the trigger to its other partners.

To start replication immediately, in the Replication Partners dialog box, click Replicate Now.

Managing Static Mappings for WINS Servers

You can change the IP addresses in static mappings owned by the WINS server you are currently administering. To edit a static mapping entry, using the WINS Manager, follow these steps:

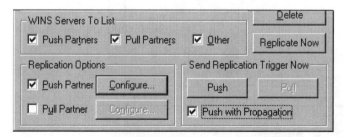

Figure 6.19 Sending a replication trigger using the WINS Manager.

1. On the Mappings menu, click Static Mappings.

2. In the Static Mappings dialog box, click the mapping you want to change, then click Edit Mapping (see Figure 6.20).

3. In the IP Address box, type a new address for the selected computer, then click OK. The change is made in the WINS database immediately. If the change you enter is not allowed for the database because that address is already in use, a message asks you to enter another address.

You can view, but not edit, the Computer Name and Mapping Type mapping option in the Edit Static Mappings dialog box. If you want to change the Computer Name or Mapping Type related to a specific IP address, you must delete the entry and redefine it in the Add Static Mappings dialog box. It is important to note that, because each static mapping is added to the database when you click Add, you cannot cancel work in this dialog box. If you make a mistake when entering a name or address for a mapping, you must return to the Static Mappings dialog box and delete the mapping there.

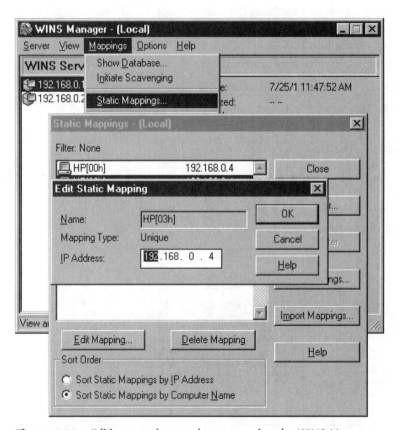

Figure 6.20   Editing a static mapping entry using the WINS Manager.

To add static mappings to the WINS database by typing entries, follow these steps:

1. On the Mappings menu, click Static Mappings.

2. In the Static Mappings dialog box, click Add Mappings (see Figure 6.21).

3. In the computer Name box, type the computer name of the system for which you are adding a static mapping.

4. In the IP Address box, type the address for the computer.

5. Click a Type option to indicate whether this entry is a unique name or a kind of group, as described in the following list:

   Unique. A unique name in the database, with one address per name.

   Group. A normal group, where addresses of individual members are not stored. The client broadcasts name packets to normal groups.

   Domain Name. A group with NetBIOS names. A domain name group stores up to 25 addresses for members.

   Internet group. User-defined, special groups that store up to 25 addresses for members. Use this to specify your own group of NetBIOS names and IP addresses.

   Multihomed. Used to specify a unique name that can have more than one address for multihomed computers.

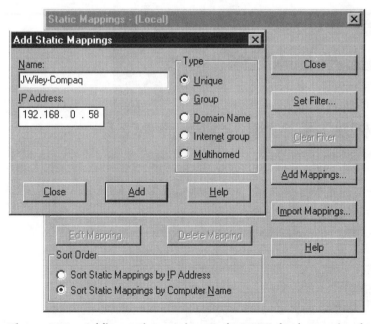

Figure 6.21 Adding static mappings to the WINS database using the WINS Manager.

6. If you specified a Domain Name, Internet group or Multihomed type, additional controls appear so that you can add multiple addresses to the list. Click an address in the list, then click Up or Down to change its order in the list.

7. Click Add. The mapping is immediately added to the database for that entry, and the boxes are cleared so that you can add another entry.

8. Repeat this process for each static mapping you want to add to the database, then click Done.

You may want to limit the range of IP addresses or computer names displayed in the Static Mappings dialog box or the Show Database dialog box. To filter mappings by address or name, follow these steps:

1. On the Mappings menu, click Static Mappings.

2. In the dialog box for Static Mappings or Show Database, click Set Filter (see Figure 6.22).

3. In the Computer Name or IP Address boxes, type a portion of the computer name or the address or both, plus asterisks for the unspecified portions of the name or address. You can use the asterisk (*) wildcard for either the name or address. However, for the address, a wildcard can be used only for a complete octet. For example, you can type 192.168.*.*, but you cannot enter 192.1*.1.1

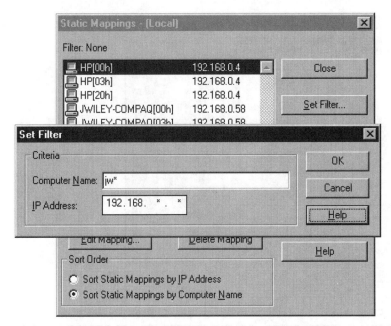

FFigure 6.22 Filtering mappings by address or name using the WINS Manager.

4. Click OK. The selected range appears in the Static Mappings or Show Database dialog box. If no mappings are found that match the range you specified, the list will be empty.

To clear the filtered range of mappings, in the Static Mappings or Show Database dialog box, click Clear Filter.

You can also import entries for static mappings from any file that has the same format as the LMHOSTS file. Scope names and keywords other than #DOM are ignored. To import a file containing static mapping entries, follow these steps:

1. In the Static Mappings dialog box, click Import Mappings.

2. Specify a filename for a static mappings file by typing its name in the box; or click one or more filenames in the list, then click OK to import the file. Each specified file is read, and a static mapping is created for each computer name and address. If the #DOM keyword is included for any record, a special group is created (if it is not already present), and the address is added to that group.

Managing the WINS Database

Like any database, the WINS database of address mappings needs to be maintained and backed up periodically to clear it of released entries and old entries that were registered at another WINS server but were not removed from this database for some reason. This process, called *scavenging*, is done automatically over intervals defined by the relationship between the Renewal and Extinction intervals defined in the Configuration dialog box.

WINS Manager provides the tools you need for maintaining the database. For example, if you want to verify old replicas immediately instead of waiting the time interval specified for verification, you can manually scavenge the database. To scavenge the WINS database, using the WINS Manager, on the Mappings menu, click Initiate Scavenging (see Figure 6.23).

The following files are stored in the \\WINNT\System32\WINS folder, which is created when you set up a WINS server:

Jet.log. Log of all transactions done with the database. If necessary, this file is used by WINS to recover data.

System.mdb. Used by WINS for holding information about the structure of its database.

Wins.mdb. The WINS database file.

Winstmp.mdb. A temporary file that WINS creates as a database swap file during index maintenance operations. This file may remain in the \\WINS folder after a crash.

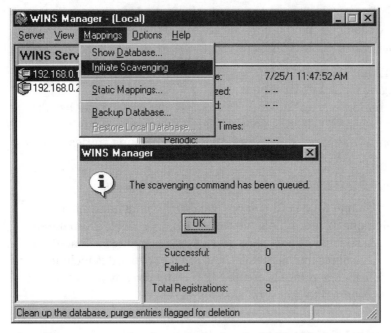

Figure 6.23   Scavenging the WINS database using the WINS Manager.

You should back up these files when you back up other files on the WINS server. After WINS has been running for a while, the database might need to be compacted to improve WINS performance. For example, you should always compact the WINS database whenever it approaches 30 MB. To compact the WINS database, follow these steps:

1. To stop the Windows Internet Name Service on the WINS server, click Services from the Control Panel and follow the steps for stopping services as explained in Chapter 3, or type `net stop wins` at a command prompt.

2. From a command prompt, run the Jetpack.exe program (found in the \\WINNT\System32 folder), as shown in Figure 6.24.

3. Restart the Windows Internet Name Service on the WINS server.

 Do not remove nor tamper with the Jet.log, System.mdb, Wins.mdb, and Winstmp.mdb files in any manner.

Backing Up and Restoring the Database

The WINS Manager provides backup tools so that you can back up and restore the WINS database. After you specify a backup folder for the database, WINS

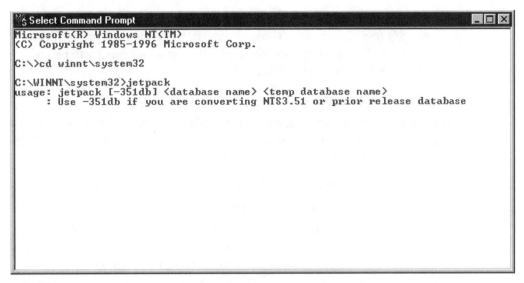

Figure 6.24   Compacting the WINS database with Jetpack.exe.

performs complete database backups every 3 hours, using the specified folder. To back up a WINS database, follow these steps:

1. On the Mappings menu, click Backup Database.

2. Enter the location for saving the backup files, then click OK. *Note*: Do not specify a network drive as the backup location.

To restore a WINS database, follow these steps:

1. On the Mappings menu, click Restore Database.

2. Enter the location where the backup files are stored, then click OK. In case of database corruption, the WINS database can be restored from the backup. Regardless of whether the WINS database is restored, use WINS Manager to do the following before invoking WINS after such a corruption:

   • In the Show Database dialog box, check the highest version number of records owned by this WINS server in the database of its present and past partners (that is, check all WINS servers to which the records may have been replicated). If a WINS server is currently down, you will need to start it to check its database for the version number information.

   • In the WINS Server Configuration dialog box, set a value for Starting Version Count that is higher than the highest version number on the other WINS servers. This number will not be accepted by WINS if it is set to more than 2^{31}. Also note that WINS may adjust the value you specify to a higher one to ensure that database records are replicated to other WINS servers quickly. Typically, the adjustment will be an increment in the range of 0 to 500.

Viewing the WINS Database

You can view the actual active and static mappings stored in the WINS database based on the WINS server that owns the entries. To view the entire WINS database at a specific server, follow these steps:

1. On the Mappings menu, click Show Database (see Figure 6.25).

2. Click Show Only Mappings from Specific Owner.

3. In the Select Owner list, click the WINS server whose database you want to view. By default, the Show Database dialog box shows all mappings for the WINS database on the currently selected WINS server.

4. Click one of the Sort Order options by which to sort the mapping: IP Address, Computer Name, Version ID, Type, or Expiration Date.

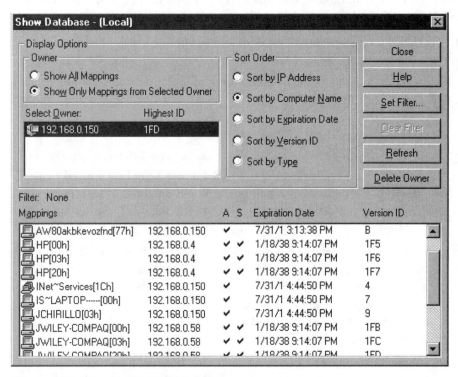

Figure 6.25 Viewing the WINS database.

5. Use the scrollbars in the Mappings box to view entries in the database. To view a specified range of mappings within the WINS database, click Set Filter and follow the procedures described in Filtering the Range of Mappings. To turn off filtering, click Clear Filter.

Remote Access Service Step by Step

RAS is another service included with the Windows NT operating system, but it is not installed by default. RAS enables remote users to log in to the local network using a modem or wide area network (WAN) link. On the server side, RAS can be configured to support modem pools with as many as 256 ports. Both dial-in and dial-back operations are provisioned with this service. For all practical purposes, RAS supports the following network communication protocols: TCP/IP, Internetwork Packet Exchange (IPX), and NetBEUI. On the client side, RAS supports the dial-up networking function of most Windows systems.

According to Microsoft, RAS lets workstations at remote sites access network servers transparently, as though they were physically connected to the network. Dial-Up Networking is the client version of Windows NT RAS. Remote access connections can be established over public telephone lines, X.25 networks, Integrated Services Digital Network (ISDN) networks, or Point-to-Point Tunneling Protocol (PPTP) connections.

An X.25 network transmits data with a packet-switching protocol, bypassing noisy telephone lines. ISDN offers a much faster communication speed than a telephone line. The phone line communicates at 9,600 bits per second (bps), whereas ISDN communicates at speeds of 64 or 128 KB per second. Businesses that need this kind of speed usually have a large telecommuting workforce or need to do extensive administrative tasks remotely, such as install software on off-site workstations.

RAS also allows remote users access through the Internet via PPTP. PPTP is a new networking technology that supports multiprotocol virtual private networks (VPNs). These networks enable remote users to access corporate networks securely across the Internet by dialing in to an Internet service provider (ISP) or by connecting directly to the Internet. PPTP offers the following advantages:

Lower transmission costs. PPTP uses the Internet as a connection instead of a long-distance telephone number or 800 service. This can greatly reduce transmission costs.

Lower hardware costs. PPTP enables modems and ISDN cards to be separated from the RAS server. Instead, they can be located at a modem pool or at a communications server (requiring less hardware for an administrator to purchase and manage).

Lower administrative overhead. With PPTP, network administrators centrally manage and secure their remote access networks at the RAS server. Instead of supporting complex hardware configurations, they have to manage only user accounts.

Enhanced security. Above all, the PPTP connection over the Internet is encrypted and secure, and it works with any protocol (including, IP, IPX, and NetBEUI).

Remote access protocols control transmission of data over the WAN. The operating system and local area network (LAN) protocol(s) used on remote access clients and servers dictate which remote access protocol your clients will use. The remote access protocols are of four types: Point-to-Point Protocol (PPP), Serial Line Internet Protocol (SLIP), Microsoft RAS Protocol, and NetBIOS Gateway. These are defined in the following subsections.

Point-to-Point Protocol

Windows NT supports the PPP in RAS. PPP is a set of industry standard framing and authentication protocols that enable remote access solutions to interoperate in a multivendor network. Microsoft recommends that you use PPP because of its flexibility and its role as an industry standard, as well as for future flexibility with client and server hardware and software.

PPP support enables computers running Windows NT to dial in to remote networks through any server that complies with the PPP standard. PPP compliance also enables a Windows NT Server computer to receive calls from, and provide network access to, other vendors' remote access software. The PPP architecture also enables clients to load any combination of IPX, TCP/IP, and NetBEUI. Applications written to the Windows Sockets, NetBIOS, or IPX interface can be run on a remote Windows NT Workstation computer.

PPP has become the standard for remote access. Remote-access protocol standards are defined in Requests for Comments (RFCs), which are published by the Internet Engineering Task Force (IETF) and other working groups. The RFCs supported in this version of Windows NT RAS include:

RFC 1549	PPP in HDLC Framing
RFC 1552	PPP Internetwork Packet Exchange Control Protocol (IPXCP)
RFC 1334	PPP Authentication Protocols
RFC 1332	PPP Internet Protocol Control Protocol (IPCP)

RFC 1661	Link Control Protocol (LCP)
RFC 1717	PPP Multilink Protocol
RFC 1144	Compressing TCP/IP Headers for Low-Speed Serial Links
RFC 1055	A Nonstandard for Transmission of IP Datagrams Over Serial Lines: SLIP

Serial Line Internet Protocol

SLIP is an older remote access standard typically used by UNIX remote access servers. Windows NT Dial-Up Networking clients support SLIP and can connect to any remote access server using the SLIP standard. This permits Windows NT version 3.5 clients to connect to the large installed base of UNIX servers. But note that the Windows NT remote access server does not support SLIP clients.

Microsoft RAS Protocol

The Microsoft RAS protocol is a proprietary remote access protocol supporting the NetBIOS standard. The Microsoft RAS protocol is supported in all previous versions of Microsoft RAS and is used on Windows NT version 3.1, Windows for Workgroups, MS-DOS, and LAN Manager clients.

A RAS client dialing in to an older version of Windows (Windows NT version 3.1 or Windows for Workgroups) must use the NetBEUI protocol. The RAS server then acts as a gateway for the remote client, providing access to servers that use the NetBEUI, TCP/IP, or IPX protocols.

NetBIOS Gateway

Windows NT continues to support NetBIOS gateways, the architecture used in previous version of Windows NT and LAN Manager. Remote users connect using NetBEUI; the RAS server translates packets, if necessary, to IPX or TCP/IP. This enables users to share network resources in a multiprotocol LAN but prevents them from running applications that rely on IPX or TCP/IP on the client. The NetBIOS gateway is used by default when remote clients are using NetBEUI.

An example of the NetBIOS gateway capability is remote network access for Lotus Notes users. Although Lotus Notes does offer dial-up connectivity, dial-up is limited to the Notes application. RAS complements this connectivity by providing a low-cost, high-performance remote network connection for Notes users that connects Notes and offers file and print services and access to other network resources.

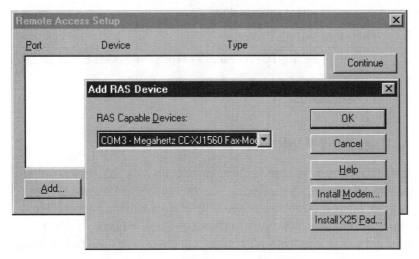

Figure 6.26 Adding a port for RAS by selecting from the list box.

RAS Installation and Configuration

The easiest method of installing RAS is carried out from the Network utility, by following these steps:

1. From Start/Settings/Control Panel, double-click the Network icon.

2. From within the Services tab, click Add.

3. Select Remote Access Service from the Network Service list and click OK to continue.

4. When prompted, insert the Microsoft Windows NT Server disc and click Continue. The driver files are located on the Windows NT CD-ROM, so be sure to have the compact disc handy. If you want Setup to look in a different place, type in the location.

5. After Setup copies the appropriate files, you'll be required to assign a communication port (i.e., external modem). To add a port for RAS, select a RAS device and port from the list box, and click OK (see Figure 6.26). Ports not in the list cannot be installed with Remote Access Setup. You must install them before running Remote Access Setup, using the manufacturer's installation program. For further information, refer to the manufacturer's documentation.

6. To have RAS Setup automatically detect your modem on the specified port, click Install Modem to use the Install New Modem Wizard (see Figure 6.27). Additionally, to install an X.25 PAD for the specified port, click Install X.25 PAD.

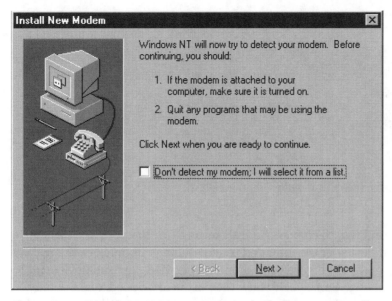

Figure 6.27   Directing RAS Setup to automatically detect your modem.

7. Next, the Remote Access Setup program (see Figure 6.28) lets you install the RAS drivers, select ports for RAS to use, and determine how each port will be used (for dialing out, receiving calls, or both). In this window, you have the following options:

  • Click Add to make another port available to RAS and install a modem or X.25 PAD for the port and proceed to Step 8. Conversely, click Remove to make a port unavailable to RAS.

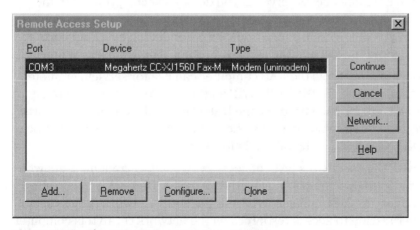

Figure 6.28   The Remote Access Setup program.

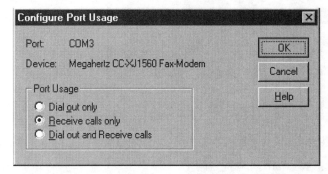

Figure 6.29 Changing the RAS settings for a port.

- Click Configure to change the RAS settings for the port, such as the attached device or the intended usage (dialing out only, receiving calls only, or both; see Figure 6.29). For the specified port and device, in the Port Usage box, specify how the port is to be used: dial out only, receive calls only, or both. Click OK when you are finished configuring the port.

- Click Clone to copy the same modem setup from one port to another.

- Click Network to configure RAS server-wide settings (see Figure 6.30). Network protocol configuration applies to all RAS operations for all RAS-enabled ports. The RAS computer may access a LAN as a client or as a server. You must select the LAN protocols RAS will use in each role.

- A RAS computer's role is determined when you specify how RAS-enabled ports will be used. Select the protocols to use when dialing out to a remote access server. If you do not select a protocol in the Dial Out Protocols box, you will be unable to select that protocol later when you configure a phone book entry for dialing out. If no ports are configured for dial out, the Dial out Protocols box appears dimmed.

- Select the protocols the RAS computer can use for servicing remote clients, whether NetBEUI, TCP/IP and/or IPX. You must also configure parameters for each protocol the RAS server will support. If no ports are configured to receive calls, the Server Settings box will not appear in the Network Configuration dialog box.

  NetBEUI. Specify the level of access you want to grant all users who dial in to this computer using the NetBEUI protocol. You can allow remote NetBEUI clients to access the entire network (grants users permission to access resources on the network) or to this computer only (grants users permission to access only the resources on this computer).

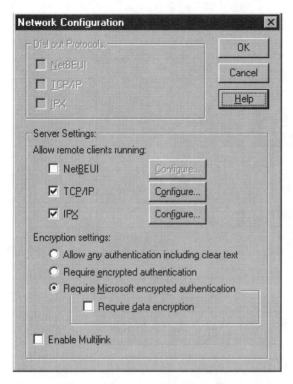

Figure 6.30 Configuring RAS server-wide settings.

TCP/IP. Use this dialog (Figure 6.31) to specify the level of access
for RAS TCP/IP clients and to specify the IP addresses for assignment to RAS clients. You can allow remote TCP/IP clients to
access the entire network (grants users permission to access
resources on the network) or to this computer only (grants users
permission to access only the resources on this computer). By
selecting use DHCP to assign remote TCP/IP client addresses,
RAS servers can obtain IP addresses for remote clients from a
DHCP server. You should select this option if a DHCP server is
available. The use static address pool is selected if a DHCP server
is not available, where a range of IP addresses can be given to a
RAS server for assignment to clients. The range must be valid for
the subnet the RAS server is in. Type the beginning and ending
addresses of the range in the appropriate box. You must assign at
least two IP addresses—one for a remote client and one for
assignment to the network adapter on the RAS server. You can
exclude addresses within the range given to the RAS server by
completing the From and To addresses and then clicking Add.
Remove excluded ranges by selecting the range to exclude and

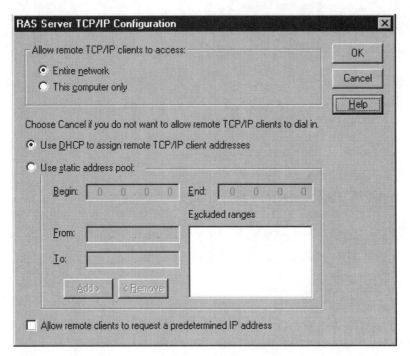

Figure 6.31   Configuring RAS for TCP/IP.

then clicking Remove. By allowing remote clients to request a pre-determined IP address, clients must specify the address by an entry in Dial-Up Networking.

IPX. Use this dialog to specify the level of access for RAS IPX clients and to specify an IPX network number assignment method for RAS clients. The RAS server provides clients connecting to an IPX network with an IPX network number and must act as their Service Advertisement Protocol (SAP) agent. Use this dialog box to specify how the RAS server provides IPX net numbers to clients and whether the RAS server should also provide access to the network (act as an IPX router for RAS clients only). You can allow remote IPX clients to access the entire network (grants users permission to access resources on the network) or to this computer only (grants users permission to access only the resources on this computer). By selecting to allocate network numbers automatically, an IPX network number not currently in use is determined by the RAS server and assigned to the RAS client. By selecting to allocate network numbers, ranges of IPX network numbers can be given to a RAS server for assignment to clients. Allocated IPX address pools are useful if you want to identify RAS clients on the network by number. You must then provide the beginning network number in the From box. RAS automatically determines the number of available ports and calculates the end number. Optionally, you can elect to assign the same network number to all IPX clients by selecting its check box. If this box is selected, only one network number is added to your routing table for all active RAS clients, which means less overhead. If this box is not selected, a network number is added to your routing table for each active RAS client. Furthermore, if you elect to allow remote clients to request IPX node number, they will do so rather than use the node number provided by the RAS server. Allowing remote clients to specify their own node number is a potential security threat to your network. It enables a client to impersonate a previously connected client and access network resources accessed by the other client.

- Select the Allow any authentication including cleartext option to permit connection using any authentication requested by the client (MS-CHAP, SPAP, PAP). This option is useful if you have RAS clients using different client software. MS-CHAP is the most secure protocol supported by RAS. The Password Authentication Protocol (PAP) uses a cleartext authentication process associated with the PPP protocol. PAP authentication should be used only when dialing in to servers that do not support encrypted authentication (i.e., SLIP and PPP servers). The Shiva Password Authentication Protocol (SPAP) uses a PAP implementation for Shiva remote client software support.

- Select the Require encrypted authentication option to permit connection using any authentication requested by the client except PAP. This option requires encrypted passwords from all clients. Select the Require Microsoft encrypted authentication option to permit connection using MS-CHAP authentication only. You can also select the Require data encryption check box to ensure that all data sent over the wire is encrypted. Windows NT RAS provides data encryption using the RSA Data Security Incorporated RC4 algorithm.

- Dial-Up Networking Multilink combines multiple physical links into a logical bundle. This aggregate link increases your bandwidth. The most common use is bundling ISDN channels, but you can also bundle two or more modems or a modem and an ISDN line. To use Multilink, both the clients and servers must have Multilink enabled. Select the Enable Multilink check box to use Multilink functionality.

- Click OK when you are finished.

8. Click Continue to proceed to the next step in Setup when you have finished with this dialog. When prompted, insert the Microsoft Windows NT Server disc and click Continue—the driver files are located on the Windows NT CD-ROM, so be sure to have the compact disc handy. If you want setup to look in a different place, type in the location.

9. Click OK to confirm the end of the setup process, then Close and Yes to restart the computer.

RAS Administration

Connecting to a Microsoft RAS server is a simple process that uses the credentials specified when you logged on to Windows NT. If you use Windows NT RAS to connect to computers that are not running Windows NT RAS, the remote computer might require a specific sequence of commands and responses through a terminal window to successfully log you on to the remote system. If the client is a Windows NT computer and the remote server is any Microsoft RAS server, logon is completely automated using Windows NT security.

Administering RAS and monitoring its service activity is easy with the Remote Access Admin utility. The program can be executed from Start/Programs /Administrative Tools by clicking Remote Access Admin. For convenience this RAS administration section is divided into two categories, *Working with the Server Service* and *Working with User Accounts*.

Working with the Server Service

One of the primary features of the RAS Admin utility is checking communication ports and port status. To check communication ports, on the Server menu, click Communication Ports (see Figure 6.32). The following options are available, some depending on the RAS configuration:

Server. The name of the server to which the computer is connected.

Port. Each serial communication port configured for RAS.

User. The user connected to each active port.

Started. The date and time of each connection.

Port Status. Statistics for a particular port.

Disconnect User. Disconnects a user on a particular port.

Send Message. Sends a message to a user on a selected port.

Send To All. Send a message to all users.

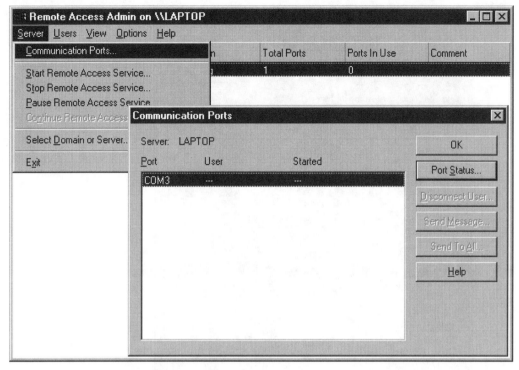

Figure 6.32   Checking RAS communication ports.

To check port status, in the Port list, select the port whose status you want to check, then click Port Status. In the Port Status dialog box, click Reset to return all statistics back to zero. The following information can be displayed from the Port Status dialog box (Figure 6.33):

PORT STATISTICS

Bytes in. The number of bytes received before decompression.

Bytes out. The number of bytes sent after compression.

CONNECTION STATISTICS

Bytes in. The number of bytes received after decompression.

Bytes out. The number of bytes sent before compression.

Frames in. The number of logical network frames received from the client.

Frames out. The number of logical network frames sent to the client.

Compression in. The ratio of compression achieved on received data, where higher is better.

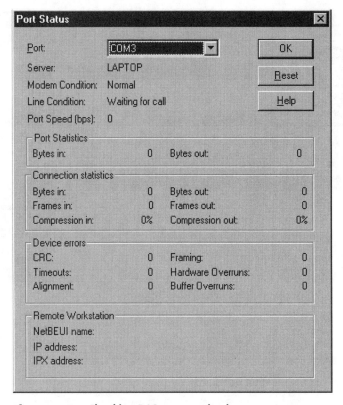

Figure 6.33   Checking RAS communication port status.

Compression out. The ratio of compression achieved on transmitted data, where higher is better.

DEVICE ERRORS

CRC. Error caused by a failed CRC—one or more characters in the data packet arrived garbled from the server.

Framing. Error caused by invalid start or stop bits—typically, the modem rate is incorrect or it's the wrong modem type.

Timeouts. Error caused when an expected character is not received in time.

Hardware Overruns. Errors caused when the sending computer has sent characters faster than the receiving computer can process at the hardware level.

Alignment. Error when a character is received but not expected—usually happens when an expected character is lost or received out of place.

Buffer Overruns. Errors caused when the sending computer has sent characters faster than the receiving computer can process at the software level.

Remote Workstation. The remote computer connected to this port.

Additionally, the Dial-Up Networking Monitor (located in the Control Panel and shown in Figure 6.34) identifies the status of a call and allows you to see the speed at which you connected, the duration of the connection, the names of users connected to a RAS server, protocols used during the connection, and which devices are part of a connection. You also use the Dial-Up Networking Monitor to hang up active connections. If you have multilink connections, you can hang up a specific device if you want to use it for another call.

By default, the Dial-Up Networking Monitor appears on the taskbar as you dial out. Use the Preferences tab to change the view and configure it to appear as window. The Dial-Up Networking Monitor displays lights to indicate traffic over dial-up lines: A button flashes blue when sending or receiv-

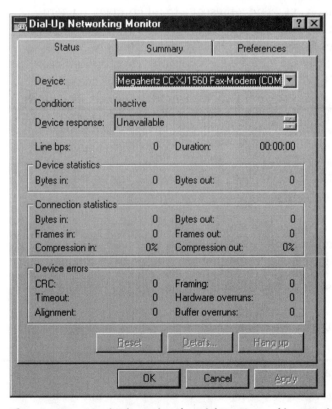

Figure 6.34   Monitoring using the Dial-Up Networking Monitor.

ing data and red when an error occurs. Also, when Dial-Up Networking Monitor is viewed as a window, you can configure it to show rows of lights for multiple devices. To do this, in the Preferences tab, click Lights.

To control RAS communication, you can pause, stop, and start the service right from the Remote Access Admin module. Pausing the Remote Access Service blocks new incoming calls; however, existing connections remain intact. To pause Remote Access, in the Remote Access Admin dialog box, select the server you want to pause. Then, on the Server menu, click Pause Remote Access Service. As a result, on the main screen, the condition of the server you selected changes from Running to Paused.

Continuing RAS resumes acceptance of new incoming calls. To continue Remote Access, in the Remote Access Admin dialog box, select the paused server you want to continue. Next, on the Server menu, click Continue Remote Access Service. On the main screen the condition of the server you selected changes back from Paused to Running.

Stopping Remote Access Service can cause connected users to lose valuable data. Therefore, it is essential to make sure everyone has disconnected first. To stop Remote Access, first Pause the Remote Access Service to block new incoming calls. Next, send a message to all connected users informing them that you are about to stop RAS and that they should save their data and disconnect from the LAN. Finally, in the Remote Access Admin dialog box, select the server on which you want to stop Remote Access Service, and on the Server menu, click Stop Remote Access Service. A list of connected users is displayed. This list is updated every 5 seconds. You should monitor the list and wait for all users to disconnect before clicking Yes. To start Remote Access again, on the Server menu, click Start Remote Access Service.

Working with User Accounts

The following procedure assumes that the user has an account for the domain or server in focus. To grant or revoke dial-in permission, on the Users menu, click Permissions (see Figure 6.35). The following options are available:

Grant Dialin Permission to User. Select to grant dial-in permission to the selected user.

No Call Back. Select to disable call back from the server for this user.

Set By Caller. Select to prompt the user for a call back number.

Preset To. Select to call back at a predefined phone number.

Grant All. Select to grant these permissions to all accounts in user list.

Revoke All. Select to revoke these permissions to all accounts in user list.

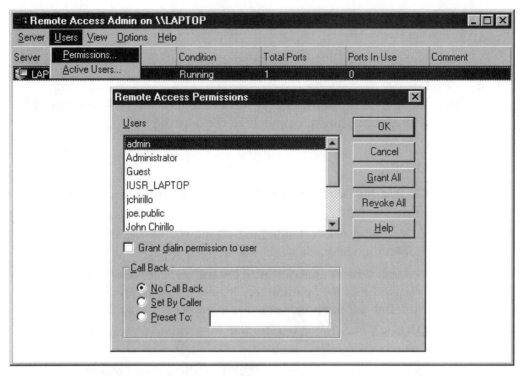

Figure 6.35   Setting user permissions from RAS.

 Do not assign callback permission to users who are connecting to the network through a switchboard. Because browsing for users and their permissions over a remote connection takes a long time, it is often more convenient to turn browsing off by default. To turn off browsing, on the Options menu, click Low-Speed Connection.

Once users are active, to see details about their accounts, on the Users menu, click Active Users. Then select the username of the account you want to see and click User Account. The following information can be displayed:

Username and Full Name. The username and full name of the account you are viewing.

Password Last Changed and Password Expires. The date/time the password was last changed and the interval set between required password changes.

Privilege Level. The user account privilege level.

Call Back Privilege and Call Back Number. Callback privilege and the number the server calls back.

Think It Over

Before moving on the Chapter 7, test your comprehension of the material in this chapter. The answers to these questions can be found in Appendix A.

6.1. Using dynamic addressing, a device can be assigned a different IP address each time it connects to the network.

   ○ True

   ○ False

6.2. Configuring DHCP servers for a network provides which of the following benefits?

   ○ Simplifies network administration because the server keeps a real-time tally of assigned IP addresses.

   ○ Allows the administrator to centrally specify global and subnet-specific TCP/IP parameters for the entire internetwork and define parameters for clients using reserved addresses.

   ○ Uses a distributed database that contains information for each node currently available.

   ○ Does not require manual TCP/IP configuration for client computers. When a client computer moves between subnets, it is automatically reconfigured for TCP/IP when the computer is started.

6.3. Most routers can't forward DHCP configuration requests, so DHCP servers are required on every subnet in the internetwork.

   ○ True

   ○ False

6.4. At the command prompt, which command can be used to start the DHCP Server service?

   ○ `net continue dhcp`

   ○ `net begin dhcp server`

   ○ `net start dhcpserver`

   ○ `dhcpserver /start`

6.5. Which of the following best defines a DHCP scope?

   ○ A DHCP scope is a grouping of computers running the DHCP client service in a subnet. The scope is used to define parameters for each subnet.

    ○ A DHCP scope contains lease duration values to be assigned to DHCP clients with dynamic addresses.

    ○ A DHCP scope contains address pools that make up the properties of subnet identifiers.

6.6. When a DHCP scope is deactivated, it does not acknowledge lease or renewal requests, so existing clients lose their leases at renewal time and reconfigure with another available DHCP server.

    ○ True

    ○ False

6.7. To ensure that all clients migrate smoothly to a new scope, you should deactivate the old scope for at least half of the lease time or until all clients have been moved off the scope manually. To move a client manually, at the command prompt, which command can be used?

    ○ `ipconfig renew`

    ○ `net dhcpserver /renew`

    ○ `ipconfig /renew`

    ○ `net dhcpserver /ipconfig renew`

6.8. If you are using a third-party DHCP server, be aware that Microsoft DHCP clients do not support option overlays. If your option set is too large, be sure that the settings used by Microsoft DHCP clients are included at the beginning of the option list. Microsoft DHCP clients do not read settings beyond which number of bytes?

    ○ The first 312 bytes

    ○ The first 624 bytes

    ○ 936 bytes

6.9. A computer running the WINS server does not require a fixed IP address; it can be a DHCP client.

    ○ True

    ○ False

6.10. Using WINS servers can offer which of the following benefits on your internetwork?

    ○ Dynamic database maintenance to support computer name registration and name resolution. Although WINS provides dynamic name services, it offers a NetBIOS namespace, making it much more flexible than DNS for name resolution.

○ Centralized management of the computer name database and the database replication policies, thereby alleviating the need for managing LMHOSTS files.

○ Dramatic increase of IP broadcast traffic in LAN Manager internetworks.

○ Clients running Windows NT and Windows for Workgroups on a Windows NT Server network can browse domains on the far side of a router without a local domain controller being present on the other side of the router.

○ A nonscaleable design, making it a good choice for name resolution only for very large internetworks.

6.11.   At the command prompt, which of the following commands can be used to start the WINS service manager?

○ `start winsadmn`

○ `start winsadmn 192.168.0.2`

○ `start winsadmn mywinsserver`

○ `net start wins`

6.12.   At the command prompt, which of the following commands can be used to start the WINS server service?

○ `start winsadmn`

○ `start winsadmn 192.168.0.2`

○ `start winsadmn mywinsserver`

○ `net start wins`

6.13.   When configuring multiple WINS servers to increase the availability and to balance the load among servers, which of the following is an obligatory step?

○ Each WINS server must be configured with another as its replication partner.

○ Each WINS server must also be configured as its own replication partner.

○ For each WINS server, you must configure threshold intervals for triggering database replication, based on a specific time, a time period, or a certain number of new records.

6.14.   Which of the following is the file in which database update operations are saved?

○ JET.LOG

○ LMHOSTS

○ SYSTEM.MDB

○ WINS.MDB

○ WINSTMP.MDB

6.15. Which of the following files is used by WINS for holding information about the structure of its database?

○ JET.LOG

○ LMHOSTS

○ SYSTEM.MDB

○ WINS.MDB

○ WINSTMP.MDB

6.16. Which of the following files is the WINS database file?

○ JET.LOG

○ LMHOSTS

○ SYSTEM.MDB

○ WINS.MDB

○ WINSTMP.MDB

6.17. Which of the following files remains in the \\WINS folder after a crash?

○ JET.LOG

○ LMHOSTS

○ SYSTEM.MDB

○ WINS.MDB

○ WINSTMP.MDB

6.18. You should always compact the WINS database whenever it approaches what size?

○ 10 MB

○ 20 MB

○ 30 MB

○ 60 MB

6.19. On the server side, RAS can be configured to support modem pools with up to how many ports?

○ 4

    ○ 64

    ○ 128

    ○ 256

6.20. RAS supports which of the following network communication protocols?

    ○ TCP/IP

    ○ IPX

    ○ NetBIOS

    ○ NetBEUI

    ○ PPTP

    ○ PPP

6.21. Remote access connections can be established over which of the following?

    ○ Public telephone lines

    ○ X.25 networks

    ○ ISDN networks

    ○ PPTP connections

6.22. Which of the following authentication methods uses a cleartext process?

    ○ MS-CHAP

    ○ SPAP

    ○ PAP

6.23. Which of the following authentication methods is the most secure protocol supported by RAS?

    ○ MS-CHAP

    ○ SPAP

    ○ PAP

6.24. Which of the following authentication methods is an implementation for Shiva remote client software support?

    ○ MS-CHAP

    ○ SPAP

    ○ PAP

6.25. Browsing for users and their permissions over a remote connection takes a long time. Which of the following processes is used to turn browsing off by default?

○ On the Options menu, click Low-Speed Connection.

○ Select Remote Access Service from the Network Service list and click OK to turn browsing off.

○ On the Options menu, click Configure and select the check box to turn browsing off.

○ On the Server menu, click Stop Remote Access Service.

Advanced Gateway Configurations

In Chapter 6, we examined three Windows NT services and stepped through their installation and administration: Dynamic Host Configuration Protocol (DHCP), the Windows Internet Naming Service (WINS), and Remote Access Service (RAS). In this chapter we install and configure the most common gateway services: the Domain Name Service (DNS), Novell NetWare, and the Internet Information Server (IIS), which features Internet services such as the World Wide Web (WWW), File Transfer Protocol (FTP), and Gopher.

 Hands-on simulations of the information in this chapter can be found on the book's companion CD-ROM.

Domain Name Service Step by Step

A domain name is a character-based handle that identifies one or more IP addresses. The DNS is a gateway service to the Internet that translates domain names into IP addresses. Its primary purpose is to aid human beings, who find it easier to remember alphabetic domain names than numeric IP addresses. The DNS translates the user-friendly character domain names into their respective numeric IP addresses. As explained in Chapter 2, datagrams that travel through the Internet use addresses; therefore every time a domain name is specified, a DNS service daemon must translate the name into the corresponding IP address. When a domain name is entered into a browser—say, TigerTools.net—a DNS server maps this alphabetic domain name into an IP address, which is where the user is forwarded to view the Web site. DNS works in a similar manner on local networks. By using DNS, administrators and users do not have to rely on IP addresses when accessing systems on their networks.

DNS is also used to control Internet email delivery, Web page requests, and domain forwarding. The DNS directory service consists of DNS data, DNS servers, and Internet protocols for fetching data from the servers. The records in the DNS directory are split into files called *zones*. Zones are kept on authoritative servers distributed all over the Internet, which answer queries according to the DNS network protocol. Most servers are authoritative for some zones, and perform a caching function for all other DNS information. The industry standard DNS resource record types include:

A: Address. Defined in RFC 1035

AAAA: IPv6 address. Defined in RFC 1886

AFSDB: AFS Database location. Defined in RFC 1183

CNAME: Canonical name. Defined in RFC 1035

HINFO: Host information. Defined in RFC 1035

ISDN: Integrated Service Digital Network. Defined in RFC 1183

KEY: Public key. Defined in RFC 2065

KX: Key Exchanger. Defined in RFC 2230

LOC: Location. Defined in RFC 1876

MB: Mailbox. Defined in RFC 1035

MG: Mail Group Member. Defined in RFC 1035

MINFO: Mailbox or Mail List Information. Defined in RFC 1035

MR: Mail Rename Domain Name. Defined in RFC 1035

MX: Mail Exchanger. Defined in RFC 1035

NS: Name Server. Defined in RFC 1035

NSAP: Network Service Access Point Address. Defined in RFC 1348. Redefined in RFC 1637 and 1706

NULL. Defined in RFC 1035

NXT: Next. Defined in RFC 2065

PTR: Pointer. Defined in RFC 1035

PX: Pointer to X.400/RFC822 information. Defined in RFC 1664

RP: Responsible Person. Defined in RFC 1183

RT: Route Through. Defined in RFC 1183

SIG: Cryptographic Signature. Defined in RFC 2065

SOA: Start of Authority. Defined in RFC 1035

SRV: Server. Defined in RFC 2052

TXT: Text. Defined in RFC 1035

WKS: Well-Known Service. Defined in RFC 1035

X25: International Telecommunication Union-Telecommunication Standardization Sector (ITU-T) protocol standard for wide area network (WAN) communications. Defined in RFC 1183.

DNS Installation and Configuration

Windows NT includes a DNS server, but it is not installed by default. The easiest way to add the service is to work from the Network utility. Follow these steps:

1. From Start/Settings/Control Panel, double-click the Network icon.

2. From within the Services tab, click Add.

3. Select Microsoft DNS Server from the Network Service list and click OK to continue.

4. When prompted, insert the Microsoft Windows NT Server disc and click Continue. The driver files are located on the Windows NT CD-ROM, so be sure to have the compact disc handy. If you want Setup to look in a different place, type in the location.

5. After Setup copies the appropriate files, click Close to continue.

6. Click Yes to complete the installation and restart the system.

Working with DNS Servers

Similar to previously mentioned NT services, DNS has its own administrator utility (shown in Figure 7.1) accessible from Start/Programs/Administrative Tools/DNS Manager. The first configuration step for our new DNS service is to add a new server.

 Be sure to have Administrator privileges on the server before attempting DNS administration.

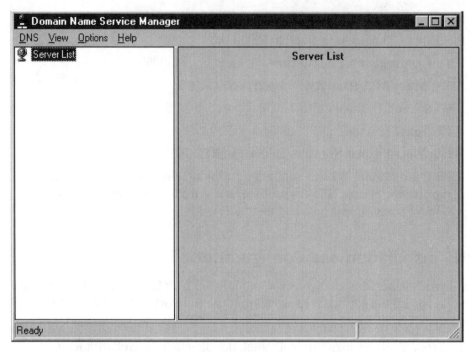

Figure 7.1 Windows NT DNS Manager.

To add a new server to the DNS Manager list, using the DNS Manager, follow these steps:

1. In the left pane of the DNS Manager window, right-click Server List or click on the DNS menu above it.

 When using the DNS menu option, be sure to first select the zone you wish to configure from the server list. By default, the three reverse lookup zones—inverse structure with strict reliance on the specific subnet structure—(zones in the In-addr.arpa domain) that are associated with each DNS server are 0.In-addr.arpa, 127.In-addr.arpa, and 255.In-addr.arpa. You do not need to do anything with them; they are added for performance reasons.

2. Click New Server (see Figure 7.2). To remove a server, click Delete.

3. In the DNS Server box, type the name or IP address of a server that is running the Microsoft DNS Service. An icon representing the server appears in the Server List.

If an icon with a red letter X appears, this indicates that DNS Manager was unable to connect with the DNS Service on the specified server. For more

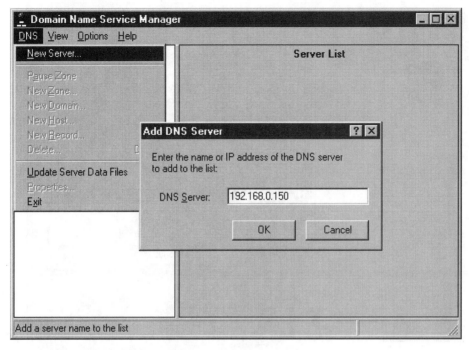

Figure 7.2   Adding a server to the DNS Manager.

information about the type of error that occurred, see the Error box at the bottom of the right pane in the DNS Manager window.

To view server statistics, in the Server List, click the new server icon—the one just created in step 3. The statistics for the selected DNS Server appear in the right pane of the DNS Manager window. At this point, the information should be grayed out. To have DNS Manager refresh statistics automatically, thus activating the statistics, on the Options menu, click Preferences. Next click Auto Refresh Server Statistics, shown in Figure 7.3. You have the option to change the value for Interval as well. This automatically updates only the server statistics, which are visible when you click a server in the Server List. To show zones created automatically by the DNS Server, select the Show Automatically Created Zones check box—this displays zones in the zone list that were set up automatically by the DNS server.

Working with DNS Zones

The *zone name* is the name of the domain (for example, microsoft.com) that is at the root of the DNS namespace section whose resource records will be managed in the resulting zone file. If you are uncertain about what to enter for the zone name, ask your system administrator.

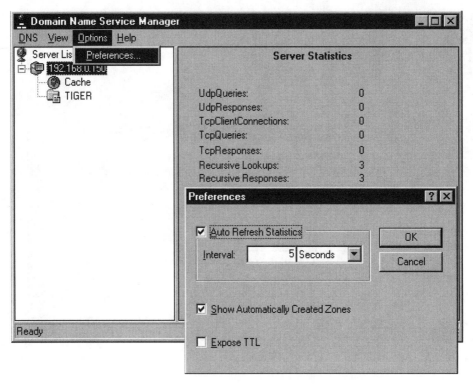

Figure 7.3 Refreshing the DNS server statistics.

To create a primary zone, follow these steps:

1. In the Server List, right-click the server icon for which you are creating a zone or click the DNS menu above.

2. Click New Zone (see Figure 7.4).

3. Click Primary, then click Next.

4. Type the appropriate name in the Zone Name box (see Figure 7.5).

5. Click the Zone File text box. The zone filename will be created automatically. You can accept the default zone filename (for example, tiger.com.dns) or type a different one.

6. Click Next, then Finish to create the new zone.

After completing this procedure, check that the information contained in the automatically created zone resource records is correct. You'll notice the new zone, and accompanying records will be displayed in the left and right panes of the DNS Manager, as shown in Figure 7.6.

It is a good idea to create a secondary zone that is a read-only copy of a primary zone. To create a secondary zone, follow these steps:

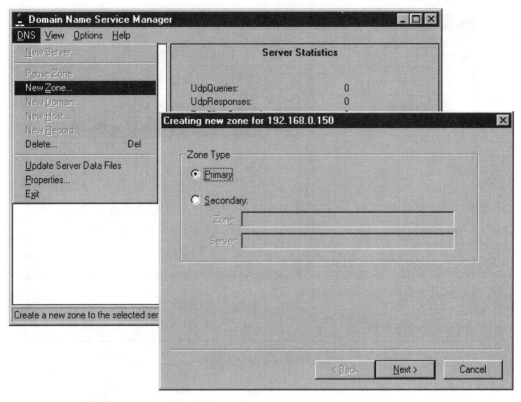

Figure 7.4 Selecting to create a primary zone.

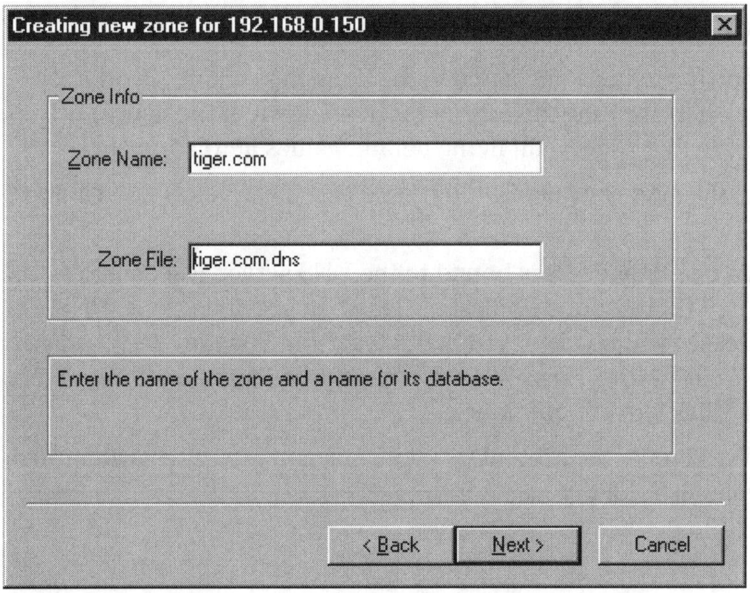

Figure 7.5 Creating the primary zone and filename.

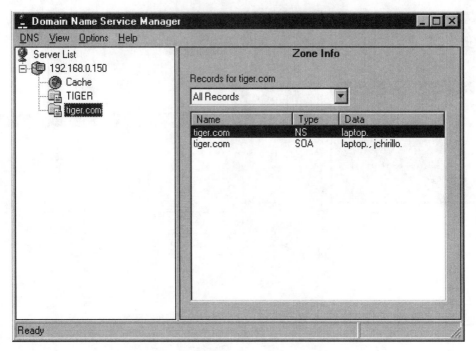

Figure 7.6 Verifying the newly created primary zone.

1. In the Server List, right-click the server icon or click the DNS menu above.

2. Select New Zone, click Secondary, then Next (see Figure 7.7).

3. Enter the newly created zone name in the Zone field and its IP address in the Server field; or drag the hand icon (not shown in the figure) to point to an existing zone to fill in the default values automatically.

4. Click Next and enter the names of the zone and file. Click Next again to continue.

5. If more than one IP address is bound to the DNS server, a secondary zone must have at least one IP Master. Based on previous steps, DNS server addresses will be displayed in the text box. You may select an address and click Move Up or Move Down to reorder the addresses (see Figure 7.8). Click Next to continue.

6. Click Finish to create the secondary zone. A secondary zone is identified by the double file folder icon.

Adding a Host

To add a new host to a primary zone, follow these steps:

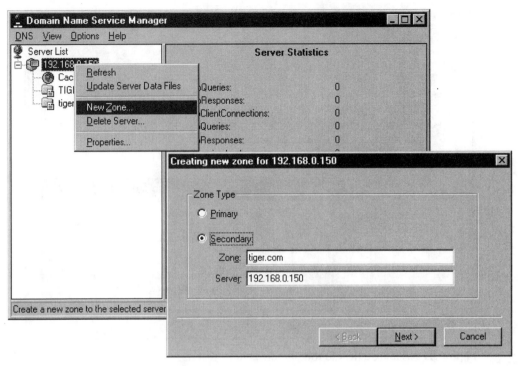

Figure 7.7   Creating a secondary zone.

1. In the Server List, right-click the zone icon or click the DNS menu.
2. Click New Host (see Figure 7.9).

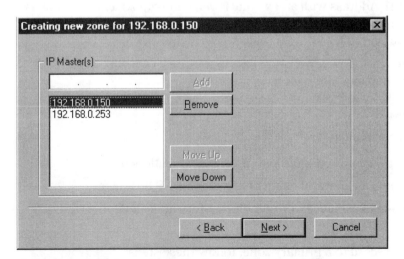

Figure 7.8   Selecting an IP Master for the secondary zone.

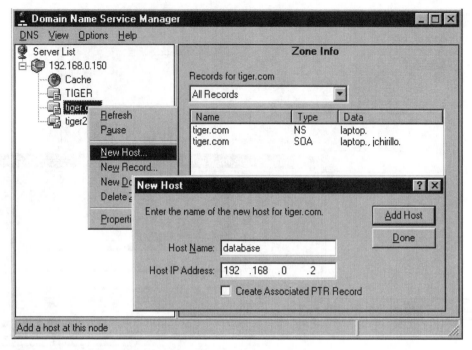

Figure 7.9   Adding a host to the primary zone.

3. In the Host Name box, type the single-part (exclusive of an extension) computer name. In the Host IP Address box, type the corresponding IP address. Optionally, you may select the Create Associated PTR Record check box, after which DNS Manager will attempt to associate the specified Host IP Address with an existing reverse lookup zone. If the zone is found, the DNS Manager will use this information to construct the associated pointer (PTR) record in the reverse lookup zone.

4. Click Add Host. The newly added computer (host) appears as an A record in the Zone Info window.

Adding Records

Typical zone records include:

A. To add an address record or host (previously mentioned).

CNAME. To add a canonical name or alias for a DNS host name.

MX. To add a mail exchanger or pointer that forwards email to a mail server.

To add a new record to a primary zone, follow these steps:

1. In the Server List, right-click the zone icon or click on the DNS menu.

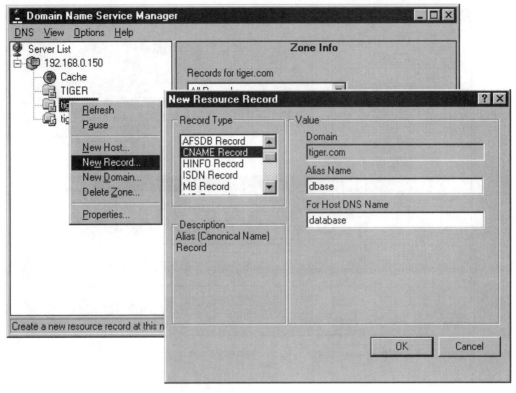

Figure 7.10   Adding a record to the primary zone.

2. Click New Record (see Figure 7.10).

3. In the Record Type list, click a type of resource record to add; fill in the associated information and click OK. The right side of the dialog box changes to show the appropriate fields for the selected record type.

If you wish to correct a mistake or to modify or delete an existing host and/or record, simply right-click it, then click Properties or Delete Record.

Adding Subdomains and Subzones

Adding a domain to a primary zone creates a subdomain within the existing zone. Resource records created in the subdomain will be part of the authoritative data of the existing zone. New records will default to using the time-to-live (TTL) interval specified in the Start of Authority (SOA) record for the zone and will be included in any zone transfers for the zone. The SOA is the most important record of the zone file—the serial number is critical to maintaining secondary servers. If a new zone is desired to enable WINS lookups for hosts in this domain or for some other administrative purpose, create a new zone.

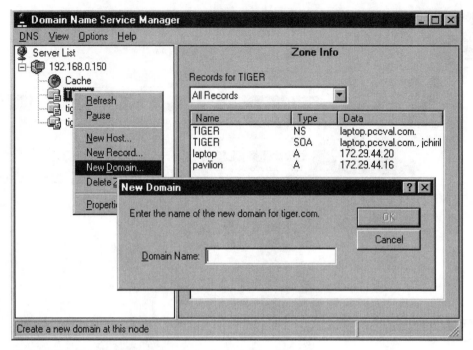

Figure 7.11 Adding a subdomain to the primary zone.

It's important to note that the new subdomain will not work with WINS Lookup. WINS Lookup will only resolve names that are direct descendents of the zone root domain. For example, if you create a domain called subdomain1 within the mycompany.com zone root domain, WINS Lookup will not work for names such as Hostx.subdomain1.mycompany.com because Hostx is not a direct descendent of the zone root domain mycompany.com. In this scenario, you should create and delegate the subdomain. When you do, it becomes its own zone root domain, and WINS Lookup functions properly within it.

To create a domain within a primary zone, follow these steps:

1. In the Server List, right-click the zone icon or click the DNS menu.

2. Click New Domain (see Figure 7.11).

3. In the Domain Name box, type the name for the new domain and click OK.

To create and delegate a new subzone for a new domain, follow these additional steps:

1. In the Server List, add the server that will be authoritative for the new subzone.

2. Click this server and create the subzone as a new primary zone.

3. In the Server List, double-click the primary server.

4. If a domain doesn't exist for the new subzone, right-click the existing zone, click New Domain, and add a new domain for the subzone.

5. Right-click the new domain and click New Record.

6. Under Record Type, click NS Record. For Domain Server DNS Name, type the fully qualified domain name of the DNS server that is authoritative for the new subzone.

7. Under Record Type, create an address (A) record for the server that will manage the zone file (authoritative) for the new subzone by following the respective previously delineated steps and click OK. You only need to create an A record if the authoritative server for the new subzone is within the domain of the authoritative zone on the primary server. For example, if you are *authoritative* for tiger.com and are delegating nt.tiger.com to bob.tiger.com, you need to create an A record. If, on the other hand, you are delegating nt.tiger.com only to bob.tiger.com, there is no need to create the A record.

Additional DNS Administration

For global name resolution queries to take effect, you must add the DNS address with the server Network utility, under Protocols/TCP/IP DNS Properties, in accordance with these network administration procedures from Chapters 3 and 5:

1. Double-click the Network icon from Start/Settings/Control Panel.

2. Click the Protocols tab.

3. In the Network Protocol list, click TCP/IP Protocol, and then click Properties.

4. Click the DNS tab.

5. Optionally, type a hostname in the Host Name box and a domain name in the Domain Name box.

6. Under DNS Server Search Order, click Add and type the IP address of a DNS server that will provide name resolution.

7. Click Add on the TCP/IP DNS Server window to accept the new entry.
   If you are using DHCP, it may already be set up to automatically configure the DNS Server Search Order. Contact your network administrator to find out if this is the case. If you are not using DHCP, or DHCP is not set up to provide this information, type the IP address of the DNS

server that will provide name resolution, and then click Add to move the address to the DNS Server Search Order box.

8. Under Domain Suffix Search Order, click Add, type the DNS domain suffix to append to host names during name resolution, and then click Add to move the suffix to the Domain Suffix Search Order box.

9. Click OK.

The settings take effect after you restart the computer. You can add up to three IP addresses for DNS servers. The servers running DNS will be queried in the order listed. To change the order in which they appear, click an address to move, and then click Up or Down. To remove an IP address, click it, and then click Remove. You can also add up to six DNS domain suffixes. The suffixes will be appended in the order listed. To change the order in which they appear, select a suffix to move, and then click Up or Down. To remove a domain suffix, click it, and then click Remove.

Next, from the DNS Manager's DNS menu option, click Update Server Data Files. This causes DNS to immediately write all changes to the zone data files. Normally these changes are written at predefined intervals and whenever DNS Server or DNS Manager is shut down.

Optionally, you can test the changes. Let's say you want to test a newly created host. You can do this by pinging the host from the command prompt, as shown in Figure 7.12.

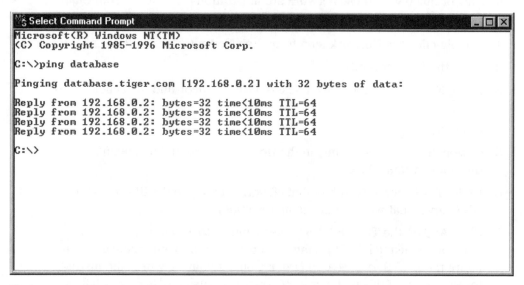

Figure 7.12   Testing new host configuration.

Novell NetWare Integration Step by Step

Novell, Inc., is a leading provider of system operation software for all types of corporate and private networks, including intranets, extranets, and the Internet. Since 1983, Novell NetWare has come into widespread corporate use; currently it is popular with many U.S. Fortune 500 companies. As you already know from previous chapters, both Windows NT and NetWare support include TCP/IP; more importantly, they support the protocols known as the Internetwork Packet Exchange and Sequenced Packet Exchange (IPX/SPX). IPX/SPX have been the primary communication protocols used for internetwork collaboration between the two operating systems.

Internetwork Packet Exchange and Sequenced Packet Exchange

NetWare provides a variety of server daemon services and support, based on the *client/server* architecture. A client is a station that requests services, such as file access, from a server. IPX was the original NetWare protocol used to route packets through an internetwork. It is a connectionless datagram protocol; as such, it is similar to unreliable datagram delivery offered by the IP. And like IP address schemes, Novell IPX network addresses must be unique; they are represented in hexadecimal format and consist of two parts, a network number and a node number. The IPX network number is an assigned 32-bit long number; the node number is a 48-bit long hardware or Media Access Control (MAC) address for one of the system's network interface cards (NICs). As defined earlier, the NIC manufacturer assigns the 48-bit long hardware or MAC address. Because the host portion of an IP network address has no equivalent to a MAC address, IP nodes must use the Address Resolution Protocol (ARP) to determine the destination MAC address—the second part of an IPX network address.

ARP uses a packet that is broadcasted to all hosts attached to a physical network. This packet contains the IP address of the node or station with which the sender wants to communicate. Other hosts on the network ignore this packet after storing a copy of the sender's IP/hardware address mapping. The target host replies with its hardware address, which will be returned to the sender, to be stored in its ARP *response cache*. In this way, communication between these two nodes can ensue.

IPX network numbers play a primary role in the foundation for IPX internetwork packet exchange between network segments. Every segment is assigned a unique network address to which packets are routed for node destinations. For a protocol to identify itself with IPX and communicate with the network, it must request a *socket number*. Socket numbers ascertain the identity of processes within a station or node.

The most common NetWare transport protocol is the Sequenced Packet Exchange (SPX). It transmits on top of IPX. SPX provides reliable delivery service, which supplements the datagram service in IPX. For Internet access, Novell utilizes IPX datagrams encapsulated in the User Datagram Protocol (UDP)—covered in Chapter 10—(which is encapsulated in IP) for transmission. SPX is a packet-oriented protocol that uses a transmission window size of one packet. Applications that generally use SPX include R-Console and P-Console.

Service Advertisement Protocol

The Service Advertisement Protocol (SAP) is a method by which Novell network resources, such as file servers, advertise their addresses and the services they provide. By default, these advertisements are sent every 60 seconds. A SAP identifier (a hexadecimal number) indicates the provided services; for example, Type 0x0007 specifies a print server. SAP packets can contain service messages for up to seven servers. Should there be more than seven, multiple packets will be sent. SAP messages may include the following identifiers:

Type 0x0004: File Server

Type 0x0005: Job Server

Type 0x0007: Print Server

Type 0x0009: Archive Server

Type 0x000A: Job Queue

Type 0x0021: SNA Gateway

Type 0x002D: Time Sync

Type 0x002E: Dynamic SAP

Type 0x0047: Advertising Print Server

Type 0x004B: Btrieve VAP

Type 0X004C: SQL VAP

Type 0x0077: Unknown

Type 0x007A: NetWare VMS

Type 0x0098: NetWare Access Server

Type 0x009A: Named Pipes Server

Type 0x009E: NetWare-UNIX

Type 0x0107: NetWare 386

Type 0x0111: Test Server

Type 0x0166: NetWare Management

Type 0x026A: NetWare Management

Gateway Service for NetWare

According to Microsoft, Gateway Service for NetWare (Gateway Service) lets you access file and print resources on NetWare servers from your computer. You can access resources on NetWare servers that use NetWare Directory Service (NDS) and bindery-style security—the database that resides on a NetWare server that contains profiles of network users to define each user's name, password, and permission(s). NDS is a distributed database that maintains information about every resource on the network and access to such. From Windows NT, you can create a gateway so that you can share NetWare resources (e.g., file and print services) with Microsoft networking clients that do not have NetWare client software. You can create gateways to both NDS and bindery resources.

Installing and Configuring the Gateway Service

Assuming your NetWare administrator prepared a NetWare server for communication with an NT gateway (i.e., adding accounts that enable the gateway users to "talk" to the NetWare LAN), we're now ready to install the gateway service. First, we'll install the IPX/SPX communication protocol with the following steps:

1. From Start/Settings/Control Panel, double-click the Network icon.
2. In the Protocols tab, click Add.
3. Select NWLink IPX/SPX Compatible Transport from the Network Service list and click OK to continue.
4. When prompted, insert the Microsoft Windows NT Server disc and click Continue. The driver files are located on the Windows NT CD-ROM, so be sure to have the compact disc handy. If you want Setup to look in a different place, type in the location. After Setup copies the appropriate files, proceed to configure the new protocol.
5. To configure NWLink, select the new NWLink IPX/SPX Compatible Transport, then click Properties (see Figure 7.13).

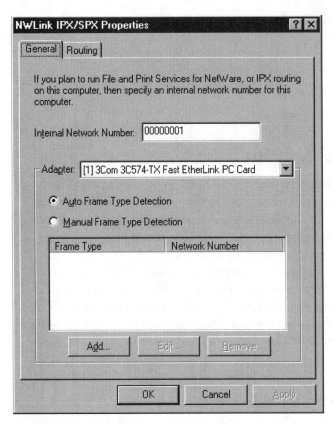

Figure 7.13 Installing the Gateway (and Client) Service for NetWare.

6. Select either Auto Frame Type Detection or Manual Frame Type Detection. If you select Manual, click Add, and enter a Frame Type and Network Number for each type you want to add; then click Add. When you're finished, click OK.

 Additional tunable parameters for NWLink are stored in the Registry. In most situations, you should not have to modify the defaults. Use this procedure only if you want to bind NWLink to a different network adapter card or to manually change the frame type. Also, by default, NWLink automatically detects the frame type used by the network adapter card to which it is bound. If NWLink detects no network traffic or any frames of type 802.2, it sets the frame type to 802.2. Otherwise, it sets the frame type to match the frames it detects.

7. Click Close to continue.

8. Click Yes to complete the installation and restart the system.

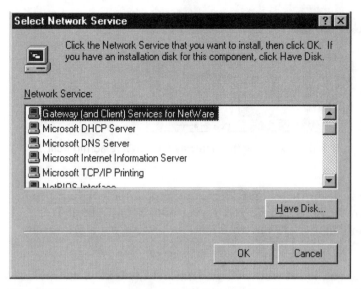

Figure 7.14   Selecting to install the Gateway (and Client) Service for NetWare.

After the system restarts, we're ready to install the Gateway Service for Net-Ware. As with several of the other services we've explored, Windows NT includes but does not by default install this service. The easiest method of adding the service is carried out from the Network utility by following these steps:

1. From Start/Settings/Control Panel, double-click the Network icon.

2. From within the Services tab, click Add.

3. Select Gateway (and Client) Service for NetWare from the Network Service list and click OK to continue (see Figure 7.14).

4. When prompted, insert the Microsoft Windows NT Server disc and click Continue—the driver files are located on the Windows NT CD-ROM, so be sure to have the compact disc handy. If you want setup to look in a different place, type in the location.

5. After setup copies the appropriate files, click Close to continue.

6. Click Yes to complete the installation and restart the system.

If you do not want to set a preferred server, you'll be logged onto the nearest available NetWare server, and your interaction with the NetWare network will be through that server. To set your Default Tree and Context or preferred server, using the gateway for NetWare admin utility, follow these steps:

1. From Start/Settings/Control Panel, double-click the GSNW icon.

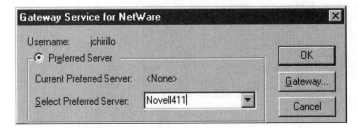

Figure 7.15   Setting a preferred server using the Gateway for NetWare admin utility.

2. Click Preferred Server (see Figure 7.15) and type or select your preferred server in the Select Preferred Server box. Set a Default Tree and Context only in an NDS environment; otherwise, set a preferred server.

In an NDS environment, to set your Default Tree and Context using the Gateway for NetWare admin utility, click Default Tree and Context, and type your tree and context in Tree and Context as shown in Figure 7.16.

To set the printing options shown in Figure 7.17, click to select or clear the following settings, then click OK:

- To eject a page at the end of each print job, select the Add Form Feed check box.
- To receive notification when your document has been printed, select the Notify When Printed check box.
- To print a banner page before each print job, select the Print Banner check box.

To enable gateways on the server to share NetWare file and printing resources over the Microsoft network, follow these steps from the Gateway for NetWare admin utility:

1. Click Gateway.
2. Select the Enable Gateway check box, as shown in Figure 7.18.

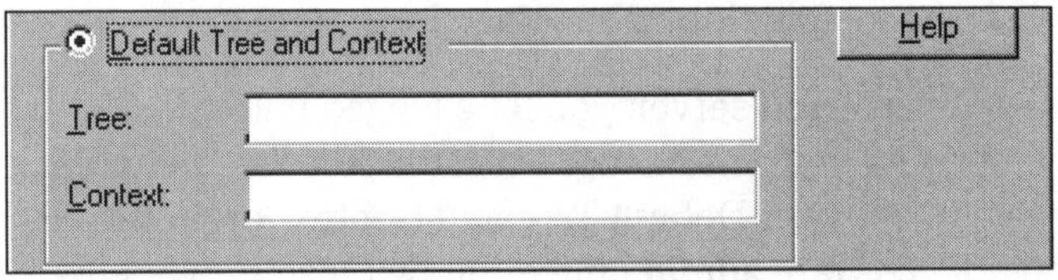

Figure 7.16   Setting a Default Tree and Context using the Gateway for NetWare admin utility.

Figure 7.17 Setting printing options using the Gateway for NetWare admin utility.

3. In Gateway Account, type the name of your gateway account (previously configured by your NetWare administrator).

4. In Password and Confirm Password, type the password for the gateway account.

All access to NetWare resources is in the context of the gateway account. The gateway account must be a member of the NetWare NTGATEWAY group on all NetWare servers for which this server will act as a gateway. Access to

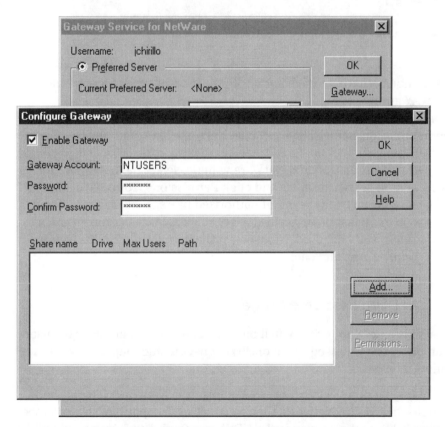

Figure 7.18 Enabling gateways on the server using the Gateway for NetWare admin utility.

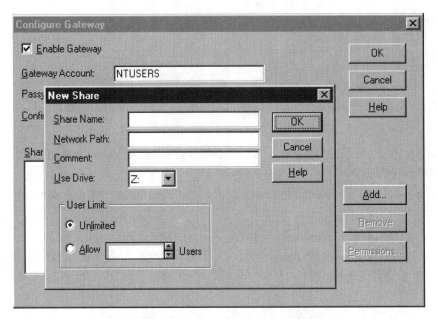

Figure 7.19   Creating a share for a specified NetWare volume.

NetWare is subject to trustee rights for both the gateway user account and the NTGATEWAY group.

To create a share for a specified NetWare volume, click Add and fill in the required information, namely, Share Name, Network Path, and Use Drive (see Figure 7.19).

To set permissions on a shared NetWare volume, select the new share for which you want to set permissions and click Permissions. To remove a selected user or group from the list of authorized users, click Remove. To add a user or group to the list of authorized users, click Add, select the group or user from Names, and click Add. Next, select the permission for this user or group in Type of Access and click OK.

General NetWare Resource Usage

When you map a network drive, you'll be connected by default under the user-name and password you used to log on. To connect to and map a NetWare volume, follow these steps:

1. From the Windows NT Explorer, or in this case Network Neighborhood, double-click Entire Network, then NetWare or Compatible Network (see Figure 7.20). In the next window, NDS trees (with a tree icon) and individual NetWare computers (with a computer icon) will be shown.

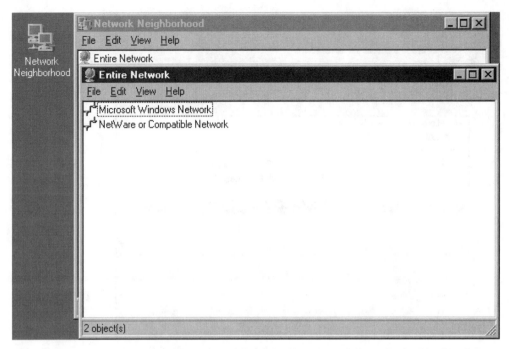

Figure 7.20   Connecting to and mapping a NetWare volume in Network Neighborhood.

2. Double-click a tree or volume to see the contents; subsequently, you can double-click those contents to see other computers or volumes.

3. When you find the volume or folder you want to access, double-click it to expand it. Or, to map a local drive to it, select the volume or folder, then click Map Network Drive on the File menu.

When you map a network drive, you are connected by default under the username and password you used to log on. To connect under a different username, type it in Connect As.

Connecting to a NetWare Print Queue

To connect to a NetWare print queue, from Start/Settings, click Printers.

1. Double-click Add Printer.

2. Click Network Printer Server, then click Next.

3. If only Microsoft network printers and computers are shown, double-click Entire Network and double-click NetWare or Compatible network (see Figure 7.21).

4. To see the contents of an NDS tree or NetWare server, double-click it, then double-click other computers displayed, as necessary.

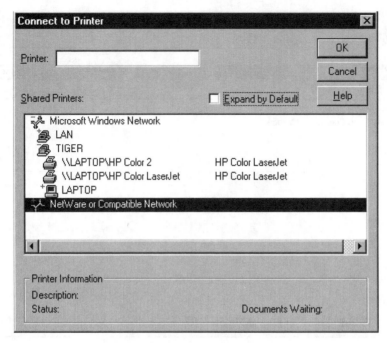

Figure 7.21 Searching for a NetWare print queue.

5. When you find the printer you want to access, select it and click OK. If a printer driver is not available locally for a NetWare print queue, you'll be prompted to install a printer driver.

Connecting to NetWare Resources Using the Command Prompt

The *net use* command is equivalent to using the NetWare map command on MS-DOS–based NetWare workstations. You can connect to individual NetWare volumes that use bindery-style security and to NDS trees. NetWare server volumes, directories, and print queues are represented by Universal Naming Convention (UNC) names and use the same command syntax as networks based on Microsoft Windows. To connect to an individual NetWare volume from the command prompt, use the following syntax:

```
net use <drive>: <UNCname or NetWarename>
```

For example, to redirect the H drive to the directory \data\mydata of the SERVER volume on a server called NetWare411 using the UNC naming syntax, type:

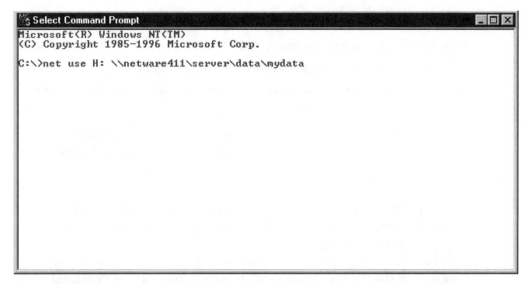

Figure 7.22 Connecting to an individual NetWare volume from the command prompt.

```
net use H: \\netware411\SERVER\data\mydata
```

as shown in Figure 7.22.

If the following error message appears:

```
The password is invalid for \\<server name>\<volume name>[\<directory
    name>...]
```

It indicates that your username and password are not authenticated. To connect under a valid username and password, add your username and password to the command line, using the following syntax:

```
/user: <username> <password>
```

For example, to connect as *jchirillo* with the password *tigertools* to the directory \data\mydata within the SERVER volume on a server called Net-Ware411 using the H drive, you would type:

```
net use H: \\netware411\server\data\mydata /user:jchirillo tigertools
```

To connect to an NDS tree from the command prompt, you would type the following syntax:

```
net use <drive>: \\treename\VolumeName.OrgName.OrgName
    [/u:UserName.OrgName.OrgName [password]]
```

where:

> *treename* is the name of the tree VolumeName.
>
> *OrgName* is the tree location to which you want to connect.
>
> *UserName.OrgName.OrgName* is the username and context for this tree (unless it is your default tree).

To use the next available drive letter when connecting at the command prompt, replace the drive letter with an asterisk (*) in the syntax. For example:

```
net use *: <UNCname or NetWarename>
```

If you prefer to be prompted for a password, replace the password in the command line with an asterisk (*). When you type your password at the prompt, it will not appear on screen.

When you run any application that writes directly to a predefined port, *net use* works like the NetWare capture utility, associating the NetWare print queue with the port. To redirect output from a port to a print queue, invoke net use followed by the server and print queue. For example:

```
net use lpt1 \\netware411\files
```

redirects output from LPT1 to the NetWare print queue called FILES on the server NetWare411. This is equivalent to the NetWare capture q=files s=netware411 l=1 command line.

To send files that do not require formatting to LPT1, after you redirect output with *net use*, use the *copy* command. For example:

```
copy myfile.txt lpt1
```

To copy a file directly to a print queue, after you redirect output with *net use*, use *copy*. For example:

```
copy myfile.txt \\netware411\files
```

To connect to a printer in an NDS tree, use the following syntax:

```
net use <drive>: \\treename\PrintName.OrgName.OrgName
  [/u:UserName.OrgName.OrgName [password]]
```

Additionally, you can use the following commands for gathering information:

> *net view /network:nw*, to display a list of NetWare file servers
>
> *net view \\<nwservername> /network:nw*, to display volumes on a specific NetWare file server)

Managing Passwords from the Command Prompt

To change your password on more than one server, connect to all the servers before executing the next procedure. Whenever you press Ctrl-Alt-Del to change your password on the Windows NT Server domain, and your network runs Directory Service Manager for NetWare, your password on NetWare servers that participate in the domain is automatically changed. To change your password on a NetWare bindery server from the Command Prompt, follow these steps:

1. At the command prompt, change to the drive for the NetWare server and type cd\public.

2. Type setpass, followed by the name of the NetWare server on which you want to change your password.

3. When you are prompted, enter your old password.

4. When you are prompted, enter a new password.

5. When you are prompted, type your new password again. The server confirms that you have successfully changed your password.

6. If prompted, type Y and press Enter to change your password on other NetWare servers that also use your old password, or type N and press Enter to leave your old password unchanged on the other NetWare servers.

If you change your password on a NetWare NDS tree, your password will be changed on all NDS trees to which you are currently connected. If the old password you specify does not match your current password on any of those trees, you are prompted to supply the old password for those trees. To change your password on a NetWare NDS tree, follow these steps:

1. Press Ctrl-Alt-Del.

2. Click Change Password.

3. In Domain, click NetWare or Compatible Network (see Figure 7.23).

4. Type your current password in Old Password.

5. Type your new password in New Password and again in Confirm New Password.

Internet Information Server Step by Step

The Internet Information Server (IIS) is Microsoft's Web server that runs on the Windows NT operating system. According to Microsoft, with Microsoft IIS,

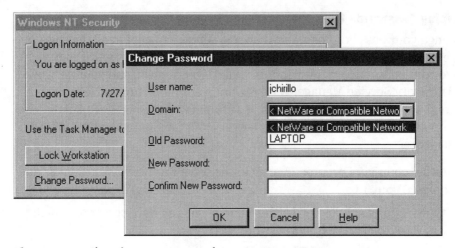

Figure 7.23   Changing your password on a NetWare NDS tree.

a computer running Windows NT Server becomes a high-volume, robust Web server that can publish information to users down the hall or around the world. IIS is ideal for corporate networks on Windows NT-based computers because it enables you to set up powerful Web servers on your existing hardware. IIS is integrated to the Windows NT Server operating system and takes advantage of its security features and performance capabilities.

IIS includes the following components:

- Internet services: WWW, FTP, and Gopher
- Internet Service Manager, the tool for administering the Internet services
- Internet Database Connector, the component for sending queries to databases
- Key Manager, the tool for installing Secure Sockets Layer (SSL) keys

IIS Installation and Configuration

Depending on the initial NT setup, this service may or may not have been installed by default on your computer. If it has not been, the easiest method of adding the service is via the Network utility. Follow these steps:

1. From Start/Settings/Control Panel, double-click the Network icon.
2. From within the Services tab, click Add.

3. Select Microsoft Internet Information Server from the Network Service list and click OK to continue.

4. When prompted, insert the Microsoft Windows NT Server disc and click Continue. The driver files are located on the Windows NT CD-ROM, so be sure to have the compact disc handy. If you want Setup to look in a different place, type in the location. After Setup locates the files, you'll be prompted by the Internet information Server Setup program. Click OK to continue.

5. From the next screen you can select Internet Information Server Components to install or remove (see Figure 7.24). The following components are selected for installation by default. If you do not want to install a particular item, click the box next to it to clear it.

   • Internet Service Manager installs the administration program for managing the services.

   • World Wide Web creates a WWW publishing server.

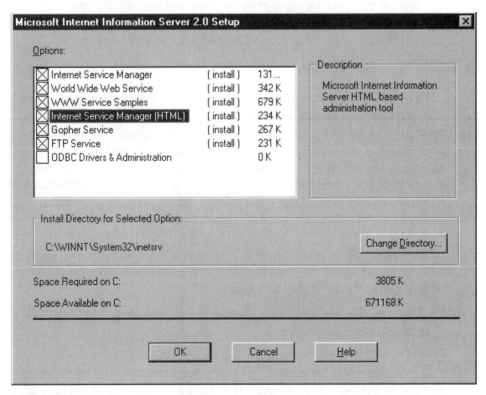

Figure 7.24   Selecting IIS components to install.

- WWW Service Samples installs sample Hypertext Markup Language (HTML) files.

- Internet Service Manager (HTML) installs the HTML version of Internet Service Manager to administer the services through a browser.

- Gopher Service creates a Gopher publishing server.

- FTP Service creates a File Transfer Protocol (FTP) publishing server.

- ODBC Drivers and Administration installs Open Database Connectivity (ODBC) drivers. These are required for logging to ODBC files and for enabling ODBC access from the WWW service.

 If you want to provide access to databases through the Microsoft Internet Information Server, you will need to set up the ODBC drivers and data sources using the ODBC applet in the Windows NT Control Panel. If you have an application running that uses ODBC, you may see an error message telling you that one or more components are in use. Before continuing, close all applications and services that use ODBC.

To install a Microsoft Internet Information Server component, make sure the box next to the component option you want to install is selected. The word *install* will appear in parentheses next to the component name. If *install* does not appear, it means the component is already installed on the computer; you can remove it by clearing the box next to the component option by clicking on it. The word *remove* will then appear next to the component name. Likewise, if *remove* does not appear, it indicates that component is not installed on the computer.

To change the directory in which to install Microsoft Internet Information Server, click the Change Directory button and type the complete directory path in the dialog box.

6. Click OK to continue and select the directories for the World Wide Web, FTP, and Gopher directories.

7. Click OK. After Setup copies the appropriate files and detects that your Guest account is enabled on the system, for security purposes it will ask to disable the account. Click Yes to disable the Guest account, then OK.

8. Click Close to complete the installation.

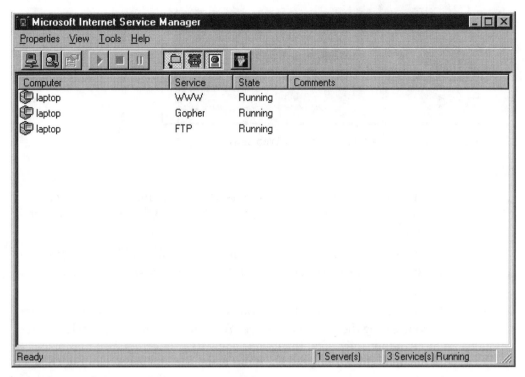

Figure 7.25   IIS admin utility for Internet services.

IIS Administration Utility

As with most of the services we've already investigated, IIS has its own unique management utility. Named Microsoft Internet Service Manager, the IIS admin program can be accessed from Start/Programs/Microsoft Internet Server (Common)/Internet Service Manager (see Figure 7.25).

IIS offers scores of configuration possibilities to provide intranet, Internet, and extranet services. So extensive are these possibilities that entire books have been written about the Internet Information Server. But for our purposes here, we'll cover only the technical specifics of common configuration and administration methods using the Microsoft Internet Service Manager.

We'll begin by taking a look at the 10 toolbar icons shown in Figure 7.26 to learn their functions. Starting from the left:

Figure 7.26   IIS admin utility toolbar icons.

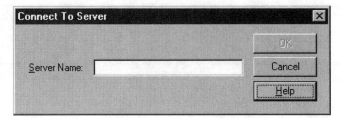

Figure 7.27   Connecting to a specific Web server.

- Shown in Figure 7.27, the first icon is used to connect to one specific Web server. Simply type in the name of the remote IIS server you wish to administer.

- Shown in Figure 7.28 the second icon is used to find all Web servers on the network. This is useful for central management when multiple IIS servers reside on a network.

- Shown in Figure 7.29, the third icon is used to display property windows for configuring the selected service. You must first select a service in the main window, then click the icon to view its properties. You may also double-click the service or select the service in the main window, then click the Properties menu Service Properties option. In the figure, we're looking at the FTP service configuration options.

- The fourth, fifth, and sixth icons are used, respectively, to start, stop, or pause a selected service. In Figure 7.30, we've selected the fifth icon to stop the FTP service.

- The seventh, eighth, and ninth icons are used to select the services you want to display—FTP, Gopher, and WWW Servers services, respectively. By clicking the icon to toggle on/off, the selected services will appear/disappear in the Internet Service Manager main window.

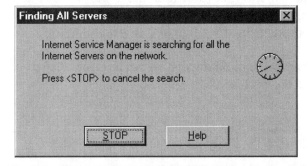

Figure 7.28   Finding all Web servers.

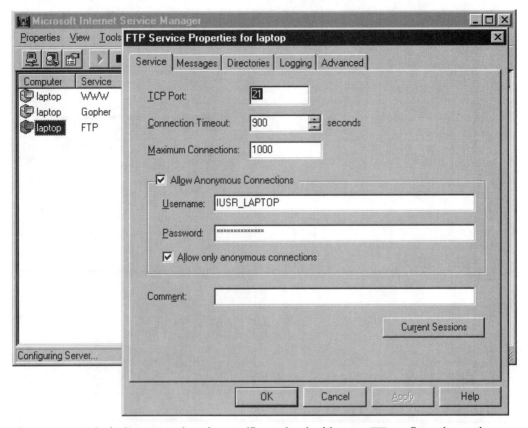

Figure 7.29   Displaying properties of a specific service, in this case, FTP configuration options.

- Shown in Figure 7.31, the tenth icon is used to start Key Manager to create a Secure Sockets Layer (SSL) key. We'll discuss how to use Key Manager to secure data transmissions with SSL later in this chapter.

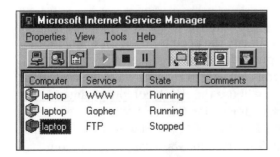

Figure 7.30   Starting, stopping, or pausing a specific service.

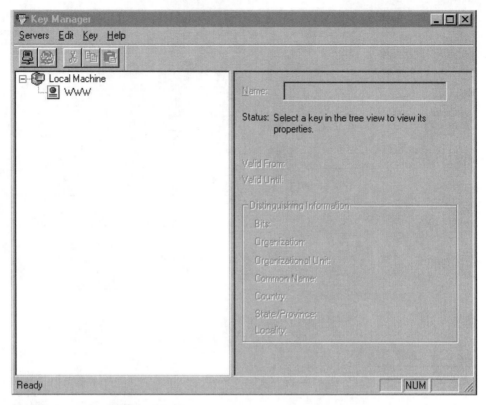

Figure 7.31 Starting Key Manager.

Configuring the WWW Service

To configure the WWW service, you must first select the service in the main window, then click the third menu icon to view its properties. Alternatively, you may double-click the service or select the service in the main window, and then click the Properties menu Service Properties option. We'll advance through the WWW Service property tabs—Service, Directories, Logging, and Advanced—in sequence.

Service. You use the Service Properties window, shown in Figure 7.32, to control who can use your server and to specify the account used for anonymous client requests to log on to the computer. Most Internet sites allow anonymous logons. If you allow anonymous logons, all user permissions for the user, such as permission to access information, will use the IUSR_computername account. When you installed Internet Information Server, Setup created the account IUSR_computername in the Windows NT User Manager for Domains and in the Internet Service Manager. This account was assigned a random password. The password for this account must be the same in both Internet

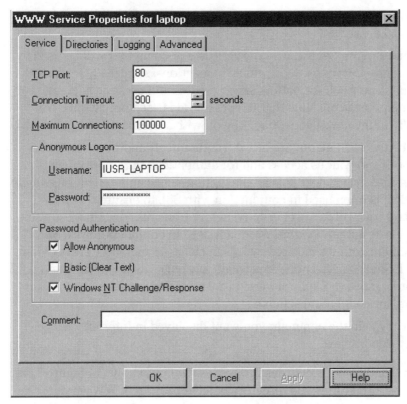

Figure 7.32 WWW service configuration properties: Service window.

Service Manager and the Windows NT User Manager for Domains. If you change the password, you must change it in both places and make sure it matches. *Note*: This account *must* have a password; you cannot assign a blank password. The IUSR_computername is granted *Log on locally* user rights by default. This right is necessary as long as you want to grant anonymous logon access to your site. If you want to use your current security system to control information access, change the anonymous logon account from IUSR_computername to an existing account on your network.

Use the other elements in the Service window as follows:

TCP Port. Identify the port on which the WWW service is running. The default is port 80. You can change the port to any unique TCP port number. For a new port number to take effect, you must restart your computer.

Connection Timeout. Set the length of time before the server disconnects an inactive user. This value ensures that all connections are closed if the HTTP protocol fails to close a connection.

Maximum Connections. Set the maximum number of simultaneous connections to the server.

Anonymous Logon. Set the Windows NT user account that will be used to assign permissions of all anonymous connections. As already explained, by default, Internet Information Server creates and uses the account IUSR_computername. Note that the password is used only within Windows NT; anonymous users do not log on with a username and password.

Password Authentication. Specify the authentication process to use to define both anonymous access and for authenticating remote client requests. You must select at least one option. Basic authentication, which is encoded, is often used in conjunction with SSL to ensure that usernames and passwords are encrypted before transmission. Most browsers support Basic authentication. When not used in conjunction with SSL, Basic authentication sends passwords in clear (unencrypted) text. Windows NT Challenge/Response automatically encrypts usernames and passwords. Internet Explorer version 2.0 and later versions support this password authentication scheme.

Comment. Type in the comment you want displayed in Internet Service Manager Report view.

Directories. The WWW Directories properties window, shown in Figure 7.33, is where you set directories and directory behavior for the WWW service, as follows:

Directory listing box. List the directories used by the WWW service.

- *Directory.* Lists the path of directories used by the WWW service.
- *Alias.* The path used for virtual directories.
- *Address.* Lists the IP address for the virtual server using that directory.
- *Error.* Indicates system errors, such as difficulty reading a directory.

Add, Remove, and Edit Properties buttons. To set up a directory, press the Add button (see Figure 7.34); or select a directory in the Directories listing box and press the Edit button. Use the Remove button to delete directories you no longer want.

Press the Add button in the Directory Properties window to set up new directories:

- *Directory.* Type the path to the directory to use for the WWW service.
- *Browse button.* Use to select the directory to use for the WWW service.
- *Home Directory.* Specify the root directory for the WWW service. Internet Information Server provides a default home directory,

Figure 7.33   WWW service configuration properties: Directories window

\wwwroot, for the WWW service. The files that you place in the WWW home directory and its subdirectories are available to remote browsers. You can change the location of the default home directory.

- *Virtual Directory.* Specify a subdirectory for the WWW service. Enter the directory name or "alias" that service users will use to gain access. You can add other directories outside the home directory that are accessed by browsers as subdirectories of the home directory. That is, you can publish from other directories and have those directories accessible from within the home directory. Such directories are called *virtual directories.* The administrator can specify the physical location of the virtual directory and the virtual name (alias), which is the directory name used by remote browsers.

    Virtual directories will not appear in WWW directory listings; you must create explicit links in HTML files in order for users to access virtual directories. Users can also type in the URL if they know the alias for the virtual directory.

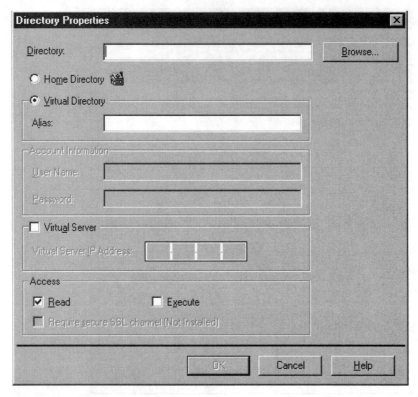

Figure 7.34   Setting up a directory in the WWW service configuration properties: Directories/Add window.

The published directories can be located on local or network drives. If the virtual directory is a network drive, provide the username and password with access to that network drive. Virtual directories on network drives must be on computers in the same Windows NT domain as the Internet Information Server.

- *Account Information.* This box is active only if the directory specified in the first line of this dialog box is a UNC server and sharename, for example, \\webserver\htmlfiles. Enter the username and password that has permission to use the network directory. Virtual directories on network drives must be on computers in the same Windows NT domain as the Internet Information Server.

If you specify a username and password to connect to a network drive, all Internet Information Server access to that directory will use that username and password. Therefore, you should be careful when using UNC connections to network drives, to prevent possible security breaches.

- *Virtual Server (World Wide Web only)*. Select the Virtual Server check box and enter an IP address to create a directory for the virtual server. The IP address must be bound to the network card providing the service. Use the Network applet in Control Panel to bind additional IP addresses to your network card.

  You can have multiple domain names on a single Internet Information Server-based computer so that it will appear that there are additional servers—that is, virtual servers. This feature makes it possible to service WWW requests for two domain names (such as http://www.tiger1.com/ and http://www.tiger2.com/) from the same computer. Enter the IP address for the home directory, and virtual directories for each virtual server that you create.

  If the path for a virtual directory is a network drive, provide a username and password with access to that network drive. Virtual directories on network drives must be on computers in the same Windows NT domain as the Internet Information Server-based computer.

  If you have assigned more than one IP address to your server, when you create a directory, you must specify which IP address has access to that directory. If no IP address is specified, that directory will be visible to all virtual servers. The default directories created during Setup do not specify an IP address. You may need to specify IP addresses for the default directories when you add virtual servers.

- *Access*. The Access check boxes control the attributes of the directory. If the files are on an NT File System (NTFS) drive, NTFS settings for the directory must match these settings:

  Read must be selected for information directories. Do not select this box for directories containing programs.

  Execute allows clients to run any programs in this directory. This box is selected by default for the directory created for programs. Put all your scripts and executable files into this directory. Do not select this box for directories containing static content.

  Require secure SSL channel must be selected if you are using SSL security to encrypt data transmissions.

Enable Default Document and Directory Browsing Allowed. The Default Document and Directory Browsing settings in the Directories property window of the WWW service are used to set up default displays that will appear if a remote user does not specify a particular file. Allowing directory browsing means that the user is presented with a hypertext listing of the directories and files so that he or she can navigate through your directory structure.

You can place a default document in each directory so that when a remote user does not specify a particular file, the default document in that directory is displayed. A hypertext directory listing is sent to the user if directory browsing is enabled and no default document is in the specified directory.

Note that virtual directories will not appear in directory listings; users must know a virtual directory's alias and type in its Uniform Resource Locator (URL) address or click a link in an HTML page to access virtual directories.

Logging. The Logging properties window, shown in Figure 7.35, is where you set valuable logging information for the selected service regarding how a server is used. You can send log data to files or to an ODBC-supported database. If you have multiple servers or services on a network, you can log all their activity to a single file or database on any network computer.

If you want to log to a file, you can specify how often to create new logs and in which directory to put the log files. Additionally, by running the

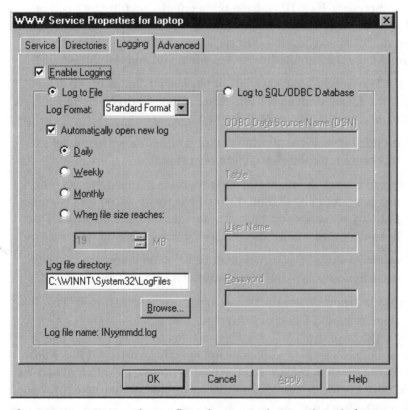

Figure 7.35   WWW service configuration properties: Logging window.

Convlog.exe command from a command prompt, you'll be able to convert log files to either European Microsoft Windows NT Academic Centre (EMWAC) or the common log file format. If you log to an ODBC data source, you must specify the ODBC DSN, table, and valid username and password to the database.

Use the options in the Logging window as described here:

Enable Logging. Select this box to start or stop logging for the selected information service.

Log to File. Choose this option to log to a text file for the selected information service.

Log Format. Click the down arrow and choose either Standard format or National Center for Supercomputing Applications (NCSA) format.

Automatically open new log. Select this box to generate new logs at the specified interval. If you do not select this option, the same log file will grow indefinitely.

Log file directory. Give the path to the directory containing all log files. To change directories, click Browse and select a different directory.

Log filename. The default name of the log file automatically set by Windows NT. Lowercase letters yy will be replaced with the year, mm with the month, and dd with the day.

Log to SQL/ODBC Database. Choose to log to any ODBC data source. Set the data source name and table name (not the filename of the table) and specify a username and password that is valid for the computer on which the database resides. You must also use the ODBC applet in Control Panel to create a system data source.

Advanced. The Advanced properties window, shown in Figure 7.36, is used to enable access by a specific IP address. This lets you block individuals or groups from gaining access to your server. You can also set the maximum network bandwidth for outbound traffic, to control the maximum amount of traffic on your server.

You can control access to each Internet service by specifying the IP address of the computers to be granted or denied access. If you choose to grant access to all users by default, you can specify the computers to be denied access. For example, let's say you have a form on your WWW server and a particular user on the Internet is entering multiple forms with fictitious information; you can prevent the computer at that IP address from connecting to your site. Conversely, if you choose to deny access to all users by default, you can then allow specific computers to have access.

The Advanced options are:

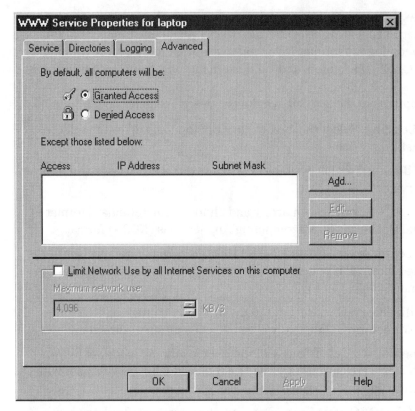

Figure 7.36 WWW service configuration properties: Advanced window.

Granted Access. Choose this option and press the Add button to list computers that will be denied access.

Denied Access. Choose this option and press the Add button to list computers that will be granted access.

Add. To add computers to which you want to deny access, select the Granted Access button and click Add. Conversely, to add computers to which you want to grant access, select the Denied Access button and click Add (see Figure 7.37).

- Choose Single Computer and provide the IP address to exclude a single computer.
- Choose Group of Computers and provide an IP address and subnet mask to exclude a group of computers.
- Press the button next to the IP address to use a DNS name instead of an IP address. Your server must have a DNS server address specified in its TCP/IP settings. You are specifying, by IP address or domain name,

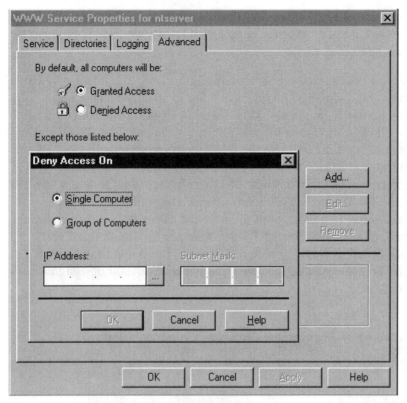

Figure 7.37   WWW service configuration properties: Advanced window/Add option.

which computer or group of computers will be granted or denied access. If you choose, by default, to grant access to all users, you will specify the computers to be denied access. If you choose, by default, to deny access to all users, you will then specify the specific computers to be allowed access. *Note*: Before using this option, you should fully understand TCP/IP networking, IP addressing, and the use of subnet masks.

Limit Network Use by all Internet Services on this computer. You can control your Internet services by limiting the network bandwidth allowed for all of the Internet services on the server. Set the maximum kilobytes of outbound traffic permitted on this computer.

Configuring the FTP Service

To configure the FTP service, you must first select the service in the main window and then click the third menu icon to view its properties. Or you may double-click the service or select the service in the main window, then click the Properties menu Service Properties option. There you'll find the following tabs: Service, Messages, Directories, Logging, and Advanced. We'll explore the offerings on each tab in sequence.

Service. Click on the Service tab, shown in Figure 7.38, to control who can use your server and to specify the account used for anonymous client requests to log on to the computer. Most Internet sites allow anonymous logons. If you allow anonymous logons, all user permissions, such as permission to access information, will use the IUSR_computername account. When you installed Internet Information Server, Setup created the account IUSR_computername in the Windows NT User Manager for Domains and in the Internet Service Manager. This account was assigned a random password. The password for this account must be the same, both in Internet Service Manager and in the Windows NT User Manager for Domains. If you change the password, you must change it in both places and make sure it matches. *Note*: This account must have a password. You cannot assign a blank password.

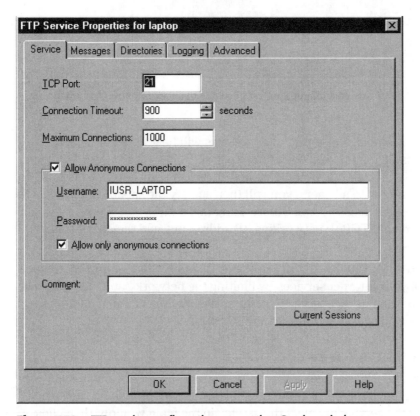

Figure 7.38   FTP service configuration properties: Service window.

To use your current security system to control information access, change the anonymous logon account from IUSR_computername to an existing account on your network.

This list explains how to use the features in this tab window:

TCP Port. Determine the port on which the FTP service is running. The default is port 21. You can change the port to any unique TCP port number. For a new port number to take effect, you must restart your computer.

Connection Timeout. Set the length of time in seconds before the server disconnects an inactive user. It is recommended that you do not set this number lower than 100 seconds. The maximum you can set is 32,767 seconds. This value ensures that all connections are closed if the FTP protocol fails to close a connection.

Maximum Connections. Set the maximum number of simultaneous connections to the server.

Allow Anonymous Connections. Set the Windows NT user account to use for permissions of all anonymous connections. As stated, by default, Internet Information Server creates and uses the account IUSR_computername for all anonymous logons. Note that the password is used only within Windows NT; anonymous users do not log on using this username and password.

Typically, anonymous FTP users will use "anonymous" as the username and their email address as the password. The FTP service then uses the IUSR_computername account as the logon account for permissions. The IUSR_computername is granted *Log on locally* user rights by default. This right is necessary as long as you want to grant anonymous logon access to your site. To grant access to a specific user, you must grant that user *Log on locally* rights.

Allow only anonymous connections. Select this box to allow only anonymous connections. When this box is selected, users cannot log on with usernames and passwords. This option prevents access by using an account with administrative permission; only the account specified for anonymous access is granted access.

Comment. Specify the comment to be displayed in Internet Service Manager's Report view.

Current Sessions. Click to display the current FTP users, as shown in Figure 7.39.

- *Connected Users.* Lists the currently connected users by IP address and the time at which they connected.

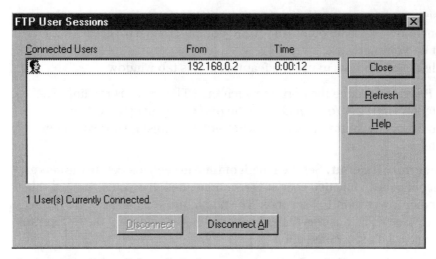

Figure 7.39   FTP service configuration properties: Service window.

- *Refresh Button.* Press to update the display of connected users.
- *Disconnect Buttons.* Press to disconnect the selected user, selected users, or all users.

Messages. By clicking on this tab, shown in Figure 7.40, you can view messages sent to clients and edit these messages as you like:

Welcome message. Displays the text displayed in the figure to clients when they first connect to the FTP server.

Exit message. Displays this text to clients when they log off the FTP server.

Maximum connections message. Displays this text to clients who try to connect when the FTP service already has the maximum number of client connections allowed.

Directories. The FTP Directories tab window, shown in Figure 7.41, is for setting directories and directory behavior for the FTP service. There you supply this information:

Directory listing box. List the directories used by the FTP service, divided into these columns:

- *Directory.* Lists the path of directories used by the FTP service.
- *Alias.* Gives the path that FTP uses for virtual directories.
- *Error.* Indicates system errors, such as difficulty reading a directory.

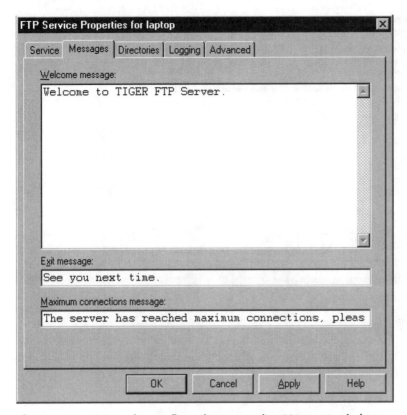

Figure 7.40 FTP service configuration properties: Messages window.

Add, Remove, and Edit buttons. To set up a directory, press the Add button or pick a directory in the Directory listing box and press the Edit button. Use the Remove button to delete directories you no longer want to list. Click Add, then configure the FTP service directories by using the dialog box shown in Figure 7.42. Use its contents as follows:

- *Directory*. Set the path to the directory to use for the FTP service.

- *Browse button*. Select the directory to use for the FTP service.

- *Home Directory*. Specify the root directory for the FTP service. Internet Information Server provides a default home directory, \ftproot, for the FTP service. The files that you place in the FTP home directory and its subdirectories are available to remote browsers. You can change the location of the default home directory.

- *Virtual Directory*. Specify a subdirectory for the FTP service.

- *Alias*. Enter a name for the virtual directory. This is the name that is used to connect to the directory. Enter either the directory name or the

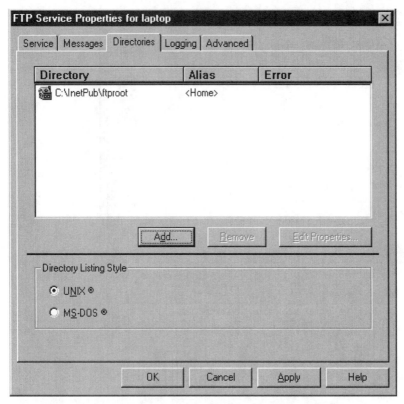

Figure 7.41 FTP service configuration properties: Directories window.

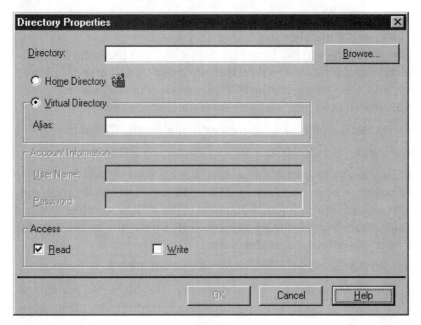

Figure 7.42 FTP service configuration properties: Directories/Add window.

alias that service users will use. You can add other directories outside the home directory that are accessible to browsers as subdirectories of the home directory. That is, you can publish from other directories and have those directories accessible from within the home directory. Such directories are called virtual directories. Note that virtual directories will not appear in FTP directory listings; FTP users must know the virtual directory's alias and type in its URL address in the FTP application or browser. The administrator can specify the physical location of the virtual directory and the virtual name (alias), which is the directory name used by remote browsers. The published directories can be located on local or network drives. If the virtual directory is a network drive, provide the username and password with access to that network drive. Virtual directories on network drives must be on computers in the same Windows NT domain as the Internet Information Server.

- *Account Information.* This box is active only if the directory specified in the first line of this dialog box is a UNC server and sharename, for example, \\webserver\htmlfiles. Enter the username and password that has permission to use the network directory. Virtual directories on network drives must be on computers in the same Windows NT domain as the computer running Internet Information Server. If you specify a username and password to connect to a network drive, all Internet Information Server access to that directory will use that username and password. Take care when using UNC connections to network drives to prevent security breaches.

- *Access check boxes.* The Access check boxes control the attributes of the directory. If the files are on an NTFS drive, NTFS settings for the directory must match these settings. Read must be selected for FTP directories. Write allows clients to write files to the FTP server. Select this only for directories that are intended to accept files from users.

Directory Listing Style. Choose the directory listing style (not shown for brevity) to send to FTP users, whether you want files listed in UNIX or MS-DOS format. Note, many browsers expect UNIX format, so you should select UNIX for maximum compatibility.

Logging. Via the Logging tab (refer to Figure 7.35), you set valuable logging information for the selected service regarding how a server is used. You can send log data to files or to an ODBC-supported database. If you have multiple servers or services on a network, you can log all their activity to a single file or database on any network computer.

If you want to log to a file, you can specify how often to create new logs and in which directory to put the log files. The Convlog.exe command prompt command converts log files to either EMWAC log files or the common log file format. If you log to an ODBC data source, you must specify the ODBC DSN, table, and valid username and password to the database. Use the Logging window contents as follows:

Enable Logging. Select this box to start or stop logging for the selected information service.

Log to File. Choose this option to log to a text file for the selected information service.

Log Format. Click the down arrow and choose either Standard format or NCSA format.

Automatically open new log. Select to generate new logs at the specified interval. If you do not select this, the same log file will grow indefinitely.

Log file directory. Identify the path to the directory containing all log files. To change directories, click Browse and select a different directory.

Log filename. The default name of the log file automatically set by Windows NT. Lowercase letters yy will be replaced with the year, mm with the month, and dd with the day.

Log to SQL/ODBC Database. Choose to log to any ODBC data source. Set the data source name and table name (not the filename of the table) and specify a username and password that is valid for the computer on which the database resides. You must also use the ODBC applet in Control Panel to create a system data source.

Advanced. Using the contents of the Advanced properties window (refer to Figure 7.36), you can set access by specific IP address to block individuals or groups from gaining access to your server. You can also set the maximum network bandwidth for outbound traffic to control the maximum amount of traffic on your server.

You can control access to each Internet service by specifying the IP address of the computers to be granted or denied access. If you choose to grant access to all users by default, you can then specify the computers to be denied access. Let's assume, for example, that you have a form on your WWW server, and a particular user on the Internet is entering multiple forms with fictitious information. You can prevent the computer at that IP address from connecting to your site. Conversely, if you choose to deny access to all users by default, you can then specify which computers are allowed access.

Use the options in this window as described here:

Granted Access. Choose this option and press the Add button to list computers that will be denied access.

Denied Access. Choose this option and press the Add button to list computers that will be granted access.

Add. To add computers to which you want to deny access, select the Granted Access button and click Add. Conversely, to add computers to which you want to grant access, select the Denied Access button, and click Add (refer to Figure 7.37).

- Choose Single Computer and provide the IP address to exclude a single computer.

- Choose Group of Computers and provide an IP address and subnet mask to exclude a group of computers.

- Press the button next to the IP address to use a DNS name instead of IP address. Your server must have a DNS server specified in its TCP/IP settings. You are specifying, by IP address or domain name, which computer or group of computers will be granted or denied access. If you choose, by default, to grant access to all users, you will specify the computers to be denied access. If you choose, by default, to deny access to all users, you will then specify the specific computers to be allowed access. Before you use this option, be sure you fully understand TCP/IP networking, IP addressing, and the use of subnet masks.

Limit Network Use by all Internet Services on this computer. You can control your Internet services by limiting the network bandwidth allowed for all of the Internet services on the server. Set the maximum kilobytes of outbound traffic permitted on this computer.

Configuring the Gopher Service

To configure the Gopher service, first select the service in the main window and then click the third menu icon to view its properties. You may also double-click the service or select the service in the main window and then click the Properties menu Service Properties option. A window with four tab options will appear: Service, Directories, Logging, and Advanced.

Service. The Gopher Service window, shown in Figure 7.43, is where you'll set user properties for this service. Fill in the items as described here:

TCP Port. Identify the port on which the Gopher service is running. The default is port 70. You can change the port to any unique TCP port number. For a new port number to take effect, you must restart your computer.

Connection Timeout. Set the length of time before the server disconnects an inactive user. This value ensures that all connections are closed if the Gopher protocol fails to close a connection.

Maximum Connections. Set the maximum number of simultaneous connections to the Gopher service.

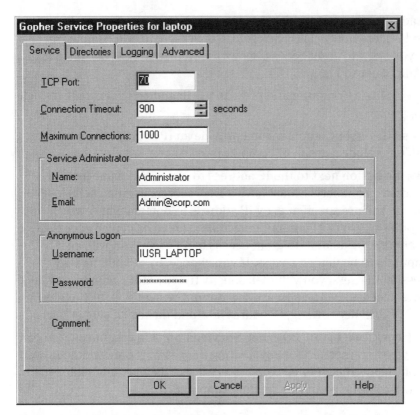

Figure 7.43 Gopher service configuration properties: Service window.

Service Administrator. Specify the values the Gopher service will report to users.

Anonymous Logon. Set the Windows NT user account to use for permissions of all anonymous connections. By default, the Internet Information Server creates and uses the account IUSR_computername. Note that the password is used only within Windows NT; anonymous users do not log on with a username and password. When you installed Internet Information Server, Setup created the account IUSR_computername in the Windows NT User Manager for Domains and in the Internet Service Manager. This account was assigned a random password. The password for this account must be the same in Internet Service Manager and the Windows NT User Manager for Domains. If you change the password, you must change it in both places and make sure it matches. The IUSR_computername is granted *Log on locally* user rights by default. This right is necessary as long as you want to grant anonymous logon access to your site. To grant access to a specific user, you must grant that user *Log on locally* rights. Note, this account must have a password; you cannot assign a blank password.

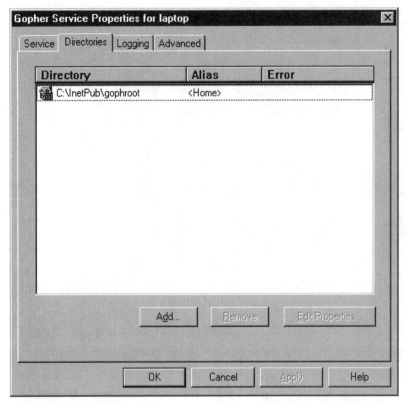

Figure 7.44 Gopher service configuration properties: Directories window.

Comment. Type the comment you want displayed in Internet Service Manager Report view.

Directories. Selecting the Gopher's Directories tab (see Figure 7.44) gives you the opportunity to set directories and directory behavior, as follows:

Directory listing box. List the directories used by the Gopher service:

- *Directory*. Lists the path of directories used by the service.

- *Alias*. The path for Gopher service users. Note that aliases do not appear in Gopher listings; you must create tag files to include virtual directories in Gopher listings.

- *Error*. Indicates system errors, such as difficulty reading a directory.

Add, Remove, and Edit buttons. To set up a directory, press the Add button or select a directory in the Directory listing box and press the Edit button. Select the Remove button to delete directories you no longer want. Configure the Gopher service directories by pressing the Add button, as shown in Figure 7.45:

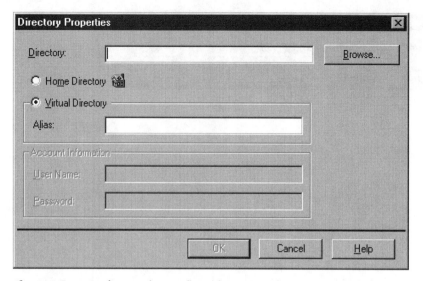

Figure 7.45 Gopher service configuration properties: Directories/Add window.

- *Directory.* Set the path to the directory to use for the Gopher service.

- *Browse button.* Select the directory to use for the Gopher service.

- *Home Directory.* Specify the root directory for the Gopher service. The Internet Information Server provides a default home directory, \Goph-root, for the Gopher service. The files that you place in the Gopher home directory and its subdirectories are available to remote browsers. You can change the location of the default home directory.

- *Virtual Directory.* Specify a subdirectory for the Gopher service. Enter the directory name or alias that service users will use. These directories are accessed using the alias in the URL as if the alias were a subdirectory of the home directory. That is, you can publish from other directories and have those directories accessible from within the home directory. Such directories are called virtual directories. Note that virtual directories will not appear in Gopher directory listings; you must create explicit links in tag files in order for users to access virtual directories. Users can also type in the URL if they know the alias for the virtual directory; however, they must precede the alias name with "11/." For example, to access the virtual directory "books" from your Gopher server that is named gopher.company.com, you would use the following URL: gopher://gopher.company.com/11/books. The administrator can specify the physical location of the virtual directory and the virtual name (alias), which is the directory name used by remote browsers. The published directories can be located on local or network drives. If the virtual directory is a network drive, provide the username and password with access to that network drive. Virtual directories on network drives must be on computers in the same Windows NT domain as the Internet Information Server.

- *Account Information.* This box is active only if the Directory specified in the first line of this dialog box is a UNC server and sharename, for example, \\webserver\htmlfiles. Enter the username and password that has permission to use the network directory. Virtual directories on network drives must be on computers in the same Windows NT domain as the Internet Information Server. If you specify a username and password to connect to a network drive, all Internet Information Server access to that directory will use that username and password. Take care when using UNC connections to network drives to prevent security breaches.

Logging. The Logging properties window (refer to Figure 7.35) is where you set logging information for the selected service regarding how a server is used. You can send log data to files or to an ODBC-supported database. If you have multiple servers or services on a network, you can log all their activity to a single file or database on any network computer.

If you want to log to a file, you can specify how often to create new logs and in which directory to put the log files. The Convlog.exe command prompt command converts log files to either EMWAC log files or the common log file format. If you log to an ODBC data source, you must specify the ODBC DSN, table, and valid username and password to the database.

Use the Logging window contents as described here:

Enable Logging. Select this box to start or stop logging for the selected information service.

Log to File. Choose this option to log to a text file for the selected information service.

Log Format. Click the down arrow and choose either Standard format or NCSA format.

Automatically open new log. Select this box to generate new logs at the specified interval. If you do not select this, the same log file will grow indefinitely.

Log file directory. Give the path to the directory containing all log files. To change directories, click Browse and select a different directory.

Log filename. The default name of the log file is automatically set by Windows NT. Lowercase letters yy will be replaced with the year, mm with the month, and dd with the day.

Log to SQL/ODBC Database. Choose to log to any ODBC data source. Set the data source name and table name (not the filename of the table) and specify a username and password that is valid for the computer on which the database resides. You must also use the ODBC applet in Control Panel to create a system data source.

Advanced. Clicking the Advanced tab (refer to Figure 7.36) lets you set access by specific IP address to block individuals or groups from gaining access to your server. You can also set the maximum network bandwidth for outbound traffic to control the maximum amount of traffic on your server.

You can control access to each Internet service by specifying the IP address of the computers to be granted or denied access. If you choose to grant access to all users by default, you can then specify the computers to be denied access. For example, if you have a form on your WWW server, and a particular user on the Internet is entering multiple forms with fictitious information, you can prevent the computer at that IP address from connecting to your site. Conversely, if you choose to deny access to all users by default, you can then specify which computers are allowed access.

Here's how the options in this window work:

Granted Access. Choose this option and press the Add button to list computers that will be denied access.

Denied Access. Choose this option and press the Add button to list computers that will be granted access.

Add. To add computers to which you want to deny access, select the Granted Access button and click Add. Conversely, to add computers to which you want to grant access, select the Denied Access button and click Add (refer to Figure 7.37).

- Choose Single Computer and provide the IP address to exclude a single computer.

- Choose Group of Computers and provide an IP address and subnet mask to exclude a group of computers.

- Press the button next to the IP address to use a DNS name instead of IP address. Your server must have a DNS server specified in its TCP/IP settings. You are specifying, by IP address or domain name, which computer or group of computers will be granted or denied access. If you choose, by default, to grant access to all users, you will specify the computers to be denied access. If you choose, by default, to deny access to all users, you will then specify the specific computers to be allowed access. Before you use this option, make sure you fully understand TCP/IP networking, IP addressing, and the use of subnet masks.

Limit Network Use by all Internet Services on this computer. You can control your Internet services by limiting the network bandwidth allowed for all of the Internet services on the server. Set the maximum kilobytes of outbound traffic permitted on this computer.

Think It Over

Test your knowledge of the material covered in this chapter before moving on to the next. The answers to these questions can be found in Appendix A.

7.1. DNS is a gateway service to the Internet that translates domain names into IP addresses.

    ○ True

    ○ False

7.2. The records in the DNS directory are split into files called what?

    ○ DNS records

    ○ DNS record types

    ○ DNS zones

    ○ DNS servers

7.3. Which of the following best describes the function of a DNS server that is authoritative for some zone?

    ○ Performs a caching function for all other DNS information

    ○ Consists of DNS data, DNS servers, and Internet protocols for providing data from the servers

    ○ Maps an alphabetic domain name into an IP address, and forwards users to view Web sites

7.4. Which of the following, by default, consists of three reverse lookup zones that are associated with each DNS server?

    ○ 0.In-addr.arpa

    ○ 127.In-addr.arpa

    ○ Zone.In-addr.arpa

    ○ 255.In-addr.arpa

7.5. What is the name of the domain that is at the root of the DNS namespace section whose resource records will be managed in the resulting zone file?

    ○ Zone name

    ○ Primary zone

    ○ Host name

7.6. A new subdomain will work with WINS Lookup.

    ○ True

    ○ False

7.7. Which of the following is a connectionless datagram protocol and, as such, is similar to unreliable datagram delivery offered by the Internet Protocol?

    ○ ARP

    ○ SPX

    ○ IPX

    ○ SAP

7.8. Which of the following is a method by which network resources, such as file servers, advertise their addresses and the services they provide?

    ○ ARP

    ○ SPX

    ○ IPX

    ○ SAP

7.9. Which of the following is a packet that is broadcast to all hosts attached to a physical network?

    ○ ARP

    ○ SPX

    ○ IPX

    ○ SAP

7.10. Which of the following is the most common NetWare transport protocol?

    ○ ARP

    ○ SPX

    ○ IPX

    ○ SAP

7.11. A SAP packet can contain service messages for up to how many servers?

    ○ 1

    ○ 3

    ○ 5

    ○ 7

7.12.   Which of the following is a distributed database that maintains infor-
        mation about every resource on the network and access to such?

        ○ NDS

        ○ NWLINK

        ○ Bindery

        ○ Tree

7.13.   With Windows NT you can create gateways to both NDS and bindery
        resources.

        ○ True

        ○ False

7.14.   If NWLink detects no network traffic or any frames of type 802.2, to
        what does it set the frame type?

        ○ Auto

        ○ 802.3

        ○ 802.2

7.15.   Access to NetWare is subject to trustee rights for which of the following?

        ○ Gateway user account

        ○ NTGATEWAY group

        ○ Admin group

7.16.   To redirect the H drive to the directory \data\mydata of the SERVER
        volume on a server called NetWare411 using UNC naming syntax,
        what syntax would you use from the command prompt?

        ○ `net use H: \\SERVER\netware411\data\mydata`

        ○ `net use H: \\netware411\SERVER\data\mydata`

        ○ `net use \\netware411\SERVER\data\mydata H:`

7.17.   To connect as user *jchirillo* with the password *tigertools* to the direc-
        tory \data\mydata within the SERVER volume on a server called Net-
        Ware411 using the H drive, what syntax would you use from the
        command prompt?

        ○ `net use /user:jchirillo tigertools\\netware411`
          `\SERVER\data\mydata H:`

        ○ `net use H: \\netware411\server\data\mydata`
          `/user:jchirillo tigertools`

        ○ `net use H: \\SERVER\netware411\data\mydata`
          `/user:jchirillo tigertools`

7.18. IIS includes which of the following components?

○ Internet services: WWW, FTP, and Gopher

○ Internet Service Manager

○ Key Manager

○ A tool for installing SSL keys

7.19. What must you do if you want to provide access to databases through the Microsoft Internet Information Server?

○ Set up the ODBC drivers and data sources using the ODBC applet in the Windows NT Control Panel

○ Close all applications and services that use ODBC

○ Configure the WWW service to have *Log on locally* rights in Windows NT Server User Manager for Domains, then set up the ODBC drivers and data sources

7.20. Which of the following password authentication types is often used in conjunction with Secure Sockets Layer (SSL) to ensure that usernames and passwords are encrypted before transmission?

○ Basic

○ Windows NT Challenge/Response

○ Clear Text

7.21. Which of the following password authentication types automatically encrypts usernames and passwords?

○ Basic

○ Windows NT Challenge/Response

○ Clear Text

7.22. In regard to the Universal Naming Convention (UNC), if you specify a username and password to connect to a network drive, all Internet Information Server access to that directory will use that user name and password.

○ True

○ False

PART

Two

Windows 2000 Server

In Part 1, we explored the mechanical details of the conventional Windows NT Server suite, and we examined configuration details, from both a nontechnical standpoint and a certified engineer's perspective. In Part 2, we'll compare the Windows NT Server suite to the more recent Windows 2000 (Win 2K for short) Server, paying particular attention to the differences embedded within this innovative new operating system.

Win 2K Server

What's New

According to Microsoft, Windows 2000 (Win 2K) Server includes improved network, application, and Web services, with increased reliability and more flexible management services. Win 2K Server is based on the Windows NT technology; therefore in this chapter—and throughout Part 2—we will investigate only the most significant differences between the two. Specifically, we will address these new improvements to the operating system:

File server. Active Directory, disk, and file management features.

Print server. Active Directory, printer, and protocol support.

Internet server. Internet Information Services features, application support, and security.

Multimedia server. Multimedia support.

Application server. Terminal Services features, management and deployment of applications, and performance and tuning features.

Development. Development support.

Networking. Network protocols and technologies, and performance and tuning features.

Server foundation. Server reliability, availability, and scalability.

Server security. Authentication and smart card support.

Configuration and management. Active Directory, IntelliMirror, remote management, disk and file management, and Internationalization features.

Win 2K Server Boot CD-ROM Installation

To launch the Win 2K Server, power up the system with the Microsoft Windows 2000 Server CD in your primary CD-ROM drive. Be sure your system's Setup specifies the primary boot process starting with CD-ROM. Then follow these steps:

1. From the Welcome to Setup screen you can choose to do one of the following:

   - Press Enter to set up Win 2K.
   - Press R to repair a Win 2K installation.
   - Press F3 to quit Setup without installing Win 2K.

      In this case, press Enter to continue with the installation process.

LICENSE AGREEMENT

2. View the entire Windows 2000 Licensing Agreement by pressing Page Down. At the end of the agreement, press F8 to accept its terms and continue.

LOCATION SELECTION AND DRIVE FORMAT

3. Select an installation location for Windows NT. In this step, you may create/delete active hard drive partitions. After which, select the partition to which you want to install the operating system and press Enter. You may now choose to format the partition using the File Allocation Table (FAT) or NT File System (NTFS) by pressing Enter. In this case, select NTFS.

4. Setup will copy the installation files to the selected partition. When Setup is finished, press Enter to restart the system and continue with the installation.

WIN 2K SETUP WIZARD

5. The Windows 2000 Server Setup Wizard will complete the installation process. Press Next to acknowledge. The Setup Wizard will detect and install devices on the system.

REGIONAL SETTINGS

6. You can customize the Win 2K server for different regions and settings. For local settings, click Customize and set the current local time, date, and currency. Click OK to accept the changes. For keyboard settings, click Customize and select your keyboard properties. Click OK to accept the settings. Click Next when you are ready to continue with the installation.

PERSONALIZING WIN 2K

7. Type your full name and the name of your company or organization, then click Next.

8. *Licensing Mode.* Based on Microsoft's definitions given in Chapter 2, on page 16, choose either the *Per Seat* or *Per Server* licensing type and click Next.

9. *Server Name and Password.* Enter a name for the computer and the Administrator password (up to 14 characters); click Next.

WIN 2K COMPONENTS

10. To add or remove a component, click the check box. A shaded box means that only part of the component will be installed. To see what's included in a component, click Details. You may elect to install services such as Domain Name Service (DNS) from the Components window; however, for our purposes here, we'll accept the default settings for accessories, utilities, and services (including Internet Information Server, or IIS) and click Next to continue.

DATE AND TIME

11. Verify the correct date, time, and time zone and click Next to confirm and accept.

NETWORKING SETTINGS

12. The Setup wizard will install the networking components. Choose whether to use typical (auto install of common services) or custom settings (to manually configure networking components). Again, for now, select Typical settings and click Next.

13. *Workgroup or Computer Domain.* Select to make this computer a member of a domain or workgroup. Click Next to continue.

INSTALLING COMPONENTS AND COMPLETING SETUP

14. Setup will install your component selection. This may take several minutes. Setup will also perform final tasks, such as registering components,

saving settings, and removing temporary files. Click Finish to complete the Setup Wizard and restart the computer.

 Be sure to remove the CD-ROM before restarting the computer in step 14.

15. *Logging in.* After you restart the system, you'll have to log in with the administrative password configured during the Setup process. For security, the password will display as asterisks when you type it in.

 Hands-on simulations of the material in this chapter can be found on the companion CD-ROM.

Basic Win 2K Server Configuration Step by Step

Thanks to a slightly enhanced user interface and updated management utilities, configuring Win 2K Server can be a breeze using new and improved configuration wizards. You will notice changes, however, compared to the NT setup. The major changes include the following:

- Plug-and-play setup integration is enabled.
- User-friendly Network Interface Card (NIC) modifications and settings dialog box has been added.
- Upgrades can only be initiated using Winnt32.exe.
- Conflicting services are disabled before setup begins.
- Upgrades and Setup run in VGA mode.
- Creation of Emergency Repair Disk (ERD) has been moved to Ntbackup.exe.

 This step-by-step overview of the installation and configuration processes assumes your system complies with the Microsoft Windows 2000 (Win 2K) Server hardware compatibility list and system requirements, which are: Pentium 133 or higher, 128 MB of RAM (minimum); 4 GB (maximum) RAM, 2-GB hard disk with 1 GB free, and up to 4 processors.

If this is your first bootup of the new operating system, you'll see the utility Configure your Server, shown in Figure 8.1. This utility will facilitate some of

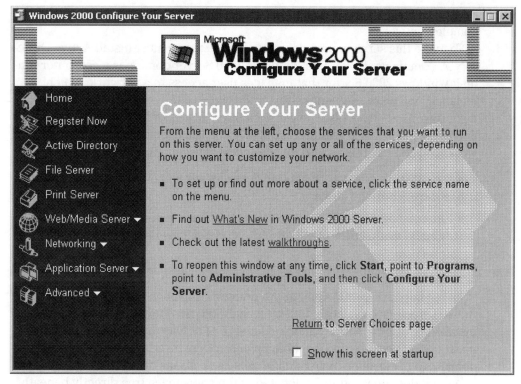

Figure 8.1   Win 2K Server configuration utility.

the basic configuration techniques. From the flexible interface, at the left menu, simply choose the services that you want to run on this server. We'll start with Active Directory.

 If it's not the first bootup, and you've elected not to be greeted by the configuration utility, you can retrieve it from Start/Programs /Administrative Tools/Configure Your Server. It's a good idea to do that so that you can follow along here.

Active Directory

Active Directory stores information about network objects, such as user accounts and shared printers, and provides access to that information. Security is integrated with Active Directory through logon authentication and access control to objects in the directory. With a single network logon, administrators can manage directory data and organization throughout their network, and authorized network users can access resources anywhere on the network. Policy-based administration eases the management of even the most complex network.

To make this server a new *domain controller*, you must install Active Directory. A domain controller in a Windows 2000 Server domain is a computer running Windows 2000 Server that manages user access to a network, which includes logging on, authentication, and access to the directory and shared resources. The Active Directory Installation wizard configures this server as a domain controller and sets up DNS if it is not already available on the network. You can use this wizard for the following scenarios:

- *No existing domain controller.* Sets up your server as the first domain controller on the network

- *Domain controller already on network.* Sets up your server as an additional domain controller, new child domain, new domain tree, or new forest

An additional domain controller is a Windows 2000 domain controller installed into an existing domain. All domain controllers participate equally in Active Directory replication but, by default, the first domain controller installed in a domain is assigned ownership of at least three floating single-master operations. Additional domain controllers installed into an existing domain do not assume ownership of these operations by default.

A child domain is a domain located in the namespace tree directly beneath another domain name (the parent domain). For example, example.microsoft.com would be a child domain of the parent domain microsoft.com. A child domain is also known as a subdomain.

The domain tree is the hierarchical structure that is used to index domain names. Domain trees are similar in purpose and concept to directory trees, which are used by computer filing systems for disk storage. For example, when numerous files are stored on disk, directories can be used to organize the files into logical collections. When a domain tree has one or more branches, each branch can organize domain names used in the namespace into logical collections.

A forest is a set of one or more trees that do not form a contiguous namespace. All trees in a forest share a common schema, configuration, and global catalog. The trees must trust each other through transitive, bidirectional trust relationships. Unlike a tree, a forest does not need a distinct name. A forest exists as a set of cross-reference objects and trust relationships known to the member trees. Trees in a forest form a hierarchy for the purposes of trust.

 You need a partition formatted with the version of NTFS used in Windows 2000 to host Active Directory.

Figure 8.2 Active Directory wizard front end.

Creating a New Domain

To create a new domain, we'll install Active Directory using the Active Directory Installation Wizard. Click the Active Directory icon in the menu listing of the configuration utility shown in Figure 8.1, click Next in Figure 8.2, then start the Active Directory wizard by clicking Start the Active Directory Wizard shown in Figure 8.3. Click Next to continue.

As just stated, a domain controller is a computer running Windows 2000 Server, which stores directory data and manages user-domain interactions, including user logon processes, authentication, and directory searches. Windows 2000 Server domain controllers provide an extension of the capabilities and features provided by Windows NT Server 4.0 domain controllers. A domain can have one or more domain controllers. For high availability and fault tolerance, a small organization using a single local area network (LAN) might need only one domain with two domain controllers, whereas a large

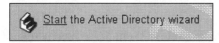

Figure 8.3 Starting the Active Directory wizard.

company with many network locations would need one or more domain controllers in each location.

A domain controller in Win 2K is configured using the Active Directory Installation wizard. This wizard installs and configures components that provide Active Directory service to network users and computers. Active Directory supports *multimaster replication* of directory data between all domain controllers in the domain. Multimaster replication is an evolution of the primary and backup domain controller model used in Windows NT Server 4.0, in which only one server, the primary domain controller, had a read-and-write copy of the directory. Windows 2000 Server multimaster replication synchronizes directory data on each domain controller, ensuring consistency of information over time. Primary domain controller changes can be impractical to perform in multimaster fashion; therefore, only one domain controller, called the *operations master*, accepts requests for such changes. In any Active Directory forest, there are at least five different operations master roles that are assigned to one or more domain controllers.

Let's create a new domain in Active Directory:

1. Once Active Directory is installed, from the Configure Your Server utility click Active Directory, and from the Active Directory window choose the domain controller type to create a new domain by selecting Domain controller for a new domain, and then click Next.

2. In the next window, choose to create a new domain tree by selecting Create a new domain tree; click Next.

3. Next, choose to create a new forest of domain trees by selecting Create a new forest of domain trees; click Next.

4. Specify a name for the new domain by typing the full DNS name (see Figure 8.4); click Next.

5. In Figure 8.5, specify the NetBIOS name for the new domain. Earlier versions of Windows will use this to identify the new domain. Click Next.

6. On the next window, in the fields provided, specify the locations of the Active Directory database and log either by accepting the default locations or by clicking Browse to find new ones. Click Next to continue.

7. You must specify the folder to be shared as the system volume in the next window. The Sysvol folder stores the server's copy of the domain's public files. Either accept the default location or click Browse to find a new one. Click Next to continue.

8. *Installing DNS.* If DNS is not available, the wizard will configure it for the new domain. Select Yes to install DNS, as shown in Figure 8.6, then click Next.

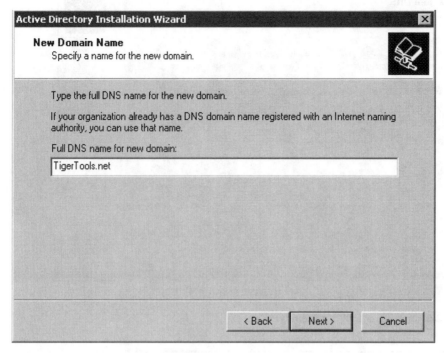

Figure 8.4   Specifying a new domain.

9. In the next window you must select the default permissions for user and group objects. You do this by selecting Permissions compatible with pre-Windows 2000 servers over Permissions compatible only with Windows 2000 servers to be compatible with our NT server programs. Click Next to continue.

10. In Figure 8.7, specify an Administrator password to use when starting the computer in restore mode; click Next

11. In the next window, review and confirm the previously selected options and click Next. The wizard will then configure Active Directory, as shown in Figure 8.8.

12. Finally in the next window click Finish to close the wizard and then Restart Now to reboot the server.

Now you're ready to learn how to manage Active Directory.

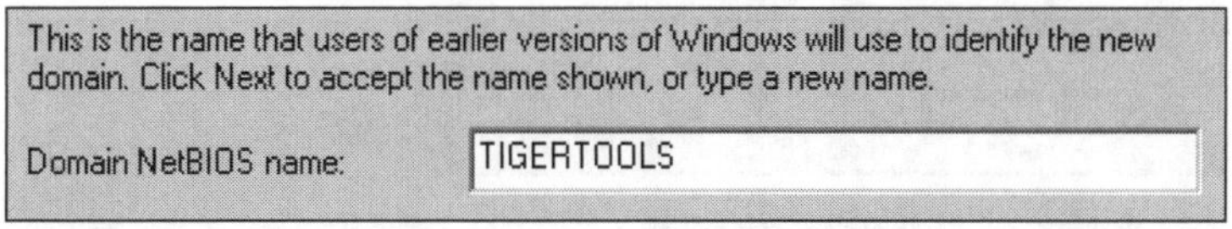

This is the name that users of earlier versions of Windows will use to identify the new domain. Click Next to accept the name shown, or type a new name.

Domain NetBIOS name: TIGERTOOLS

Figure 8.5   Specifying the NetBIOS name for the new domain.

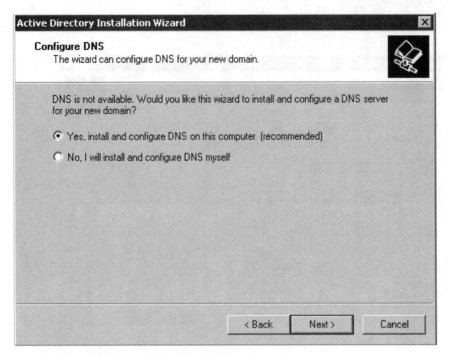

Figure 8.6 Installing DNS for the new domain.

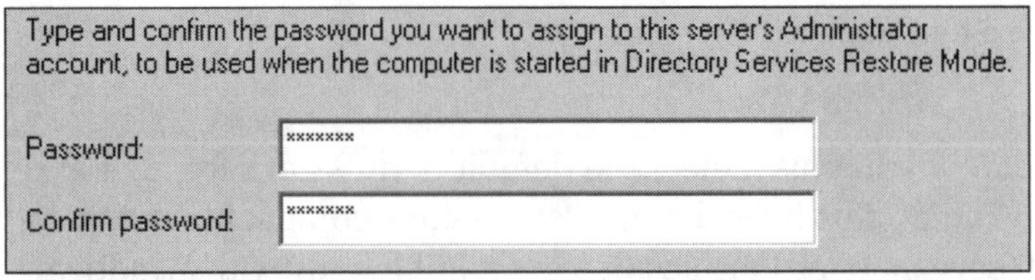

Type and confirm the password you want to assign to this server's Administrator account, to be used when the computer is started in Directory Services Restore Mode.

Password: ××××××××

Confirm password: ××××××××

Figure 8.7 Specifying an Administrator password for directory restore mode.

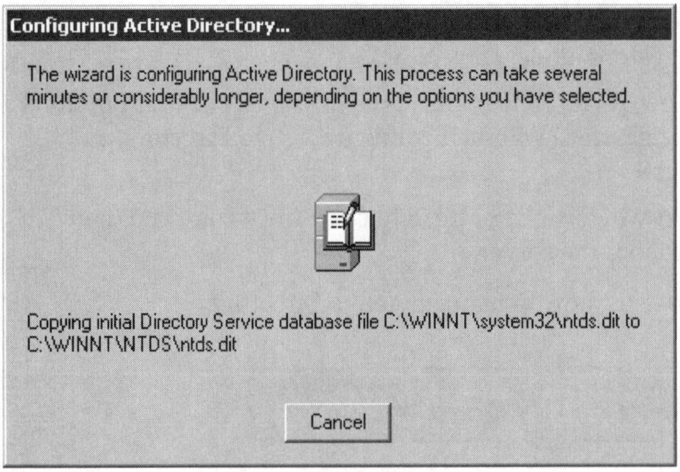

Configuring Active Directory...

The wizard is configuring Active Directory. This process can take several minutes or considerably longer, depending on the options you have selected.

Copying initial Directory Service database file C:\WINNT\system32\ntds.dit to C:\WINNT\NTDS\ntds.dit

Cancel

Figure 8.8 Configuring the Active Directory installation.

Figure 8.9 Starting the Active Directory admin utility.

Managing Active Directory

From Start/Programs/Administrative Tools/Configure Your Server, start the wizard again by clicking Active Directory in the menu listing on the left (refer to Figure 8.1). Click Manage user accounts and group settings, shown in Figure 8.9, to start the Active Directory admin utility.

The Active Directory admin utility, shown in Figure 8.10, is used to manage domain controllers, user accounts, computer accounts, groups, organizational units, and published resources. We'll begin our investigation of these processes by learning to manage domain controllers.

Managing Domain Controllers

To find a domain controller, using the Active Directory admin utility, follow these steps:

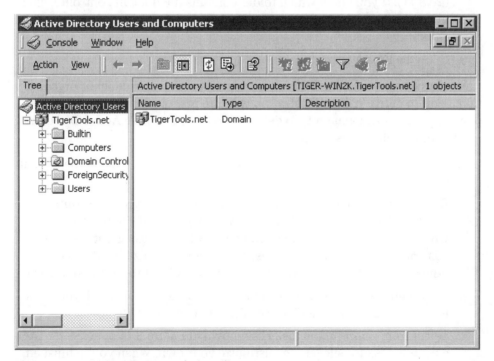

Figure 8.10 Active Directory admin utility.

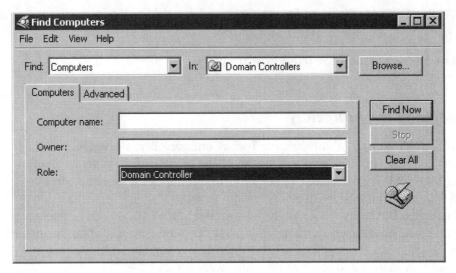

Figure 8.11 Searching for a domain controller.

1. In the Console Tree, right-click any node or folder, then click Find.

2. Under Find, click Computers; in Role, click Domain Controller (see Figure 8.11). If you know which folder contains the domain controller, click the folder in the In field or, to search the entire directory, click Entire Directory.

3. Click the Find Now button.

You can delegate administrative control of a particular domain or organizational unit to individual administrators who are responsible for only that domain or organizational unit. To delegate control, using the Active Directory admin utility, follow these steps:

1. In the Console Tree, double-click the domain node to expand the domain tree.

2. Right-click the folder that you want another user or group to control, and click Delegate Control to start the Delegation of Control wizard, whose welcome page is shown in Figure 8.12. You can grant users permission to manage users, groups, computers, organizational units, and other objects stored in Active Directory. Click Next to begin the wizard.

3. Click Add and/or select one or more users or groups to which you want to delegate control (see Figure 8.13), then click Next.

4. Select from the common tasks list shown in Figure 8.14 or select Create a custom task to delegate to customize your own. When you're finished, click Next and then Finish to complete the control delegation.

Figure 8.12 Delegation of Control Wizard.

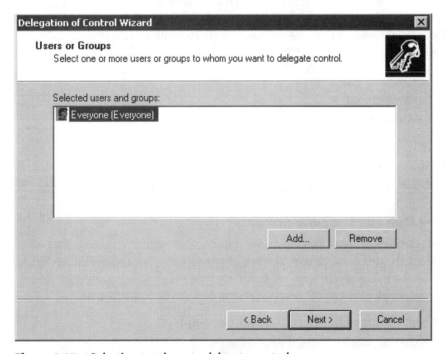

Figure 8.13 Selecting to whom to delegate control.

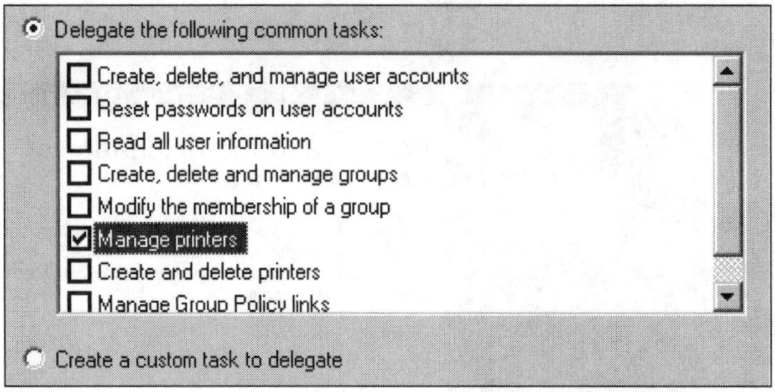

Figure 8.14   Selecting control from the common tasks list.

By default, domain controllers are installed in the Domain Controllers folder. Certain properties (for example, Name, Role, and Operating System) are automatically assigned when the computer is added to the domain or whenever it is started, and these properties cannot be modified by the administrator. Other domain controller properties can be modified using the Active Directory admin utility. To do so, follow these steps:

1. In the Console Tree, double-click the domain node.

2. Click the folder containing the domain controller. In the Details pane, right-click the domain controller that you want to modify, then click Properties. As you can see in Figure 8.15, the following property tabs display:

   - General
   - Operating System
   - Member Of
   - Location
   - Managed By

3. Click the property tab that contains the property you want to modify.

Managing User and Computer Accounts

Microsoft defines Active Directory user and computer accounts as representing physical entities such as a computer or person. Accounts provide security credentials for users or computers, enabling those users and computers to log on to the network and access domain resources. An account is used to:

- Authenticate the identity of the user or computer.
- Authorize access to domain resources.
- Audit actions performed using the user or computer account.

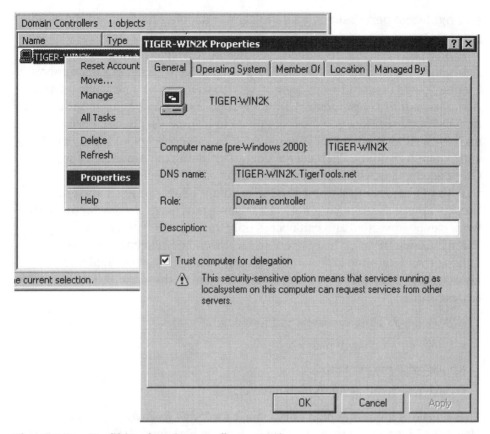

Figure 8.15 Modifying domain controller properties.

An Active Directory user account enables a user to log on to computers and domains with an identity that can be authenticated and authorized for access to domain resources. Each user who logs on to the network should have his or her own unique user account and password. User accounts can also be used as service accounts for some applications.

By default, Windows 2000 provides predefined user accounts that you can use to log on to a computer running Windows 2000. These predefined accounts are:

- Administrator account
- Guest account

Predefined accounts are designed to let users log on to a local computer and access resources from that computer. As such, these accounts are designed primarily for initial logon and configuration of a local computer. Each predefined account has a different combination of rights and permissions. As you might assume, the Administrator account has the most extensive rights and permissions, while the Guest account has limited rights and permissions.

Though convenient, predefined accounts pose a significant problem: If their rights and permissions are not modified or disabled by a network administrator, they could be used by any user or service to log on to a network using the Administrator or Guest identity. To implement the security of user authentication and authorization, you must create an individual user account for each user who will participate on your network by using the Active Directory Users and Computers utility. Each user account (including the Administrator and Guest account) can then be added to Window 2000 groups to control the rights and permissions assigned to the account. Using accounts and groups that are appropriate for your network ensures that users logging on to a network can be identified and can access only the permitted resources.

Each Active Directory user account has a number of security-related options that determine how someone logging on with that particular user account is authenticated on the network. Several of these options are specific to passwords:

- User must change password at next logon.
- User cannot change password.
- Password never expires.
- Save password as encrypted clear text.

These options are self-explanatory except for "Save password as encrypted clear text." If you have users logging on to your Windows 2000 network from Apple computers, select this option for those user accounts.

User and computer accounts are added, disabled, reset, and deleted using the Active Directory Users and Computers utility. Note the following in regard to these actions:

- If you create a new user account with the same name as a previously deleted user account, it does not automatically assume the permissions and memberships of the deleted account because the security descriptor for each account is unique.
- To duplicate a deleted user account, all permissions and memberships must be manually re-created.

To add a user account from the Active Directory admin utility, follow these steps:

1. In the Console Tree, double-click the domain node. In the details pane, right-click the organizational unit where you want to add the user, point to New, and click User (see Figure 8.16).
   - In First name, type the user's first name.

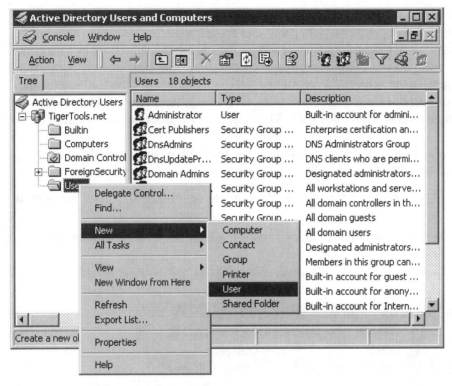

Figure 8.16 Adding a user account.

- In Initials, type the user's initials.
- In Last name, type the user's last name.
- Modify Full name as desired.
- In User logon name, type the name that the user will log on with; and, from the drop-down list, click the user principal name (UPN) suffix that must be appended to the user logon name (following the @ symbol). If the user will use a different name to log on from computers running Windows NT, Windows 98, or Windows 95, change the user logon name as it appears in User logon name (pre-Windows 2000) to the different name.
- In Password and Confirm password, type the user's password.
- Select the appropriate password options.

2. After creating the user account, right-click the new user and click Properties to edit the user account and/or enter additional user account information, as shown in Figure 8.17. You can edit general user information, group memberships, dialin access, terminal server access, and session settings.

Rather than deleting an unused user account, it can be disabled as a security measure to prevent a particular user from logging on. Disabled accounts can also serve a useful purpose. By creating disabled user accounts with common group memberships, they can be used as account templates to simplify user account creation. Therefore instead of manually creating the exact same type of account for, say, 20 new users, an account template can be copied, renamed, and activated for each. This could save a great deal of administrative time.

To disable/enable a user account, using the Active Directory admin utility, follow these steps:

1. In the Console Tree, double-click the domain node to expand the domain tree.

2. In the Console Tree, click Users or click the folder that contains the desired user account.

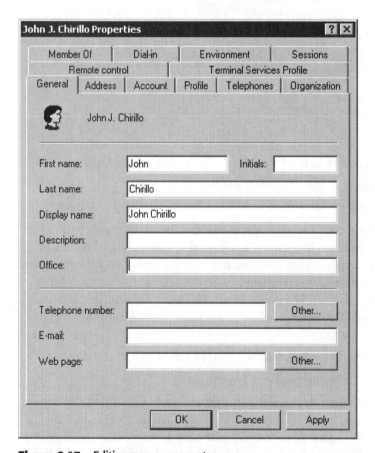

Figure 8.17   Editing a user account.

3. In the details pane, right-click on the user and click Disable or Enable Account (see Figure 8.18).

To copy, delete, rename, or move a user account, using the Active Directory admin utility, follow these steps:

1. In the Console Tree, double-click the domain node to expand the domain tree.

2. In the Console Tree, click Users or click the folder that contains the desired user account.

3. In the details pane, right-click on the user and select the appropriate course of action.

Managing Computer Accounts

As set up by Microsoft, every computer running Windows 2000 or Windows NT that joins a domain has a computer account. Similar to user accounts, computer accounts provide a means for authenticating and auditing the computer's access to the network and to domain resources. Each computer connected to the network should have its own unique computer account.

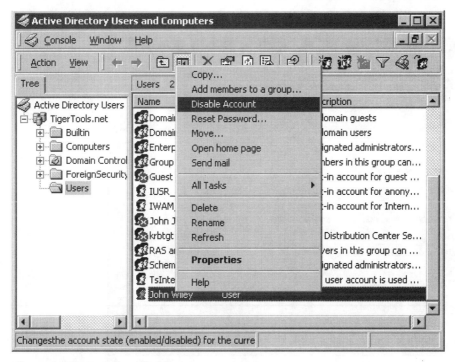

Figure 8.18   Enabling/disabling a user account.

Computers running Windows 98 and Windows 95 do not have the advanced security features of those running Windows 2000 and Windows NT and cannot be assigned computer accounts in Windows 2000 domains. However, you can log on to a network and use Windows 98 and Windows 95 computers in Active Directory domains.

By default, domain policy settings enable only domain administrators (members of the group *Domain Admins)* to add a computer account to a domain.

To add a computer account to a domain, using the Active Directory admin utility, follow these steps:

1. In the Console Tree, click Computers, or click the container (the directory service object that includes subcontainers for computer and user Group Policy information) in which you want to add the computer.

2. Right-click Computers or the container in which you want to add the computer, point to New, then click Computer.

3. Type the computer name (see Figure 8.19).

4. Click the Change button to specify a different user or group that can add this computer to the domain.

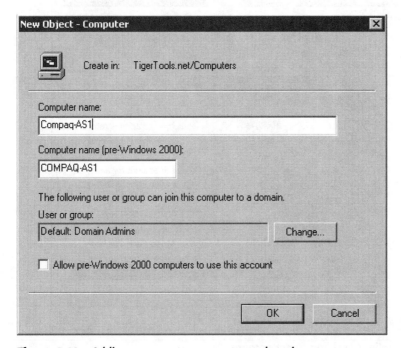

Figure 8.19 Adding a computer account to a domain.

To view or change the full computer name of a computer and the domain that a computer belongs to, on the desktop, right-click My Computer, click Properties, and then the Network Identification tab.

Group Policy settings are components of a user's desktop environment that a system administrator needs to manage—programs and Start menu options. Group Policy settings are contained in a Group Policy object, which is associated with selected Active Directory objects—sites, domains, or organizational units. They are settings for User or Computer Configuration, which affect users and computers, respectively.

Adding a computer to a group allows you to assign permissions to all of the computer accounts in that group and to filter Group Policy settings on all accounts in that group. To add a computer account to a group, using the Active Directory admin utility, follow these steps:

1. In the Console Tree, click Computers or click the folder in which the computer is located.

2. In the details pane, right-click the computer, then click Properties (see Figure 8.20).

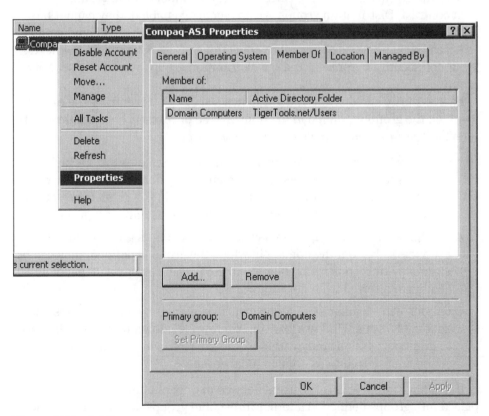

Figure 8.20 Adding a computer to a group.

3. Click the Member Of tab, then Add, then the group to which you want to add the computer; click Add again. To add the computer to more than one group, press the Ctrl key and simultaneously click the groups to which you want to add the computer, and then click Add.

To disable/enable, move, or delete a computer account, using the Active Directory admin utility, follow these steps:

1. In the Console Tree, click Computers or click the folder in which the computer is located.

2. In the details pane, right-click on the computer and select the appropriate course of action.

Managing Groups

Microsoft has set up two types of groups in Windows 2000: Security and Distribution. Security groups are listed in *discretionary access control lists* (DACLs) that define permissions on resources and objects. Security groups can also be used as an email entity—that means that sending an email message to the group sends the message to all the members of the group.

In contrast, Distribution groups are not security-enabled; they cannot be listed in DACLs. Distribution groups can be used only with email applications (such as Exchange) to send email to collections of users. If you do not need a group for security purposes, create a distribution group instead of a security group.

Each security and distribution group has a scope that identifies the extent to which the group is applied in the domain tree or forest. There are three different scopes: *universal, global,* and *domain local.*

- Groups with universal scope can have as their members groups and accounts from any Windows 2000 domain in the domain tree or forest; they can be granted permissions in any domain in the domain tree or forest. Groups with universal scope are referred to as universal groups.

- Groups with global scope can have as their members groups and accounts only from the domain in which the group is defined; they can be granted permissions in any domain in the forest. Groups with a global scope are referred to as global groups.

- Groups with domain local scope can have as their members groups and accounts from a Windows 2000 or Windows NT domain; they can be used to grant permissions only within a domain. Groups with a domain local scope are referred to as domain local groups.

If you have multiple forests, users defined in only one forest cannot be placed into groups defined in another forest, and groups defined in only one forest cannot be assigned permissions in another forest.

When you install a domain controller, several default groups are installed in the Builtin and Users folders of the Active Directory Users and Computers console. These are security groups that represent common sets of rights and permissions that you can use to grant certain roles, rights, and permissions to the accounts and groups that you place into the default groups.

Default groups with domain local scope are located in the Builtin folder. Predefined groups with global scope are located in the Users folder. You can move the built-in and predefined groups to other group or organizational unit folders within the domain, but you cannot move them to other domains.

The default groups placed in the Builtin folder for Active Directory Users and Computers are:

Account Operators

Administrators

Backup Operators

Guests

Print Operators

Replicator

Server Operators

Users

These built-in groups have domain local scope and are primarily used to assign default sets of permissions to users who will have some administrative control in that domain. For example, the Administrators group in a domain has a broad set of administrative authority over all accounts and resources in the domain.

In addition to the groups in the Builtin and Users folder, Windows 2000 Server includes three special identities. For convenience, these identities also are generally referred to as groups. These special groups do not have specific memberships that you can modify, but they can represent different users at different times, depending on the circumstances. The three special groups are:

Everyone. Represents all current network users, including guests and users from other domains. Whenever users log on to the network, they are automatically added to the Everyone group.

Network. Represents users currently accessing a given resource over the network (as opposed to users who access a resource by logging on locally at the computer where the resource is located). Whenever users access a given resource over the network, they are automatically added to the Network group.

Interactive. Represents all users currently logged on to a particular computer and accessing a given resource located on that computer (as opposed to users who access the resource over the network). Whenever users access a given resource on the computer to which they are currently logged on, they are automatically added to the Interactive group.

Although the special identities can be assigned rights and permission to resources, as stated, you cannot modify or view the memberships of these special identities. You do not see them when you administer groups and you cannot place the special identities into groups. Group scopes do not apply to special identities. Users are automatically assigned to these special identities whenever they log on or access a particular resource.

Using *nesting*, you can add a group as a member of another group. You can nest groups to consolidate group management by increasing the affected member accounts and to reduce replication traffic caused by replication of group membership changes. Your nesting options depend on whether the domain is in *native-mode* (comprising Windows 2000 systems) or *mixed-mode* (comprising both Windows NT and 2000 systems). Groups in native-mode domains or distribution groups in mixed-mode domains have their membership determined as follows:

- Groups with universal scope can have the following as their members: user accounts, computer accounts, other groups with universal scope, and groups with global scope from any domain.

- Groups with global scope can have the following as their members: accounts from the same domain and other groups with global scope from the same domain.

- Groups with domain local scope can have the following as their members: user and/or computer accounts, groups with universal scope, and groups with global scope, all from any domain. They can also have as members other groups with domain local scope from within the same domain.

Security groups in a mixed-mode domain are restricted to the following types of membership:

- Groups with global scope can have as members only user and/or computer accounts.

- Groups with domain local scope can have as their members other groups with global scope and accounts.

Security groups with universal scope cannot be created in mixed-mode domains because universal scope is supported only in Windows 2000 native-mode domains.

By creating a group to assign permissions to all of the computer accounts in that group and to filter Group Policy settings on all accounts in that group, using the Active Directory admin utility, follow these steps:

1. In the Console Tree, double-click the domain node.

2. Right-click the folder in which you want to add the group, point to New, then click Group.

3. Type the name of the new group. By default, the name you type is also entered as the pre-Windows 2000 name of the new group (see Figure 8.21).

4. Click the Group scope and the Group type you want.

5. Click OK.

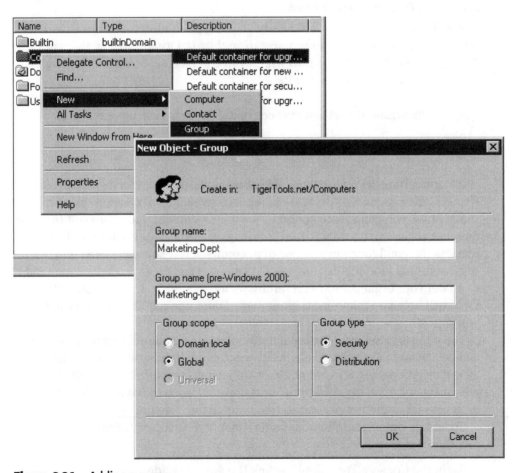

Figure 8.21   Adding a group.

If the domain in which you are creating the group is in mixed-mode, you can only select security groups with Domain local or Global scopes.

6. (Optional) To add a member to the group, right-click the new group name, click Properties, then click the Members tab followed by Add. Finally, click the users and computers to be added, then click Add again.

To move, delete, or rename a group, using the Active Directory admin utility, follow these steps:

1. In the Console Tree, double-click the domain node.
2. Click the folder that contains the group.
3. In the details pane, right-click the group and select the appropriate course of action.

Managing Organizational Units

According to Microsoft, a particularly useful type of directory object contained within domains is the *organizational unit*. Organizational units are Active Directory containers into which you can place users, groups, computers, and other organizational units.

 An organizational unit may not contain objects from other domains.

An organizational unit is the smallest scope or unit to which you can assign Group Policy settings or delegate administrative authority. Using organizational units, you can create containers within a domain that represent the hierarchical, logical structures within your organization. This enables you to manage the configuration and use of accounts and resources based on your organizational model. A hierarchy of containers can be extended as necessary to model your organization's hierarchy within a domain. Using organizational units will help you minimize the number of domains required for your network.

You can also use organizational units to create an administrative model that can be scaled to any size. A user can be granted administrative authority for all organizational units in a domain or for a single organizational unit. An administrator of an organizational unit does not need to have administrative authority for any other organizational units in the domain.

To add an organizational unit, using the Active Directory admin utility, follow these steps:

1. In the Console Tree, double-click the domain node.

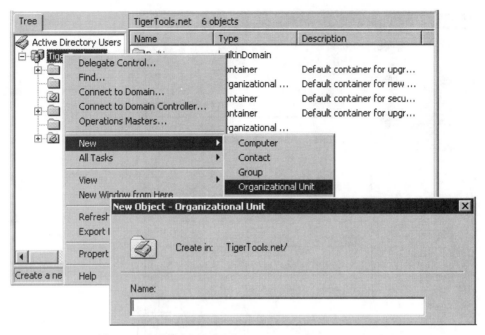

Figure 8.22 Adding an organizational unit.

2. Right-click the domain node or the folder in which you want to add the organizational unit, point to New, then click Organizational Unit.

3. Type the name of the organizational unit (see Figure 8.22).

4. Click OK.

5. To modify an organizational unit's properties, in the details pane, right-click the organizational unit and click Properties (see Figure 8.23).

6. Customize the unit's properties and, when you're done, click OK.

To delegate control of an organizational unit, using the Active Directory admin utility, follow these steps:

1. In the Console Tree, double-click the domain node.

2. In the details pane, right-click the organizational unit and click Delegate control to start the Delegation of Control wizard. Follow the instructions in the Delegation of Control Wizard as previously described in "Managing Domain Controllers."

To move, delete, or rename an organizational unit, using the Active Directory admin utility, follow these steps:

1. In the Console Tree, double-click the domain node.

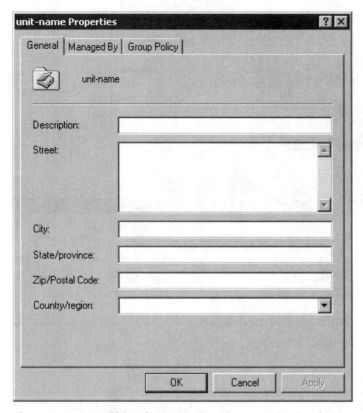

Figure 8.23 Modifying the properties of an organizational unit.

2. Click the folder that contains the group.

3. In the details pane, right-click the organizational unit and select the appropriate course of action.

Managing Domains and Trusts

Microsoft explicitly states that in Active Directory, each user account has a *user principal name* that is based on the Internet Engineering Task Force's (IETF's) RFC 822, "Standard for the Format of ARPA Internet Text Messages." The user principal name has two parts: the prefix (a user logon name) and the suffix (a domain name). These parts are joined by the "at" symbol (@) to form the complete user principal name.

For existing Windows NT accounts, the first part of the user principal name, the user logon name, is by default the same as the name used to log on to a Windows NT 4.0 domain. For new Windows 2000 user accounts, the user logon name must be created and assigned by an administrator.

The second part of the user principal name, the user principal name suffix, identifies the domain in which the user account is located. This second part can be the DNS domain name or an alternative name created by an administrator and used just for logon purposes. This logon name does not need to be a valid DNS name.

In Active Directory, the default user principal name suffix is the DNS name of the root domain in the domain tree. In most cases, this is the domain name registered as the enterprise domain on the Internet. Using alternative domain names as the user principal name suffix can provide additional logon security and simplify the names used to log on to another domain in the forest.

For example, if your organization uses a deep domain tree, organized by department and region, domain names can become quite long. The default user principal name for a user in that domain might be sales.westcoast.microsoft.com. The logon name for a user in that domain would be user@sales.westcoast.microsoft.com. Creating a user principal name suffix of microsoft would allow that same user to log on with the much simpler logon name of user@microsoft.com.

You can add or remove user principal name suffixes using the Active Directory Domains and Trusts utility. To add user principal name suffixes, follow these steps:

1. From Start/Programs/Administrative Tools, click Active Directory Domains and Trusts.

2. In the Console Tree, right-click Active Directory Domains and Trusts, then click Properties.

3. Click on the UPN Suffixes tab, type an alternative UPN suffix for the domain, then click Add (see Figure 8.24). Repeat this step to add additional alternative user principal name suffixes.

4. Click Apply and OK.

A *domain trust* is a relationship established between two domains that enables users in one domain to be authenticated by a domain controller in another domain. All domain trust relationships have only two domains in the relationship: the trusting domain and the trusted domain.

In earlier versions of Windows, trusts were limited to the two domains involved in the trust, and the trust relationship was one-way. In Windows 2000, all trusts are transitive and two-way. Both domains in a trust relationship automatically trust each other.

As an example, given Domains A, B, and C, if Domain A trusts Domain B, and Domain B trusts Domain C, users from Domain C (when granted the proper permissions) can access resources in Domain A. When a user is authenticated by a domain controller, this does not imply any access to

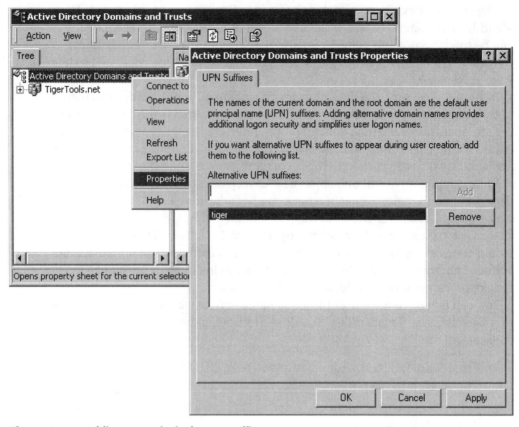

Figure 8.24 Adding user principal name suffixes.

resources in that domain. This is determined solely by the rights and permissions granted to the user account by the domain administrator for the trusting domain.

Explicit trusts are trust relationships that you create yourself, as opposed to trusts created automatically during installation of a domain controller. You create and manage explicit trusts using the Active Directory Domains and Trusts utility. There are two kinds of explicit trusts: *external* and *shortcut*. External trusts enable user authentication to a domain outside of a forest. Shortcut trusts shorten the trust path in a complex forest.

External trusts establish trust relationships to domains outside the forest. The benefit of creating external trusts is to enable user authentication to a domain not encompassed by the trust paths of a forest. All external trusts are one-way nontransitive trusts. You can combine two one-way trusts to create a two-way trust relationship.

Before an account can be granted access to resources by a domain controller of another domain, Windows 2000 must determine whether the domain containing the desired resources (*target domain*) has a trust relationship with the domain in which the account is located (*source domain*). To make this determination for two domains in a forest, Windows 2000 computes a *trust path* between the domain controllers for these source and target domains. A trust path is the series of domain trust relationships that must be traversed by Windows 2000 security to pass authentication requests between any two domains. Computing and traversing a trust path between domain trees in a complex forest can take time, which can be reduced with shortcut trusts.

Shortcut trusts are two-way transitive trusts that enable you to shorten the path in a complex forest. You explicitly create shortcut trusts between Windows 2000 domains in the same forest. A shortcut trust is a performance optimization that shortens the trust path for Windows 2000 security to take for authentication purposes. The most effective use of shortcut trusts is between two domain trees in a forest. You can also create multiple shortcut trusts between domains in a forest, if necessary.

To create an explicit trust, you must know the domain names and a user account with permission to create trusts in each domain. Each trust is assigned a password that must be known to the administrators of both domains in the relationship. To create an explicit domain trust, using the Active Directory admin utility, follow these steps:

1. From Start/Programs/Administrative Tools, click Active Directory Domains and Trusts.

2. In the Console Tree, right-click the domain node for the domain you want to administer, then click Properties.

3. Click the Trusts tab (see Figure 8.25).

4. Depending on your requirements, in either Domains trusted by this domain or Domains that trust this domain, click Add. If the domain to be added is a Windows 2000 domain, type the full DNS name of the domain; if the domain is running an earlier version of Windows, type the domain name.

5. Type the password for this trust, confirm the password, and click OK.

Repeat this procedure on the domain that forms the second half of the explicit trust relationship. Note that the password must be accepted in both the trusting and trusted domains.

To verify/revoke a trust, click the trust to be verified, click Edit, then click Verify/Reset.

Managing Site Settings

Active Directory uses multimaster replication to enable any Windows 2000 domain controller in the forest to service requests, including modifications to

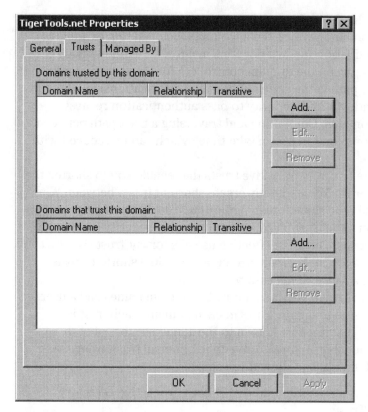

Figure 8.25 Creating an explicit domain trust.

the directory, by users. If you have a small deployment of well-connected computers, arbitrary selection of a domain controller may not cause problems. However, a deployment that comprises a wide area network (WAN) could be extraordinarily inefficient when, for example, users in, say, Sydney, Australia, attempt to authenticate to domain controllers in New York using a dial-up connection. Active Directory Sites and Services can improve the efficiency of directory services for most deployments through the use of *sites*.

You provide information about the physical structure of your network by publishing sites to Active Directory using Active Directory Sites and Services. Active Directory uses this information to determine how to replicate directory information and handle service requests.

Computers are assigned to sites based on their location in a *subnet* or in a set of well-connected subnets. Subnets provide a simple way to represent network groupings, much the same way that postal codes conveniently group mailing addresses. Subnets are formatted in terms that make it easy to post physical information about network connectivity to the directory. Having all computers in one or more well-connected subnets also reinforces the standard that all computers in a site must be well-connected, because computers in the same subnet typically have better connections than do an arbitrary selection of computers on a network.

Sites facilitate:

Authentication. When clients log on using a domain account, the logon mechanism first searches for domain controllers that are in the same site as the client. Attempting to use domain controllers in the client's site first localizes network traffic, increasing the efficiency of the authentication process.

Replication. Directory information is replicated both within and among sites. Active Directory replicates information within a site more frequently than across sites. This balances the need for up-to-date directory information with the limitations imposed by available network bandwidth. You customize how Active Directory replicates information using *site links* to specify how your sites are connected. Active Directory uses the information about how sites are connected to generate *Connection objects* that provide efficient replication and fault tolerance. You provide information about the cost of a site link, times when the link is available for use, and how often the link should be used. Active Directory uses this information to determine which site link will be used to replicate information. Customizing replication schedules so that replication occurs during specific times, such as when network traffic is low, makes replication more efficient. Ordinarily, all domain controllers are used to exchange information between sites, but you can further control replication behavior by specifying a *bridgehead server* for intersite replicated information. Establish a bridgehead server when you have a specific server you want to dedicate for intersite replication, rather than using any server available. You can also establish a bridgehead server when your deployment uses proxy servers, such as for sending and receiving information through a firewall.

Active Directory-enabled services. Information such as service bindings and configurations can be made available through the directory to make administration and use of network resources easier and more efficient. Sites help structure and optimize distribution of service information, so the current information is available to clients and distributed efficiently throughout your network.

To create a site, follow these steps:

1. From Start/Programs/Administrative Tools, click Active Directory Sites and Services.

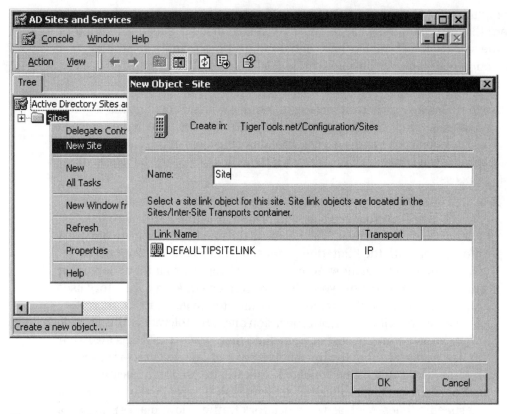

Figure 8.26 Creating a site.

2. Right-click the Sites folder, then click New Site.

3. In Name, type the name of the new site and click a site link object; click OK (see Figure 8.26).

Active Directory Sites and Services can be used only from a computer that has access to a Windows 2000 domain. Active Directory Sites and Services is installed on all Windows 2000 domain controllers. To use Active Directory Sites and Services on a computer that is not a domain controller, such as one running Windows 2000 Professional, install the Windows 2000 Administration Tools.

To create a subnet, using the Active Directory Sites and Services, follow these steps:

1. In the Console Tree, double-click Sites.

2. Right-click Subnets, then click New Subnet (see Figure 8.27).

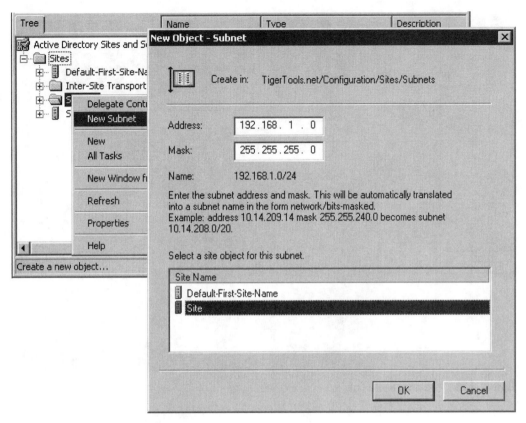

Figure 8.27 Creating a subnet.

3. In Address, enter the subnet address. In Mask, enter the subnet mask that describes the range of addresses included in this site's subnet.

4. Choose a site with which to associate this subnet; click OK.

Managing Replication

Creating a site link between two or more sites is a way to influence replication topology. By creating a site link, you provide Active Directory with information about which connections are available, which are preferred, and how much bandwidth is available. Active Directory uses this information to choose times and connections for replication that will afford the best performance.

To create a site link, using the Active Directory Sites and Services, follow these steps:

1. In the Console Tree, right-click the intersite transport protocol you want the site link to use, then click New Site Link (see Figure 8.28).

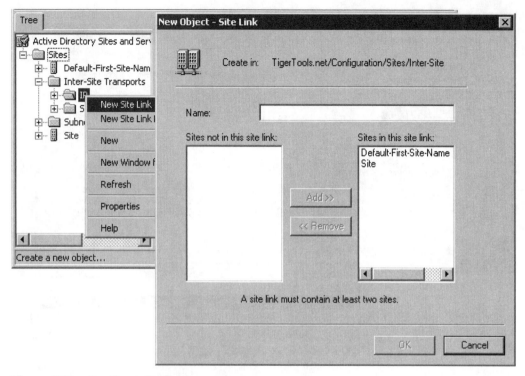

Figure 8.28 Creating a site link.

2. A new object site link window appears. From within this window, in Name, type the name to be given to the link.

3. Next, click two or more sites to connect, then click Add.

4. From the next window, configure the site link's cost, schedule, and replication frequency.

 If you create a site link that uses Simple Mail Transfer Protocol (SMTP), you must have an enterprise certification authority (Enterprise CA) available, and SMTP must be installed on all domain controllers that will use the site link.

File Server

In Windows 2000, Shared Folders replaces resource-related components in the Windows NT 4.0 Server Control Panel. With Shared Folders, you can perform the following tasks:

- Create, view, and set permissions for shares, including shares on computers running Windows NT 4.0.

- View a list of all users who are connected to the computer over a network and disconnect one or all of them.

- View a list of files opened by remote users and close one or all of the open files.

- Configure Services for Macintosh. This enables personal computer users and Macintosh users to share files and other resources, such as printing devices, through a computer running Windows 2000 Server. (This is available *only* on computers running Windows 2000 Server.) Macintosh clients need to run an Apple networking protocol to access Macintosh volumes and Macintosh printers.

Shared Folders provides information, arranged in columns, about all the shares, sessions, and open files on the local computer. A computer's shared resources include those resources (such as folders) that have been shared by a user or an administrator, plus any special shares that may have been created by the system.

Depending on the configuration of the computer being administered, some or all of the following special shares may appear when Windows 2000 presents a list of the computer's shared resources. Special shares are created by the system. In most cases, special shares should not be deleted or modified, including:

drive letter$. A share that allows administrative personnel to connect to the root directory of a storage device. Shown as A$, B$, C$, D$, and so on. For example, D$ is a sharename by which drive D might be accessed by an administrator over the network. For a Windows 2000 Professional computer, only members of the Administrators or Backup Operators group can connect to these shares. For a Windows 2000 Server computer, members of the Server Operators group can also connect to these shares.

ADMIN$. A resource used by the system during remote administration of a computer. The path of this resource is always the path to the Windows 2000 system root (the directory in which Windows 2000 is installed; for example, *C:\Winnt*).

IPC$. A resource sharing the named pipes that are essential for communication between programs. It is used during remote administration of a computer and when viewing a computer's shared resources.

PRINT$. A resource used during remote administration of printers.

NETLOGON. A resource used by the Net Logon service of a Windows 2000 Server computer while processing domain logon requests. This resource is provided only for Windows 2000 Server computers. It is not provided for Windows 2000 Professional computers.

FAX$. A share on a server used by fax clients in the process of sending a fax. The share is used to temporarily cache files and access cover pages stored on the server.

The following types of access permissions can be applied to shared folders:

Read. Allows viewing filenames and subfolder names, traversing to subfolders, viewing data in files, and running program files.

Change. Allows all Read permissions, plus adding files and subfolders, changing data in files, and deleting subfolders and files.

Full Control. The default permission applied to any new shares you create. It allows all Read and Change permissions, plus changing permissions (NTFS files and folders only) and taking ownership (NTFS files and folders only).

The Shared Folder Wizard is used to create folders that can be shared with other Windows systems and operating systems. From Start/Programs/Administrative Tools/Configure Your Server, start the wizard by clicking File Server from the left menu, and then follow these simple steps:

1. Click Start the Shared Folder Wizard.

2. Enter the folder to share, or click Browse to locate one manually.

3. Enter the Share name and description, then click Next (see Figure 8.29).

4. Choose one of the basic share permissions, as listed in Figure 8.30, or select Customize share and folder permissions and click Custom to create your own. The basic share permissions include:

   • All users have full control.

   • Administrators have full control; other users have read-only access.

   • Administrators have full control; other users have no access.

5. Click Finish to complete the share setup; click Yes to create another or No to exit.

To view a list of shares, sessions, or open files, double-click Shared Folders from Start/Programs/Administrative Tools/Computer Management, as shown in Figure 8.31.

To disconnect a user or users, in the Console Tree, click Sessions. To disconnect one user, right-click the username and click Close Session. To disconnect all users, click Action, then Disconnect All Sessions.

Figure 8.29   Using the Shared Folder Wizard to create a share.

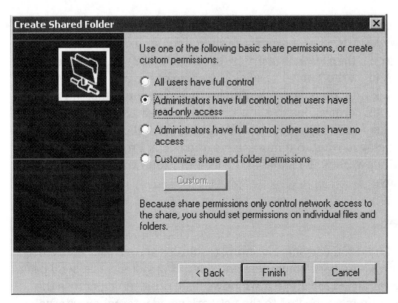

Figure 8.30   Using the Shared Folder Wizard to assign permissions to a share.

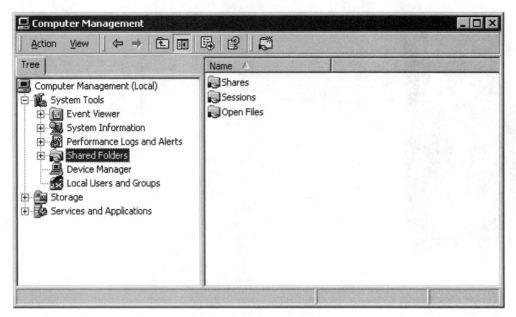

Figure 8.31 Accessing the shared folders utility.

 Disconnecting users who are using resources may result in loss of data. It is a good idea to warn connected users before disconnecting them.

To add a user or group to a shared folder, in the Console Tree, click Shares (refer to Figure 8.31). Next, right-click the shared folder to which you want to add a user or group, then click Properties (see Figure 8.32). In the Security tab window, click Add. In the Name list, click the name of the user or group you want to add, click Add, then click OK. Finally, on the Security tab, in Permissions, select which permissions to allow or deny the new user or group.

To remove a user or group from a shared folder, right-click the shared folder from which you want to remove users, then click Properties. In the Security tab window, click the name of the user or group you want to remove, and click Remove.

Print Server

With Windows 2000, you can share printing resources across your entire network. Clients on a variety of computers and operating systems can send print jobs to printers attached locally to a Windows 2000 print server, across the Internet, or to printers connected to the network using internal or external network adapters or another server.

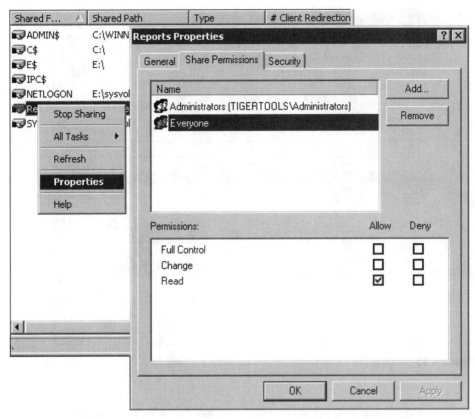

Figure 8.32 Adding a user or group to a shared folder.

Windows 2000 supports several advanced printing features. For example, you can administer a Windows 2000 print server that exists anywhere on your network. Another advanced feature is that you do not have to install a printer driver on a Windows 2000 client computer to enable it to use a printer. The driver is downloaded automatically when the client connects to a Windows 2000 print server.

 It is important to distinguish between a printer (the device that does the actual printing) and a logical printer (its software interface on the print server). When you initiate a print job, it is spooled on the logical printer, which is also called a printer, before it is sent to the printer itself.

The Add Printer Wizard helps you set up a local or network printer and publish to Active Directory. Run the wizard for each printer and platform you want to set up. After you run the wizard, network users can begin using the printer immediately. You can also administer the print server from any com-

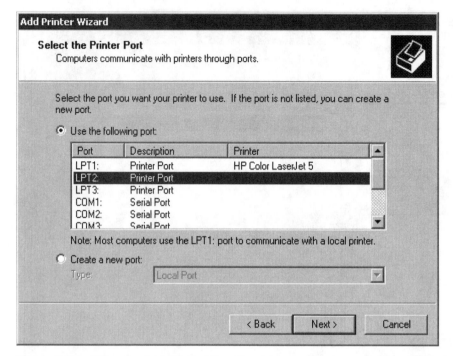

Figure 8.33 Using the Add Printer Wizard to share a printer.

puter on the network by using the Printers folder or a Web browser. From Start/Programs/Administrative Tools/Configure Your Server, start the wizard by clicking Print Server from the left menu; and then follow these simple steps:

1. Click Start the Add Printer Wizard and click Next.

2. Choose whether the printer will be a local (directly attached to the server) or network printer, then click Next.

3. Select the port you want the printer to use, or create a new one by selecting Create a new port (see Figure 8.33). Click Next to continue.

4. Select the manufacturer and model of the local printer; or click Have Disk to load drivers from an external source such as CD-ROM, floppy, or network drive. Click Next to continue.

5. Specify a printer name and click Next.

6. Indicate whether to share the printer with others. In this case, select Share as, and click Next.

7. Optionally, enter the printer location and/or comment to help others distinguish this printer from others; click Next.

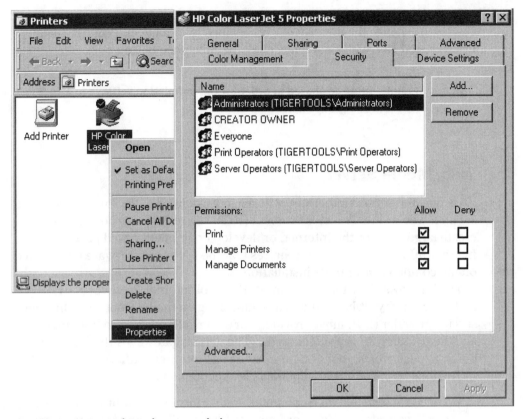

Figure 8.34 Managing printer permissions.

8. Select whether to print a test page; click Next and then Finish.

To set or remove permissions for a printer, open Printers from Start/Settings and follow these steps:

1. Right-click the printer for which you want to set permissions, click Properties (see Figure 8.34).

2. In the Security tab window, do one of the following:

   - To change or remove permissions from an existing user or group, click the name of the user or group.

   - To set up permissions for a new user or group, click Add. In Name, type the name of the user or group for which you want to set permissions, click Add, and then click OK to close the dialog box.

   - In Permissions, click Allow or Deny for each permission you want to allow or deny, or to remove the user or group from the permissions list, click Remove.

To change device settings, you must have the Manage Printers permission. To view or change the underlying permissions that make up Print, Manage Printers, and Manage Documents, click the Advanced button.

 A printer must be shared in order for the permission settings to affect the users and groups listed.

Web/Media Server

IIS is the Web service integrated with Windows 2000 Server. You can use IIS to set up a Web or File Transfer Protocol (FTP) site on your corporate intranet, create large sites for the Internet, or develop component-based programs. Internet Information Services requires that the following software be installed on the computer prior to its installation:

The Windows Transmission Control Protocol/Internet Protocol (TCP/IP) and Connectivity Utilities. If you are publishing on the Internet, your Internet service provider (ISP) must provide your server's IP address, subnet mask, and the default gateway's IP address. (The default gateway is the ISP computer through which your computer routes all Internet traffic.)

The following optional components are recommended:

- The DNS, installed on a computer in your intranet. If your intranet is small, you can use Hosts or Lmhosts files on all computers in your network. This step, although optional, is important because it enables users to use memory-friendly text names instead of harder-to-remember numeric IP addresses. On the Internet, Web sites usually use DNS. If you register a domain name for your site, users can type your site's domain name in a browser to contact your site.

- For security purposes, Microsoft recommends that all drives used with IIS be formatted with NTFS.

- Microsoft FrontPage to create and edit Hypertext Markup Language (HTML) pages for your Web site. FrontPage is a "what you see is what you get"—WYSIWYG—editor that provides a friendly, graphical interface for tasks such as inserting tables, graphics, and scripts.

- Microsoft Visual InterDev, a Web development tool designed for programmers to create and develop interactive Web applications.

Internet Information Services 5.0 is installed on Windows 2000 Server by default. You can remove IIS or select additional components by using the Add/Remove Programs application in Control Panel. If you remove the service and wish to install IIS again:

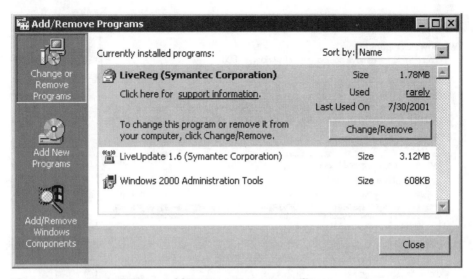

Figure 8.35   Win 2K Server Add/Remove Programs utility.

1. From Start/Settings/Control Panel, double-click Add/Remove Programs (see Figure 8.35).

2. Select the Add/Remove Windows Components button and then follow the on-screen instructions to Add or remove components (see Figure 8.36).

To begin the IIS install process, simply check to install Internet Information Service from the components list and click Next. If prompted for the location of the service files, insert your Windows 2000 Server CD-ROM and click OK. After Setup copies the necessary files, click Finish to complete the installation.

To manage your Web services, start the Internet Information Services utility from Start/Programs/Administrative Tools/Internet Services Manager shown in Figure 8.37. You can view the product documentation by typing `http://localhost/iisHelp/` in your browser address bar and pressing Enter on the keyboard.

Streaming Media Server

As an enhancement to IIS, Windows Media Services enables you to stream multimedia content over your Internet/intranet and/or networks that range from low-bandwidth, dial-up Internet connections to high-bandwidth, local area networks. When you install Windows Media Services, you can choose Windows Media Services in the Windows Components Wizard to install the Windows Media component services and Windows Media Administrator. Click

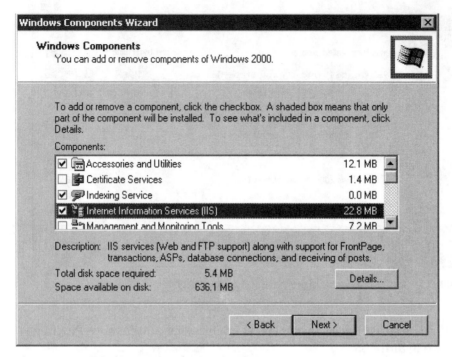

Figure 8.36   Windows Components Wizard.

Details and select only Windows Media Services Admin to install only Windows Media Administrator. Install only Windows Media Administrator if you want to remotely administer a Windows Media server.

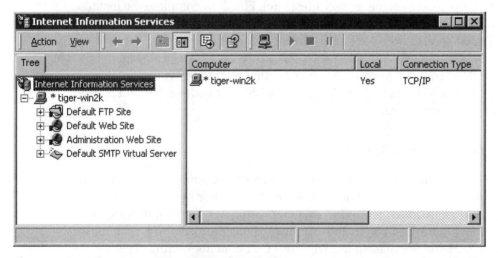

Figure 8.37   Win 2K Server Internet Services Manager.

The Windows Components Wizard helps you create and publish streaming multimedia presentations (i.e., real-time audio and video presentations) with your intranet or Internet services via Windows Media Services. From Start/Programs/Administrative Tools/Configure Your Server, start the wizard by clicking Web/Media Server from the left menu and then follow these simple steps:

1. Click Start the Windows Components Wizard.

2. Check to install Windows Media Services from the components list, and then click Next. If prompted for the location of the service files, insert your Windows 2000 Server CD-ROM and click OK.

3. After Setup copies the necessary files, click Finish to complete the installation.

When you employ Windows Media Services on your Web site, you will see that it works similarly to a Web server. You will also see that it can add capabilities to your Web site, such as enabling radio and television programs, slide show presentations, file transfers, movies, and multimedia shows.

 It is recommended that you dedicate a separate NTFS volume for storing on-demand content. For best results, this volume should be on a separate physical disk. NTFS volumes are more efficient than FAT16 partitions, in terms of storage space used and disk-read operations. An NTFS volume also permits use of access control list (ACL) checking on your content files.

To start Windows Media Administrator, from Start/Programs/Administrative Tools, click Windows Media (see Figure 8.38). Follow the on-screen steps to configure the new media services.

As a component of the Windows media system, Windows Media Encoder encodes audio and video content into an Advanced Streaming Format (ASF) stream that can be delivered to a Windows Media server or written to an .asf file. The content can be from a live source or an existing .avi, .wav, or .mp3 file. The output from Windows Media Encoder is a stream of information that can be heard or viewed with Microsoft Windows Media Player or sent to a Windows Media server for multicasting, unicasting, or storage.

 Because the process of encoding and compressing video and audio content requires a high percentage of the computer's processing capability, it is advised that you run Windows Media Encoder on a separate computer from the one that is running the Windows Media server components.

Figure 8.38 Windows Media Administrator.

Windows Media Encoder

Windows Media Encoder is used to create an .asd file, which contains information about the media types, **co**mpressors/**dec**ompressors (codecs), and bandwidth setting used to create an ASF stream—the *stream format*. If you are delivering the stream to a Windows Media server and do not use a template stream format (TSF) to create your content stream, it is necessary to propagate the .asd file to the Windows Media server so that the Windows Media component services can recognize the stream format. Template stream formats are known to the Windows Media component services, so you do not have to supply the .asd file to the server for it to interpret a stream that was encoded using a template.

To start Windows Media Encoder, from Start/Programs/Windows Media Tools, click Windows Media Encoder (see Figure 8.39). Follow the on-screen steps to configure the encoder with the media server.

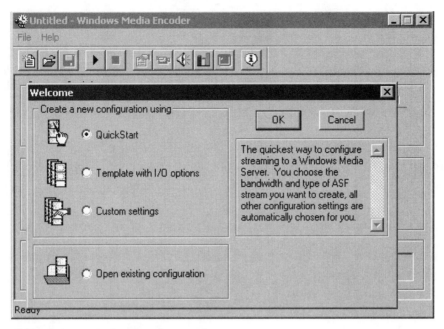

Figure 8.39　Windows Media Encoder.

Moving Forward

Now that you're familiar with the differences between Windows 2000 Server and its Windows NT predecessor we can move on to the next chapter where we delve into a number of Win 2K Server networking services and their configurations. We'll start with TCP/IP as a suite of standard protocols for connecting computers and building networks, and work our through the accompanying services of the Dynamic Host Configuration Protocol (DHCP), remote access, routing, terminal services, and managing the previously installed DNS.

Win 2K Networking Services Configuration

In this chapter we'll configure the Transmission Control Protocol/Internet Protocol (TCP/IP), as well as the networking services of Dynamic Host Configuration Protocol (DHCP). We'll also cover remote access and routing and learn to manage the Domain Name Service (DNS), which we installed previously.

Step-by-Step TCP/IP Customization

The Networking Configuration Wizard, accessible from Start/Programs/Administrative Tools/Configure Your Server, allows for the configuration of most of the services we're exploring in this chapter. Typically, during the standard Windows 2000 (Win 2K) Server installation, simple TCP/IP services, including network interface card (NIC) configurations (using a DHCP client), are installed. In this section, you'll learn how to customize that configuration to conform to your own network operating standards.

To begin, from Start/Settings/Control Panel/Network and Dial-up Connections, double-click Local Area Connection (see Figure 9.1) to access the Local Area Connection Status box. Right off the bat you'll notice general packet activity status (helpful when troubleshooting connectivity) and that you have the capability to halt communications by clicking Disable.

Next to the Disable button is the Properties button, which is what we'll use to customize TCP/IP configuration. Click on Properties to open the LAN

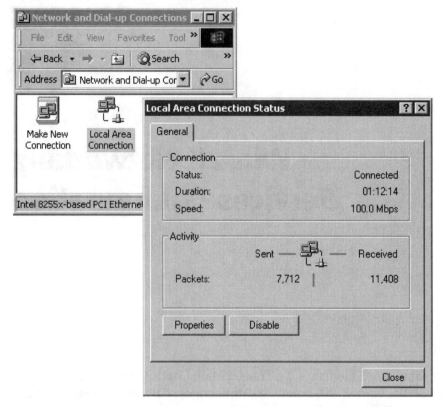

Figure 9.1   Simple TCP/IP management utility.

Connection Properties window shown in Figure 9.2. To configure TCP/IP for static addressing, on the General tab (for a local area connection) or the Networking tab (all other connections), click to select Internet Protocol (TCP/IP), then click Properties. That will lead you to the screen shown in Figure 9.3. From there do the following:

1. In the IP Properties screen, click Use the following IP address, and do one of the following:

   • For a local area connection, type the IP address, subnet mask, and default gateway addresses (described in Chapter 2) in the appropriate fields.

   • For all other connections, type the IP address in that field.

2. Click Use the following DNS server addresses. In Preferred DNS server and Alternate DNS server, type the primary and secondary DNS server addresses (described in Chapter 7).

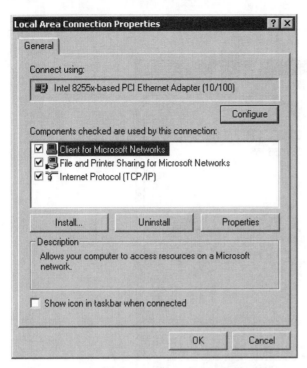

Figure 9.2   LAN Connection Properties window.

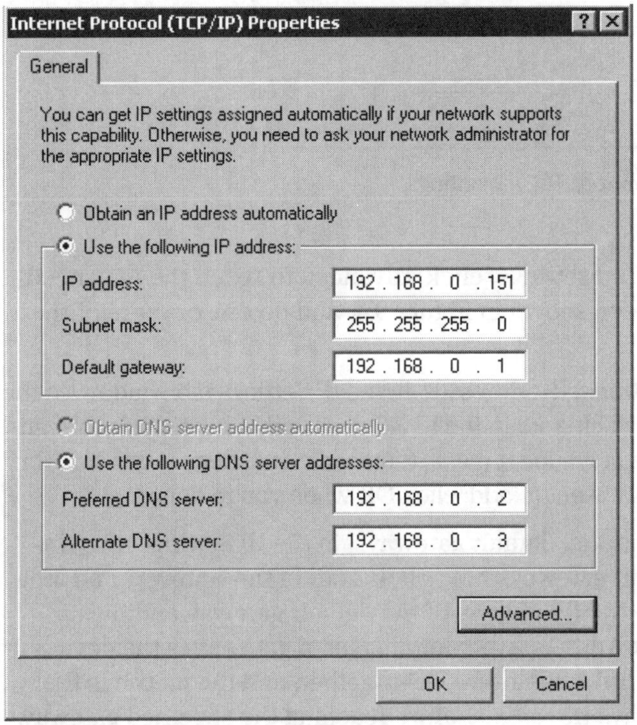

Figure 9.3   Configuring static IP addressing.

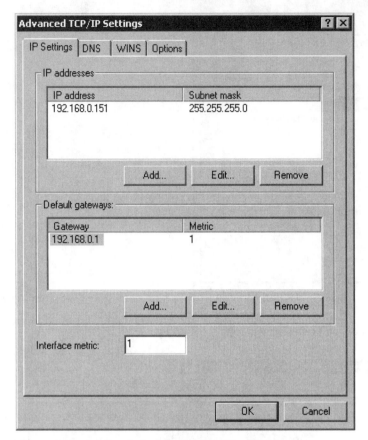

Figure 9.4 Configuring advanced TCP/IP settings.

3. To configure advanced settings, click Advanced to reach the Advanced TCP/IP Settings screen shown in Figure 9.4, and do one or more of the following:

- To configure additional IP addresses, in the IP Settings tab window, in the IP addresses box, click Add. In the IP Address and Subnet mask columns, type an IP address and subnet mask, then click Add. Repeat this step for each IP address you want to add; click OK when you're done.

- To configure additional default gateways, in the IP Settings tab window, in the Default gateways box, click Add. In the Gateway and Metric columns, type the IP address of the default gateway and the metric, then click Add. As a memory jogger, a gateway is the device (i.e., router) that links two networks together, and the metric is the number of gateways traversed before reaching the specified gateway. Repeat this step for each default gateway you want to add; click OK when you're done.

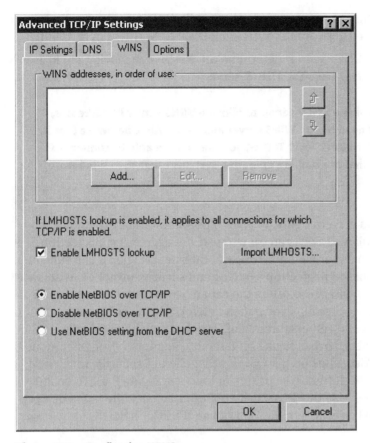

Figure 9.5 Configuring WINS.

- To configure a custom metric for this connection, type a metric value in Interface metric.

4. Optionally, you can configure TCP/IP to use the Windows Internet Naming Service (WINS). To do that, click the WINS tab to access the screen shown in Figure 9.5 and then click Add. In TCP/IP WINS server window, type the IP address of the WINS server, and click Add. Repeat this step for each WINS server IP address you want to add; click OK.

   - To enable the use of the LMHOSTS file to resolve remote NetBIOS names, select the Enable LMHOSTS lookup check box. This option is enabled by default.

   - To specify the location of the file that you want to import into the LMHOSTS file, click Import LMHOSTS, and select the file in the Open dialog box.

   - To modify the behavior of NetBIOS over TCP/IP behavior by enabling the use of NetBIOS over TCP/IP, click Enable NetBIOS over TCP/IP.

- To modify the behavior of NetBIOS over TCP/IP behavior by disabling the use of NetBIOS over TCP/IP, click Disable NetBIOS over TCP/IP.
- To have the DHCP server determine the NetBIOS behavior, click Use NetBIOS setting from the DHCP server.

 If you are using a DHCP server to allocate WINS server IP addresses, you do not need to add WINS server addresses. Also, be aware that if you disable NetBIOS over TCP/IP, you may not be able to connect to computers that are running operating systems other than Windows 2000.

5. Optionally, you can configure TCP/IP to use an Internet Protocol security (IPSec) policy. IPSec is an easy-to-use, yet aggressive, protection mechanism against private network and Internet attacks. It is a suite of cryptography-based protection services and security protocols with end-to-end security. IPSec also offers the capability to protect communications between workgroups, local area network (LAN) computers, domain clients and servers, branch offices that may be physically remote, extranets, roving clients, and remote administration of computers. To add IPSec, click on the Options tab, click IP security, then click Properties to reach the IP Security window (see Figure 9.6). To enable IP security, click Use this IP security policy, then click the name of a policy. To disable IP security, click Do not use IPSEC. Click OK.

 The Windows 2000 implementation of IPSec is based on industry standards in development by the Internet Engineering Task Force (IETF) IPSec working group.

6. TCP/IP filtering is a security measure that specifies the types of incoming traffic that are to be passed to the TCP/IP protocol suite for processing. You can opt to configure TCP/IP to use TCP/IP filtering. To do so, again in the Options tab window, click TCP/IP filtering, then Properties (see Figure 9.7).

- To enable TCP/IP filtering for all adapters, select the Enable TCP/IP Filtering (All adapters) check box.
- To disable TCP/IP filtering for all adapters, clear the Enable TCP/IP Filtering (All adapters) check box.

Based on your requirements for TCP/IP filtering, configure TCP ports, User Datagram Protocol (UDP) ports, or IP protocols for the allowed traffic. Click OK when finished.

7. Click OK again, then Close to finish.

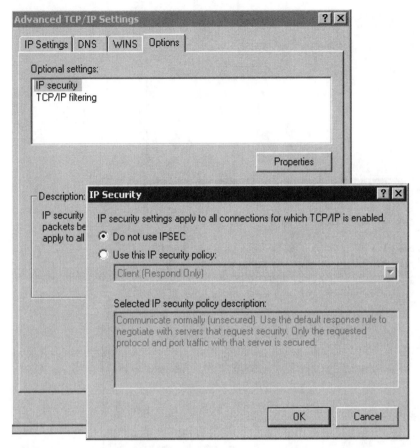

Figure 9.6   Configuring IPSec.

Dynamic Host Configuration Protocol

The DHCP is a TCP/IP standard designed to reduce the complexity of administering address configurations. It implements a server computer to centrally manage IP addresses and other related configuration details used on your network. Windows 2000 Server provides the DHCP service, which enables the server computer to perform as a DHCP server and enables you to configure DHCP-enabled client computers on your network, as described in the current DHCP draft standard, RFC 2131.

As discussed early in this book, every computer on a TCP/IP network must have a unique computer name and IP address. The IP address (together with its related subnet mask) identifies the host computer and the subnet to which it is attached. When you move a computer to a different subnet, the IP address must be changed. DHCP allows you to dynamically assign an IP address to a client from a DHCP server IP address database on your local network.

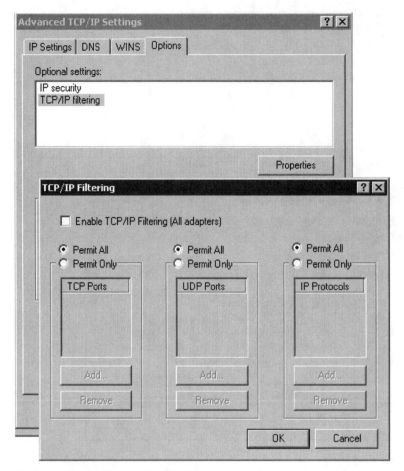

Figure 9.7 Configuring TCP/IP filtering.

DHCP uses a client/server model, meaning that the network administrator establishes one or more DHCP servers that maintain TCP/IP configuration information and provide it to clients. The server database includes the following:

- Valid configuration parameters for all clients on the network.
- Valid IP addresses maintained in a pool for assignment to clients, plus reserved addresses for manual assignment.
- Duration of a lease offered by the server. The lease defines the length of time for which the assigned IP address can be used.

With a DHCP server installed and configured on your network, DHCP-enabled clients can obtain their IP address and related configuration parameters dynamically each time they join your network. DHCP servers provide this configuration in the form of an address-lease offer to requesting clients.

DHCP Terminology

Before explaining how to install and configure DHCP, it's essential that you get some related terminology under your belt to help you understand all that we'll be doing in this section.

Scope. The full consecutive range of possible IP addresses for a network. Scopes typically define a single physical subnet on your network to which DHCP services are offered. Scopes also provide the primary way for the server to manage distribution and assignment of IP addresses and any related configuration parameters to clients on the network.

Superscope. An administrative grouping of scopes that can be used to support multiple logical IP subnets on the same physical subnet. Superscopes only contain a list of member scopes or child scopes that can be activated together. Superscopes are not used to configure other details about scope usage. For configuring most properties used within a superscope, you need to configure member scope properties individually.

Exclusion range. A limited sequence of IP addresses within a scope, excluded from DHCP service offerings. Exclusion ranges assure that addresses in these ranges are not offered by the server to DHCP clients on your network.

Address pool. After you define a DHCP scope and apply exclusion ranges, the remaining addresses form the available address pool within the scope. Pooled addresses are eligible for dynamic assignment by the server to DHCP clients on your network.

Lease. A length of time, specified by a DHCP server, during which a client computer can use an assigned IP address. When a lease is made to a client, the lease is active. Before the lease expires, the client typically needs to renew its address lease assignment with the server. A lease becomes inactive when it expires or is deleted at the server. The duration of a lease determines when it will expire and how often the client needs to renew it with the server.

Reservation. Used to create a permanent address lease assignment by the DHCP server. Reservations assure that a specified hardware device on the subnet can always use the same IP address.

Option types. Other client configuration parameters a DHCP server can assign when serving leases to DHCP clients. For example, some commonly used options include IP addresses for default gateways (routers), WINS servers, and DNS servers. Typically, these option types are enabled and configured for each scope. The DHCP console also permits you to configure default option types that are used by all scopes added and configured at the server. Most options are predefined through RFC 2132, but you can use the DHCP console to define and add custom option types if needed.

Options class. A way for the server to further manage option types provided to clients. When an options class is added to the server, clients of that class can be provided class-specific option types for their configuration. For Windows 2000, client computers can also specify a class ID when communicating with the server. For earlier DHCP clients that do not support the class ID process, the server can be configured with default classes to use instead when placing clients in a class. Options classes can be of two types: vendor classes and user classes.

The primary tool that you use to manage DHCP servers is the DHCP console, which is added to the Administrative Tools folder in Control Panel when you install a DHCP server for Windows 2000 Server. The DHCP console appears as a Microsoft Management Console (MMC) snap-in and further integrates DHCP administration into your total network management.

This version of the DHCP console also contains new features and enhancements, many of which were suggested by network managers. These include enhanced server performance monitoring, more predefined DHCP option types, dynamic update support for clients running earlier versions of Windows, and detection of unauthorized DHCP servers on your network.

DHCP Installation

To set up DHCP, use the Windows Components Wizard. From Start/Programs/Administrative Tools/Configure Your Server, click Networking/DHCP in the left menu, and then follow these simple steps:

1. Click-start the Windows Components Wizard.

2. Under Networking Services, check to install Dynamic Host Configuration Protocol (DHCP) from the components list, click OK, then Next. If prompted for the location of the service files, insert your Windows 2000 Server CD-ROM and click OK.

3. After Setup copies the necessary files, click Finish to complete the installation.

To open the DHCP console, from Start/Programs/Administrative Tools, click DHCP (see Figure 9.8). The DHCP console is an administrative tool for managing DHCP servers.

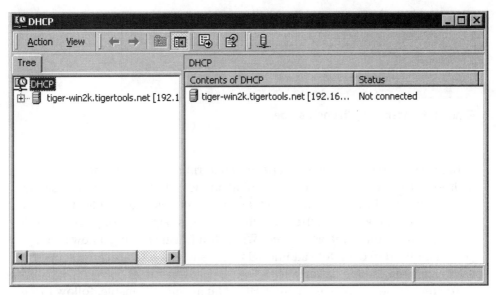

Figure 9.8 DHCP management console.

DHCP Configuration

After you install a DHCP server, you can use the DHCP console to perform these basic administrative server tasks: create scopes, add and configure superscopes (for grouping multiple scopes as a single administrative entity) and multicast scopes (new proposed standard for performing multicast address allocation), view and modify scope properties for scopes (such as setting additional exclusion ranges), activate scopes or superscopes, monitor scope leasing activity occasionally by reviewing the active leases for each scope, and create reservations in scopes as needed for DHCP clients that require a permanent IP address for leased use.

In addition, you can use the DHCP console to perform the following optional or advanced setup tasks:

- Add new custom default option types
- Add and configure any user- or vendor-defined option classes
- Further configure other server properties, such as audit logging or BOOTP tables

Creating Scopes

 In many of the steps to follow, the Next and Finish buttons have been cut out from the figures in this book for brevity.

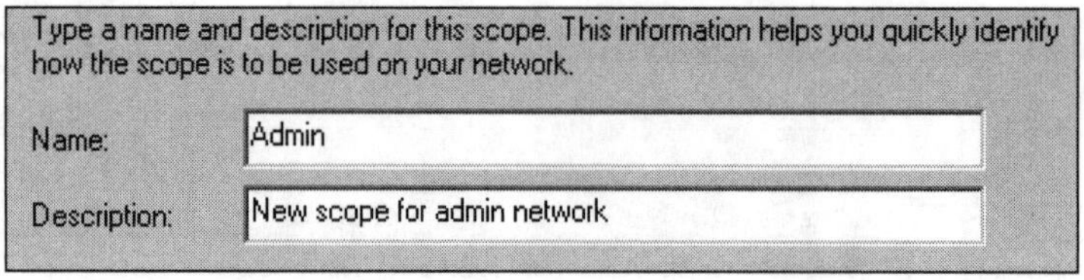

> Type a name and description for this scope. This information helps you quickly identify
> how the scope is to be used on your network.
>
> Name: Admin
>
> Description: New scope for admin network

Figure 9.9   Identifying the new scope.

Before you create a scope, you need to determine start and end IP
addresses to be used within it. Depending on these addresses for your scope,
the DHCP console suggests a default subnet mask that is useful for most networks. If you know that a different subnet mask is required for your network,
you can modify the value as needed. When you finish creating a new scope,
you might need to complete additional tasks, such as activating the scope for
use or assigning scope options.

To create a new scope using the DHCP Management Console, follow these
steps:

1. On the Action menu, click New Scope to start the New Scope Wizard.

2. The wizard will help set up a new scope for distributing IP addresses.
   Click Next to begin.

3. Provide a scope name and optional description in the fields provided
   (see Figure 9.9), then click Next.

4. Define the scope range with consecutive IP addresses in the Start IP and
   End IP address fields, then select the appropriate subnet mask and click
   Next (see Figure 9.10).

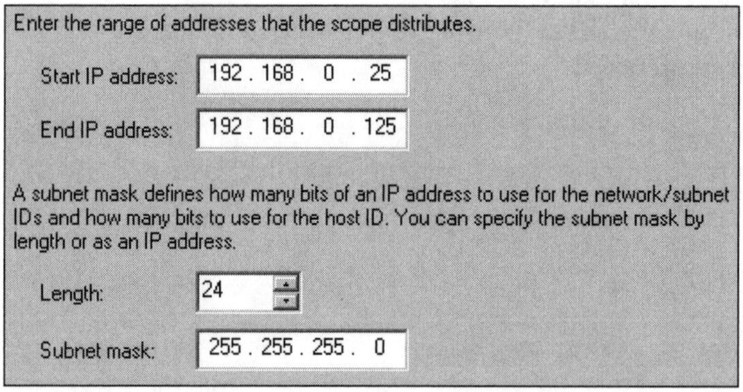

> Enter the range of addresses that the scope distributes.
>
> Start IP address: 192 . 168 . 0 . 25
>
> End IP address: 192 . 168 . 0 . 125
>
> A subnet mask defines how many bits of an IP address to use for the network/subnet
> IDs and how many bits to use for the host ID. You can specify the subnet mask by
> length or as an IP address.
>
> Length: 24
>
> Subnet mask: 255 . 255 . 255 . 0

Figure 9.10   Identifying the scope IP address range with mask.

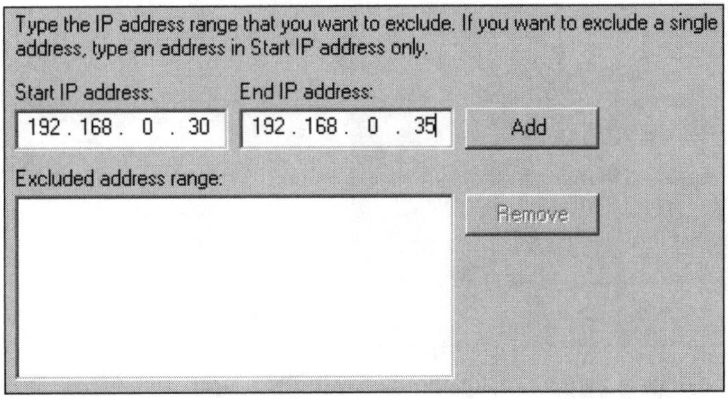

Figure 9.11 Identifying exclusive IP addresses.

5. Optionally, as shown in Figure 9.11, define the exclusive IP addresses or those within the scope range that should not be distributed (because they may be already in use); click Add. Click Next when you're finished.

6. Define the lease duration, or how long a client can use an IP address from the scope, in days/hours/minutes, as shown in Figure 9.12, then click Next.

7. On the next screen, configure the most common DHCP options, such as router, DNS, and WINS settings, by selecting Yes, I want to configure these now, then click Next.

8. Define the router(s) or default gateways that should be distributed to clients using the scope. Enter the IP address and click Add (see Figure 9.13); repeat as necessary. If there is more than one address listed, you can set the address delegation priority by selecting an address and clicking Up or Down to maneuver it about the list. Click Next when you're ready to continue.

9. Define the DNS domain and servers that should be distributed to the clients. Enter the parent domain name in the Parent domain field and the

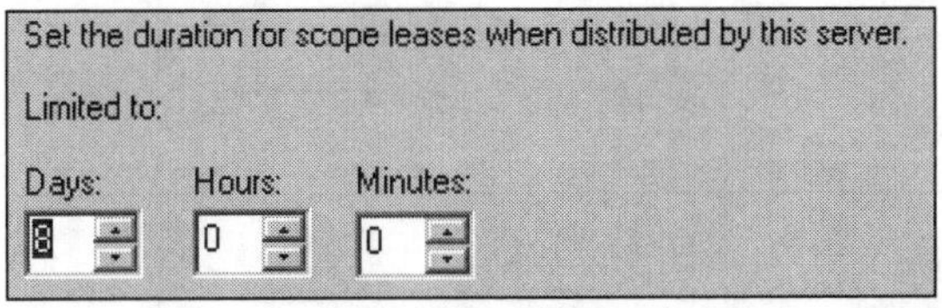

Figure 9.12 Identifying the IP address lease duration.

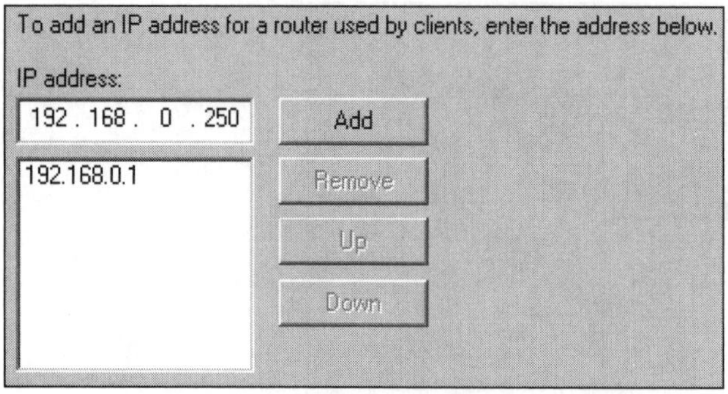

Figure 9.13   Defining the default gateway(s) distributed with the scope.

IP address of any DNS servers on the network (see Figure 9.14). You may optionally enter the DNS server name in the Server name field and click Resolve to have Setup automatically find the IP address of the server. Click Add to insert each address. If there is more than one address listed, you can set the address delegation priority by selecting an address and clicking Up or Down to maneuver it about the list. Click Next to continue.

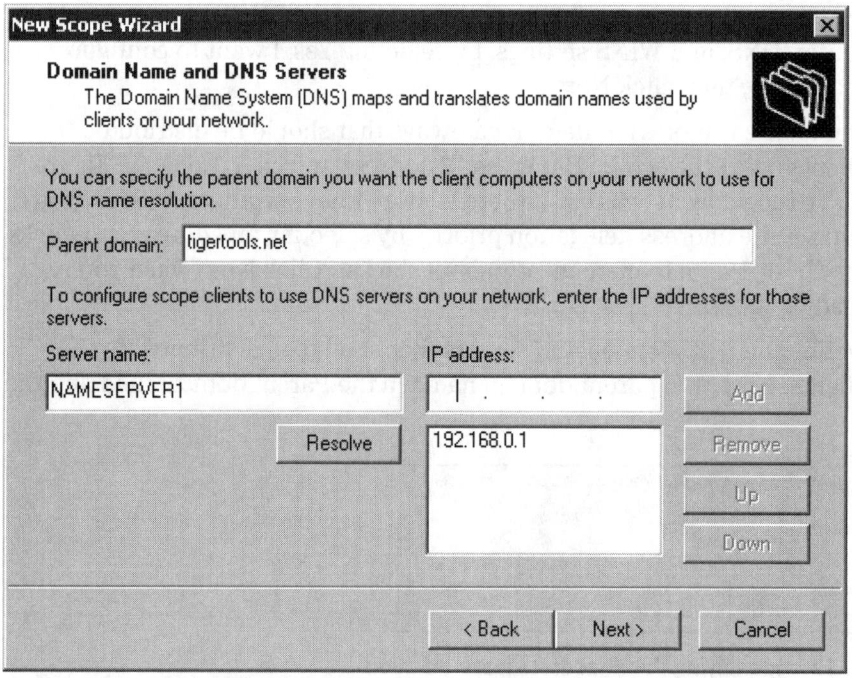

Figure 9.14   Defining DNS server addresses.

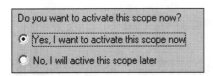

Figure 9.15 Activating the new scope.

10. Define the WINS server(s) that should be distributed to the clients. You may opt to enter the DNS server name in the Server name field and click Resolve to have Setup automatically find the IP address of the server. Click Add to insert each address. If there is more than one address listed, you can set the address delegation priority by selecting an address; click Up or Down to maneuver in the list. Click Next to continue.

11. To activate the scope so that clients can start obtaining IP addresses, select Yes, I want to activate this scope now, and click Next (see Figure 9.15). Click Finish to acknowledge the configuration.

12. A DHCP server must be authorized in the Active Directory before it can distribute IP addresses. To authorize the DHCP server, in the management console select the DHCP server in question and, on the Action menu, click Authorize.

Editing or Viewing Scope Properties

To change or view scope properties, in the Console Tree, click the applicable scope (see Figure 9.16), and on the Action menu, click Properties. Click the tab to view DNS options, and click the fields within to enter any changes.

The subnet identifiers and address pool (defined by the Start and End IP addresses used to create the scope) make up the basic properties of a scope. Some, but not all, properties can be changed:

- You can change only certain properties of an existing scope: exclusion ranges, client reservations, configured scope option type values, or the time set for leasing scope addresses to clients.

- You cannot exclude a range of addresses that includes an active lease. You must first delete the active lease and then retry the exclusion.

- You can extend the address range of the scope, but you cannot reduce it. However, you can at any time selectively exclude any unwanted addresses from the full scope range of addresses.

Creating Superscopes

A superscope is an administrative feature of Windows 2000 DHCP servers that you can create and manage through the DHCP console. Using a superscope,

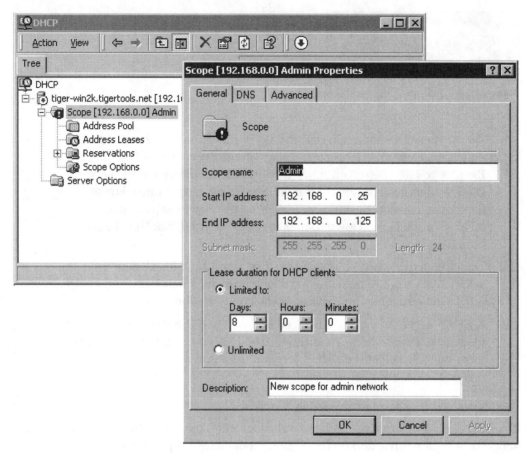

Figure 9.16 Editing the new scope.

you can group multiple scopes as a single administrative entity. With this feature, a DHCP server can:

- Support DHCP clients on a single physical network segment (such as a single Ethernet LAN segment) where multiple logical IP networks are used. When more than one logical IP network is used on each physical subnet or network, such configurations are often called *multinets*.
- Support remote DHCP clients located on the opposite side of DHCP and BOOTP relay agents (where the network on the far side of the relay agent uses multinets).

In multinet configurations, you can use DHCP superscopes to group and activate individual scope ranges of IP addresses used on your network. In this way, a DHCP server computer can activate and provide leases from more than one scope to clients on a single physical network.

Superscopes can resolve certain types of DHCP deployment issues for multinets, including situations in which:

- The available address pool for a currently active scope is nearly depleted and more computers need to be added to the network. The original scope includes the full addressable range for a single IP network of a specified address class. You need to use another IP network range of addresses to extend the address space for the same physical network segment.

- Clients must be migrated over time to a new scope (such as to renumber the current IP network from an address range used in an existing active scope to a new scope that contains another IP network range of addresses).

- You want to use two DHCP servers on the same physical network segment to manage separate logical IP networks.

A superscope can have scopes added to it, either during or after its creation. Scopes that are contained within superscopes are sometimes called *child scopes* or *member scopes*. To create a superscope using the DHCP management console, on the Action menu, click New Superscope to start the wizard. *Note*: This menu option only appears if at least one scope that is not currently part of a superscope has been created at the server.

1. Click Next to begin.

2. Provide a superscope name (see Figure 9.17), click Next.

3. Select a current scope to add to the superscope (see Figure 9.18); click Next, then Finish.

Only new superscopes need to be activated. When you activate a superscope, it activates all of its member scopes on your network. You must activate a superscope to make IP addresses for all of its member scopes available for use by DHCP clients.

 Do not activate a superscope until you specify the options you want for each of its member scopes.

The Action menu command changes to Deactivate when the selected scope is currently activated. Do not deactivate a superscope unless you

Name:	TigerLAN

Figure 9.17 Identifying the new superscope.

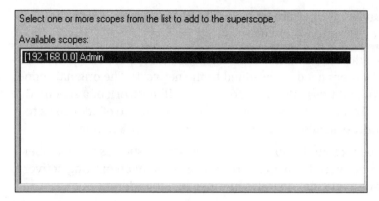

Figure 9.18 Building the superscope collection of scopes.

intend to permanently retire all of its member scopes from use on your network.

To activate/deactivate a superscope, in the Console Tree, locate and select the applicable superscope, then click Activate/Deactivate on the Action menu (see Figure 9.19).

Creating Multicast Scopes

According to Microsoft, multicast scopes are supported through the use of the Multicast Address Dynamic Client Allocation Protocol (MADCAP), a new pro-

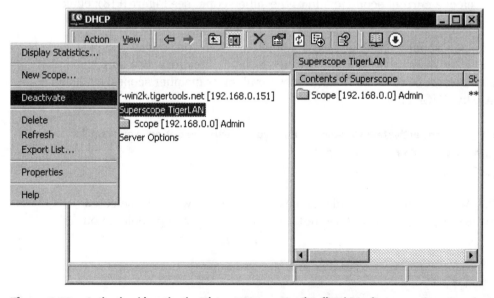

Figure 9.19 Activating/deactivating the superscope and collection of scopes.

posed standard for performing multicast address allocation. The MADCAP protocol describes how multicast address allocation (or MADCAP) servers can dynamically provide IP addresses to other computers (MADCAP clients) on your network.

Typically, a MADCAP client might also be a multicast server (MCS) used to support IP multicasting. An MCS, such as a server computer running the Site Server Internet Location Server (ILS) service, manages the shared or group use of the allocated multicast IP address and streams data traffic to members that share the use of the specified group address.

Once an MCS is configured and allocated a group IP address to use, any multicast clients that have registered their membership with the MCS can receive streams sent to this address. By registering with the MCS, clients can participate efficiently in the stream process, such as for real-time video or audio network transmissions. The MCS also manages the multicast group list, updating its membership and status so that multicast traffic is received by all current members.

Ordinarily, you use DHCP scopes to provide client configurations by allocating ranges of IP addresses from the standard address classes, A, B, or C. Using DHCP scopes, you can assign IP addresses from the ranges provided by these addresses to your DHCP clients for configuration as unicast- (or point-to-point) directed communication between other TCP/IP networked computers. The multicast address range uses an additional address class, D, that includes IP addresses that range from 224.0.0.0 to 239.255.255.255 for use in IP multicasting—and multicasting only, not for regular DHCP scopes.

In all TCP/IP networks, each host is required to be configured first with its own IP address, taken from one of the standard address classes. You must assign this required unicast IP address before you can configure a host to support and use secondary IP addresses, such as a multicast IP address.

Another difference between unicast and multicast addresses is that a group of TCP/IP host computers are able to share the use of a multicast IP address. This is not normally the case with unicast IP addresses, which are assigned individually to only one configured host and not shared with other hosts.

When the destination address for an IP datagram is an IP multicast address, the datagram is forwarded to all members of a multicast group, which is a set of zero or more hosts identified by the address. The membership of a multicast group is dynamic in that individual hosts can join or leave the group at any time.

Membership and use of multicast groups is unrestricted and can be compared to membership and use of a group email address: Group membership can be any size, and hosts can be members of many multicast groups.

You can permanently reserve multicast group addresses or temporarily assign and use them as needed on your network. For a permanent group IP address to be reserved for Internet use, you must register it with the Internet Assigned Numbers Authority (IANA).

For multicast IP addresses not permanently reserved with the IANA, all Class D addresses that remain unreserved can then be used dynamically to assign and form temporary multicast groups. These temporary groups can exist as long as one or more hosts on the network are configured with the group address and actively share its use.

The Windows 2000 DHCP Server service supports both the DHCP and MADCAP protocols. These protocols function separately and are not dependent on each other. For example, a DHCP client might or might not be a MADCAP client, and a MADCAP client might or night not be a DHCP client.

 Multicast scopes and MADCAP only provide a mechanism for dynamically allocating IP address configuration for multicast-ranged IP addresses.

To create a multicast scope using the DHCP management console, go to the Action menu and click New Multicast Scope to start the wizard. *Note*: This menu option appears only if at least one scope that is not currently part of a superscope has been created at the server.

1. Click Next to begin.

2. Provide a multicast scope name and optional description in the fields provided; click Next.

3. Define the scope range with addresses in the Start IP and End IP address fields (the valid range is 224.0.0.0 to 239.255.255.255.255), then select the Time to Live (TTL), which is the number of routers the multicast traffic must traverse, and click Next (see Figure 9.20).

4. Optionally, define the exclusive addresses, those within the scope range that should not be distributed because they may be already in use, and click Add. Click Next when finished.

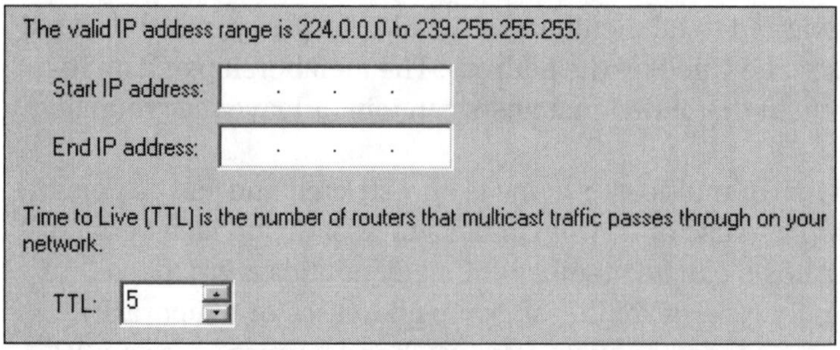

The valid IP address range is 224.0.0.0 to 239.255.255.255.

Start IP address: _____

End IP address: _____

Time to Live (TTL) is the number of routers that multicast traffic passes through on your network.

TTL: 5

Figure 9.20   Identifying the scope address range with TTL.

5. Define the lease duration, or how long a client can use an IP address from the scope, in days/hours/minutes, and click Next.

6. To activate the scope so that clients can start obtaining IP addresses, select Yes, I want to activate this scope now, and click Next. Click Finish to acknowledge the configuration.

7. By default, multicast scopes do not expire. Once created, they typically exist until they are manually removed. You can manually remove a multicast scope by selecting the scope and clicking Remove from the Action menu. The following procedure, however, can be used to have the DHCP server automatically remove the multicast scope at an appointed future date and time. To specify a finite lifetime for a multicast scope, in the Console Tree, click the applicable multicast scope; then on the Action menu, click Properties. In the Lifetime tab window, click Multicast scope expires on and specify a date and time when the multicast scope is to be expired and removed from the applicable DHCP server (see Figure 9.21).

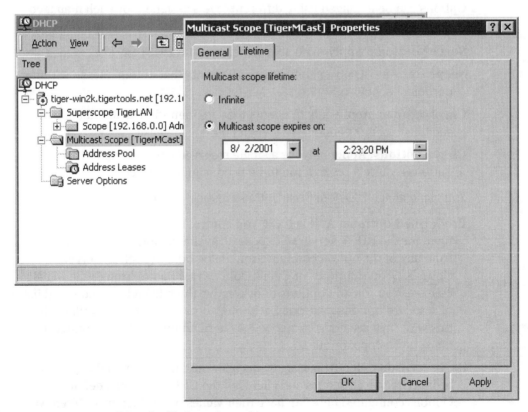

Figure 9.21 Specifying the lifetime of a multicast scope.

Managing DHCP Options

DHCP provides an internal framework for passing on configuration information to clients on your network. Configuration parameters and other control information are carried in *tagged data items* stored within protocol messages exchanged between the DHCP server and its clients. These data items are called *options*.

 Most standard DHCP options are currently defined in Requests for Comments (RFCs) published by the IETF. The full set of standard DHCP options is described specifically in RFC 2132, "DHCP Options and BOOTP Vendor Extensions." All DHCP options mentioned in RFC 2132 are predefined for you to configure and use at any Windows 2000 DHCP server. If needed, you can also use the DHCP console to define new DHCP options at each server. Even though most DHCP servers can assign many options, most DHCP clients are typically designed to request or support only a subset of the full RFC-specified standard options set.

Options can be managed using different levels assigned for each managed DHCP server:

Server options. Apply to all scopes defined at a DHCP server.

Scope options. Apply specifically to all clients that obtain a lease within a particular scope.

Class options. Apply only to clients that are identified as members of a specified user or vendor class when obtaining a lease.

Client options. Apply only for a single reserved client computer. These options require a reservation to be used in an active scope.

You can manage DHCP options at these distinct levels:

Predefined options. At this level, you control the types of options predefined for the DHCP server to expose as available options for assigning from any of the option configuration dialog boxes (such as Server Options, Scope Options, or Client Options) available through the DHCP console. You can add options to or remove them from the predefined list of standard options as needed. Although options are made available in this way, they are not assigned values until administratively configured at the server, scope, or client.

Server options. Here you assign values for options that should apply to or be inherited by all scopes and clients of the DHCP server as defaults. Options configured here can have their values overridden by different values if those values are set at a scope, options class, or reserved client level.

Scope options. Assign values here for options that should apply only to clients of an applicable scope selected in the DHCP Console Tree. Options configured here can have their values overridden by different values if those values are set at either an options class or reserved client level.

Client options. Assign values here for options that should apply only to a specific reserved DHCP client. To use this level of assignment, you must first add a reservation for the applicable client to the applicable DHCP server and scope where the client is to obtain its IP address. These options are set for an individual DHCP client configured with an address reservation in a scope. Only properties manually configured at the client computer can override options assigned at this level.

Class options. When using any of the option configuration dialog boxes (Server Options, Scope Options or Client Options), you can click the Advanced tab of the applicable dialog box to configure and enable options for assignment and to identify member clients of a specified user or vendor class.

Depending on the context, only those DHCP clients identified according to the selected class are distributed options data you have configured specifically for that class. For example, if a class-assigned option is set at a scope, only clients of that scope that indicate class membership during leasing activity are configured with class-assigned option values. Other nonmember clients are configured using scope option values set from the General tab.

These options can override values assigned and set at the same context (server, scope, or client options) or values inherited from options configured at a higher context. However, the capability of the client to indicate membership in a specific options class is typically the decisive criterion for using this level of options assignment.

The following guidelines can help you determine what level to assign the options you use for clients on your network:

- Add or define new custom option types only if you have new software or applications that require a nonstandard DHCP option.

- If your DHCP server manages many scopes for a large network, be selective when assigning Server Options. These options apply by default to all clients of a DHCP server computer unless otherwise overridden.

- Use Scope Options for assigning most options that clients use. In most networks, this level is typically preferred for assigning and enabling the use of DHCP options.

- Use Class Options if you have a mixture of DHCP clients with diverse needs that are able to identify a specific class on the DHCP server when obtaining a lease. For example, if you have a limited number of client computers running Windows 2000 DHCP clients, these clients can be configured to receive vendor-specific options that other clients do not use.

- Use Client Options for individual DHCP clients in your network that have special configuration requirements.

- For any hosts (that is, computers or other networked devices) that do not support DHCP or are not recommended to use it, you can also consider excluding IP addresses for those computers and devices and manually setting the IP address configuration directly at the applicable host. For example, you often need to statically configure the IP address for routers.

After you set basic TCP/IP configuration settings for clients (such as IP address, subnet mask, and default gateway), most clients also need the DHCP server to provide other information through DHCP options. The most common of these include the following:

Routers. A preferred list of IP addresses for routers on the same subnet as DHCP clients. The client can then contact these routers as needed to forward IP packets destined for remote hosts.

DNS servers. IP addresses for DNS name servers that DHCP clients can contact and use to resolve a domain host name query.

DNS domain. Specifies the domain name that DHCP clients should use when resolving unqualified names during DNS domain name resolution.

WINS node type. A preferred NetBIOS name resolution method for the DHCP client to use (such as b-node for broadcast only or h-node for a hybrid of point-to-point and broadcast methods).

WINS server. IP addresses of primary and secondary WINS servers for the DHCP client to use.

Option classes offer an additional method for grouping DHCP-provided configuration details for clients within a scope. For Windows 2000 Server, there are two types of option classes that can be used for submanaging options:

- User classes, for assigning options to clients identified as sharing a common need for similar DHCP options configuration.

- Vendor classes, for assigning vendor-specific options to clients identified as sharing a commonly defined vendor type.

User classes make it possible to differentiate DHCP clients by specifying a User Class option. When available for client use, this option includes a user-determined class ID that can help to group clients of similar configuration needs within a scope. For example, you might support users and computers with mobile computing needs by configuring a user class at the DHCP server and setting the related class ID at the client computers.

A user class is helpful when you need to maintain separate options for special-needs client computers, such as providing a shorter lease time for portable computers that move frequently or often use remote access. In this example, you could configure the DHCP server to distribute different options that are specific to the needs of clients.

The user class feature gives you greater flexibility in configuring DHCP clients on your network, but it is not required for standard DHCP use. If user-defined option classes are not configured, options are provided through the applicable server, scope, or client option settings instead.

Windows 2000 DHCP servers, which support recognition of user class IDs, perform the following added steps to lease clients that are identified according to this process:

1. The server determines whether the user class identified by the client in its lease request is a recognized class previously defined on the server. If a predefined user classes exists at the server, and is configured, class-based assignment is enabled. For other user classes, you must first add and configure them at the server before they are available for use.

2. If the user class is recognized, the server determines whether any additional DHCP options are configured for this class in the active lease context (either the scope or a client reservation) where the server is leasing the client.

3. If the scope or reserved client options are configured to provide options for the user-defined class of the client, the server returns those options to the client as part of its DHCP acknowledgment message (DHCPACK), which is sent to confirm the lease.

For Windows 2000 computers, you can define specific user class identifiers to convey information about client software configuration, its physical location in a building, or its user preferences. For example, an identifier can specify that DHCP clients are members of a user-defined class called "2nd floor, West," which has need for a special set of router, DNS, and WINS server settings. You can also use the Microsoft predefined user classes for isolating configuration details specific for clients with special needs, such as BOOTP or Routing and Remote Access service.

Vendor-defined option classes can be used by DHCP clients that are configured to, optionally, be identified by their vendor type to the DHCP server when obtaining a lease. For a client to identify its membership in a vendor class, the client provides a value in the Vendor class identifier option when it requests or selects a lease from the server.

The vendor class identifier information is a string of character data interpreted by a DHCP server. Microsoft supports vendor class identification for its DHCP clients running Windows 2000 or Windows 98. Most vendor types are derived from standard reserved hardware and operating system type abbreviation codes listed in RFC 1700. Other vendors might choose to define their own specific vendor class IDs for conveying vendor-specific information or handling special needs for their DHCP clients.

Windows 2000 DHCP servers, which support recognition of vendor class IDs, perform the following additional steps to lease the clients that are identified according to this process:

1. The server determines whether the vendor class identified by the client in its lease request is a recognized class, previously defined on the server. Only Microsoft vendor classes are predefined at the server. For other vendor classes, you must manually add and configure these options at your Windows 2000 DHCP servers before they are available for use.

2. If the vendor class is a recognized one, the server determines whether any additional DHCP options are configured for this class in the active lease context (either the scope or a client reservation) where the server is leasing the client.

3. If the scope or reserved client options are configured to provide options for the vendor-defined class of the client, the server returns them using the vendor-specific information option as part of its DHCP acknowledgment message (DHCPACK), which is sent to confirm the lease.

Vendor classes permit other system vendors to support custom applications for DHCP in mixed-vendor environments. Vendor-specific options, when provided, are used in addition to any of the standard DHCP options assigned or required for DHCP. When you add new vendor classes at the DHCP server, be sure that the vendor class ID data you set at the server matches the actual vendor class ID used by clients for your vendor.

Assigning Server/Scope-Based Options

Scope options are inherited as default values for all clients of the applicable scope. Option values configured as Scope-based options are overridden by any reserved client-based values assigned for the same options. Server options are inherited as default values for all scopes created at the applicable DHCP server. Option values configured as Server-based options are overridden by any scope-based or client-based values assigned for the same options.

To assign a server/scope-based option using the DHCP management console, in the Console Tree, click Server Options or Scope Options; then on the Action menu, click Configure Options (see Figure 9.22).

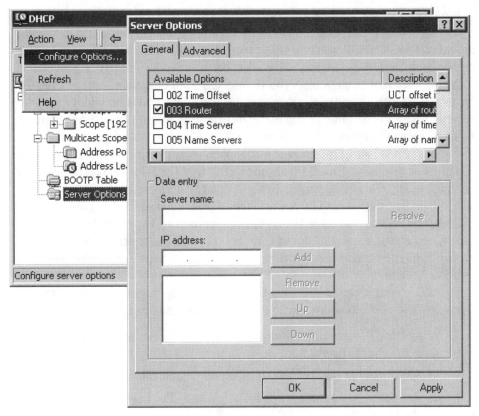

Figure 9.22   Assigning server-based options from the DHCP console.

In list of Available Options, select the check box for the first option you want to configure. Under Data entry, type the information required for this option. Repeat this for any other server options you want to specify, then click OK.

You can click the Advanced tab and specify additional server options to be applied only for members of select user or vendor classes. Options assigned at this level are provided only to clients identified as members of the classes specified at this tab.

Managing Reservations

When you make a client *reservation*, you can reserve a specific IP address for permanent use by a DHCP client. Typically, you will need to do this if the client uses an IP address that was assigned using another method for TCP/IP configuration.

If multiple DHCP servers are configured with a scope that covers the range of the reserved IP address, the client reservation must be made and duplicated at each of these DHCP servers. Otherwise, the reserved client computer can receive a different IP address, depending on the responding DHCP server.

If you want to change a reserved IP address for a current client, you have to remove the existing address reservation of the client and then add a new reservation. You can change any other information about a reserved client while keeping the reserved IP address.

If you are reserving an IP address for a new client, or an address that is different from its current one, you should verify that the address has not already been leased by the DHCP server. Reserving an IP address in a scope does not automatically cause a client currently using that address to stop using it.

Reserved clients can have DHCP options configured specifically for their use. When options are configured for a reserved client, these values override any option type parameters distributed via server-, scope-, or class-based options assignment.

To add a client reservation using the DHCP management console, in the Console Tree, click Reservations; on the Action menu, click New Reservation.

1. In the New Reservation window, fill in the information required to complete the client reservation.

2. To add the client reservation to the scope, click Add (see Figure 9.23).

3. Repeat the two previous steps for any other client reservations you want to add; click Close.

When adding a reservation, the DHCP server checks for the address you enter in the database to make sure it is not currently in use by another client. Reservations are applied on the basis of the DHCP client Media Access Control (MAC) address for the applicable network connection. To locate this address, at the client computer, type `ipconfig /all` at a command prompt and view the Physical Address for the connection. Alternately, you can right-click the connection in the Network and Dial-up Connections folder and select Properties to view this information.

Domain Name Service

As you know by now, DNS is a system for naming computers and network services; these names are organized into a hierarchy of domains. DNS is used in TCP/IP networks, such as the Internet, to locate computers and services through user-friendly names. When a user enters a DNS name in an application, DNS services can resolve the name to other information associated with the name, such as an IP address.

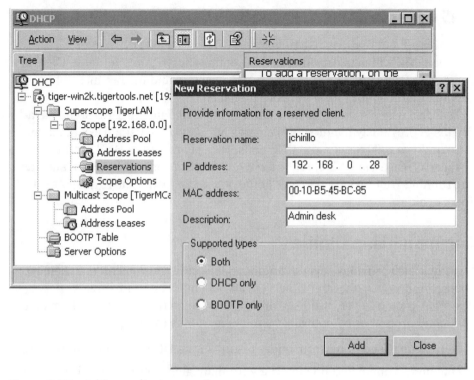

Figure 9.23 Adding a client reservation.

For example, most users prefer an easy-to-remember name such as example.microsoft.com to locate a computer, say, a mail or Web server on a network. However, computers communicate over a network using numeric addresses, which are more difficult for users to remember. In short, name services such as DNS provide a way to map the user-friendly name for a computer or service to its numeric address. If you have ever used a Web browser, you have used DNS.

Windows 2000 provides a number of utilities for administering, monitoring, and troubleshooting both DNS servers and clients. These utilities include:

- The DNS console, which is part of Administrative Tools.

- Command-line utilities, such as Nslookup, which can be used to troubleshoot DNS problems.

- Logging features, such as the DNS server log, which can be viewed using Event Viewer. File-based logs can also be used temporarily as an advanced debugging option to log and trace selected service events.

- Performance-monitoring utilities, such as statistical counters to measure and monitor DNS server activity with System Monitor.

DNS Console

The primary tool that you use to manage Windows 2000 DNS servers is the DNS console, which is provided in the Administrative Tools folder in Control Panel. The DNS console appears as a MMC snap-in and further integrates DNS administration to your total network management.

The DNS console provides new ways to perform familiar DNS administrative tasks previously handled in Windows NT Server 4.0 using DNS Manager. For Windows 2000 Server, the DNS console appears after a DNS server is installed. To use the DNS console from another nonserver computer, such as one running Windows 2000 Professional, you must install the Administrative Tools pack.

Command-Line Utilities

Windows 2000 provides several command-line utilities. You can use them to manage and troubleshoot DNS servers and clients. The following list describes each of these utilities, which can be run either by typing them at a command prompt or by entering them in batch files for scripted use.

Nslookup. Used to perform query testing of the DNS domain namespace.

Dnscmd. A command-line interface for managing DNS servers. This utility is useful in scripting batch files to help automate routine DNS management tasks or to perform simple unattended setup and configuration of new DNS servers on your network.

Ipconfig. This command is used to view and modify IP configuration details used by the computer. For Windows 2000, additional command-line options are included with this utility to provide help in troubleshooting and supporting DNS clients.

Event-Monitoring Utilities

Windows 2000 Server includes two options for monitoring DNS servers:

Default logging of DNS server event messages to the DNS server log. For Windows 2000 Server, server event messages are separated and kept in their own system event log, the DNS server log, which can be viewed using Event Viewer. The DNS server log contains basic events logged by the DNS Server service. For example, when the DNS server starts or stops, a corresponding event message is written to this log. Some additional critical DNS service events are also logged here; an example is when the server starts but cannot locate initializing data, such as zones or boot information stored in the Windows 2000 Registry or (in some cases) Active Directory. The event types logged by Windows 2000 DNS servers are predetermined.

You can also use Event Viewer to view and monitor client-related DNS events. These appear in the System log and are written by the DNS Client service at any computers running Windows 2000 (all versions).

Optional debug options for trace logging to a text file on the DNS server computer. You can use the DNS console to selectively enable additional debug logging options for temporary trace logging to a text-based file of DNS server activity. The file created and used for this feature, Dns.log, is stored in the systemroot\System32\Dns folder.

Performance-Monitoring Utilities

Performance monitoring for Windows 2000 DNS servers can be done using additional service-specific counters that measure DNS server performance. These counters are accessible through System Monitor, which is provided in the Performance console. When using System Monitor, you can create charts and graphs of server performance trends over time for any of your Windows 2000 DNS servers. These can be studied and analyzed to determine whether additional server tuning is needed. By measuring and reviewing server metrics over a period of time, it is possible to determine performance benchmarks and decide whether further adjustments can be made to optimize the system.

DNS Management Console

In Chapter 7, we installed and configured a DNS server; in this section of this chapter we'll use the DNS console to accomplish some basic administrative server tasks:

- Connect to and manage a local DNS server on the same computer or on remote DNS servers on other computers.
- Add and remove forward and reverse lookup zones as needed.
- Add, remove, and update resource records in zones.
- Modify security for specific zones or resource records.

In addition, you'll learn to use the DNS console to perform the following tasks:

- Perform maintenance on the server. You can start, stop, pause, or resume the server or manually update server data files.
- Monitor the contents of the server cache and, as needed, clear it.

- Tune advanced server options.
- Configure and perform aging and scavenging of stale resource records stored by the server.

Connecting to and Managing a Local DNS Server

To open the DNS management console, click Start/Programs/Administrative Tools/DNS and the screen in Figure 9.24 appears.

To start, stop, pause, resume, or restart a DNS server from the console, in the Console Tree, click the applicable DNS server; on the Action menu, point to All Tasks and click one of the following (Figure 9.25):

- To start the service, click Start.
- To stop the service, click Stop.
- To interrupt the service, click Pause.
- To stop and then automatically restart the service, click Restart.

After you pause or stop the service, on the Action menu, in All Tasks, you can click Resume to immediately continue service. You can also perform most of these tasks at a command prompt by using the following commands:

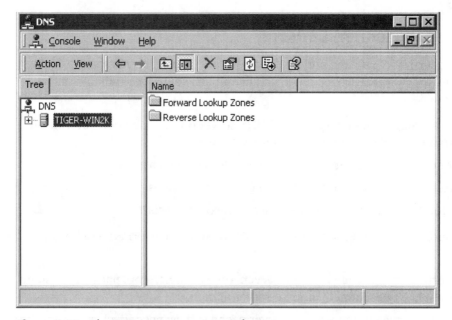

Figure 9.24   The DNS management console.

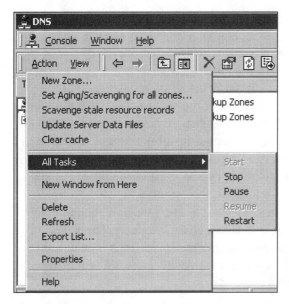

Figure 9.25 Controlling the DNS service operation.

```
net start dns
net stop dns
net pause dns
net continue dns
```

Adding Forward and Reverse Lookup Zones

The DNS allows a DNS namespace to be divided into *zones*, which store name information about one or more DNS domains. For each DNS domain name included in a zone, the zone becomes the authoritative source for information about that domain.

A zone starts as a storage database for a single DNS domain name. If other domains are added below the domain used to create the zone, these domains can either be part of the same zone or belong to another zone. Once a subdomain is added, it can then either be managed and included as part of the original zone records or be delegated to another zone created to support the subdomain. For example, if the microsoft.com zone does not use delegation for a subdomain, any data for the subdomain remains part of the microsoft.com zone. Thus, the subdomain dev.microsoft.com is not delegated away but is managed by the microsoft.com zone.

Because of the important role that zones play in DNS, it is intended that they be available from more than one DNS server on the network to provide availability and fault tolerance when resolving name queries. Otherwise, if a single server is used and that server is not responding, queries for names in the zone can fail. For additional servers to host a zone, zone transfers are required to replicate and synchronize all copies of the zone used at each server configured to host the zone.

When a new DNS server is added to the network and is configured as a new secondary server for an existing zone, it performs a full initial transfer of the zone to obtain and replicate a full copy of resource records for the zone. For most earlier DNS server implementations, this same method of full transfer for a zone is also used when the zone requires updating after changes are made to the zone. For Windows 2000 Server, the DNS service supports *incremental zone transfer*, a revised DNS zone transfer process for intermediate changes.

 Incremental zone transfers are described in RFC 1995 as an additional DNS standard for replicating DNS zones. When incremental transfers are supported by both a DNS server acting as the source for a zone and any servers that copy the zone from it, they provide a more efficient method of propagating zone changes and updates.

In earlier DNS implementations, any request for an update of zone data required a full transfer of the entire zone database using an AXFR query. With incremental transfer, an alternate query type (IXFR) can be used instead. This allows the secondary server to pull only those zone changes it needs to synchronize its copy of the zone with its source, either a primary or secondary copy of the zone maintained by another DNS server.

With IXFR zone transfers, differences between the source and replicated versions of the zone are first determined. If the zones are identified to be the same version—as indicated by the serial number field in the start of authority (SOA) resource record of each zone—no transfer is made.

If the serial number for the zone at the source is greater than at the requesting secondary server, a transfer is made of only those changes to resource records (RRs) for each incremental version of the zone. For an IXFR query to succeed and changes to be sent, the source DNS server for the zone must keep a history of incremental zone changes to use when answering these queries. The incremental transfer process requires substantially less traffic on a network, and zone transfers are completed much faster.

A zone transfer might occur during any of the following scenarios:

- When the refresh interval expires for the zone.

- When a secondary server is notified of zone changes by its master server.

- When the DNS Server service is started at a secondary server for the zone.

- When the DNS console is used at a secondary server for the zone to manually initiate a transfer from its master server.

Zone transfers are always initiated at the secondary server for a zone and sent to their configured master servers, which act as their source for the zone. Master servers can be any other DNS server that loads the zone, such as either the primary server for the zone or another secondary server. When the master server receives the request for the zone, it can reply with either a partial or full transfer of the zone to the secondary server.

During new configuration, the destination server sends an initial "all zone" transfer (AXFR) request to the master DNS server configured as its source for the zone. The master (source) server responds and fully transfers the zone to the secondary (destination) server.

The zone is delivered to the destination server requesting the transfer with its version established by use of a serial number field in the properties for the SOA RR. The SOA RR also contains a stated refresh interval in seconds (by default, 900 seconds, or 15 minutes) to indicate when the destination server should next request to renew the zone with the source server.

When the refresh interval expires, an SOA query is used by the destination server to request renewal of the zone from the source server. The source server answers the query for its SOA record. This response contains the serial number for the zone in its current state at the source server.

The destination server checks the serial number of the SOA record in the response and determines how to renew the zone. If the value of the serial number in the SOA response is equal to its current local serial number, it concludes that the zone is the same at both servers and that a zone transfer is not needed. The destination server then renews the zone by resetting its refresh interval based on the value of this field in the SOA response from its source server.

If the value of the serial number in the SOA response is higher than its current local serial number, it concludes that the zone has been updated and that a transfer is needed. If the destination server concludes that the zone has changed, it sends an IXFR query to the source server, containing its current local value for the serial number in the SOA record for the zone. The source server responds with either an incremental or full transfer of the zone. If the source server supports incremental transfer by maintaining a history of recent incremental zone changes for modified resource records, it can answer with an incremental zone transfer (IXFR) of the zone. If the source server does not support incremental transfer, or does not have a history of zone changes, it can answer with a full (AXFR) transfer of the zone instead.

Incremental zone transfer through IXFR query is supported for Windows 2000 Server. For earlier versions of the DNS service running on Windows NT Server 4.0, and for many other DNS server implementations, incremental zone transfer is not available; in these versions, only full-zone (AXFR) queries and transfers are used to replicate zones.

Windows DNS servers support DNS Notify, an update to the original DNS protocol specification that permits a means of initiating notification to secondary servers when zone changes occur (RFC 1996). DNS notification implements a push mechanism for notifying a select set of secondary servers for a zone when it is updated. Servers that are notified can then initiate a zone transfer as just described to pull zone changes from their master servers and update their local replicas of the zone.

For "secondaries" to be notified by the DNS server acting as their configured source for a zone, each secondary server must first have its IP address in the notify list of the source server. When using the DNS console to manage zones loaded at Windows 2000 DNS servers, this list is maintained in the Notify dialog box, which is accessible from the Zone Transfer tab located in zone Properties.

In addition to notifying the listed servers, the DNS console permits you to use the contents of the Notify list as a means to restrict or limit zone transfer access to only those secondary servers specified in the list. This can help prevent an undesired attempt by an unknown or unapproved DNS server to pull, or request, zone updates. The following is a brief summary of the typical DNS notification process for zone updates:

1. The local zone at a DNS server acting as a master server, a source for the zone to other servers, is updated. When the zone is updated at the master or source server, the serial number field in the SOA RR is also updated, indicating a new local version of the zone.

2. The master server sends a DNS notify message to other servers that are part of its configured Notify list.

3. All secondary servers that receive the Notify message can then respond by initiating a zone transfer request back to the notifying master server.

The normal zone transfer process can then continue as described previously.

To add a forward lookup zone, from the DNS management console, in the Console Tree, click Forward Lookup Zones. On the Action menu, click New Zone to start the wizard. You can also right-click on Forward Lookup Zones and then click New Zone (see Figure 9.26).

1. Click Next to begin.

2. Select the type of zone: Active Directory-integrated, Standard primary, or Standard secondary. For this example, choose Standard primary, as shown in Figure 9.27, then click Next.

3. Enter the name of the zone and click Next (see Figure 9.28).

4. Select whether to create a new zone file or use one previously created, then click Next (see Figure 9.29). Click Finish.

DNS
Console Window Help
Action View
Tree
DNS
TIGER-WIN2K
Forward Lookup Zones
tigertools
Reverse Look
New Zone...
View
New Window from Here
Refresh
Export List...
Help
Name
Type
Status
tigertools.net
Active Direct...
Running
Create a new zone

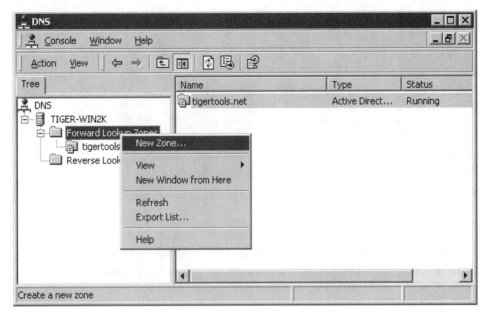

Figure 9.26 Adding a forward lookup zone.

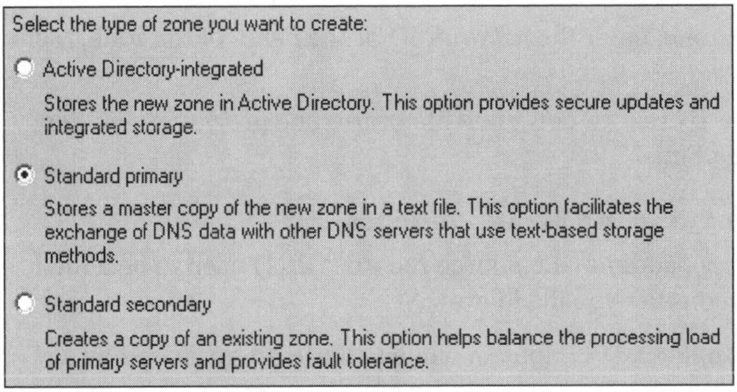

Select the type of zone you want to create:
Active Directory-integrated
Stores the new zone in Active Directory. This option provides secure updates and integrated storage.
Standard primary
Stores a master copy of the new zone in a text file. This option facilitates the exchange of DNS data with other DNS servers that use text-based storage methods.
Standard secondary
Creates a copy of an existing zone. This option helps balance the processing load of primary servers and provides fault tolerance.

Figure 9.27 Selecting the zone type.

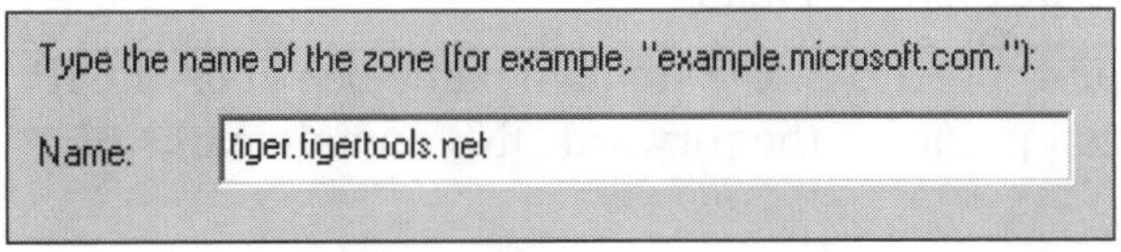

Type the name of the zone (for example, "example.microsoft.com."):
Name:
tiger.tigertools.net

Figure 9.28 Entering the zone name.

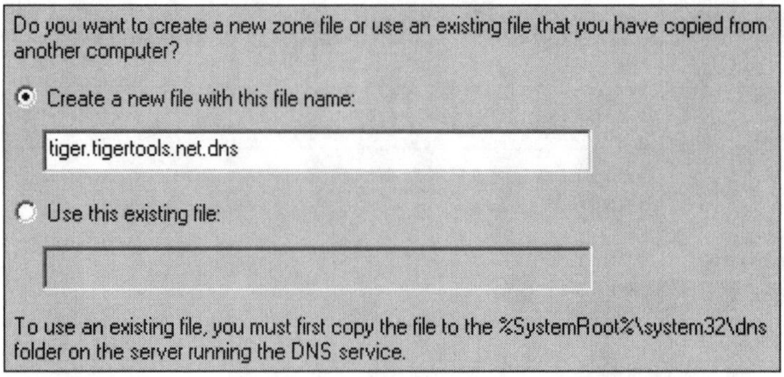

Do you want to create a new zone file or use an existing file that you have copied from another computer?

☑ Create a new file with this file name:

tiger.tigertools.net.dns

○ Use this existing file:

To use an existing file, you must first copy the file to the %SystemRoot%\system32\dns folder on the server running the DNS service.

Figure 9.29   Creating a new zone file.

To add a reverse lookup zone, from the DNS management console, in the Console Tree, click Reverse Lookup Zones; on the Action menu, click New Zone to start the wizard. You can also right-click on Reverse Lookup Zones, then click New Zone.

1. Click Next to begin.
2. Select the type of zone from Active Directory-integrated, Standard primary, or Standard secondary. Here, again, choose Standard primary, then click Next.
3. To identify the zone, enter the network ID or the name of the zone, then click Next.
4. Select whether to create a new zone file or use one previously created; click Next, then Finish.

Adding and Updating Resource Records in Zones

After you create a zone, additional resource records (RRs) need to be added to it. The most common RRs you'll add are:

Host (A). For mapping a DNS domain name to an IP address used by a computer.

Alias (CNAME). For mapping an alias DNS domain name to another primary or canonical name.

Mail Exchanger (MX). For mapping a DNS domain name to the name of a computer that exchanges or forwards mail.

Pointer (PTR). For mapping a reverse DNS domain name based on the IP address of a computer that points to the forward DNS domain name of that computer.

Service location (SRV). For mapping a DNS domain name to a specified list of DNS host computers that offer a specific type of service, such as Active Directory domain controllers.

To add a resource record—in this case a host (A) resource record to a zone—from the DNS console, in the Console Tree, click the applicable forward lookup zone.

1. On the Action menu, click New Host.

2. In the Name text box, type the DNS computer name for the new host.

3. In the IP address text box, type the IP address for the new host (see Figure 9.30). As an option, select the Create associated pointer (PTR) record check box to create an additional pointer record in a reverse zone for this host, based on the information you entered in the Name and IP address boxes.

4. Click Add Host to add the new host record to the zone.

5. Repeat the process or click Done to finish.

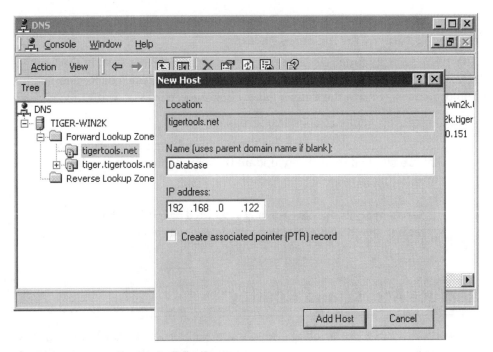

Figure 9.30 Creating a zone record.

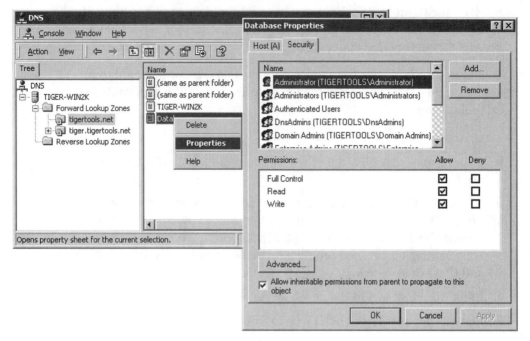

Figure 9.31   Specifying security options for a resource record.

Modifying Security for Resource Records

To modify security for a resource record using the DNS console, in the Console Tree, click the applicable zone—Forward Lookup Zones or Reverse Lookup Zones—and in the details pane, click the record you want to view.

1. On the Action menu, click Properties.

2. In the Security tab window, modify the list of member users or groups that are allowed to securely update the applicable record and reset their permissions as needed (see Figure 9.31).

   Secure dynamic updates are only supported or configurable for resource records stored with Active Directory-integrated zones.

Remote Access and Routing

Microsoft describes the Routing and Remote Access service for Windows 2000 Server as a full-featured software router and an open platform for routing and internetworking. It offers routing services to businesses in LAN and wide area network (WAN) environments or over the Internet by using secure virtual private network (VPN) connections. The Routing and Remote Access service combines and integrates the separate routing and remote access services of Windows NT 4.0 and is an enhancement of the Routing and Remote Access Service (RRAS) for Windows NT 4.0.

An advantage of the Routing and Remote Access service is integration with the Windows 2000 Server operating system. The service delivers many cost-saving features and works with a wide variety of hardware platforms and hundreds of network adapters. It is extensible with application programming interfaces (APIs), which developers can use to create custom networking solutions and new vendors can use to participate in the growing business of open internetworking.

 Hereafter, a computer running Windows 2000 and the Routing and Remote Access service that provides LAN and WAN routing services will be referred to as the Windows 2000 router.

The Windows 2000 router is intended for use by system administrators who are already familiar with routing protocols and routing services. With it, they can view and manage both routers and remote access servers on their networks. Some of the advantages of the Windows 2000 routing services include the following:

- Multiprotocol unicast routing for Internet Protocol (IP), Internetwork Packet Exchange (IPX), and AppleTalk.

- Industry-standard unicast IP routing protocols: Open Shortest Path First (OSPF) and Routing Information Protocol (RIP), versions 1 and 2.

- Industry-standard IPX routing protocols and services: Routing Information Protocol (RIP) for IPX and Service Advertising Protocol (SAP) for IPX.

- IP multicast services (Internet Group Management Protocol, or IGMP, router mode and IGMP proxy mode) to enable the forwarding of IP multicast traffic.

- IP network address translation (NAT) services to simplify home networking and the connection of small office or home office (SOHO) networks to the Internet.

- IP and IPX packet filtering for security and performance.

- Demand-dial routing over dial-up WAN links.

- VPN support with the Point-to-Point Tunneling Protocol (PPTP) and the Layer Two Tunneling Protocol (L2TP) over Internet Protocol security (IPSec).

- Industry standard support for a Dynamic Host Configuration Protocol (DHCP) Relay Agent for IP.

- Industry standard support for router advertisement by using Internet Control Message Protocol (ICMP) router discovery.

- Tunneling support by using IP-in-IP tunnels.

- A graphical user interface for remote monitoring and configuration.

- A command-line interface for running scripts and automating configuration and remote monitoring.

- Support for Windows 2000 power management capabilities.

- Simple Network Management Protocol (SNMP) management capabilities with support for popular management information bases (MIBs).

- Extensive support for media, including Ethernet, Token Ring, Fiber Distributed Data Interface (FDDI), asynchronous transfer mode (ATM), Integrated Services Digital Network (ISDN), T-Carrier, Frame Relay, xDSL, cable modems, X.25, and analog modems.

- APIs for routing protocols, administration, and the user interface to enable value-added development on the Windows 2000 router platform.

Windows 2000 Server remote access, part of the integrated Routing and Remote Access service, connects remote or mobile workers to organization networks. Remote users can work as if their computers are physically connected to the network.

Users run remote access software and initiate a connection to the remote access server. The remote access server, which is a computer running Windows 2000 Server and the Routing and Remote Access service, authenticates users and services sessions until terminated by the user or network administrator. All services typically available to a LAN-connected user (including file and print sharing, Web server access, and messaging) are enabled by means of the remote access connection.

Remote access clients use standard tools to access resources. For example, on a computer running Windows 2000, clients can use Windows Explorer to make drive connections and to connect to printers. Connections are persistent: Users do not have to reconnect to network resources during their remote sessions. Because drive letters and universal naming convention (UNC) names are fully supported by remote access, most commercial and custom applications work without modification.

A remote access server running Windows 2000 provides two different types of remote access connectivity:

Dial-up networking. A remote access client makes a nonpermanent, dial-up connection to a physical port on a remote access server using the service of a telecommunications provider such as analog phone, ISDN, or X.25. The best example is a dial-up networking client who dials the phone number of one of the ports of a remote access server. Dial-up networking over an analog phone or ISDN is a direct physical connection between the dial-up networking client and the dial-up networking server. You can encrypt data sent over the connection, but it is not required.

Virtual private networking. The creation of secured, point-to-point connections across a private network or a public network such as the Internet. A virtual private networking client uses special TCP/IP-based protocols called tunneling protocols to make a virtual call to a virtual port on a virtual private networking server. The best example is a virtual private networking client who makes a virtual private network connection to a remote access server that is connected to the Internet. The remote access server answers the virtual call, authenticates the caller, and transfers data between the virtual private networking client and the corporate network. In contrast to dial-up networking, virtual private networking is always a logical, indirect connection between the virtual private networking client and the virtual private networking server. To ensure privacy, you must encrypt data sent over the connection.

Installing and Configuring Remote Access and Routing

Before you install the Routing and Remote Access service, you must have installed and have working all relevant hardware, which, depending on your network and requirements, might include the following:

- Network adapter with a certified Network Driver Interface Specification (NDIS) driver
- One or more compatible modems and an available COM port
- Multiport adapter for acceptable performance with multiple remote connections
- X.25 smart card (if you are using an X.25 network)
- ISDN adapter (if you are using an ISDN line)

 To verify the compatibility of all hardware in a computer running Windows 2000 Server, access the Microsoft Windows Hardware Compatibility List at the Microsoft Web site (www.microsoft.com/).

When you install Windows 2000 Server, typically the remote access component is automatically installed; however, it is installed in a disabled state. To

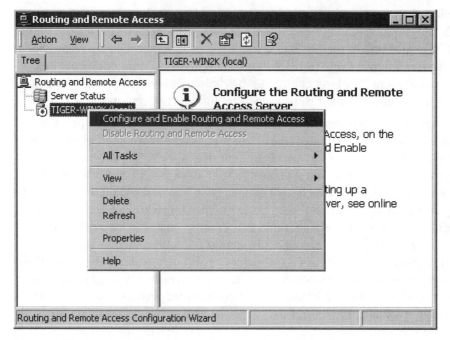

Figure 9.32 Starting the Routing and Remote Access Wizard.

enable the Routing and Remote Access service, you must start the Routing and Remote Access management console from Start/Programs/Administrative Tools/Routing and Remote Access.

By default, the local computer is listed as a server. In the Console Tree, right-click the server, then click Configure and Enable Routing and Remote Access to start the wizard (Figure 9.32).

1. Click Next to begin.

2. Select the Remote access server configuration choice and click Next. The choice include:

   - *Internet connection server.* Enable all computers on this network to connect to the Internet

   - *Remote access server.* Enable remote computers to dial in to this network

   - *Virtual private network server.* Enable remote computers to connect to this network through the Internet

   - *Network router.* Enable this network to communicate with other networks

3. Verify that the communication protocols for this service are available in the list shown in Figure 9.33 by selecting either Yes, all of the required

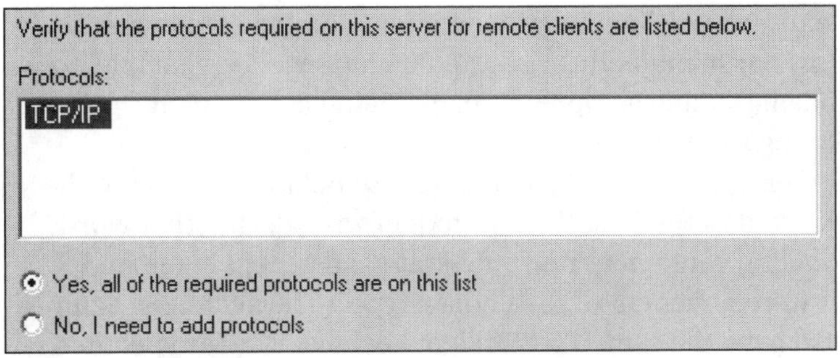

Verify that the protocols required on this server for remote clients are listed below.

Protocols:

TCP/IP

⊙ Yes, all of the required protocols are on this list
○ No, I need to add protocols

Figure 9.33 Verifying the communication protocols.

protocols are on this list, or No, I need to add protocols. Click Next to continue. If you've elected to add protocols, the wizard will exit for you to add and configure protocols such as the TCP/IP suite discussed in the first section of this chapter.

4. Select the method from which clients will be assigned IP addressing: Automatically via DHCP or From a specified range of addresses (see Figure 9.34); click Next.

5. Select whether remote access will use an existing Remote Authentication Dial-In User Service (RADIUS) server (see Figure 9.35); click Next, then Finish.

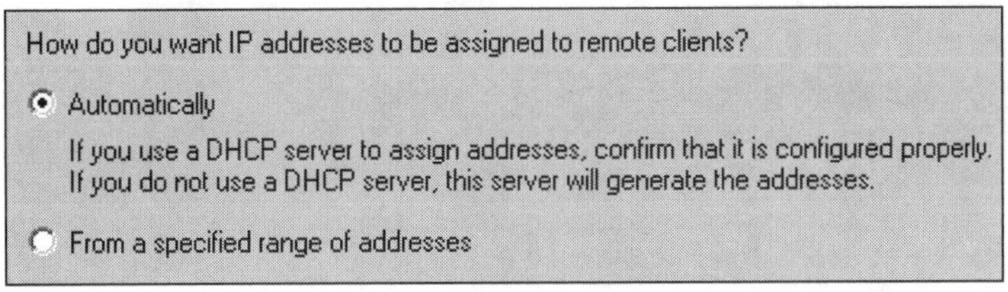

How do you want IP addresses to be assigned to remote clients?

⊙ Automatically

If you use a DHCP server to assign addresses, confirm that it is configured properly. If you do not use a DHCP server, this server will generate the addresses.

○ From a specified range of addresses

Figure 9.34 Selecting how clients will be assigned addresses.

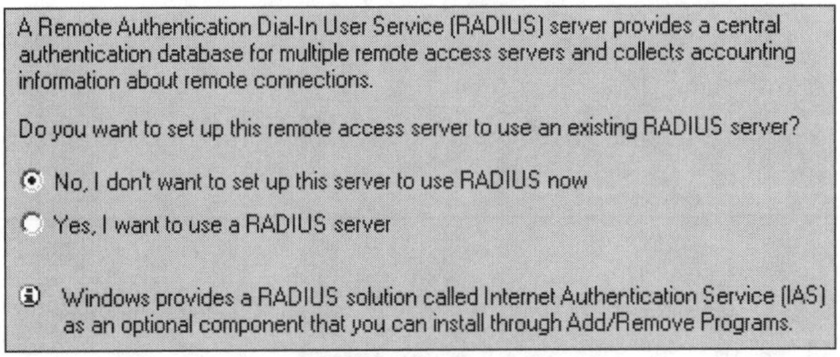

A Remote Authentication Dial-In User Service (RADIUS) server provides a central authentication database for multiple remote access servers and collects accounting information about remote connections.

Do you want to set up this remote access server to use an existing RADIUS server?

⊙ No, I don't want to set up this server to use RADIUS now

○ Yes, I want to use a RADIUS server

ⓘ Windows provides a RADIUS solution called Internet Authentication Service (IAS) as an optional component that you can install through Add/Remove Programs.

Figure 9.35 Selecting whether or not to use RADIUS.

6. Configure the direct serial connection, modem-pooling equipment, or X.25 smart card per manufacturer recommendations. For example, to configure modem-pooling equipment, click Phone and Modem Options from Start/Setting/Control Panel.

Configure your modem-pooling equipment to behave like one of the modem types listed in the Install New Modem wizard. (In other words, the modem-pooling equipment must generate and accept command strings as if it were a modem of the chosen type.) The switching equipment must also have the same RS-232 signal behavior as the specified modem. Connect COM ports to the equipment and configure the ports for remote access in Routing and Remote Access.

7. Choose an authentication method (such as Windows authentication) from the Routing and Remote Access service management console by right-clicking the server name for which you want to configure Windows 2000 authentication; click Properties. In the Security tab window, in the Authentication provider box, click Windows authentication (see Figure 9.36).

8. Using the steps for configuring Users and Groups from Chapter 8, grant the appropriate dial-in permissions.

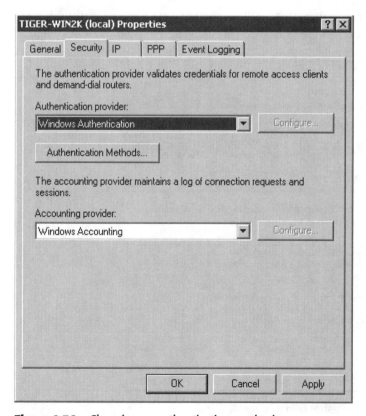

Figure 9.36   Choosing an authentication method.

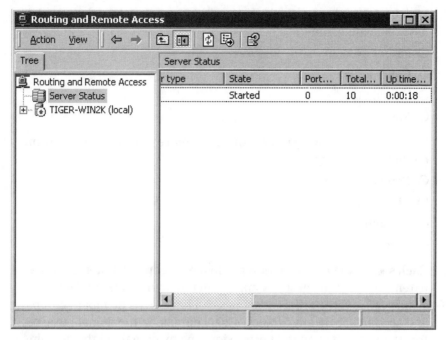

Figure 9.37 Monitoring the remote access service.

To monitor the Routing and Remote Access service, from the Console Tree, double-click Routing and Remote Access, then click Server Status (see Figure 9.37). The Routing and Remote Access window shows the server name, the state of the Routing and Remote Access service (started or stopped), the total ports on the server, the ports in use, and the amount of time that the server has been up since the Routing and Remote Access service was last started. To view connected remote access clients, in the Console Tree, click Remote Access Clients. In the details pane, right-click a username, then click Status.

Think It Over

Test your comprehension of the topics covered in this chapter before moving on to Chapter 10. You'll find the answers to these questions in Appendix A.

9.1. Which of the following is a domain located in the namespace tree directly beneath another domain name?

  ○ Parent domain

  ○ Child domain

  ○ Domain tree

  ○ Forest

9.2. Which of the following is the hierarchical tree structure that is used to index domain names?

○ Parent domain

○ Child domain

○ Domain tree

○ Forest

9.3. Which of the following is a set of one or more trees that do not form a contiguous namespace?

○ Parent domain

○ Child domain

○ Domain tree

○ Forest

9.4. Each security and distribution group has a scope that identifies the extent to which the group is applied in the domain tree or forest. Which of the three different scopes can have as its members groups and accounts from any Windows 2000 domain in the domain tree or forest and can be granted permissions in any domain in the domain tree or forest?

○ Universal

○ Global

○ Domain local

9.5. Each security and distribution group has a scope that identifies the extent to which the group is applied in the domain tree or forest. Which of the three different scopes can have as its members groups and accounts from a Windows 2000 or Windows NT domain and can be used to grant permissions only within a domain?

○ Universal

○ Global

○ Domain local

9.6. Each security and distribution group has a scope that identifies the extent to which the group is applied in the domain tree or forest. Which of the three different scopes can have as its members groups and accounts only from the domain in which the group is defined and can be granted permissions in any domain in the forest?

○ Universal

○ Global

○ Domain local

9.7. Groups in native-mode domains or distribution groups in mixed-mode domains have their membership determined as which of the following for groups with universal scope?

○ They can have as their members: user accounts, computer accounts, other groups with universal scope, and groups with global scope from any domain.

○ They can have as their members: user accounts from the same domain and other groups with global scope from the same domain.

○ They can have as their members: user accounts, groups with universal scope, and groups with global scope, all from any domain. They can also have as members other groups with domain local scope from within the same domain.

9.8. Groups in native-mode domains or distribution groups in mixed-mode domains have their membership determined as which of the following for groups with global scope?

○ They can have as their members: user accounts, computer accounts, other groups with universal scope, and groups with global scope from any domain.

○ They can have as their members: user accounts from the same domain and other groups with global scope from the same domain.

○ They can have as their members: user accounts, groups with universal scope, and groups with global scope, all from any domain. They can also have as members other groups with domain local scope from within the same domain.

9.9. Groups in native-mode domains or distribution groups in mixed-mode domains have their membership determined as which of the following for groups with domain local scope?

○ They can have as their members: user accounts, computer accounts, other groups with universal scope, and groups with global scope from any domain.

○ They can have as their members: user accounts from the same domain and other groups with global scope from the same domain.

○ They can have as their members: user accounts, groups with universal scope, and groups with global scope, all from any domain. They can also have as members other groups with domain local scope from within the same domain.

9.10. Explicit trusts create trust relationships to domains outside the forest.

○ True

○ False

9.11. Shortcut trusts are two-way transitive trusts that enable you to shorten the path in a complex forest.

○ True

○ False

9.12. Which of the following terms represents a limited sequence of IP addresses within a scope, excluded from DHCP service offerings?

○ Scope

○ Superscope

○ Exclusion range

○ Reservation

○ Option types

○ Options class

9.13. Which of the following terms represents a way for the server to further manage option types provided to clients?

○ Scope

○ Superscope

○ Exclusion range

○ Reservation

○ Option types

○ Options class

9.14. Which of the following terms represents a permanent address lease assignment by the DHCP server?

○ Scope

○ Superscope

○ Exclusion range

○ Reservation

○ Option types

○ Options class

9.15. Which of the following terms represents an administrative grouping of scopes that can be used to support multiple logical IP subnets on the same physical subnet?

○ Scope

○ Superscope

○ Exclusion range

○ Reservation

○ Option types

○ Options class

9.16. Which of the following terms represents a way for the server to further manage option types provided to clients?

○ Scope

○ Superscope

○ Exclusion range

○ Reservation

○ Option types

○ Options class

9.17. Which of the following terms represents the full consecutive range of possible IP addresses for a network?

○ Scope

○ Superscope

○ Exclusion range

○ Reservation

○ Option types

○ Options class

9.18. A superscope can have scopes added to it either during or after its creation.

   ○ True

   ○ False

9.19. Which of the following DHCP options are applied for all scopes defined at a DHCP server?

   ○ Server options

   ○ Scope options

   ○ Class options

   ○ Client options

9.20. Which of the following DHCP options are applied only to clients that are identified as members of a specified user or vendor class when obtaining a lease?

   ○ Server options

   ○ Scope options

   ○ Class options

   ○ Client options

9.21. Which of the following DHCP options are applied specifically to all clients that obtain a lease within a particular scope?

   ○ Server options

   ○ Scope options

   ○ Class options

   ○ Client options

9.22. To manage and troubleshoot DNS servers and clients, which of the following best describes the *Nslookup* command?

   ○ This command is used to perform query testing of the DNS domain namespace.

   ○ This utility is useful in scripting batch files to help automate routine DNS management tasks or to perform simple unattended setup and configuration of new DNS servers on a network.

   ○ This command is used to view and modify IP configuration details used by the computer.

9.23. To manage and troubleshoot DNS servers and clients, which of the following best describes the *Ipconfig* command?

○ This command is used to perform query testing of the DNS domain namespace.

○ This utility is useful in scripting batch files to help automate routine DNS management tasks or to perform simple unattended setup and configuration of new DNS servers on a network.

○ This command is used to view and modify IP configuration details used by the computer.

9.24. A zone transfer might occur during which of the following scenarios?

○ When the refresh interval expires for the zone

○ When a secondary server is notified of zone changes by its master server

○ When the DNS Server service is started at a secondary server for the zone

○ When the DNS console is used at a secondary server for the zone to manually initiate a transfer from its master server

PART

Three

Internetworking with Cisco

To this point, we've been investigating the server platform: In Part 1, we explored the mechanical details of the conventional Windows NT Server suite, including configuration details; in Part 2 we compared Windows 2000 Server to its Windows NT predecessor, specifically addressing the Transmission Control Protocol/Internet Protocol (TCP/IP) and the accompanying services of Dynamic Host Configuration Protocol (DHCP), Domain Name Service (DNS), and remote access and routing.

Now it's time to move on to internetworking. In this part, we'll delve into Cisco router fundamentals and operations and cover the specifics of both local area network (LAN) and wide area network (WAN) internetworking. You'll learn the technical objectives used to facilitate the certification process, as well as gain hands-on configuration experience through this book's interactive CD-ROM.

Cisco Router Fundamentals

To ensure you've acquired a high standard of technical expertise, Cisco has formed a grueling list of objectives at which you *must* become skilled. To address the required technical objectives, this chapter covers a lot of ground. To begin, it covers:

- The Open Systems Interconnection (OSI) Reference Model and Layered Communications model

- Data links and network addresses and key differences between them

- The function of the Media Access Control (MAC) address

- The key internetworking functions for the OSI Network layer and reasons why the industry uses a layered model

- The two parts of network addressing; the parts in specific protocol address examples

- The five conversion steps of data encapsulation

- Connection-oriented and connectionless network services and their key differences

- LAN segmentation, using bridges, routers, and switches, and the benefits of each.

We'll then move on to examine router elements and the Internetworking Operating System (IOS); manage configuration files from the privilege EXEC mode; control router passwords, identification, and banners; identify the main Cisco IOS software commands for router startup, log in to a router in both user and privilege modes; check an initial configuration using the setup command; use the context-sensitive help facility and the command history and editing features; list the commands to load Cisco IOS software from Flash memory, a trivial file transfer protocol (TFTP) server, or ROM; and, finally, prepare the initial configuration of your router and enable IP.

 Hands-on simulations of the material in this chapter can be found on the book's companion CD-ROM.

Open Systems Interconnection Reference Model and Layered Communications

The International Standards Organization (ISO) developed the OSI layered model to describe the functions performed during data communications. Seven layers comprise the OSI model, and it is important to understand how each layer functions, because together they work to achieve successful communications (see Figure 10.1). Layering helps divide networking complexity into manageable segments, making problems easier to troubleshoot; moreover, layering allows specialization—that is, it enables vendors to develop new products to target a specific area. In other words, the OSI model functions as like a mediator, allowing different hardware and applications to play nice together.

We begin, then, by defining the seven layers:

Layer 7: Application. Providing the user interface, this layer brings networking to the application and performs application synchronization and system processes. Common services defined at this layer include File Transfer Protocol (FTP), Simple Mail Transfer Protocol (SMTP), and World Wide Web (WWW).

Layer 6: Presentation. This layer is responsible for presenting data to layer 7. Data encoding, decoding, compression, and encryption are accomplished at this layer, using coding schemes such as GIF, JPEG, ASCII, and MPEG.

Layer 5: Session. Session establishment, used at layer 6, is formed, managed, and terminated by this layer. Basically, this layer defines the data coordination between nodes at the Presentation layer. Novell Service Access Points (SAPs) and NetBEUI are protocols that function at the Session layer.

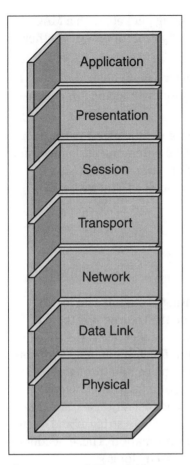

Figure 10.1 OSI model layers.

Layer 4: Transport. TCP and User Datagram Protocol (UDP) are network protocols that function at this layer. For that reason, this layer is responsible for reliable, connection-oriented communication between nodes and for providing transparent data transfer from the higher levels, with error recovery.

Layer 3: Network. Routing protocols and logical network addressing operate at this level of the OSI model. Examples of logical addressing include IP and Internetwork Packet Exchange (IPX) addresses. An example of a routing protocol defined at this layer is the Routing Information Protocol (RIP, discussed later).

Layer 2: Data Link. This layer provides the reliable transmission of data into bits across the physical network through the Physical layer. This layer has the following two sublayers:

- **MAC:** This sublayer is responsible for framing packets with a MAC address, error detection, and defining the physical topology, whether bus, star, or ring.

- **Logical Link Control (LLC):** This sublayer's main objective is to maintain upper-layer protocol standardization by keeping it independent over differing LANs.

Layer 1: Physical. The Physical layer is in charge of the electrical and mechanical transmission of bits over a physical communication medium. Examples of physical media include network interface cards (NICs), shielded or unshielded wiring, and topologies such as Ethernet and Token Ring.

Internetworking Functions of the Network Layer

The network layer of the OSI model is where routing protocols and logical network addressing operate. An example would be the Internet Protocol (IP), part of the TCP/IP suite. The IP is designed to interconnect networks to form an Internet, through which data is passed back and forth. It contains addressing and control information that enables *packets* to be routed through this Internet. (A packet is defined as a logical grouping of information, which includes a header containing control information and, usually, user data. The equipment—that is, routers—that encounter these packets strip off and examine the *headers* that contain the sensitive routing information. These headers are modified and reformulated as a packet to be passed along.)

One of the IP's primary functions is to provide a permanently established connection (called *connectionless*) and unreliable, best-effort delivery of *datagrams* through an internetwork. Datagrams can be described as a logical grouping of information sent as a network layer unit over a communication medium. IP datagrams are the primary information units in the Internet. Another of IP's principal responsibilities is the fragmentation and reassembly of datagrams to support links with different transmission sizes.

IP datagrams are the very basic, or fundamental, transfer unit of the Internet. An IP datagram is the unit of data commuted between IP modules. IP datagrams have headers with fields that provide routing information used by infrastructure equipment such as routers. Be aware that the data in a packet is not really a concern for the IP. Instead, IP is concerned with the control information as it pertains to the upper-layer protocol. This information is stored in the IP header, which tries to deliver the datagram to its destination on the local network or over the Internet. To understand this relationship, think of IP as the method and the datagram as the means.

Encapsulation and Fragmentation

It is important to understand the methods a datagram uses to travel across networks. To sufficiently travel across the Internet, over physical media, we want some guarantee that each datagram travels in a physical frame. The process of a datagram traveling across media in a frame is called *encapsulation*.

Using the OSI model, we can define the encapsulation process in five steps:

1. When a user sends information, at the Presentation layer, the information is converted to data.

2. At the Transport layer, data is converted to segments.

3. At the Network layer, segments are converted to packets/datagrams.

4. At the Data Link layer, packets/datagrams are converted to frames.

5. At the Physical layer, frames are converted to bits (0s and 1s) and transmitted.

When a user receives the transmission, the encapsulation process is reversed until the information is converted back from data (step 1).

An ideal situation is one in which an entire IP datagram fits into a frame, and the network it is traveling across supports that particular transfer size. But as we all know, ideal situations are rare. One problem with our traveling datagram is that networks enforce a maximum transfer unit (MTU) size, or limit, on the size of transfer. To further confuse the issue, different types of networks enforce their own MTU; for example, Ethernet has an MTU of 1,500, Fiber Distributed Data Interface (FDDI) uses 4,470 MTU, and so on. When datagrams traveling in frames cross network types that have different specified size limits, routers must sometimes divide the datagram to accommodate a smaller MTU. This process is called *fragmentation*.

Connection-Oriented/Connectionless Network Services and TCP/UDP Ports

The input/output ports on a computer are the channels through which data is transferred between an input or output device and the processor. They are also what hackers scan to find open, or "listening," ports and therefore are potentially susceptible to an attack. Hacking tools such as port scanners can, within minutes, easily scan every one of the more than 65,000 ports on a computer; however, they specifically scrutinize the first 1,024, those identified as the *well-known ports*. These first 1,024 ports are reserved for system services; as such, outgoing connections will have port numbers higher than 1023. This means that all incoming packets that communicate via ports higher than 1023 are replies to connections initiated by internal requests. When a port scanner scans computer ports, essentially, it asks one by one if a port is open or closed.

TCP and UDP ports (which are elucidated in RFC 793 and RFC 768, respectively) name the ends of logical connections that mandate service conversations on and between systems. Mainly, these lists specify the port used by the service daemon process as its contact port. The contact port is the acknowledged "well-known port."

A TCP connection is initialized through what's called a *three-way handshake*, whose purpose is to synchronize the sequence number and acknowledgment numbers of both sides of the connection while exchanging TCP window sizes. This is referred to as a *connection-oriented reliable service*. The handshake process starts with a one-node TCP request by a SYN/ACK bit and the second node TCP response with a SYN/ACK bit. At this point, communication between the two nodes will proceed. When there is no more data to send, a TCP node may send a FIN bit, indicating a close control signal. At this intersection, both nodes will close simultaneously. We'll examine the three-way handshake comprehensively in Chapter 11.

On the other side of the spectrum, UDP provides a *connectionless datagram service* that offers unreliable, best-effort delivery of data. This means that there is no guarantee of datagram arrival or of the correct sequencing of delivered packets.

Data Link and Network Addresses: The Differences Between Them

A MAC address is defined in the MAC sublayer of the Data Link layer of the OSI model. This address is referred to as the *hardware* or *data link address* because the MAC address identifies a physical hardware network interface. The MAC address is programmed in the read-only memory (ROM), for example, on an NIC.

Each interface must have a unique address in order to participate on communication media, primarily only on its local network (nonroutable). MAC addresses play an important role in the Internetwork Packet Exchange (IPX) protocol, described in Chapter 7. Remember, the address itself is 6 bytes, or 48 bits, in length and is divided in the following manner:

- The first 24 bits equal the manufacturer or vendor code.

- The last 24 bits equal a unique serial number assigned by the vendor.

An easy way to determine the MAC address on a Windows system is by using the Windows IP Configuration (WINIPCFG) command. From Start/Run,

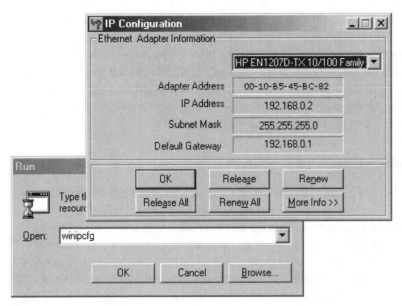

Figure 10.2   Locating the MAC address on a Windows station.

type *winipcfg* and press Enter (see Figure 10.2). The adapter address, shown in the figure, represents the physical hardware, MAC, or data link address.

A network address, on the other hand, can be defined as either a logical, dynamic, virtual, or static address that is assigned by network administrators and bound by software configurations to NICs, for example, as an IP address. This address is used to communicate on both local and remote networks; therefore, it can be easily routed.

To make a direct comparison, a network address (used on IP networks) is a logical (routable) address, whereas a data link address (used on IPX networks) is a physical hardware or MAC address (nonroutable) that is assigned by the NIC manufacturer.

MAC Address Functionality

We know that every interface or NIC in a station, server, or piece of infrastructure equipment has a unique physical address that is programmed and bound internally by the manufacturer—the MAC address.

One goal of infrastructure software is to communicate using an assigned IP or Internet address, while hiding the unique physical address of the hardware. Underneath all of this is the address mapping of the assigned address to the actual physical hardware address. To map these addresses, programmers use the Address Resolution Protocol (ARP).

Basically, ARP is a packet that is broadcast to all hosts attached to a physical network. This packet contains the IP address of the node or station with which the sender wants to communicate. Other hosts on the network ignore this packet after storing a copy of the sender's IP/hardware address mapping. The target host, however, will reply with its hardware address, which will be returned to the sender, to be stored in its ARP *response cache*. In this way, communication between these two nodes can ensue.

Network Addressing with Protocols

As you know by now, communicating on the Internet would be almost impossible if a system of unique addressing were not used. With TCP/IP, to prevent the use of duplicate addresses, routing between nodes is based on addresses assigned from a pool of classes, or range of available addresses, from the InterNetwork Information Center (InterNIC). InterNIC assigns and controls all network addresses used over the Internet by assigning addresses in three classes (A, B, and C), which consist of 32-bit numbers. By default, the usable bits for Classes A, B, and C are 8, 16, and 24, respectively. Addresses from this pool have been assigned and used since the 1970s, and they include the ranges shown in Figure 10.3; an example of an IP address is also shown.

IP Address: 206.0.125.0

Class	First Octet or Series	Octets as Network vs. Host	Netmask Binary
A	1 – 126	Network.Host.Host.Host	1111 1111 0000 0000 0000 0000 0000 0000 or 255.0.0.0
B	128 – 191	Network.Network.Host.Host	1111 1111 1111 1111 0000 0000 0000 0000 or 255.255.0.0
C	192 – 223	**Network.Network.Network.Host**	**1111 1111 1111 1111 1111 1111 0000 0000 or 255.255.255.0**
D	*Defined for multicast operation and not used for normal operation*		
E	*Defined for experimental use and not used for normal operation*		

Figure 10.3 IP address chart by class.

In the sample IP address, the first octet (206) indicates a Class C (Internet-assigned) IP address range with the format *Network.Network.Network.Host* with a standard mask binary indicating 255.255.255.0. This means that we have 8 bits in the last octet for hosts. The 8 bits that make up the last, or fourth, octet are understood by infrastructure equipment such as routers and software in the following manner:

Bit:	1	2	3	4	5	6	7	8	
Value:	128	64	32	16	8	4	2	1	= 255

(254 usable hosts)

In this example of a full Class C, we only have 254 usable IP addresses for hosts; 0 and 255 cannot be used as host addresses because the network number is 0 and the broadcast address is 255.

In the early 1990s, to cope with the widespread use of Class B address space and the flooding of requested Class C addresses, a Classless Interdomain Routing (CIR) system was introduced. Under CIR, basically, a route is no longer an IP address; a route is now an IP address and mask, allowing us to break a network into *subnets* and *supernets*. This also drastically reduces the size of Internet routing tables.

IP Subnetting

Subnetting is the process of dividing an assigned or derived address class into smaller, individual, but related, physical networks. *Variable-length subnet masking* (VLSM) is the broadcasting of subnet information through routing protocols. A subnet mask is a 32-bit number that determines the network split of IP addresses on the bit level. Let's take a look at a real-world scenario of allocating IP addresses for a routed network (see Figure 10.4).

Given: 206.0.125.0 (NIC-assigned Class C). In this scenario, we need to divide our Class C address block to accommodate three usable subnets (for offices A, B, and C) and two subnets for future growth. Each subnet or network must have at least 25 available node addresses.

This process can be divided into five steps. First, four host addresses will be required for each of the office's router interfaces:

SUBNET	INTERFACES
1	Router 1 (Ethernet 0 or E0)
	Router 1 (Serial 0 or S0 IP address will be provided by the ISP)
	Router 2 (Ethernet 0 or E0)
2	Router 1 (Ethernet 1 or E1)

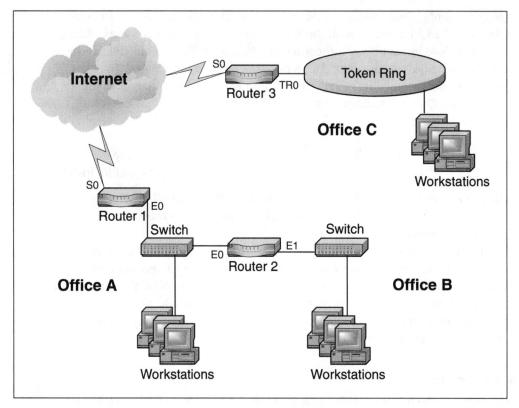

Figure 10.4   Real-world IP network example.

3   Router 3 (Token Ring 0 or TR0)

                     Router 3 (Serial 0 or S0 IP address will be provided by the ISP)

Second, using a Class C subnet cheat sheet, only one option will support our scenario of five subnets with at least 25 IP addresses per network (as shown in Figure 10.5).

Bits in Subnet Mask: Keeping in mind the information given earlier, let's further explore the subnet mask bit breakdown. When a bit is used, we indicate this with a 1:

3 Bits:	1	1	1				
Value:	128	64	32	16	8	4	2	1

When a bit is not used, we indicate this with a 0:

3 Bits:				0	0	0	0	0
Value:	128	64	32	16	8	4	2	1

Bits in Subnet Mask	Subnet Mask	# of Subnets	# of Hosts Per Subnet
2	255.255.255.192	2	62
3	**255.255.255.224**	6	30
4	255.255.255.240	14	14
5	255.255.255.248	30	6
6	255.255.255.252	62	2

Figure 10.5   Class C subnet chart by number of subnets versus number of hosts per subnet.

Put the bits together and add the values:

3 Bits:	1	1	1	0	0	0	0	0
Value:	128	64	32	16	8	4	2	1

Value: 128 + 64 + 32   = 224

(subnet mask = 255.255.255.224)

Number of Subnets: Remember, in this scenario we need to divide our Class C address block to accommodate three usable subnets (for offices A, B, and C) and two subnets for future growth with at least 25 available node addresses per each of the five networks.

To make this process as simple as possible, let's start with the smaller number, that is, 5 for the required subnets or networks as opposed to 25 for the available nodes needed per network. To explain the addresses required for each of the office's router interfaces, we'll start with the following equation, where we'll solve for n in $2^n - 2$, being sure to cover the required five subnets or networks.

Let's start with the power of 2 and work our way up:

$$2^2 - 2 = 2, 2^3 - 2 = 6, 2^4 - 2 = 14$$

The (third power) in the equation indicates the number of bits in the subnet mask. Here we see that $2^3 - 2 = 6$ subnets if we use these 3 bits. This will cover the required five subnets with an additional subnet (or network) left over.

Number of Hosts per Subnet: Now let's determine the number of bits left over for available host addresses. In this scenario, we will be using 3 bits in the mask for subnetting. How many are left over?

Out of the given 32 bits that make up IP addresses, the default availability (for networks versus hosts), as previously explained, for Classes A, B, and C blocks are as follows:

Class A: 8 bits

Class B: 16 bits

Class C: 24 bits

Our scenario involves a Class C block assigned by InterNIC. If we subtract our default bit availability for Class C of 24 bits (as shown) from the standard 32 bits that make up IP addresses, we have 8 bits remaining for networks versus hosts for Class C blocks.

Next, we subtract our 3 bits used for subnetting from the total 8 bits remaining for network versus hosts, which gives us 5 bits left for actual host addressing:

3 Bits:	1	1	1	0	0	0	0	0
Value:	128	64	32	(16	8	4	2	1)

5 bits left

Let's solve an equation to see if 5 bits are enough to cover the required available node addresses of at least 25 per subnet or network:

$$2^5 - 2 = 30$$

Placing the remaining 5 bits back into our equation gives us the available node addresses per subnet or network, $2^5 - 2 = 30$ host addresses per six subnets or networks (remember, we have an additional subnet left over).

From these steps, we can divide our Class C block using 3 bits to give us six subnets with 30 host addresses each.

Now that we have determined the subnet mask, in this case 255.255.255.224 (3 bits), we need to calculate the actual network numbers or range of IP addresses in each network. This is the third step. An easy way to accomplish this is by setting the host bits to 0. Remember, we have 5 bits left for hosts:

3 Bits:	1	1	1	0	0	0	0	0
Value:	128	64	32	(16	8	4	2	1)

5 host bits left

With the 5 host bits set to 0, we set the first 3 bits to 1 *in every variation* and then calculate the value (for a shortcut, take the first subnet value = 32 and add it in succession to reveal all six subnets):

3 Bits:	0	0	1	0	0	0	0	0	
Value:	128	64	32	(16	8	4	2	1)	
			32						= **32**

3 Bits:	0	1	0	0	0	0	0	0	
Value:	128	64	32	(16	8	4	2	1)	
		64							= **64**

3 Bits:	0	1	1	0	0	0	0	0	
Value:	128	64	32	(16	8	4	2	1)	
		64 +	32						= **96**

3 Bits:	1	0	0	0	0	0	0	0	
Value:	128	64	32	(16	8	4	2	1)	
	128								= **128**

3 Bits:	1	0	1	0	0	0	0	0	
Value:	128	64	32	(16	8	4	2	1)	
	128	+	32						= **160**

3 Bits:	1	1	0	0	0	0	0	0	
Value:	128	64	32	(16	8	4	2	1)	
	128 +	64							= **192**

Now let's take a look at the network numbers of our subnetted Class C block with mask 255.255.255.224:

192.168.1.32	192.168.1.64	192.168.1.96
192.168.1.128	192.168.1.160	192.168.1.192

Now that we have solved the network numbers, we take the fourth and final step in the process: to resolve each network's *broadcast address* by setting host bits to all 1s. The broadcast address is defined as the system that copies and delivers a single packet to all addresses on the network. All hosts attached to a network can be notified by sending a packet to a common broadcast address:

3 Bits:	0	0	1	1	1	1	1	1	
Value:	128	64	32	(16	8	4	2	1)	
			32 +	16 +	8 +	4 +	2 +	1	= **63**

3 Bits:	0	1	0	1	1	1	1	1	
Value:	128	64	32	(16	8	4	2	1)	
		64	+	16	+ 8	+ 4	+ 2	+ 1	**= 95**

3 Bits:	0	1	1	1	1	1	1	1	
Value:	128	64	32	(16	8	4	2	1)	
		64 +	32 +	16 +	8 +	4 +	2 +	1	**= 127**

3 Bits:	1	0	0	1	1	1	1	1	
Value:	128	64	32	(16	8	4	2	1)	
	128		+	16	+ 8	+ 4	+ 2	+ 1	**= 159**

3 Bits:	1	0	1	1	1	1	1	1	
Value:	128	64	32	(16	8	4	2	1)	
	128	+	32 +	16 +	8 +	4 +	2 +	1	**= 191**

3 Bits:	1	1	0	1	1	1	1	1	
Value:	128	64	32	(16	8	4	2	1)	
	128 + 64		+	16	+ 8	+ 4	+ 2	+ 1	**= 223**

Let's take a look at the network broadcast addresses of our subnetted Class C block with mask 255.255.255.224:

192.168.1.63	192.168.1.95	192.168.1.127
192.168.1.159	192.168.1.191	192.168.1.223

So what are the available IP addresses for each of our six networks? They are the addresses between the network and broadcast addresses for each subnet or network (see Figure 10.6).

Taking a Shortcut

You'll be happy to know there is a shortcut we can take to determine a network address, given an IP address. Let's look at a couple of examples.

Given: 206.0.139.81 255.255.255.224. To calculate the network address for this host, let's map out the host octet (81) and the subnet-masked octet (224) by starting from the left, or largest, number:

(81)

Bits:		1		1				1	
Value:	128	64	32	16	8	4	2	1	
		64 +		16 +				1	= 81

Network Address	Broadcast Address	Valid IP Address Range
206.0.125.32	206.0.125.63	206.0.125.33 – 206.0.125.62
206.0.125.64	206.0.125.95	206.0.125.65 – 206.0.125.94
206.0.125.96	206.0.125.127	206.0.125.97 – 206.0.125.126
206.0.125.128	206.0.125.159	206.0.125.129 – 206.0.125.158
206.0.125.160	206.0.125.191	206.0.125.161 – 206.0.125.190
206.0.125.192	206.0.125.223	206.0.125.193 – 206.0.125.222

Figure 10.6   Available IP addresses for our networks.

```
(224)
Bits:      1    1    1
Value:    128  64   32   16   8    4    2    1
----------------------------------------------------------
          128 + 64 + 32                              = 224
```

Now we can perform a mathematic logical AND to obtain the network address of this host (the value 64 is the only common bit):

```
(81)
Bits:           1         1                   1
Value:    128  64   32   16   8    4    2    1

(224)
Bits:      1    1    1
Value:    128  64   32   16   8    4    2    1
----------------------------------------------------------
          64                                 = 64
```

We simply put the 1s together horizontally and record the common value (205.0.125.64).

For our second example, we'll calculate the IP subnets, network, and broadcast addresses for another IP address:

Given: 07.247.60.0 (InterNIC-assigned Class C) 255.255.255.0. In this scenario, we need to divide our Class C address block to accommodate 10 usable subnets. Each subnet or network must have at least 10 available node addresses.

This example requires four steps to complete. First we need the number of subnets. Remember, in this scenario we need to divide our Class C address block to accommodate 10 usable with at least 10 available node addresses per each of the 10 networks. Let's start with the number 10 for the required subnets and the following equation, where we'll solve for n in $2^n - 2$, being sure to cover the required 10 subnets or networks.

We'll begin with the power of 2 and work our way up:

$$2^2 - 2 = 2 \qquad 2^3 - 2 = 6 \qquad \mathbf{2^4 - 2 = 14}$$

In this equation, the ^{4} indicates the number of bits in the subnet mask. Note that $2^4 - 2 = 14$ subnets if we use these 4 bits. This will cover the required 10 subnets and leave four additional subnets (or networks).

SUBNET MASK

4 Bits:	1	1	1	1	0	0	0	0
Value:	128	64	32	16	8	4	2	1

Value:	128 + 64 + 32 + 16	= 240

(mask = 255.255.255.240)

Number of hosts per subnet: Now we'll determine the number of bits left over for available host addresses. In this scenario, we will be using 4 bits in the mask for subnetting. How many are left over? Remember, out of the given 32 bits that make up IP addresses, the default availability (for networks versus hosts), as previously explained, for Classes A, B, and C blocks is as follows:

Class A: 8 bits

Class B: 16 bits

Class C: 24 bits

Our scenario involves a Class C block assigned by InterNIC. If we subtract our default bit availability for Class C of 24 bits (as shown) from the standard 32 bits that make up IP addresses, we have 8 bits remaining for networks versus hosts for Class C blocks.

Next, we subtract the 4 bits used for subnetting from the total 8 bits remaining for network versus hosts, which gives us 4 bits left for actual host addressing:

4 Bits:	1	1	1	1	0	0	0	0
Value:	128	64	32	16	(8	4	2	1)

4 bits left

Let's solve an equation to determine whether 4 bits are enough to cover the required available node addresses of at least 10 per subnet or network:

$$2^4 - 2 = 14$$

Placing the remaining 4 bits back into our equation gives us the available node addresses per subnet or network: $2^4 - 2 = 14$ host addresses per 14 subnets or networks (remember, we have four additional subnets left over).

From these steps, we can divide our Class C block using 4 bits to give us 14 subnets with 14 host addresses each.

Now that we have determined the subnet mask, in this case 255.255.255.240 (4 bits), we need to calculate the actual network numbers or range of IP addresses in each network. This is the second step in this process. An easy way to accomplish this is by setting the host bits to 0. Remember, we have 4 bits left for hosts:

4 Bits:	1	1	1	1	0	0	0	0
Value:	128	64	32	16	(8	4	2	1)

4 host bits left

With the 4 host bits set to 0, we set the first 4 bits to 1 *in every variation*, then calculate the value:

4 Bits:	0	0	0	1	0	0	0	0
Value:	128	64	32	16	(8	4	2	1)

----
16   **= 16**

4 Bits:	0	0	1	0	0	0	0	0
Value:	128	64	32	16	(8	4	2	1)

----
32   **= 32**

and so on to reveal our 14 subnets or networks. Recall the shortcut in the first example: We can take our first value (=16) and add it in succession to equate to 14 networks:

First subnet = 16   Second subnet = 32 (16+16) Third subnet = 48 (32+16)…

207.247.60.16	207.247.60.32	207.247.60.48	207.247.60.64
207.247.60.80	207.247.60.96	207.247.60.112	207.247.60.128
207.247.60.144	207.247.60.160	207.247.60.176	207.247.60.192
207.247.60.208	207.247.60.224		

Now that we have solved the network numbers, let's resolve each network's broadcast address. This third step is easy. Remember, the broadcast address is the last address in a network before the next network address; therefore:

First Network   **Second Network**

207.247.60.16   **(31)**   207.247.60.32   **(47)**   207.247.60.48   **(63)**

        First Broadcast   **Second Broadcast**

So, what are the available IP addresses for each network? Determining this is step 4, and the answer is right in the middle of step 3. Keep in mind, the available IP addresses for each network fall between the network and broadcast addresses:

First Network   **Second Network**

207.247.60.16   **(31)**   207.247.60.32   **(47)**   207.247.60.48

        First Broadcast   **Second Broadcast**

(First Network addresses: 17 – 30)

(Second Network addresses: 33 – 46)

IPX Addressing

To review from Chapter 7, IPX is a connectionless datagram protocol and, as such, is similar to unreliable datagram delivery offered by the Internet Protocol; also, like IP address schemes, Novell IPX network addresses must be unique. They are represented in hexadecimal format and consist of two parts, a network number and a node number. The IPX network number is an assigned 32-bit-long number. The node number is a 48-bit-long hardware or MAC address for one of the system's NICs. The NIC manufacturer assigns the 48-bit-long hardware or MAC address.

An example of an IPX address using the format *Network Number.Node Number*, is shown here:

    48F30106.00A024F9173B
    (Network)   (Node)

Because the host portion of an IP network address has no equivalence to a MAC address, IP nodes must use the ARP to determine the destination MAC address.

To process upper-layer (OSI Layers 2 and 3) protocol information and data into frames, NetWare IPX supports several encapsulation schemes. Among the most popular encapsulation types are Novell Proprietary, 802.3, Ethernet Version 2, and Ethernet Subnetwork Access Protocol (SNAP), which are defined in the following list:

Novell Proprietary. Novell's initial encapsulation type, also known as Novel Ethernet 802.3 and 802.3 Raw.

802.3. The standard IEEE 802.3 format, also known as Novell 802.2.

Ethernet II. Includes a standard Ethernet Version 2 header.

Ethernet SNAP. An extension of 802.3.

IPX network numbers play a primary role in the foundation for IPX internetwork packet exchange between network segments. Every segment is assigned a unique network address to which packets are routed for node destinations. For a protocol to identify itself with IPX and communicate with the network, it must request a *socket number*. Socket numbers ascertain the identity of processes within a station or node.

Whether addressing LAN devices with IP or IPX, grouping them into large networks can be difficult to manage. More importantly, however, bandwidth will be rapidly consumed as devices attempt to simultaneously communicate. To alleviate bandwidth congestion, segmenting large networks will be crucial.

LAN Segmentation

Breaking down large networks into smaller, more manageable units is called *segmentation*. Generally speaking, the most critical benefit of segmentation is maximized bandwidth, achieved by increasing bandwidth per user, thereby reducing network congestion, or creating collision domains. A collision takes place when two or more devices attempt to send a signal simultaneously along the same channel, whereas collision domains segregate devices into smaller segments, which reduces the chances of colliding signals. In this section, we'll discuss the benefits of segmenting with routers, bridges, and switches.

Segmenting with Routers

Fundamentally, a gateway is a network point that acts as a doorway between multiple networks. In a company network, for example, a proxy server may act as a gateway between the internal network and the Internet. By the same token, an SMTP gateway would allow users on the network to exchange email. Gateways interconnect networks and are categorized according to their OSI model layer of operation; examples are repeaters at Physical Layer 1, bridges at Data Link Layer 2, routers at Network Layer 3, and so on. Gateways that function primarily as access routers operate at the Network—Layer 3—of the OSI model.

A router that connects any number of LANs (or WANs) uses information from protocol headers to build a routing table and forwards packets based on compiled decisions. Routing hardware design is relatively straightforward, consisting of network interfaces, administration or console ports, and even auxiliary ports for out-of-band management devices such as modems. As packets travel into a router's network interface card, they are placed into a queue for processing. During this operation, the router builds, updates, and maintains routing tables while concurrently checking packet headers for next-step compilations—whether accepting and forwarding the packet based on routing policies or discarding the packet based on filtering policies. At the same time, protocol performance functions provide handshaking, windowing, buffering, source quenching, and error checking.

A router can segment a large network by breaking it into multiple subnets or internetworks, as shown in Figure 10.7. These subnets are actually manageable broadcast domains. Routers make intelligent routing decisions based on filters, security, and costs or best path to a destination. In this case, it's important to note that routers route packets at the Network layer based on IP addresses.

Segmenting with Bridges

A bridge can segment a large network by creating physical and logical segments or collision domains (see Figure 10.8). Working at the MAC sublayer of

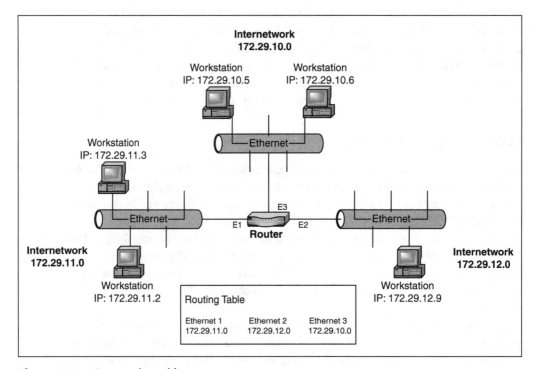

Figure 10.7 Segmenting with a router.

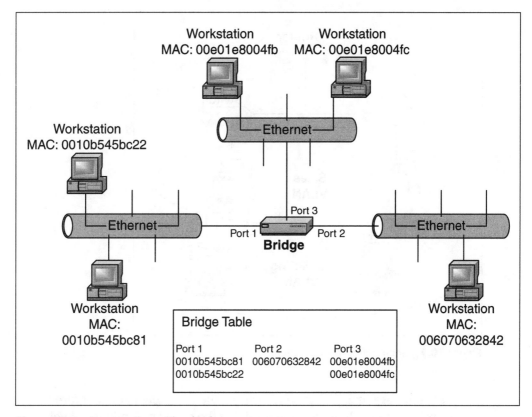

Figure 10.8 Segmenting with a bridge.

the Data Link layer, bridges check MAC addresses in each passing frame and forward them based on the destination MAC addresses. If a bridge intercepts a destination MAC address that is not known or that is not already in its bridging table, the bridge will forward the frame out all ports except the source port—the port from which the frame entered. A longstanding problem of bridging is the advent of *broadcast storms*—a state in which a message that has been broadcast across a network results in even more broadcast responses, and each response results in still more responses. For this reason, many large networks opt to implement switches for LAN segmentation.

Segmenting with Switches

A switch can segment a large network by creating *virtual LANs* (VLANs), logical groups of ports as broadcast domains, shown in Figure 10.9. For all practical purposes, a switch can be thought of as a smart bridge that forwards frames out of ports to destination MAC addresses. For increased performance, there are three switching types:

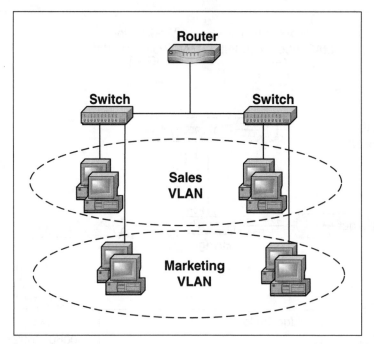

Figure 10.9 Segmenting with a switch.

Store-and-forward. The switch receives the complete packet before forwarding. After calculating and verifying the cyclic redundancy check (CRC)—for detecting data transmission errors—at the end of each frame, the destination and source addresses are read and the packet is forwarded to the destination's ports. The frame is discarded if it contains a CRC error. Latency increases in proportion to packet size when this switching technique is used because of the time it takes to receive and check the entire frame.

Cut-through. The switch does not wait for the packet to be completely received nor does it check the CRC. It simply waits for the header to be received to determine the destination address. Depending on the network transport protocol being used (connectionless or connection-oriented), there is a significant decrease in latency from input port to output port.

Fragment-free. This is a modified form of cut-through switching. The switch waits for the collision window (64 bytes) to pass before forwarding. If a packet has an error—or more accurately stated, a collision—it almost always occurs within the first 64 bytes. Fragment-free mode provides better error checking than the cut-through mode with practically no increase in latency.

Router Elements and the Internetworking Operating System

An operating system (O/S) can be defined as the collection of directives that are required before a computer system can run. Thus, the O/S is the most important software in any system. A system relies on the O/S to manage all of the hardware installed and connected to it. A good general analogy would be to think of the operating system as the post office: The post office is responsible for the flow of mail throughout your neighborhood; likewise, the O/S is in command of the flow of information through your system.

Like a server and its operating system, a Cisco router contains an IOS. In preparation to examining and configuring IOS functionality, let's take a look at the basic router elements, setup, and login modes.

 We'll be using a few different routers during our investigations, primarily from the popular 2600 series.

Router Elements

Figure 10.10 illustrates the standard interfaces of a Cisco router. From left to right, the serial ports will typically be used to connect to WAN devices, the Ethernet ports to LAN devices, the Console port to a computer for direct administration via console cable, and the Auxiliary port to a modem for remote dial-in management.

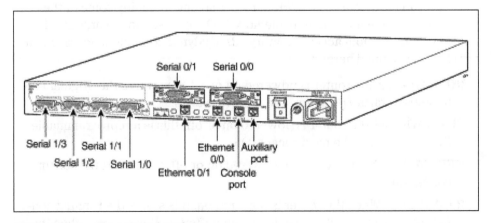

Figure 10.10   Cisco 2600 interfaces.

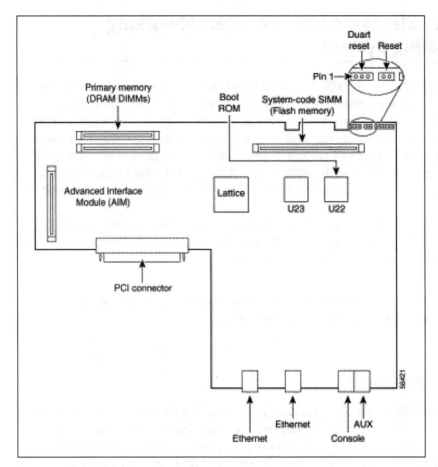

Figure 10.11   Cisco 2600 internal layout.

Figure 10.11 illustrates the internal router layout, including some of the most critical elements: read-only memory (ROM), Flash, nonvolatile RAM (NVRAM), and random access memory (RAM)/dynamic random-access memory (DRAM), defined here:

ROM. Whether the router is powered on or off, this stores the original IOS, bootstrap startup program, and hardware tests.

Flash. Whether the router is powered on or off, this is a reprogrammable ROM that stores the most recent IOS.

NVRAM. Whether the router is powered on or off, this stores the startup configuration.

RAM/DRAM. When the router is powered on, this stores the running configuration, routing tables, caching, and buffering. It is cleared when the router is powered off.

Setup

Before we log in to the router, let's review the following generic Cisco Quick Start Setup steps:

CONNECTING THE CONSOLE CABLE

1. Connect the console cable to the port labeled Console on the rear panel of the router. Connect the other end of the console cable to an RJ-45 adapter—use either the RJ-45-to-DB-9 adapter or the RJ-45-to-DB-25 adapter, depending on your local PC.

2. Attach the console adapter to a serial port on your PC running Windows. Configure and start your system's HyperTerminal program to communicate via the appropriate serial COM port with the following settings (see Figure 10.12):

> Bits per second: 9600
>
> Data bits: 8
>
> Parity: none
>
> Stop bits: 1
>
> Flow control: Hardware

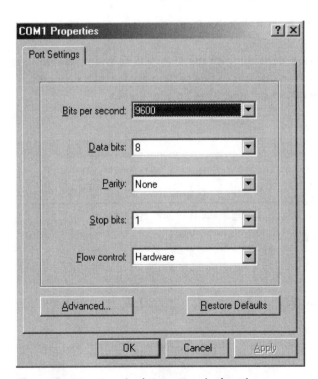

Figure 10.12   Required HyperTerminal settings.

CONNECTING TO THE LAN AND POWERING UP

3. Connect to the Ethernet network by attaching one end of an Ethernet cable to the Ethernet port labeled Ethernet 0/0 on the rear panel of your router. Connect the other end of the Ethernet cable to any available port on your network hub or switch. Make sure your PC is also connected to the Ethernet LAN.

4. Connect the power and turn on the router.

RUNNING SETUP

Depending on your router status, to start the initial Setup program, you may be required type `enable` and then `setup` at the prompt. Also note that the actual steps may vary, depending on the current IOS version— we'll be working with version 12.0. At any point you may enter a question mark (?) for help. Use Ctrl-C to abort configuration dialog at any prompt. Default settings are given in square brackets [ ].

5. The initial messages that appear in your terminal window are part of the router bootstrap process, as shown in Figure 10.13. Either press Enter to get started and/or type yes and press Enter if asked:

```
Continue with configuration dialog? [yes/no]:
```

These messages will vary, depending on the Cisco IOS software release and feature set. The screen displays in this section are for reference only and might not exactly reflect the messages on your screen.

6.
```
Basic management setup configures only enough connectivity for
management of the system; extended setup will ask you to configure
each interface on the system.

Would you like to enter basic management setup? [yes/no]:
```
Type no and press Enter.

7.
```
First, would you like to see the current interface summary? [yes]:
```
Press Enter to accept the default yes to see the current interface summary.

8.
```
Configuring global parameters:
  Enter host name [Router]:
```

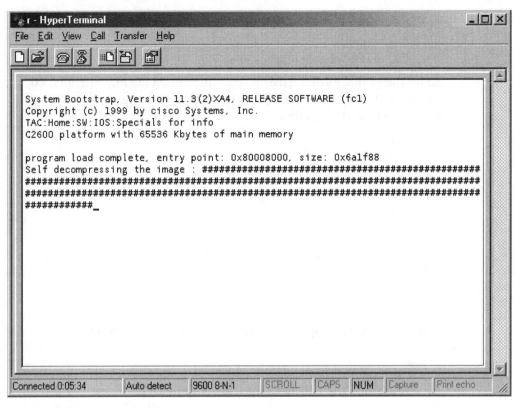

```
System Bootstrap, Version 11.3(2)XA4, RELEASE SOFTWARE (fc1)
Copyright (c) 1999 by cisco Systems, Inc.
TAC:Home:SW:IOS:Specials for info
C2600 platform with 65536 Kbytes of main memory

program load complete, entry point: 0x80008000, size: 0x6a1f88
Self decompressing the image : ###########################################
##########################################################################
##########################################################################
############
```

Figure 10.13 The router bootstrap process.

Enter a host name for the router (we'll use 2611) to represent our model. Type 2611 and press Enter.

9.

```
The enable secret is a password used to protect access to
privileged EXEC and configuration modes. This password, after
entered, becomes encrypted in the configuration.
Enter enable secret:
```

Enter an enable secret password. This password is encrypted (more secure) and cannot be seen when viewing the configuration. Type ciscosecret and press Enter.

10.

```
The enable password is used when you do not specify an
enable secret password, with some older software versions, and
some boot images.
Enter enable password:
```

The enable password is used when there is no enable secret and when using older software and some boot images. Type cisco and press Enter.

11.

```
The virtual terminal password is used to protect
access to the router over a network interface.
Enter virtual terminal password:
```

Enter the virtual terminal password, which prevents unauthenticated access to the router through ports other than the console port. Type `vterminal` and press Enter.

12.

```
Configure SNMP Network Management? [no]:
```

Press Enter to accept the default no to skip the SNMP setup—we'll cover that later.

13.

```
Configure LAT? [yes]:
```

Type no to skip the LAT setup—we'll cover that later. Press Enter to continue.

14.

```
Configure AppleTalk? [no]:
```

Type no to skip the AppleTalk setup. Press Enter to continue.

15.

```
Configure DECnet? [no]:
```

Type no to skip the DECnet setup. Press Enter to continue.

16.

```
Configure IP? [yes]:
```

Press Enter to accept the default yes to configure IP.

17.

```
Configure IGRP routing? [yes]:
```

Type no to skip the IGRP routing configuration—we'll cover that later. Press Enter to continue.

18.

```
Configure RIP routing? [no]:
```

Type no to skip the RIP routing configuration—we'll cover that later. Press Enter to continue.

19.

```
Configure CLNS? [no]:
Configure bridging? [no]:
Configure IPX? [no]:
Configure Vines? [no]:
Configure XNS? [no]:
Configure Apollo? [no]:
```

Type no or press Enter to accept the default no to skip setup of each of these—we'll cover most of them later. Press Enter to continue.

20.

```
Async lines accept incoming modems calls. If you will have
users dialing in via modems, configure these lines.
Configure Async lines? [yes]:
```

Type no to skip this configuration—we'll cover that later. Press Enter to continue.

21.

```
Configuring interface parameters:
Do you want to configure Ethernet0/0  interface? [yes]:
Configure IP on this interface? [yes]:
```

Press Enter to accept the default yes to configure our LAN-connected Ethernet interface.

22.

```
IP address for this interface:
```

Type 192.168.0.3 and press Enter.

23.

```
Subnet mask for this interface:
```

Type 255.255.255.0 and press Enter.

24.

```
Do you want to configure Serial0/0  interface? [no]:
Do you want to configure Serial0/1  interface? [no]:
```

Type no to skip the Serial interfaces setup—we'll cover that later. Press Enter to continue.

25.

```
Do you want to configure Ethernet0/1 interface? [yes]:
```

Type no to skip this configuration—we'll cover that later. Press Enter to continue.

26.

```
The following configuration command script was created:
hostname 2611
enable secret 5 $1$SQNi$S2EBRbGRX3m2mLv/A1qh00
enable password cisco
line vty 0 4
password vterminal
no snmp-server
!
no appletalk routing
no decnet routing
ip routi
no clns routing
no bridge 1
no ipx routing
no vines routing
no xns routing
```

```
no apollo routing
!
interface Ethernet0/0
ip address 192.168.0.3 255.255.255.0
no mop enabled
!
interface Serial0/0
shutdown
no ip address
!
interface Ethernet0/1
shutdown
no ip address
!
interface Serial0/1
shutdown
no ip address
dialer-list 1 protocol ip permit
dialer-list 1 protocol ipx permit
!
end

[0] Go to the IOS command prompt without saving this config.
[1] Return back to the setup without saving this config.
[2] Save this configuration to nvram and exit.
Enter your selection [2]:
```

Press Enter to accept the default option—number 2—to save the configuration to NVRAM and exit.

27.

```
Building configuration...
00:42:50: %LINK-5-CHANGED: Interface Ethernet0/1, changed state to
administratively down
Use the enabled mode configure' command to modify this configuration.
2611#
```

That's it—the initial setup was easy.

Login Modes

You now have access to the command interpreter referred to as EXEC, in full privileged mode. In this study, there are really only two operation modes to be concerned with:

User mode. Supports tasks for monitoring basic router status information. The user mode prompt looks like this:

```
2611>
```

Privileged mode. Supports tasks for modifying the router configuration and accessing advanced status information, debugging, and troubleshooting. The privileged mode can be entered by typing enable at the user mode prompt:

```
2611>enable
```

Then press Enter.
The privileged prompt looks like this:

```
2611#
```

To exit back to the user mode, type disable at the privileged mode prompt:

```
2611#disable
```

Then press Enter.
Other important router EXEC modes to know include the following:

Setup mode. The interactive prompted dialogue at the console that we just executed.

Global configuration mode. One-line command mode to perform simple configuration tasks.

RXBOOT mode. Maintenance mode used to recover lost passwords and other techniques.

Now let's power-cycle the router and view the login process from both the console and remote terminal access via Telnet. From HyperTerminal, after the initial bootstrap and configuration loading processes, you'll see the EXEC user mode prompt shown in Figure 10.14. There simply type enable and then our secret password, ciscosecret, and press Enter to return to the privileged mode.

To log in remotely via Telnet, from Start/Run on your Windows system, type: telnet 192.168.0.3 and press Enter (see Figure 10.15). At the first prompt, enter the virtual terminal password vterminal and press Enter. This will log you in again to the EXEC user mode. From there, type enable and then our secret password, ciscosecret, and press Enter to enter privileged mode.

Commands for Router Elements

The objective in this section is to examine some of the most common EXEC commands, particularly those involving the router elements: Flash, NVRAM, and RAM/DRAM.

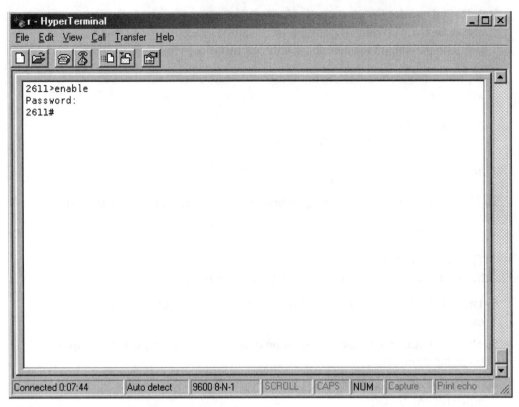

Figure 10.14 Logging in from the router console.

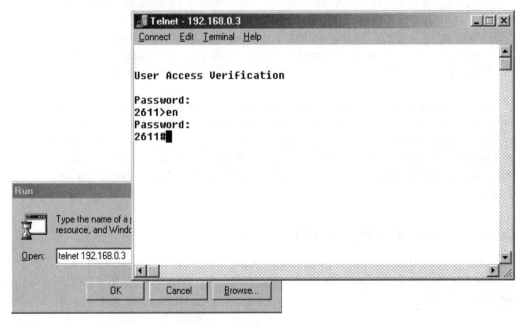

Figure 10.15 Logging in remotely using Telnet.

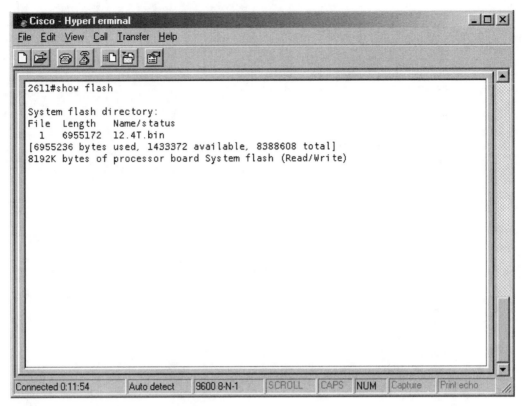

Figure 10.16 Viewing the current IOS.

Flash (show flash)

Whether the router is powered on or off, the Flash is a reprogrammable ROM that stores the most recent IOS. To view the current IOS information, as shown in Figure 10.16, from the command prompt, type:

```
show flash
```

then press Enter.

NVRAM (show startup-config)

Whether the router is powered on or off, the NVRAM stores the startup configuration. To view the current startup configuration stored in NVRAM, type:

```
show startup-config
```

and then press Enter. You'll see the following code:

```
2611#show startup-config
Using 779 out of 29688 bytes
```

```
!
version 12.0
service config
service timestamps debug uptime
service timestamps log uptime
no service password-encryption
!
hostname 2611
!
enable secret 5 $1$SQNi$S2EBRbGRX3m2mLv/A1qh00
enable password cisco
!
ip subnet-zero
!
!
!
!
!
interface Ethernet0/0
 ip address 192.168.0.3 255.255.255.0
 no ip directed-broadcast
 no mop enabled
!
interface Serial0/0
 no ip address
 no ip directed-broadcast
 shutdown
!
interface Ethernet0/1
 no ip address
 no ip directed-broadcast
 shutdown
!
interface Serial0/1
 no ip address
 no ip directed-broadcast
 shutdown
!
ip classless
no ip http server
!
dialer-list 1 protocol ip permit
dialer-list 1 protocol ipx permit
!
!
line con 0
 transport input none
line aux 0
line vty 0 4
 password vterminal
```

```
 login
 !
no scheduler allocate
end
```

RAM/DRAM (show running-config)

When the router is powered on, the RAM/DRAM stores the running configuration, routing tables, caching, and buffering. It is cleared when the router is powered off. Therefore, if you change the current configuration without saving it to NVRAM, the changes will be lost the next time the router is power-cycled. To view the running configuration, type:

```
show running-config
```

and then press Enter. This results in the following:

```
2611#show running-config
Building configuration...

Current configuration:
!
version 12.0
service config
service timestamps debug uptime
service timestamps log uptime
no service password-encryption
!
hostname 2611
!
enable secret 5 $1$SQNi$S2EBRbGRX3m2mLv/A1qh00
enable password cisco
!
ip subnet-zero
!
!
!
!
!
interface Ethernet0/0
 ip address 192.168.0.3 255.255.255.0
 no ip directed-broadcast
 no mop enabled
!
interface Serial0/0
 no ip address
 no ip directed-broadcast
 shutdown
!
interface Ethernet0/1
```

```
    no ip address
    no ip directed-broadcast
    shutdown
!
interface Serial0/1
    no ip address
    no ip directed-broadcast
    shutdown
!
ip classless
no ip http server
!
dialer-list 1 protocol ip permit
dialer-list 1 protocol ipx permit
!
!
line con 0
    transport input none
line aux 0
line vty 0 4
    password vterminal
    login
!
end
```

You can abbreviate most of the commands from the EXEC modes; for example, `sh run` would execute `show running-config`, `sh start` would execute `show startup-config`, and `sh fl` would execute `show flash`. In this chapter, however, we'll be using the full command text to help recall their meanings in the field.

Configuration Mode (config t, copy running-config startup-config)

To modify the current running configuration, shown in Figure 10.17, you would type: `config t` and then press Enter to enter the configuration mode. You enter configuration commands one per line and end by pressing Ctrl-Z. Remember, you can modify the configuration only from EXEC privileged mode. When you're ready to save the modified running configuration by moving it to NVRAM, type:

```
copy running-config startup-config
```

then press Enter.

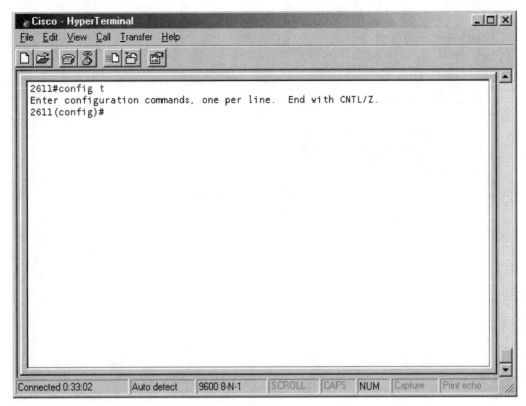

Figure 10.17 Entering the configuration mode.

Cisco Discovery Protocol

Cisco Discovery Protocol (CDP) is an independent device discovery protocol that runs on all Cisco equipment. With CDP, a device advertises its existence to other devices and in turn receives information about those devices on the same LAN or WAN. Each device configured for CDP sends periodic messages to a multicast address and advertises at least one address at which it can receive SNMP messages. These messages also contain time-to-live (TTL; hold time) information, which is the length of time a receiving device should retain CDP information before discarding it.

To configure CDP, shown in Figure 10.18, Cisco recommends performing the following tasks from the EXEC privileged, configuration mode (config t):

1. Set the CDP Transmission Timer and Holdtime by typing: cdp timer (5-254) (choose 5 to 254 seconds for the rate at which CDP packets are sent), then press Enter. Next, type cdp holdtime (10-255) (choose 10 to 255 seconds for the length of time that the receiver must keep this packet) and press Enter.

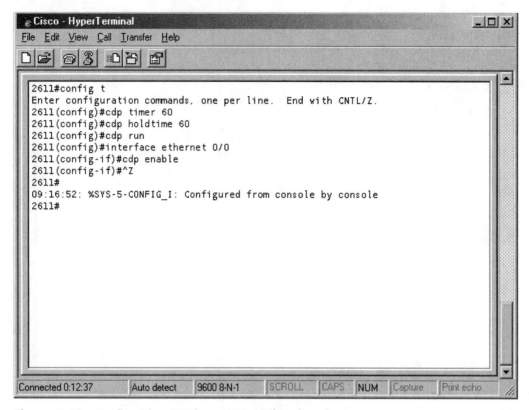

Figure 10.18 Configuration CDP from EXEC privileged mode.

2. Enable CDP by typing `cdp run`. Press Enter.

3. Enable CDP on an Interface by typing `interface ethernet0/0`. Press Enter to go into the interface-specific configuration mode, then type `cdp enable`. Press Enter again.

4. Press Ctrl-Z to exit

To monitor and maintain CDP, use one or more of these common commands in privileged EXEC mode:

clear cdp counters. Resets the traffic counters to zero.

clear cdp table. Deletes the CDP table of information about neighbors.

show cdp. Displays global information such as frequency of transmissions and the hold time for packets being transmitted. Sample output:

```
2611#show cdp
Global CDP information:
```

```
          Sending CDP packets every 60 seconds
          Sending a holdtime value of 60 seconds
          Sending CDPv2 advertisements is  enabled
     2611#
```

show cdp interface. Displays information about interfaces on which CDP is enabled. Sample output:

```
2611#show cdp interface
Ethernet0/0 is up, line protocol is up
  Encapsulation ARPA
  Sending CDP packets every 60 seconds
  Holdtime is 60 seconds
```

show cdp neighbors. Displays information about neighbors. The display can be limited to neighbors on a specific interface and expanded to provide more detailed information.

show cdp traffic. Displays CDP counters, including the number of packets sent and received and checksum errors.

Using the Context-Sensitive Help Facility

The router IOS contains an extremely accommodating and advanced context-sensitive help facility for all commands in the EXEC privileged and user modes. Simply by typing a question mark (?) at the command prompt, the router will display general command help (see Figure 10.19).

 Whenever you see —More— in the console or terminal window, you can either move forward page by page (page down) by pressing the Spacebar or move forward line by line by pressing Enter.

The IOS help facility also provides twofold assistance when you have difficulty recalling a specific command. First, if you can't remember a particular command, but know that it begins with, say, an "s," you can type s? (note that there is no space between s and ?) to see a list of potential commands, as shown in Figure 10.20.

You can also ask for help when you know part, but not all, of a command phrase. For example, if you can't remember a second or third part of particular command sentence, but know that it begins with show cdp *something*, you can type: show cdp ? (note that a space *is* required between cdp and ?) to see a list of available options, as shown here:

```
2611#show cdp ?
    entry       Information for specific neighbor entry
```

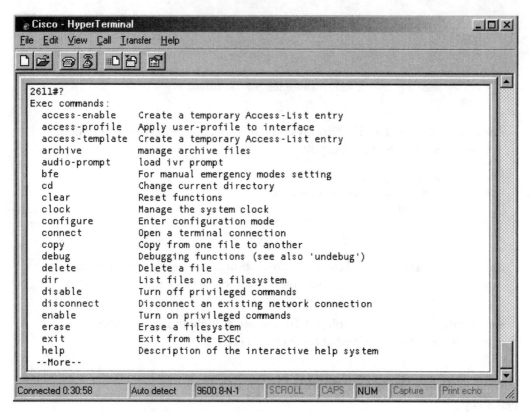

```
Cisco - HyperTerminal
File  Edit  View  Call  Transfer  Help

2611#?
Exec commands:
  access-enable     Create a temporary Access-List entry
  access-profile    Apply user-profile to interface
  access-template   Create a temporary Access-List entry
  archive           manage archive files
  audio-prompt      load ivr prompt
  bfe               For manual emergency modes setting
  cd                Change current directory
  clear             Reset functions
  clock             Manage the system clock
  configure         Enter configuration mode
  connect           Open a terminal connection
  copy              Copy from one file to another
  debug             Debugging functions (see also 'undebug')
  delete            Delete a file
  dir               List files on a filesystem
  disable           Turn off privileged commands
  disconnect        Disconnect an existing network connection
  enable            Turn on privileged commands
  erase             Erase a filesystem
  exit              Exit from the EXEC
  help              Description of the interactive help system
--More--

Connected 0:30:58   Auto detect   9600 8-N-1   SCROLL   CAPS   NUM   Capture   Print echo
```

Figure 10.19   Displaying the context-sensitive command help.

```
2611#s?
*s=show  sdlc   send        set       setup
show     slip   start-chat  systat

2611#s
```

Figure 10.20   Getting help to remember commands.

```
interface  CDP interface status and configuration
neighbors  CDP neighbor entries
traffic    CDP statistics
|          Output modifiers
<cr>

2611#show cdp
```

After viewing the available options, the help facility automatically returns you to where you left off.

Using the Command History and Editing Features

To make router administration and configuration more proficient, a number of IOS command history and editing features are available—some of which you'll find yourself using often. First, let's look at the command history features:

show history. Displays the command buffer. This is helpful for reviewing previously entered commands, especially when troubleshooting—say, if an interface goes down after someone makes modifications. Sample output:

```
2611#show history
  en
  show history
  config t
  show history
  disable
  en
  show interface ethernet 0/0
  config t
  sh cdp
  show history
2611#
```

terminal history (size). Used to set the history buffer size.

terminal no editing. Disables advanced editing features.

terminal editing. Re-enables advanced editing features.

You are likely to find the following keyboard sequence editing features much more useful during day-to-day router administration:

Crtl-A. Moves the cursor to the beginning of the command line.

Crtl-E. Moves the cursor to the end of the command line.

Crtl-F. Moves the cursor forward one character.

Crtl-B. Moves the cursor back one character.

Crtl-Z. Exits configuration mode.

Crtl-P. Recalls previous command.

Crtl-N. Recalls previous command.

Tab. Completes the rest of the command entry.

Esc-B. Moves cursor back one word.

Esc-F. Moves cursor forward one word.

Managing Configuration Files

There are several ways to display and manipulate router configurations, including configuration from either a virtual terminal or the console and loading a configuration from a LAN TFTP server—using a TFTP server will facilitate central config file management. The necessary commands for these features and many more include:

`config t` or `configure terminal`. Configures from the console.

`configure memory`. Loads the configuration from NVRAM.

`copy tftp running-config`. Loads the configuration from a network TFTP server.

`copy running-config startup-config`. Saves the current configuration in RAM to NVRAM.

`show running-config`. Displays the current configuration in RAM.

`copy running-config tftp`. Saves the current configuration in RAM to a network TFTP server.

`show startup-config`. Displays the configuration in NVRAM.

`erase startup-config`. Erases the NVRAM.

Controlling Router Passwords, Identification, and Banners

Among the most critical router administration functions are password maintenance and identification and banner management. Password management can be performed using the following commands:

- To change the virtual terminal password:

```
2611#config t
Enter configuration commands, one per line.  End with CNTL/Z.
2611(config)#line vty 0 4
2611(config-line)#login
```

```
2611(config-line)#password vterm
2611(config-line)#^Z
2611#
```

- To change the console password:

```
2611#config t
Enter configuration commands, one per line.  End with CNTL/Z.
2611(config)#line console 0
2611(config-line)#login
2611(config-line)#password ciscocon
2611(config-line)#^Z
2611#
```

- To change the enable password:

```
2611#config t
Enter configuration commands, one per line.  End with CNTL/Z.
2611(config)#enable password cisco2611
2611(config)#^Z
2611#
```

- To change the secret password:

```
2611#config t
Enter configuration commands, one per line.  End with CNTL/Z.
2611(config)#enable secret ciscosec
2611(config)#^Z
2611#
```

Router identification management includes editing the router hostname, command prompt text, and login and message of the day (MOTD) banners. These can be performed using the following commands:

- To modify the router hostname:

```
2611#config t
Enter configuration commands, one per line.  End with CNTL/Z.
2611(config)#hostname Cisco2611
Cisco2611(config)#^Z
Cisco2611#
```

- To modify the command prompt text:

```
Cisco2611#config t
Enter configuration commands, one per line.  End with CNTL/Z.
Cisco2611(config)#prompt Command:
Cisco2611(config)#^Z
Command:
```

- To set the login banner text:

```
Cisco2611#config t
Enter configuration commands, one per line.  End with CNTL/Z.
Cisco2611(config)#banner login z [Enter a character here, such as z, that will be
entered after the text message, to  indicate the end of the text.]
Enter TEXT message.  End with the character 'z'.
Welcome to the Cisco2611 z
Cisco2611(config)#^Z
Cisco2611#
```

Using this command, at the next login, you'll see the new banner shown in Figure 10.21.

- To set the MOTD:

```
Cisco2611#config t
Enter configuration commands, one per line.  End with CNTL/Z.
Cisco2611(config)#banner motd z
Enter TEXT message.  End with the character 'z'.
Please change login passwords today. Thanks. z
Cisco2611(config)#^Z
Cisco2611#
```

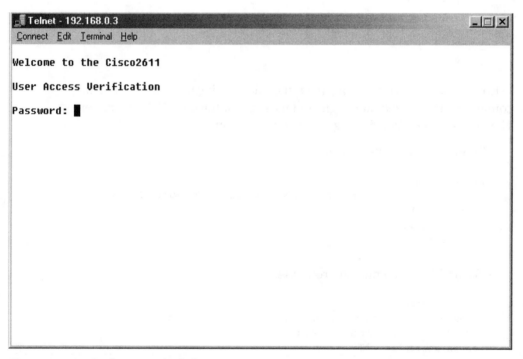

Figure 10.21   Setting a new login banner.

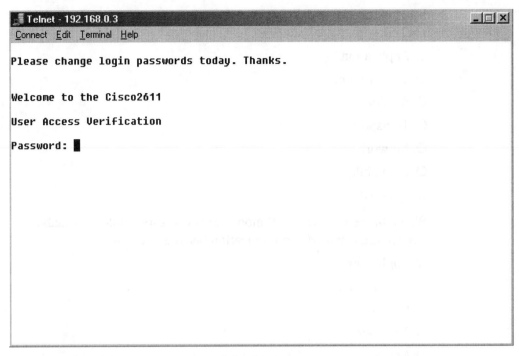

Figure 10.22   Setting a new message of the day.

Using this command, at the next login, you'll see the new MOTD shown in Figure 10.22.

Think It Over

Test your knowledge of Cisco router fundamentals by seeing how many of these questions you answer correctly. Check your results against those in Appendix A.

10.1. Which of the following OSI model layers is responsible for encoding, decoding, compression, and encryption?

O Application

O Presentation

O Session

O Transport

O Network

O Data Link

O Physical

10.2. Which of the following OSI model layers is responsible for framing packets with a MAC address?

○ Application

○ Presentation

○ Session

○ Transport

○ Network

○ Data Link

○ Physical

10.3. Which of the following OSI model layers is responsible for reliable, connection-oriented communication between nodes?

○ Application

○ Presentation

○ Session

○ Transport

○ Network

○ Data Link

○ Physical

10.4. Which of the following OSI model layers is responsible for bringing networking to the application and for performing application synchronization?

○ Application

○ Presentation

○ Session

○ Transport

○ Network

○ Data Link

○ Physical

10.5. Which of the following OSI model layers is responsible for routing protocols and logical network addressing?

○ Application

○ Presentation

○ Session

O Transport

O Network

O Data Link

O Physical

10.6. Which of the following OSI model layers is responsible for data coordination between nodes and Novell Service Access Points (SAPs)?

O Application

O Presentation

O Session

O Transport

O Network

O Data Link

O Physical

10.7. Which of the following can be best described as the primary information units in the Internet?

O Datagrams

O Packets

O Frames

10.8. Which of the following can be best described as a logical grouping of information, which includes a header containing control information and, usually, user data?

O Datagrams

O Packets

O Frames

10.9. When datagrams traveling in frames cross network types with different specified size limits, routers must sometimes divide the datagram to accommodate a smaller MTU. This defines which of the following processes?

O Encapsulation

O Fragmentation

O Segmentation

10.10. At which of the following layers is data converted to segments?

O Application

O Presentation

○ Session

○ Transport

○ Network

○ Data Link

○ Physical

10.11. At which of the following layers are segments converted to packets/datagrams?

○ Application

○ Presentation

○ Session

○ Transport

○ Network

○ Data Link

○ Physical

10.12. At which of the following layers is user information converted to data?

○ Application

○ Presentation

○ Session

○ Transport

○ Network

○ Data Link

○ Physical

10.13. At which of the following layers are frames converted to bits?

○ Application

○ Presentation

○ Session

○ Transport

○ Network

○ Data Link

○ Physical

10.14. At which of the following layers are packets/datagrams converted to frames?

○ Application

○ Presentation

○ Session

○ Transport

○ Network

○ Data Link

○ Physical

10.15. Which of the following describes a connection-oriented service?

○ Unreliable, best-effort delivery of data

○ Reliable delivery of data

○ A three-way handshake, whose purpose is to synchronize the sequence number and acknowledgment numbers of both sides of the connection, while exchanging TCP window sizes

10.16. Which of the following describes a connectionless service?

○ Unreliable, best-effort delivery of data

○ Reliable delivery of data

○ A three-way handshake, whose purpose is to synchronize the sequence number and acknowledgment numbers of both sides of the connection, while exchanging TCP window sizes

10.17. A network address is 32 bits in length.

○ True

○ False

10.18. A data link address can be defined as a logical, dynamic, virtual address.

○ True

○ False

10.19. The default availability (for networks versus hosts) for a Class B address block is which of the following?

○ 8 bits

○ 16 bits

○ 24 bits

10.20. Given 206.0.139.81 255.255.255.224, what is the network address?

    ◯ 205.0.125.64

    ◯ 205.0.125.128

    ◯ 205.0.125.32

10.21. Given IPX address 48F30106.00A024F9173B, which is the node number?

    ◯ 48F30106.00A024F9173B

    ◯ 48F30106

    ◯ 00A024F9173B

10.22. Which of the following are advantages of LAN segmentation?

    ◯ Separate collision domains

    ◯ Less congestion

    ◯ Individual broadcast domains

10.23. Of the switching types, which of the following methods represents when the switch does not wait for the packet to be completely received or checks the CRC?

    ◯ Store-and-forward

    ◯ Cut-through

    ◯ Fragment-free

10.24. Of the switching types, which of the following method represents when the switch waits for the collision window (64 bytes) to pass before forwarding?

    ◯ Store-and-forward

    ◯ Cut-through

    ◯ Fragment-free

10.25. Which of the following router elements stores the original IOS, bootstrap startup program, and hardware tests?

    ◯ ROM

    ◯ Flash

    ◯ NVRAM

    ◯ RAM/DRAM

10.26. Which of the following router elements stores the running configuration, routing tables, caching, and buffering?

O ROM

O Flash

O NVRAM

O RAM/DRAM

10.27. Which of the following router elements stores the startup configuration?

O ROM

O Flash

O NVRAM

O RAM/DRAM

10.28. The EXEC privileged mode can be entered by taking which of the following actions?

O Logging in

O Typing `enable` at the command prompt

O Typing `config t` at the command prompt

O Telnetting with the virtual terminal session

10.29. Typing which of the following EXEC commands will display the NVRAM contents?

O `show running-config,` at the privileged mode command prompt

O `show startup-config,` at the privileged mode command prompt

O `show running-config,` at the user mode command prompt

O `show flash,` at the user mode command prompt

10.30. Typing which of the following EXEC commands will display the RAM contents?

O `show running-config,` at the privileged mode command prompt

O `show startup-config,` at the privileged mode command prompt

O `show running-config,` at the user mode command prompt

O `show flash,` at the user mode command prompt

10.31. Which of the following keyboard sequence editing features will exit configuration mode?

O Crtl-A

O Crtl-E

O Crtl-F

O Crtl-B

O Crtl-Z

O Crtl-P

O Crtl-N

O Tab

O Esc-B

O Esc-F

10.32. Which of the following keyboard sequence editing features will recall the previous command?

O Crtl-A

O Crtl-E

O Crtl-F

O Crtl-B

O Crtl-Z

O Crtl-P

O Crtl-N

O Tab

O Esc-B

O Esc-F

10.33. Which of the following keyboard sequence editing features will complete the command entry?

O Crtl-A

O Crtl-E

O Crtl-F

O Crtl-B

O Crtl-Z

O Crtl-P

O Crtl-N

    O Tab

    O Esc-B

    O Esc-F

10.34. Which of the following keyboard sequence editing features will move the cursor to the beginning of the command line?

    O Crtl-A

    O Crtl-E

    O Crtl-F

    O Crtl-B

    O Crtl-Z

    O Crtl-P

    O Crtl-N

    O Tab

    O Esc-B

    O Esc-F

10.35. Which of the following EXEC commands will save the current configuration in RAM to NVRAM?

    O `configure memory`

    O `copy tftp running-config`

    O `copy running-config startup-config`

    O `show running-config`

    O `copy running-config tftp`

    O `show startup-config`

    O `erase startup-config`

10.36. Which of the following EXEC commands will display the configuration in NVRAM?

    O `configure memory`

    O `copy tftp running-config`

    O `copy running-config startup-config`

    O `show running-config`

    O `copy running-config tftp`

    O `show startup-config`

    O `erase startup-config`

10.37. Which of the following EXEC commands will load the configuration from NVRAM?

○ configure memory

○ copy tftp running-config

○ copy running-config startup-config

○ show running-config

○ copy running-config tftp

○ show startup-config

○ erase startup-config

10.38. Which of the following EXEC commands will display the startup configuration?

○ configure memory

○ copy tftp running-config

○ copy running-config startup-config

○ show running-config

○ copy running-config tftp

○ show startup-config

○ erase startup-config

10.39. Which of the following EXEC commands sequences will change the virtual terminal password?

○ 2611(config)#line vty 0 4
　2611(config-line)#login
　2611(config-line)#password xxx

○ 2611(config)#line console 0
　2611(config-line)#login
　2611(config-line)#password xxx

○ 2611(config)#enable password xxx
　2611(config)#^z
　2611#

LAN Internetworking

This chapter continues our discussion on the Cisco router fundamentals, begun in Chapter 10. We begin by examining LAN design; this will include descriptions of full- and half-duplex Ethernet operation, problems in Ethernet networks, the features and benefits of Fast/Gigabit Ethernet, and use guidelines and distance limitations of each. Next we investigate network protocols; you'll learn the functions of the TCP/IP network-layer protocol and those performed by ICMP. You'll also learn to manually configure IP addresses and IPX, and verify IP addresses. Along the way you'll discover more about IPX addresses and their required encapsulation type. This chapter concludes with a discussion of routing, specifically, to define flow control and describe basic methods used in networking, and how to add the RIP and IGRP routing protocols to your configuration.

 Hands-on simulations of the information in this chapter can be found on the book's companion CD-ROM.

LAN Design

Topologies, such as Ethernet, illustrated in Figure 11.1, make up the networking infrastructure that connects stations to LANs, LANs into wide area

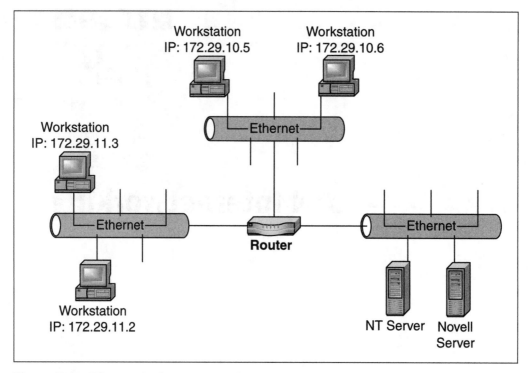

Figure 11.1   Ethernet topology.

networks (WANs), and WANs into internets. In this section we'll look at Ethernet from a half (data transmission in one direction)- and full-duplex (data transmission in two directions) perspective, a perspective that encompasses enhancements, limitations, and specifications.

Ethernet

A local area network (LAN) protocol that uses a bus or star topology, supporting data transfer rates of 10 Mbps. The first Ethernet, Ethernet DIX, was named after the companies that proposed it: Digital, Intel, and Xerox. During this time, the Institute of Electrical and Electronics Engineers (IEEE) had been working on Ethernet standardization, which became known as Project 802. Upon its success, the Ethernet plan evolved into the IEEE 802.3 standard. Based on carrier sensing, as originally developed by Robert Metcalfe, David Boggs, and their team of engineers, Ethernet became a major player in communication media, competing head-to-head with IBM's proposed Token Ring, or IEEE 802.5.

Carrier Transmissions

When a station on an Ethernet network is ready to transmit, it must first listen for transmissions on the channel. If another station is transmitting, it is said to be "producing activity." This activity, or transmission, is called a *carrier*. In a nutshell, this is how Ethernet became known as the *carrier-sensing communication medium*. With multiple stations, all sensing carriers, on an Ethernet network, this mechanism was called Carrier Sense with Multiple Access, or CSMA.

If a carrier is detected, the station will wait for a pre-programmed minuscule timeframe (9.6 microseconds), after the last frame passes, before transmitting its own frame. When two stations transmit simultaneously, a *fused signal bombardment*—otherwise known as a *collision*—occurs. Ethernet stations detect collisions to minimize problems. This capability was added to CSMA to become Carrier Sense with Multiple Access and Collision Detection or CSMA/CD.

Stations involved in a collision immediately abort their transmissions. The first station to detect the collision sends an alert to all stations. At this point, all stations execute a random collision timer to force a delay before attempting to transmit their frames. This timing-delay mechanism is termed the *backoff algorithm*. If multiple collisions are detected, the random delay timer is doubled.

Ethernet Design, Cabling, Adapters

Ethernet comes in various flavors. The actual physical arrangement of nodes in a structure is termed the *network topology*. Ethernet topology examples include bus, star, and point-to-point (see Figure 11.2).

Bus. Linear LAN where a station's transmissions are propagated and viewed by all stations.

Star. Structure wherein endpoints are connected to a common central switch or hub by direct links.

Point-to-Point. The physical connection and communication passes from one station to another.

Ethernet options also come in many variations, some of which are shown in Figure 11.3 and defined in the following list:

Ethernet, 10Base5. Ethernet with thick coaxial (coax) wire uses cable type RG08. Connectivity from the NIC travels through a transceiver cable to an external transceiver and finally through the thick coax cable (see Figure 11.4). Due to signal degradation, a segment is limited to fewer

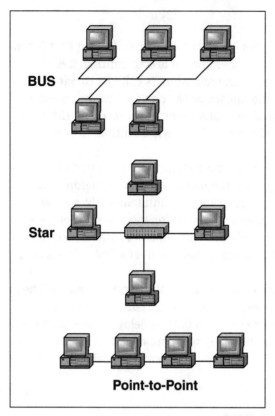

Figure 11.2   Ethernet topology breakdown.

	Ethernet	10Base2	10Base5	10BaseT	10BaseFL	100BaseT
Topology	Bus	Bus	Bus	Star	Pt-to-Pt	Bus
Data Transfer Rate	10 Mbps	10 Mbps	10 Mbps	10 Mbps	10 Mbps	100 Mbps
Maximum Segment Length	500 Meters	185 Meters	500 Meters	100 Meters	2,100 Meters	100 Meters
Media Type	Thick Coax	Thin Coax	Thick Coax	Unshielded Twisted Pair	Fiber Optic	Unshielded Twisted Pair

Figure 11.3   An Ethernet specification chart by type, for comparison.

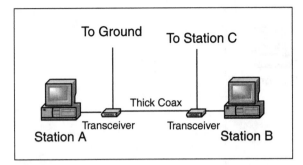

Figure 11.4   Ethernet and 10Base5 network.

than 500 meters, with a maximum of 100 stations per segment of 1,024 stations total.

10Base2. Thin-wire Ethernet, or *thinnet*, uses cable type RG-58. With 10Base2, the transceiver functionality is processed in the NIC. BNC T connectors link the cable to the NIC (see Figure 11.5). As with every media type, due to signal degradation, a thinnet segment is limited to fewer than 185 meters, with a maximum of 30 stations per segment of 1,024 stations total.

10BaseT. Unshielded twisted-pair (UTP) wire uses cable type RJ-45 for 10BaseT specifications. Twisted-pair Ethernet broke away from the electric shielding of coaxial cable, using conventional unshielded copper wire. Using the star topology, each station is connected via RJ-45 with UTP wire to a unique port in a hub or switch (see Figure 11.6). The hub simulates the signals on the Ethernet cable. Due to signal degradation, the cable between a station and a hub is limited to fewer than 100 meters.

Hardware Addresses, Frame Formats

Using that overview of Ethernet design and cabling as a foundation, we can address the underlying Ethernet addressing and formatting models. We know

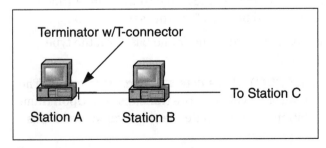

Figure 11.5   10Base2 network diagram.

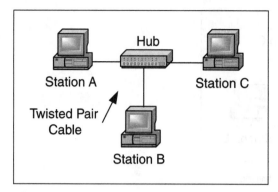

Figure 11.6   10BaseT example diagram.

that every station in an Ethernet network has a unique 48-bit address bound to each NIC (as described in Chapter 2). These addresses not only specify a unique, single station, but also provide for transmission on an Ethernet network to three types of addresses:

Unicast address. Transmission destination to a single station.

Multicast address. Transmission destination to a subset or group of stations.

Broadcast address. Transmission destination to all stations.

The Ethernet frame is variable length, which is to say that no frame will be smaller than 64 octets or larger than 1,518 octets. Each frame consists of a preamble, a destination address, a source address, the frame type, frame data, and cyclic redundancy check (CRC) fields. These fields are defined as follows:

Preamble. Aids in the synchronization between sender and receiver(s).

Destination Address. The address of the receiving station.

Source Address. The address of the sending station.

Frame Type. Specifies the type of data in the frame to determine which protocol software module should be used for processing.

Frame Data. Indicates the data carried in the frame based on the type latent in the Frame Type field.

Cyclic Redundancy Check (CRC). Helps detect transmission errors. The sending station computes a frame value before transmission. Upon frame retrieval, the receiving station must compute the same value based on a complete, successful transmission.

Congestion Problems

As a result of ongoing technological advances and the advent of complex, bandwidth-intensive applications, network congestion continues to increase dramatically. In a snowball effect, as more bandwidth becomes available, we create more complex applications, which in turn cause greater congestion. Concomitantly, network response time decreases, which of course lowers productivity.

Benefits and Guidelines of Fast Ethernet

Using the same foundation and cabling as Ethernet, Fast Ethernet operates at 100 Mbps and is designed to handle high-bandwidth network requirements. The benefits of 100BaseT Fast Ethernet include the following:

- High performance, high bandwidth at 100 Mbps.

- Can use existing cabling and most network equipment, with easy updating from 10 Mbps to 100 Mbps by adding Fast Ethernet hubs and/or switches, and 100 Mbps network interface cards (NICs).

- Fast Ethernet is based on Ethernet specifications.

To accommodate bandwidth-intensive applications and network expansion, the Fast Ethernet Alliance (composed of 3Com Corporation, DAVID Systems, Digital Equipment Corporation, Grand Junction Networks, Inc., Intel Corporation, National Semiconductor, SUN Microsystems, and Synoptics Communications) was formed to promote 100 Mbps technology

To understand the difference in transmission speed between 10BaseT and 100BaseT, let's look at the formula:

Station-to-Hub Diameter (meters) = 25,000/Transmission Rate (Mbps)

followed by examples:

Given: 10 Mbps 10BaseT Ethernet network:

Diameter (meters) = 25,000/10 (Mbps)
Diameter = 2,500 meters

Given: 100 Mbps 100BaseT Fast Ethernet network:

Diameter (meters) = 25,000 / 100 (Mbps)
Diameter = 250 meters

From these equations, we can deduce that 100 Mbps Fast Ethernet requires a station-to-hub diameter, in meters, that is one-tenth that of 10 Mbps Ethernet. This speed-versus-distance ratio in Fast Ethernet allows for a tenfold scale increase in maximum transmitted bits. Other prerequisites for Fast Ethernet include 100 Mbps station NICs, Fast Ethernet hub or switch, and Category 5 UTP (data grade) wire.

Benefits and Guidelines of Gigabit Ethernet

At 1 Gbps, Gigabit Ethernet offers 100 times the performance over Fast Ethernet. The new Gigabit Ethernet Alliance and the IEEE 802.3z specify an easy migration from Fast Ethernet to Gigabit Ethernet, without changing network protocols, server operating systems, or applications.

Three Gigabit Ethernet standards have been employed, with the following specifications:

1000BaseCX. Operates at 1,000 Mbps in half-duplex mode (2,000 Mbps in full-duplex mode), over 25 meters, or 82 feet.

1000BaseSX. Operates at 1,000 Mbps in half-duplex mode up to 316 meters, or 1,036 feet, and 2,000 Mbps in full-duplex mode up to 550 meters, or 1,804 feet.

1000BaseLX. Operates at 1,000 Mbps in half-duplex mode up to 316 meters, or 1,036 feet, and 2,000 Mbps in full-duplex mode up to 5,000 meters, or 16,404 feet.

Network Protocols

Approximately 30 years ago, networking protocols were developed so that individual stations could be connected to form a local area network (LAN). This group of computers and other devices, dispersed over a relatively limited area and connected by a communications link, enabled any station to interact with any other on the network. These networks allowed stations to share resources, such as laser printers and large hard disks.

This section is a discussion on the communication protocols—sets of rules or standards—that were designed to enable these stations to connect with one another and to exchange information. This material is intended to expand on and complement the information presented in previous chapters; specifically, we'll go into more detail on TCP/IP, IP, and IPX.

TCP/IP Transport and Network Layers

As you know by now, the protocol generally accepted for standardizing overall computer communications is the seven-layer set of hardware and software guidelines called the Open Systems Interconnection (OSI) model. At the Transport layer of the OSI model, you'll find TCP and UDP. This layer, if you recall, is responsible for reliable, connection-oriented communication between nodes, and for providing transparent data transfer from the higher levels, with error recovery. At the Network layer of the OSI model, routing protocols and logical network addressing operate. An example would be the Internet Protocol (IP), part of the TCP/IP suite.

TCP

IP has many weaknesses, one of which is unreliable packet delivery—that is, packets may be dropped due to transmission errors, bad routes, and/or throughput degradation. The Transmission Control Protocol (TCP) helps reconcile these issues by providing reliable, stream-oriented connections. In fact, TCP/IP is predominantly based on TCP functionality, which is based on IP, to make up the TCP/IP suite. These features describe a connection-oriented process of communication.

Many components result in TCP's reliable service delivery. Following are some of the main ones:

Streams. Data is systematized and transferred as a stream of bits, organized into 8-bit octets or bytes. As these bits are received, they are passed on in the same manner.

Buffer flow control. As data is passed in streams, protocol software may divide the stream to fill specific buffer sizes. TCP manages this process and assures avoidance of a buffer overflow. During this process, fast-sending stations may be stopped periodically to keep up with slow-receiving stations.

Virtual circuits. When one station requests communication with another, both stations inform their application programs and agree to communicate. If the link or communications between these stations fail, both stations are made aware of the breakdown and inform their respective software applications. In this case, a coordinated retry is attempted.

Full-duplex connectivity. Stream transfer occurs in both directions, simultaneously, to reduce overall network traffic.

Sequencing and Windowing

TCP organizes and counts bytes in the data stream using a 32-bit sequence number. Every TCP packet contains a starting sequence number (first byte) and an acknowledgment number (last byte). A concept known as a *sliding window* is implemented to make stream transmissions more efficient. The sliding window uses bandwidth more effectively, because it will allow the transmission of multiple packets before an acknowledgment is required.

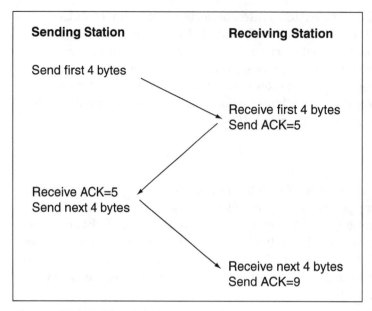

Figure 11.7 TCP windowing example.

Figure 11.7 is a real-world example of the TCP sliding window. In this example, a sender has bytes to send in sequence (1 to 8) to a receiving station with a window size of 4. The sending station places the first 4 bytes in a window and sends them, then waits for an acknowledgment (ACK=5). This acknowledgment specifies that the first 4 bytes were received. Assuming its window size is still 4 and that it is also waiting for the next byte (byte 5), the sending station moves the sliding window 4 bytes to the right, then sends bytes 5 to 8. Upon receiving these bytes, the receiving station sends an acknowledgment (ACK=9), indicating it is waiting for byte 9. And the process continues.

At any point, the receiver may indicate a window size of 0, in which case the sender will not send any more bytes until the window size is greater than 0. A typical cause for this occurring is a buffer overflow.

TCP Packet Format and Header Snapshots

Keeping in mind that it is important to differentiate between "captured" packets—that is, whether they are TCP, UDP, ARP, and so on—let's identify the parts of the TCP packet format, whose components are defined in the following list:

Source port. Specifies the port at which the source processes send/receive TCP services.

Destination port. Specifies the port at which the destination processes send/receive TCP services.

Sequence number. Specifies the first byte of data or a reserved sequence number for a future process.

Acknowledgment number. The sequence number of the very next byte of data the sender should receive.

Data offset. The number of 32-bit words in the header.

Flags. Control information, such as SYN, ACK, and FIN bits, for connection establishment and termination.

Window size. The sender's receive window or available buffer space.

Checksum. Specifies any damage to the header that occurred during transmission.

Urgent pointer. The optional first urgent byte in a packet, which indicates the end of urgent data.

Options. TCP options, such as the maximum TCP segment size.

Data. Upper-layer information.

Ports, Endpoints, Connection Establishment

TCP enables simultaneous communication between different application programs on a single machine. TCP uses port numbers to distinguish each of the receiving station's destinations. A pair of *endpoints* identifies the connection between the two stations, as mentioned earlier. Colloquially, these endpoints are defined as the connection between the two stations' applications as they communicate; they are defined by TCP as a pair of integers in this format: (host, port). The *host* is the station's IP address, and *port* is the TCP port number on that station. An example of a station's endpoint is:

206.0.125.81:1026

(host)   (port)

An example of two stations' endpoints during communication is:

STATION 1		STATION 2	
206.0.125.81:1022		207.63.129.2:26	
(host)	(port)	(host)	(port)

This technology is very important in TCP, as it allows simultaneous communications by assigning separate ports for each station connection. When a connection is established between two nodes during a TCP session, a *three-way handshake* is used. This process starts with a one-node TCP request by a SYN/ACK bit, and the second node TCP response with a SYN/ACK bit. At this point, communication between the two nodes will proceed. When there is no more data to send, a TCP node may send a FIN bit, indicating a close control signal. At this intersection, both nodes will close simultaneously. Some common and well-known TCP ports and their related connection services are shown in Table 11.1.

Table 11.1   Common TCP Ports and Services

PORT NUMBER	SERVICE
7	echo
9	discard
11	systat
13	daytime
15	netstat
17	qotd
19	chargen
20	ftp-data
21	ftp
23	telnet
25	smtp
37	time
42	name
43	whols
53	domain
57	mtp
77	rje
79	finger
80	http
87	link
95	supdup
101	hostnames
102	iso-tsap
103	dictionary
104	x400-snd
105	csnet-ns
109	pop
110	pop3

Table 11.1   Common TCP Ports and Services (*Continued*)

PORT NUMBER	SERVICE
111/135	portmap/loc-serv
113	auth
115	sftp
117	path
119	nntp
139	nbsession
144	news
158	tcprepo
170	print-srv
175	vmnet
400	vmnet0
512	exec
513	login
514	shell
515	printer
520	efs
526	tempo
530	courier
531	conference
532	netnews
540	uucp
543	klogin
544	kshell
556	remotefs
600	garcon
601	maitrd
602	busboy
750	kerberos
751	kerberos_mast
754	krb_prop
888	erlogin

Attributes

To review: TCP is a connection-oriented protocol for reliable communications; it features these important attributes:

- Handshake process
- Sliding window
- Sequence/acknowledgment numbers
- Breakup of messages into datagrams
- Reassembly of datagrams into messages

Real-world examples include HTTP, FTP, and Telnet.

UDP

The User Datagram Protocol (UDP) operates in a connectionless fashion; that is, it provides the same unreliable, datagram delivery service as IP. Unlike TCP, UDP does not send SYN/ACK bits to assure delivery and reliability of transmissions. Moreover, UDP does not include flow control or error recovery functionality. Consequently, UDP messages can be lost, duplicated, or arrive in the wrong order. And because UDP contains smaller headers, it expends less network throughput than TCP and so can arrive faster than the receiving station can process them.

UDP is typically utilized where higher-layer protocols provide necessary error recovery and flow control. Popular server daemons that employ UDP include Network File System (NFS), Simple Network Management Protocol (SMTP), Trivial File Transfer Protocol (TFTP), and Domain Name System (DNS), to name a few.

UDP Formatting, Encapsulation, and Header Snapshots

UDP messages are called *user datagrams*. These datagrams are encapsulated in IP, including the UDP header and data, as it travels across the Internet. Basically, UDP adds a header to the data sent by a user, and passes it along to IP. The IP layer then adds a header to what it receives from UDP. Finally, the network interface layer inserts the datagram in a frame before sending it from one machine to another.

As just mentioned, UDP messages contain smaller headers and consume fewer overheads than TCP. The UDP datagram format and its components are defined in the following list:

Source/destination port. A 16-bit UDP port number used for datagram processing.

Message length. Specifies the number of octets in the UDP datagram.

Checksum. An optional field to verify datagram delivery.

Data. The information handed down to the TCP protocol, including upper-layer headers.

Multiplexing, Demultiplexing, and Port Connections

UDP provides *multiplexing* (a method that enables multiple signals to be transmitted concurrently into an input stream, across a single physical channel) and *demultiplexing* (the actual separation of the streams that have been multiplexed into a common stream back into multiple output streams) between protocol and application software.

Multiplexing and demultiplexing, as they pertain to UDP, transpire through ports. Each station application must negotiate a port number before sending a UDP datagram. When UDP is on the receiving side of a datagram, it checks the header (destination port field) to determine whether it matches one of station's ports currently in use. If the port is in use by a so-called listening application, the transmission proceeds; if the port is not in use, an ICMP error message is generated, and the datagram is discarded. A number of common UDP ports and their related connection services are listed in Table 11.2.

Table 11.2   Common UDP Ports and Services

PORT NUMBER	SERVICE
7	echo
9	discard
13	daytime
17	qotd
19	chargen
37	time
39	rlp
42	name
43	whols
53	dns
67	bootp
69	tftp
111	portmap
123	ntp
137	nbname

(continues)

Table 11.2 Common UDP Ports and Services (*Continued*)

PORT NUMBER	SERVICE
138	nbdatagram
153	sgmp
161	snmp
162	snmp-trap
315	load
500	sytek
512	biff
513	who
514	syslog
515	printer
517	talk
518	ntalk
520	route
525	timed
531	rvd-control
533	netwall
550	new-rwho
560	rmonitor
561	monitor
700	acctmaster
701	acctslave
702	acct
703	acctlogin
704	acctprimter
705	acctinfo
706	acctslave2
707	acctdisk
750	kerberos
751	kerberos_mast
752	passwd_server
753	userreg_serve

Attributes

To review: UDP is a connectionless protocol for unreliable communications; its important attributes are:

- Heavy reliance on the application layer
- No error checking and no sliding window

Real-world examples include TFTP, video, and audio

IP

The Internet Protocol (IP) part of the TCP/IP suite is a four-layer model (see Figure 11.8). IP is designed to interconnect networks to form an Internet to pass data back and forth. IP contains addressing and control information that enables *packets* to be routed through this Internet. (A packet is defined as a logical grouping of information, which includes a header containing control information and, usually, user data. The equipment—that is, routers—that encounter these packets, strip off and examine the *headers* that contain the sensitive routing information. These headers are modified and reformulated as a packet to be passed along.

One of the IP's primary functions is to provide a permanent connection (termed *connectionless*), unreliable, best-effort delivery of *datagrams* through an internetwork. Recall that datagrams can be described as a logical grouping of information sent as a network layer unit over a communication medium. IP

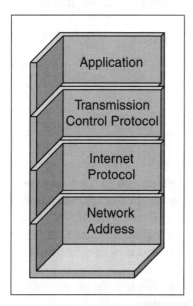

Figure 11.8   The four-layer IP model.

datagrams are the primary information units in the Internet. Another of IP's principal responsibilities is the fragmentation and reassembly of datagrams to support links with different transmission sizes.

During an analysis session, or *sniffer capture*, it is necessary to differentiate between types of packet captures. The following describes the IP packet and the 14 fields therein:

Version. The IP version currently used.

IP Header Length (Length). The datagram header length in 32-bit words.

Type-of-Service (ToS). How the upper-layer protocol (the layer immediately above, such as transport protocols like TCP and UDP) intends to handle the current datagram and assign a level of importance.

Total Length. The length, in bytes, of the entire IP packet.

Identification. An integer used to help piece together datagram fragments.

Flag. A 3-bit field, where the first bit specifies whether the packet can be fragmented. The second bit indicates whether the packet is the last fragment in a series. The final bit is not used at this time.

Fragment Offset. The location of the fragment's data, relative to the opening data in the original datagram. This allows for proper reconstruction of the original datagram.

Time-to-Live (TTL). A counter that decrements to zero to keep packets from endlessly looping. At the zero mark, the packet is dropped.

Protocol. Indicates the upper-layer protocol receiving the incoming packets.

Header Checksum. Ensures the integrity of the IP header.

Source Address/Destination Address. The sending and receiving nodes (station, server and/or router)

Options. Typically, contains security options.

Data. Upper-layer information.

ICMP

The Internet Control Message Protocol (ICMP), an extension to the IP protocol, delivers message and control packets, reporting errors (e.g., "destination unreachable"), and other pertinent information to the sending station or source at the network layer. Hosts and infrastructure equipment use this mechanism to communicate control and error information, as they pertain to IP packet processing.

ICMP message encapsulation is a twofold process. The messages are encapsulated in IP datagrams, which are encapsulated in frames, as they travel across the Internet. Basically, ICMP uses the same unreliable means of communications as a datagram. This means that ICMP error messages may be lost or duplicated.

The ICMP format includes a Message Type field, indicating the type of message; a Code field that includes detailed information about the type; and a Checksum field, which provides the same functionality as IP's Checksum field. When an ICMP message reports an error, it includes the header and data of the datagram that caused the specified problem. This helps the receiving station to understand which application and protocol sent the datagram.

There are many types of useful ICMP messages; Figure 11.9 contains a list of several, which are described in the following list.

Echo Reply (Type 0)/Echo Request (Type 8). The basic mechanism for testing possible communication between two nodes. The receiving station, if available, is asked to reply to the *ping*. An example of a ping is as follows:

Begin Echo Request—Ping 206.0.125.81 (at the command prompt)

Begin Echo Reply:

Reply from 206.0.125.81: bytes-32 time<10ms TTL=128 (from receiving station 206.0.125.81)

Reply from 206.0.125.81: bytes-32 time<10ms TTL=128

Reply from 206.0.125.81: bytes-32 time<10ms TTL=128

Reply from 206.0.125.81: bytes-32 time<10ms TTL=128

Destination Unreachable (Type 3). This message type is issued to indicate several situations, including when a router or gateway does not

Message Type	Description
0	Echo Reply
3	Destination Unreachable
4	Source Quench
5	Route Redirect
8	Echo Request
11	Datagram Time Exceeded
12	Datagram Parameter Problem
13	Timestamp Request
14	Timestamp Reply
15	Information Request
16	Information Reply
17	Address Mask Request
18	Address Mask Reply

Figure 11.9   ICMP message chart.

know how to reach the destination, when a protocol or application is not active, when a datagram specifies an unstable route, or when a router must fragment the size of a datagram and cannot because the Don't Fragment Flag is set. An example of a Type 3 message is as follows:

Begin Echo Request—Ping 206.0.125.81 (at the command prompt)

Begin Echo Reply:

Pinging 206.0.125.81 with 32 bytes of data:

Destination host unreachable.

Destination host unreachable.

Destination host unreachable.

Destination host unreachable.

Source Quench (Type 4). A basic form of flow control for datagram delivery. When datagrams arrive too quickly for a receiving station to process, the datagrams are discarded. During this process, for every datagram that has been dropped, an ICMP Type 4 message is passed along to the sending station. Thus, the Source Quench messages actually become requests, to slow down the rate at which datagrams are sent. Source Quench messages do not, however, have a reverse effect, whereas the sending station would increase the rate of transmission—only the receiving station controls the rate of delivery.

Route Redirect (Type 5). Routing information is exchanged periodically to accommodate network changes and to keep routing tables up to date. When a router identifies a host that is using a nonoptional route, the router sends an ICMP Type 5 message while forwarding the datagram to the destination network. As a result, routers can send Type 5 messages only to hosts directly connected to their networks.

Datagram Time Exceeded (Type 11). A gateway or router will emit a Type 11 message if it is forced to drop a datagram because the TTL (Time-to-Live) field is set to 0. Basically, if the router detects the TTL=0 when intercepting a datagram, it is forced to discard that datagram and send an ICMP message Type 11.

Datagram Parameter Problem (Type 12). Specifies a problem with the datagram header that is impeding further processing. The datagram will be discarded, and a Type 12 message will be transmitted.

Timestamp Request (Type 13)/Timestamp Reply (Type 14). These provide a means for delay tabulation of the network. The sending station injects a send timestamp (the time the message was sent) and the receiving station appends a receive timestamp to compute an estimated delay time and assist in their internal clock synchronization.

Information Request (Type 15)/Information Reply (Type 16). As an alternative to reverse ARP (described in Chapter 10) (RARP), stations use Type 15 and Type 16 to obtain an Internet address for a network to which they are attached. The sending station will emit the message with the network portion of the Internet address, and wait for a response, with the host portion (its IP address) filled in.

Address Mask Request (Type 17)/Address Mask Reply (Type 18). Similar to an Information Request/Reply, stations can send Type 17 and Type 18 messages to obtain the subnet mask of the network to which they are attached. Stations may submit this request to a known node, such as a gateway or router, or broadcast the request to the network.

Configuring, Verifying, and Monitoring IP

In the initial setup configuration of our router in Chapter 10, we chose to install IP and configured an IP address to be bound to our Ethernet 0/0 interface. Each interface can have one or more addresses bound to it. In this section, we'll manually configure IP addresses and verify connectivity from the router console.

To configure an IP address on an interface, we first need to enter the EXEC privileged mode, then the configuration mode, as shown in Figure 11.10.

Remember, to get a list of available commands in the configuration mode, type a question mark (?) at the config command prompt:

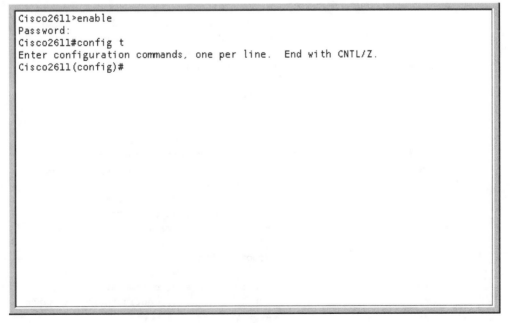

```
Cisco2611>enable
Password:
Cisco2611#config t
Enter configuration commands, one per line.  End with CNTL/Z.
Cisco2611(config)#
```

Figure 11.10   Preparing to configure an IP address.

```
Cisco2611(config)#?
Configure commands:
aaa                          Authentication, Authorization and
 Accounting.
  access-list                Add an access list entry.
  alias                      Create command alias.
  alps                       Configure Airline Protocol Support.
  apollo                     Apollo global configuration commands.
  appletalk                  Appletalk global configuration commands.
  arap                       Appletalk Remote Access Protocol.
  arp                        Set a static ARP entry.
  async-bootp                Modify system bootp parameters.
  autonomous-system          Specify local AS number to which we belong.
  banner                     Define a login banner.
  boot                       Modify system boot parameters.
  bridge                     Bridge Group.
  bstun                      BSTUN global configuration commands.
  buffers                    Adjust system buffer pool parameters.
  busy-message               Display message when connection to host
                             fails.
  call-history-mib           Define call history mib parameters.
  cdp                        Global CDP configuration subcommands.
  chat-script                Define a modem chat script.
  clns                       Global CLNS configuration subcommands.
  clock                      Configure time-of-day clock.
  cns                        CNS Event Service.
  config-register            Define the configuration register.
  controller                 Configure a specific controller.
  decnet                     Global DECnet configuration subcommands.
  default                    Set a command to its defaults.
  default-value              Default character-bits values.
  dial-control-mib           Define Dial Control Mib parameters.
  dial-peer                  Dial Map (Peer) configuration commands.
  dialer                     Dialer watch commands.
  dialer-list                Create a dialer list entry.
  dlsw                       Data Link Switching global configuration
                             commands.
  dnsix-dmdp                 Provide DMDP service for DNSIX.
  dnsix-nat                  Provide DNSIX service for audit trails.
  downward-compatible-config Generate a configuration compatible with
                             older software.
  dspu                       DownStream Physical Unit Command.
  enable                     Modify enable password parameters.
  end                        Exit from configure mode.
  endnode                    SNA APPN endnode command.
  exception                  Exception handling.
  exit                       Exit from configure mode.
  file                       Adjust file system parameters.
  frame-relay                Global frame relay configuration commands.
  gateway                    Gateway.
  gw-accounting              Enable voip gateway accounting.
```

help	Description of the interactive help system.
hostname	Set system's network name.
interface	Select an interface to configure.
ip	Global IP configuration subcommands.
ipx	Novell/IPX global configuration commands.
kerberos	Configure Kerberos.
key	Key management.
keymap	Define a new keymap.
lane	Configure LAN Emulation.
lat	DEC Local Area Transport (LAT) transmission protocol.
line	Configure a terminal line.
lnm	IBM LAN Manager
locaddr-priority-list	Establish queueing priorities based on LU address.
location	Network Management Router location Command.
logging	Modify message logging facilities.
login-string	Define a host-specific login string.
map-class	Configure static map class.
map-list	Configure static map list.
memory-size	Adjust memory size by percentage.
menu	Define a user-interface menu.
modemcap	Modem Capabilities database.
mop	Configure the DEC MOP Server.
multilink	PPP multilink global configuration.
ncia	Native Client Interface Architecture.
netbios	NETBIOS access control filtering.
no	Negate a command or set its defaults.
ntp	Configure NTP.
num-exp	Dial Map Number Expansion configuration commands.
partition	Partition device.
printer	Define an LPD printer.
priority-list	Build a priority list.
privilege	Command privilege parameters.
prompt	Set system's prompt.
queue-list	Build a custom queue list.
resume-string	Define a host-specific resume string.
rif	Source-route RIF cache.
rlogin	Rlogin configuration commands.
rmon	Remote Monitoring.
route-map	Create route-map or enter route-map command mode.
router	Enable a routing process.
rsrb	RSRB LSAP/DSAP filtering.
rtr	RTR Base Configuration
sap-priority-list	Establish queueing priorities based on SAP and/or MAC address(es).
scheduler	Scheduler parameters.
service	Modify use of network-based services.
sgbp	SGBP Stack Group Bidding Protocol configuration.

```
smrp                      Simple Multicast Routing Protocol
                          configuration commands.
sna                       Network Management Physical Unit Command.
snmp-server               Modify SNMP parameters.
source-bridge             Source-route bridging ring groups.
stackmaker                Specify stack name and add its member.
state-machine             Define a TCP dispatch state machine.
stun                      STUN global configuration commands.
subscriber-policy         Subscriber policy.
tacacs-server             Modify TACACS query parameters.
tarp                      Global TARP configuration subcommands.
terminal-queue            Terminal queue commands.
tftp-server               Provide TFTP service for netload requests.
time-range                Define time range entries.
tn3270                    tn3270 configuration command.
translate                 Translate global configuration commands.
ttycap                    Define a new termcap.
username                  Establish User Name Authentication.
vines                     VINES global configuration commands.
virtual-profile           Virtual Profile configuration.
vpdn                      Virtual Private Dialup Network.
vpdn-group                VPDN group configuration.
vty-async                 Enable virtual async line configuration
x25                       X.25 Level 3.
x29                       X29 commands.
xns                       XNS global configuration commands.
xremote                   Configure XRemote.

Cisco2611(config)#
```

Do you see the command we're looking for, the one to configure an interface? Yep, that's right, the command is:

```
interface                 Select an interface to configure
```

Let's see the available interface commands by typing `interface ?` at the prompt:

```
Cisco2611(config)#interface ?
  Async            Async interface
  BVI              Bridge-Group Virtual Interface
  Dialer           Dialer interface
  Ethernet         IEEE 802.3
  Group-Async      Async Group interface
  Lex              Lex interface
  Loopback         Loopback interface
  Multilink        Multilink-group interface
  Null             Null interface
  Port-channel     Ethernet Channel of interfaces
  Serial           Serial
```

```
Tunnel              Tunnel interface
Virtual-Template    Virtual Template interface
Virtual-TokenRing   Virtual TokenRing

Cisco2611(config)#interface ethernet 0/0
```

The next step involves the type of interface we'll be configuring—in this case, an Ethernet interface (Figure 11.11).

Now let's look at the available commands in the config interface (Ethernet) mode:

```
Cisco2611(config-if)#?
Interface configuration commands:
    access-expression   Build a bridge Boolean access expression.
    apollo              Apollo interface subcommands.
    appletalk           Appletalk interface subcommands.
    arp                 Set arp type (arpa, probe, snap) or timeout.
    backup              Modify backup parameters.
    bandwidth           Set bandwidth informational parameter.
    bridge-group        Transparent bridging interface parameters.
    carrier-delay       Specify delay for interface transitions.
    cdp                 CDP interface subcommands.
    clns                CLNS interface subcommands.
    cmns                OSI CMNS.
    custom-queue-list   Assign a custom queue list to an interface.
    decnet              Interface DECnet config commands.
```

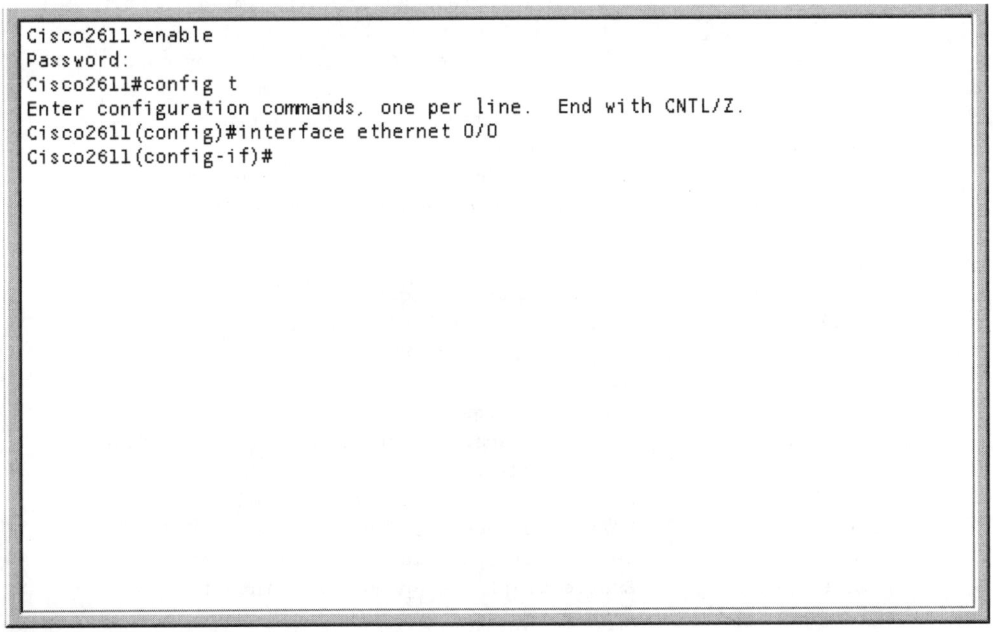

```
Cisco2611>enable
Password:
Cisco2611#config t
Enter configuration commands, one per line.  End with CNTL/Z.
Cisco2611(config)#interface ethernet 0/0
Cisco2611(config-if)#
```

Figure 11.11   Entering the config interface (Ethernet) mode.

default	Set a command to its defaults.
delay	Specify interface throughput delay.
description	Interface specific description.
dspu	Down Stream PU.
exit	Exit from interface configuration mode.
fair-queue	Enable Fair Queuing on an Interface
fras	DLC Switch Interface Command.
full-duplex	Configure full-duplex operational mode.
h323-gateway	Configure H323 Gateway.
half-duplex	Configure half-duplex and related commands.
help	Description of the interactive help system.
hold-queue	Set hold queue depth.
ip	Interface Internet Protocol config commands.
ipx	Novell/IPX interface subcommands.
isis	IS-IS commands.
iso-igrp	ISO-IGRP interface subcommands.
keepalive	Enable keepalive.
lan-name	LAN Name command.
lat	LAT commands.
llc2	LLC2 Interface Subcommands.
load-interval	Specify interval for load calculation for an interface.
locaddr-priority	Assign a priority group.
logging	Configure logging for interface.
loopback	Configure internal loopback on an interface.
mac-address	Manually set interface MAC address.
mop	DEC MOP server commands.
mtu	Set the interface Maximum Transmission Unit (MTU).
multilink-group	Put interface in a multilink bundle.
netbios	Use a defined NetBIOS access list or enable name-caching.
no	Negate a command or set its defaults.
ntp	Configure NTP.
priority-group	Assign a priority group to an interface.
random-detect	Enable Weighted Random Early Detection (WRED) on an Interface.
rate-limit	Rate Limit.
sap-priority	Assign a priority group.
shutdown	Shut down the selected interface.
smrp	Simple Multicast Routing Protocol interface subcommands.
sna	SNA pu configuration.
snapshot	Configure snapshot support on the interface.
snmp	Modify SNMP interface parameters.
standby	Hot standby interface subcommands.
tarp	TARP interface subcommands
timeout	Define timeout values for this interface.
traffic-shape	Enable traffic shaping on an interface or sub-interface.
transmit-interface	Assign a transmit interface to a receive-only interface.

```
    tx-queue-limit        Configure card-level transmit queue limit.
    vines                 VINES interface subcommands.
    xns                   XNS interface subcommands.

Cisco2611(config-if)#
```

Do you see the command to configure IP on our interface? It's:

```
    ip                    Interface Internet Protocol config commands
```

As you would have deduced, the config interface (Ethernet) IP subcommand for assigning an IP address to this interface is address. Let's now view our options for this subcommand:

```
Cisco2611(config-if)#ip address ?
  A.B.C.D  IP address
Cisco2611(config-if)#ip address
```

 The IP address subhelp asks for the IP subnet mask to follow.

Seems simple enough. Let's go ahead and configure our new IP address for this interface (see Figure 11.12).

```
Cisco2611>enable
Password:
Cisco2611#config t
Enter configuration commands, one per line.  End with CNTL/Z.
Cisco2611(config)#interface ethernet 0/0
Cisco2611(config-if)#ip address 192.168.0.4 255.255.255.0
Cisco2611(config-if)#^Z
Cisco2611#
```

Figure 11.12 Configuring the new IP address.

If the newly configured interface was previously shut down, we would add the no shutdown **command during the config interface mode to activate the interface.**

Three common methods are used to verify a new IP address and the connectivity to/from the router interface. These include PING, Traceroute, and Telnet:

PING. An acronym for Packet INternet Groper. PING is a protocol for testing whether a particular computer IP address is active; using ICMP, it sends a packet to its IP address and waits for a response. Interestingly, PING is derived from submarine active sonar, where a sound signal, called a ping, is broadcast. Surrounding objects are revealed by their reflections of the sound. PING can be executed from the router console or remote terminal window, an MS-DOS window in Microsoft Windows or a terminal console session in UNIX.

 When used as a verb, ping is shown in lowercase.

Let's ping from our router to verify network connectivity with our single active interface:

```
Cisco2611#ping 192.168.0.1

Type escape sequence to abort.
Sending 5, 100-byte ICMP Echos to 192.168.0.1, timeout is 2 seconds:
!!!!!
Success rate is 100 percent (5/5), round-trip min/avg/max = 1/2/4 ms
Cisco2611#
```

Traceroute. Displays the path for data traveling from a sending node to a destination node, returning the time in milliseconds and each hop count in between (e.g., router and/or server). Tracing a route is typically a vital mechanism for troubleshooting connectivity problems.

Let's trace route from our router to verify network connectivity with our single active interface:

```
Cisco2611#traceroute 192.168.0.2

Type escape sequence to abort.
Tracing the route to 192.168.0.2

  1 192.168.0.2 0 msec 0 msec 0 msec
Cisco2611#
```

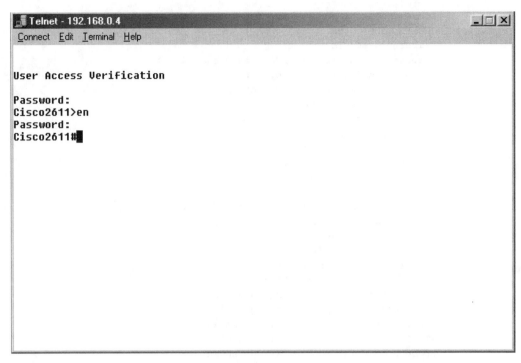

Figure 11.13   Verifying IP connectivity with Telnet.

Telnet. Before there were Web browsers with graphical compilers or even the World Wide Web, computers on the Internet communicated by means of text and command-line control using Telnet daemons. Typically, you gained access to these hosts from a "terminal," a simple computer directly connected to the larger, more complex "host system." Telnet software is "terminal emulator" software; that is, it pretends to be a terminal directly connected to the host system, even though its connection is actually made through the Internet (customarily through TCP port 23).

Let's telnet from our station to the router to verify network connectivity (see Figure 11.13).

There are several IOS commands used to monitor IP communications from the router. These include:

show ip interface (interface). Displays IP status for an interface. Sample output:

```
Cisco2611#show ip interface ethernet 0/0
Ethernet0/0 is up, line protocol is up
  Internet address is 192.168.0.4/24
  Broadcast address is 255.255.255.255
```

```
Address determined by setup command
MTU is 1500 bytes
Helper address is not set
Directed broadcast forwarding is disabled
Outgoing access list is not set
Inbound  access list is not set
Proxy ARP is enabled
Security level is default
Split horizon is enabled
ICMP redirects are always sent
ICMP unreachables are always sent
ICMP mask replies are never sent
IP fast switching is enabled
IP fast switching on the same interface is disabled
IP Flow switching is disabled
IP Fast switching turbo vector
IP multicast fast switching is enabled
IP multicast distributed fast switching is disabled
Router Discovery is disabled
IP output packet accounting is disabled
IP access violation accounting is disabled
TCP/IP header compression is disabled
RTP/IP header compression is disabled
Probe proxy name replies are disabled
Policy routing is disabled
Network address translation is disabled
WCCP Redirect outbound is disabled
WCCP Redirect exclude is disabled
BGP Policy Mapping is disabled
```

show ip route.   Displays the contents of the IP routing table. Sample output:

```
Cisco2611#show ip route
Codes: C - connected, S - static, I - IGRP, R - RIP, M - mobile, B -
BGP
       D - EIGRP, EX - EIGRP external, O - OSPF, IA - OSPF inter area
       N1 - OSPF NSSA external type 1, N2 - OSPF NSSA external type 2
       E1 - OSPF external type 1, E2 - OSPF external type 2, E - EGP
       i - IS-IS, L1 - IS-IS level-1, L2 - IS-IS level-2, * -
candidate
       default
       U - per-user static route, o - ODR, P - periodic downloaded
static
       route
       T - traffic engineered route

Gateway of last resort is not set

C    192.168.0.0/24 is directly connected, Ethernet0/0
```

show ip traffic. Displays packet types and status. Sample output:

```
Cisco2611#show ip traffic
IP statistics:
   Rcvd:  10358 total, 10358 local destination
          0 format errors, 0 checksum errors, 0 bad hop count
          0 unknown protocol, 0 not a gateway
          0 security failures, 0 bad options, 0 with options
   Opts:  0 end, 0 nop, 0 basic security, 0 loose source route
          0 timestamp, 0 extended security, 0 record route
          0 stream ID, 0 strict source route, 0 alert, 0 cipso
          0 other
   Frags: 0 reassembled, 0 timeouts, 0 couldn't reassemble
          0 fragmented, 0 couldn't fragment
   Bcast: 10267 received, 636 sent
   Mcast: 0 received, 0 sent
   Sent:  808 generated, 0 forwarded
   Drop:  0 encapsulation failed, 0 unresolved, 0 no adjacency
          0 no route, 0 unicast RPF, 0 forced drop

ICMP statistics:
   Rcvd: 0 format errors, 0 checksum errors, 0 redirects, 3 unreachable
         2 echo, 5 echo reply, 0 mask requests, 0 mask replies, 0
quench
         0 parameter, 0 timestamp, 0 info request, 0 other
         0 irdp solicitations, 0 irdp advertisements
   Sent: 0 redirects, 0 unreachable, 5 echo, 2 echo reply
      0 mask requests, 0 mask replies, 0 quench, 0 timestamp
         0 info reply, 0 time exceeded, 0 parameter problem
         0 irdp solicitations, 0 irdp advertisements

UDP statistics:
   Rcvd: 10276 total, 0 checksum errors, 1451 no port
   Sent: 729 total, 0 forwarded broadcasts

TCP statistics:
   Rcvd: 79 total, 0 checksum errors, 0 no port
   Sent: 72 total

Probe statistics:
   Rcvd: 0 address requests, 0 address replies
         0 proxy name requests, 0 where-is requests, 0 other
   Sent: 0 address requests, 0 address replies (0 proxy)
         0 proxy name replies, 0 where-is replies

EGP statistics:
   Rcvd: 0 total, 0 format errors, 0 checksum errors, 0 no listener
   Sent: 0 total

IGRP statistics:
```

```
         Rcvd: 0 total, 0 checksum errors
         Sent: 0 total

     OSPF statistics:
        Rcvd: 0 total, 0 checksum errors
              0 hello, 0 database desc, 0 link state req
              0 link state updates, 0 link state acks

        Sent: 0 total

     IP-IGRP2 statistics:
        Rcvd: 0 total
        Sent: 0 total

     PIMv2 statistics: Sent/Received
        Total: 0/0, 0 checksum errors, 0 format errors
        Registers: 0/0, Register Stops: 0/0,  Hellos: 0/0
        Join/Prunes: 0/0, Asserts: 0/0, grafts: 0/0
        Bootstraps: 0/0, Candidate_RP_Advertisements: 0/0

     IGMP statistics: Sent/Received
        Total: 0/0, Format errors: 0/0, Checksum errors: 0/0
        Host Queries: 0/0, Host Reports: 0/0, Host Leaves: 00
        DVMRP: 0/0, PIM: 0/0

     ARP statistics:
        Rcvd: 79 requests, 0 replies, 0 reverse, 0 other
        Sent: 1 requests, 214 replies (0 proxy), 0 reverse
     Cisco2611#
```

IPX

Recall that IPX is a connectionless datagram protocol. Also, not unlike IP addressing, Novell IPX network addresses must be unique; they are represented in hexadecimal format, and consist of two parts (a 32-bit long network number and a 48-bit long node number). The node number is also the Media Access Control (MAC) address for one of the system's network interface cards (NICs), assigned by the NIC manufacturer.

IPX network numbers play a primary role in the foundation for IPX internetwork packet exchange between network segments. Every segment is assigned a unique network address to which packets are routed for node destinations. For a protocol to identify itself with IPX and communicate with the network, it must request a *socket number*. Socket numbers ascertain the identity of processes within a station or node.

IPX header formatting and fields are defined as follows:

Checksum. The default for this field is no checksum; however, it can be configurable to perform on the IPX section of the packet.

Packet Length. The total length of the IPX packet.

Transport Control. When a packet is transmitted, and passes through a router, this field is incremented by 1. The limit for this field is 15 (hops or routers). The router that increments this field number to 16 will discard the packet.

Packet Type. Services include:

(Type 0) Unknown packet type

(Type 1) Routing information packet

(Type 4) IPX packet or used by the Service Advertisement Protocol (SAP; explained in the next section)

(Type 5) SPX packet

(Type 17) NetWare core protocol packet

(Type 20) IPX NetBIOS broadcast

Destination Network. The destination network to which the destination node belongs. If the destination is local, this field is set to 0.

Destination Node. The destination node address.

Destination Socket. The destination node's process socket address.

Source Network. The source network to which the source node belongs. If the source is unknown, this field is set to 0.

Source Node. The source node address.

Source Socket. The source node's process socket address, which transmits the packet.

Data. The IPX data, often including the header of a higher-level protocol.

It's important to note that in order to configure IPX on a Cisco router, a valid network address is required. The network ID must match the current network; or, if it is a new network, it must be a valid 32-bit number entered in hex.

Hex

The hexadecimal (hex) system is a form of binary shorthand. Internetworking equipment such as routers use this format while formulating headers to easily indicate Token Ring numbers, bridge numbers, networks, and so on. Using hex reduces header sizes and transmission congestion. Typically, hex is derived from the binary format, which is derived from decimal. Hex was designed so that the 8 bits in the binary 11100000 (Decimal=224) will equate to only two hex characters, each representing 4 bits.

To clarify, take a look at the binary value for 224:

1110000

In hex, we break this 8-bit number into 4-bit pairs:

1110 and 0000

Each bit in the 4-bit pairs has a decimal value, starting from left to right: 8 then 4 then 2 then 1 for the last bit:

8 4 2 1   8 4 2 1

1 1 1 0   0 0 0 0

Now we add the bits that are "on," or that have a 1 in each of the 4-bit pairs:

8 4 2 1 = 8+4+2+0 = **14**   8 4 2 1 = 0+0+0+0 = **0**

1 1 1 0   0 0 0 0

In this example, the decimal values that represent the hex characters in each of the 4-bit pairs are 14 and 0. To convert these to hex, use Table 11.3. Using this chart, the hex conversion for the decimals 14 and 0 (14 for the first 4-bit pair and 0 for the second 4-bit pair) = e0 (e for 14 and 0 for 0).

Let's look at one more example: We'll convert the decimal number 185 to binary:

Bits:	1	0	1	1	1	0	0	1
Value:	128	64	32	16	8	4	2	1 = 185

Binary for 185:   10111001

(the on/off bits indicated above each value)

Then we'll convert the binary number 10111001 to hex, which we break into 4-bit pairs:

1011 1001

Each bit in the 4-bit pairs has a decimal value, starting from left to right: 8 then 4 then 2 then 1 for the last bit:

8 4 2 1 8 4 2 1

1 0 1 1 1 0 0 1

Now we add the bits that have a 1 in each of the 4-bit pairs:

8 4 2 1 = 8+0+2+1= **11**   8 4 2 1 = 8+0+0+1 = **9**

1 0 1 1   1 0 0 1

Using the hex chart, the conversion for the decimals 11 and 9 (11 for the first 4-bit pair and 9 for the second 4=bit pair) = b9, as shown here:

Table 11.3 Decimal-to-Hex Conversion Table

DECIMAL	HEX
0	0
1	1
2	2
3	3
4	4
5	5
6	6
7	7
8	8
9	9
10	a
11	b
12	c
13	d
14	e
15	f

DECIMAL	BINARY	HEX
185	10111001	b9
224	11100000	e0

Configuring IPX

Before we discuss the IOS IPX configuration steps, let's look at Cisco's associated encapsulation types:

Arpa (for Ethernet_II)

Sap (for Ethernet_802.2)

Snap (for Ethernet_SNAP)

Novell ether (for default for Ethernet_802.3)

Token (for Token Ring)

Snap (for Token Ring_SNAP)

We configured the IP address for our Ethernet interface in one step—we entered the interface configuration mode and assigned an IP address. Configuring IPX is not much more difficult, though it does require two steps.

First, we employ the IPX routing command:

```
ipx routing   H.H.H   IPX address of this router
```

 If you do not specify the IPX address of the router, don't worry, the router will use that of the interface.

```
Cisco2611>enable
Password:
Cisco2611#config t
Enter configuration commands, one per line.  End with CNTL/Z.
Cisco2611(config)#ipx routing
Cisco2611(config)#
```

The second step to this configuration involves the interface that will take part in the IPX communications. The command text is the following:

ipx network (network number) encapsulation (encapsulation type) (secondary—to assign a secondary type)

Let's take a look at the commands for step 2:

```
Cisco2611(config)#interface ethernet 0/0
Cisco2611(config-if)#ipx network c8023 encapsulation novell-ether
Cisco2611(config-if)#ipx network c8022 encapsulation sap secondary
```

Here's output from the combined steps:

```
Cisco2611>enable
Password:
Cisco2611#config t
Enter configuration commands, one per line.  End with CNTL/Z.
Cisco2611(config)#ipx routing
Cisco2611(config)#interface ethernet 0/0
Cisco2611(config-if)#ipx network c8023 encapsulation novell-ether
Cisco2611(config-if)#ipx network c8022 encapsulation sap secondary
Cisco2611(config-if)#^Z
Cisco2611#
```

Monitoring IPX

Several IOS commands are used to monitor IPX communications from the router. They include:

show ipx interface (interface number). Displays IP status for an interface. Sample output:

```
Cisco2611#show ipx interface ethernet 0/0
Ethernet0/0 is up, line protocol is up
   IPX address is C8023.0002.16b7.af20, NOVELL-ETHER [up]
   Delay of this IPX network, in ticks is 1 throughput 0 link delay 0
   IPXWAN processing not enabled on this interface.
   IPX SAP update interval is 60 seconds
   IPX type 20 propagation packet forwarding is disabled
   Incoming access list is not set
   Outgoing access list is not set
   IPX helper access list is not set
   SAP GGS output filter list is not set
   SAP GNS processing enabled, delay 0 ms, output filter list is not
set
   SAP Input filter list is not set
   SAP Output filter list is not set
   SAP Router filter list is not set
   Input filter list is not set
   Output filter list is not set
   Router filter list is not set
   Netbios Input host access list is not set
   Netbios Input bytes access list is not set
   Netbios Output host access list is not set
   Netbios Output bytes access list is not set
   Updates each 60 seconds aging multiples RIP: 3 SAP: 3
   SAP interpacket delay is 55 ms, maximum size is 480 bytes
   RIP interpacket delay is 55 ms, maximum size is 432 bytes
   RIP response delay is not set
   IPX accounting is disabled
   IPX fast switching is configured (enabled)
   RIP packets received 0, RIP packets sent 2
   SAP packets received 0, SAP packets sent 2
```

show ipx route. Displays the contents of the IPX routing table. Sample output:

```
Cisco2611#show ipx route
Codes: C - Connected primary network,    c - Connected secondary network
       S - Static, F - Floating static, L - Local (internal), W - IPXWAN
       R - RIP, E - EIGRP, N - NLSP, X - External, A - Aggregate
       s - seconds, u - uses, U - Per-user static

1 Total IPX routes. Up to 1 parallel paths and 16 hops allowed.

No default route known.

C       C8023 (NOVELL-ETHER),  Et0/0
Cisco2611#
```

show ipx servers. Displays a list of IPX servers found on the network.

show ipx traffic. Displays IPX packet types and status. Sample output:

```
Cisco2611#show ipx traffic
System Traffic for 0.0000.0000.0001 System-Name: Cisco2611
Time since last clear: never
Rcvd:   0 total, 13 format errors, 0 checksum errors, 0 bad hop count,
        0 packets pitched, 0 local destination, 0 multicast
Bcast:  0 received, 4 sent
Sent:   4 generated, 0 forwarded
        0 encapsulation failed, 0 no route
SAP:    0 Total SAP requests, 0 Total SAP replies, 0 servers
        0 SAP general requests, 0 ignored, 0 replies
        0 SAP Get Nearest Server requests, 0 replies
        0 SAP Nearest Name requests, 0 replies
        0 SAP General Name requests, 0 replies
        0 SAP advertisements received, 0 sent
        0 SAP flash updates sent, 0 SAP format errors
RIP:    0 RIP requests, 0 ignored, 0 RIP replies, 1 routes
        0 RIP advertisements received, 0 sent
        0 RIP flash updates sent, 0 RIP format errors
Echo:   Rcvd 0 requests, 0 replies
        Sent 0 requests, 0 replies
        0 unknown: 0 no socket, 0 filtered, 0 no helper
        0 SAPs throttled, freed NDB len 0
Watchdog:
        0 packets received, 0 replies spoofed
Queue lengths:
        IPX input: 0, SAP 0, RIP 0, GNS 0
        SAP throttling length: 0/(no limit), 0 nets pending lost route
           reply
        Delayed process creation: 0
EIGRP:  Total received 0, sent 0
        Updates received 0, sent 0
        Queries received 0, sent 0
        Replies received 0, sent 0
        SAPs received 0, sent 0
Trace:  Rcvd 0 requests, 0 replies
        Sent 0 requests, 0 replies
Cisco2611#
```

Now that we've examined LAN communication protocols, let's move on to discuss how LANs communicate over WANs with routing protocols.

Routing

Recall that a router, operating at the Network layer that connects any number of LANs or WANs uses information from protocol headers to build a routing table, and forwards packets based on decisions. Then, as packets traverse through a router's NIC, they are placed into a queue for processing—during which, the router builds, updates, and maintains routing tables while concurrently checking packet headers for next-step compilations—whether accepting and forwarding the packet based on routing policies or discarding the packet based on filtering policies. While this is taking place, protocol performance functions provide handshaking, windowing, buffering, source quenching, and error checking.

Additionally, a router segments a network by breaking it into multiple subnets or internetworks. These subnets become manageable broadcast domains. Routers can make intelligent routing decisions, in multiprotocol environments, based on filters, security, and costs or best path to a destination.

The benefits of routing in a multiprotocol environment include:

- Provides path selection and packet switching for multiple protocols.
- Simplifies the administrative tasks.
- Maintains universal routing updates—usable by each protocol.
- Maintains separate routing tables for each protocol.
- Conserves resources.

Distance Vector versus Link State Routing Protocols

Distance Vector routing protocols send their entire routing tables at scheduled intervals, typically in seconds. Path determination is based on hop counts or distance (a hop takes place each time a packet reaches the next router in succession). There is no mechanism for identifying neighbors, and convergence is high.

With Link State routing protocols, only partial routing table updates are transmitted, and only when necessary; for example, when a link goes down or comes up. The metric is based on a much more complex algorithm (Dijkstra), whereby the best or shortest path is determined and then selected. An example of this type of path determination is a scenario that features a low-bandwidth dial-up connection (only one hop away), as opposed to higher-bandwidth leased lines that, by design, are two or three hops away from the destination.

With Distance Vector routing protocols, the dial-up connection may seem superior, as it is only one hop away; however, because the Link State routing protocol chooses the higher-bandwidth leased lines, it avoids potential congestion, and transmits data much faster. The primary differences between Distance Vector and Link State routing protocols are charted in Figure 11.14, and Figure 11.15 lists the five most common routing protocols and their specifications.

	Distance Vector	Link State
Path Determination (Metric)	Hop count	Best path
Routing Updates	Entire table at intervals	Partial when necessary
Neighbor Router Identification	None	Included
Metric Algorithm	Bellman-Ford	Dijkstra

Figure 11.14 Comparing Distance Vector and Link State protocol specifications.

Distance Vector and Link State routing protocols both use prioritization for determining the next best route (Administrative Distance), at the same time as implementing mechanisms to avoid routing loops.

Administrative Distance

The Administrative Distance is basically a priority mechanism for choosing between different routes to a destination. The shortest administrative distance has priority:

ROUTE	ADMINISTRATIVE DISTANCE
Attached Interface	0
Static Route	1
EIGRP Summary	5
EBGP	20
EIGRP Internal	90

Protocol	RIP	RIP v.2	IGRP	RTMP	OSPF
Type	Distance Vector	Distance Vector	Distance Vector	Distance Vector	Link State
Updates	Entire Table- 30 sec	Entire Table- 30 sec	90 sec	Hello Packets- 10 sec	Hello Packets- 10 sec/ LSA- 30 min
Class Support	Classful	Classless	Classful	Classful	Classless
Algorithm	Bellman-Ford	Bellman-Ford	Bellman-Ford	Bellman-Ford	Dijkstra

Figure 11.15 The five most common routing protocols.

IGRP	100
OSPF	110
IS-IS	115
RIP	120
EGP	140
EIGRP External	170
IBGP	200

Loop Prevention Methods

One of the primary goals of routing protocols is to attain a quick convergence, whereby each participating router maintains the same routing table states and where no loops can occur. The following list explains the most popular loop prevention mechanisms:

Split horizon. Updates are not sent back out the interface from which they were received.

Poison reverse. Updates are sent back out the interface from which they were received, but are advertised as unreachable.

Count to infinity. Specifies a maximum hop count, whereby a packet can only traverse through so many interfaces.

Holddown timers. When a link status has changed (i.e., goes down) a holddown timer sets a waiting period before a router will advertise the potential faulty route.

Triggered updates. When link topology changes (i.e., goes up), updates can be triggered to be advertised immediately.

Routing Information Protocol

The Routing Information Protocol (RIP) propagates route updates by major network numbers as a classful routing protocol—they do not carry prefix subnet masks. Version 2 of RIP introduces routing advertisements to be aggregated outside the network class boundary. The RIP Packet format fields are defined as follows:

Command. Specifies whether the packet is a request or a response to a request.

Version Number. Identifies the current RIP version.

Address Family Identifier (AFI). Indicates the protocol address being used:

1   IP (IP version 4)

2   IP6 (IP version 6)

3   NSAP

4   HDLC (8-bit multidrop)

5   BBN 1822

6   802 (includes all 802 media)

7   E.163

8   E.164 (SMDS, Frame Relay, ATM)

9   F.69 (Telex)

10   X.121 (X.25, Frame Relay)

11   IPX

12   Appletalk

13   Decnet IV

14   Banyan Vines

Route Tag. Specifies whether the route is internal or external.

Entry Address. IP address for the entry.

Subnet Mask. Subnet mask for the entry.

Next Hop. IP address of next hop router.

Metric. Lists the number of hops to destination (maximum = 15 hops).

Configuring RIP

For all practical purposes, there are two simple steps in the RIP configuration. Before we review the implementation, however, let's take a look at the command syntax:

router rip.   Enables RIP routing on the router.

```
Cisco2611(config)#router rip
Cisco2611(config-router)#
```

network (network number). Specifies the local network.

```
Cisco2611(config-router)#network 192.168.0.0
Cisco2611(config-router)#
```

The actual RIP implementation syntax from the console or virtual terminal would be:

```
Cisco2611>enable
Password:
Cisco2611#config t
Enter configuration commands, one per line.  End with CNTL/Z.
Cisco2611(config)#router rip
Cisco2611(config-router)#network 192.168.0.0
Cisco2611(config-router)#^Z
Cisco2611#
```

Interior Gateway Routing Protocol

Cisco developed the Interior Gateway Protocol (IGRP) for routing within an autonomous system, to act as a distance-vector interior gateway protocol. Merging both distance-vector and link-state technologies into one protocol, Cisco later developed the Enhanced Interior Gateway Protocol (EIGRP). The IGRP Packet format fields are defined as follows:

Version Number. Specifies the current protocol version.

Operation Code (OC) Command. Specifies whether the packet is a request or an update.

Autonomous System (AS). Lists the AS number.

AS Subnets. Indicates the subnetworks outside of the current autonomous system.

AS Nets. Indicates the number and networks outside of the current autonomous system.

Checksum. Gives the standard UDP algorithm.

The autonomous system (AS) can be defined as a combination of systems (including routers) working together as a unit under central administration. Cisco defines an autonomous system as a collection of networks under a common administration sharing a common routing strategy (see Figure 11.16). An autonomous system may comprise one or many networks, and each network may or may not have an internal structure (subnetting). All routers that belong to an autonomous system must be configured with the same autonomous system number.

Configuring IGRP

IGRP configuration also is generally a two-step process. Here's the command syntax:

`router igrp (autonomous system (AS) number (1-65545))`.
Enables IGRP routing on the router, with the specified AS number.

```
Cisco2611(config)#router igrp 1
Cisco2611(config-router)#
```

network (network number). Specifies the local network.

```
Cisco2611(config-router)#network 192.168.0.0
Cisco2611(config-router)#
```

The actual IGRP implementation syntax from the console or virtual terminal would be:

```
Cisco2611>enable
Password:
Cisco2611#config t
Enter configuration commands, one per line.  End with CNTL/Z.
Cisco2611(config)#router igrp 1
Cisco2611(config-router)#network 192.168.0.0
Cisco2611(config-router)#^Z
Cisco2611#
```

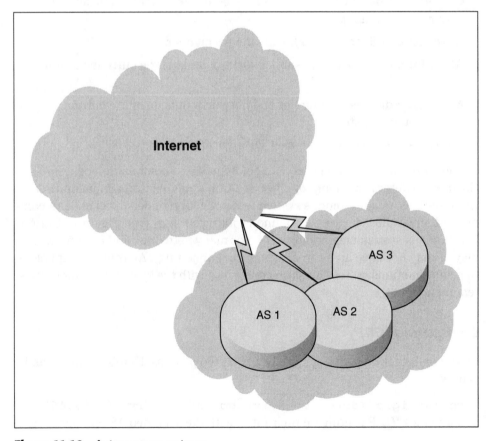

Figure 11.16 Autonomous systems.

Remember to use `show ip route` **to display the contents of the IP routing table containing both RIP and IGRP information.**

Sample output:

```
Cisco2611#sh ip route
Codes: C - connected, S - static, I - IGRP, R - RIP, M - mobile, B - BGP
       D - EIGRP, EX - EIGRP external, O - OSPF, IA - OSPF inter area
       N1 - OSPF NSSA external type 1, N2 - OSPF NSSA external type 2
       E1 - OSPF external type 1, E2 - OSPF external type 2, E - EGP
       i - IS-IS, L1 - IS-IS level-1, L2 - IS-IS level-2, * - candidate
          default
       U - per-user static route, o - ODR, P - periodic downloaded
          static route
       T - traffic engineered route

Gateway of last resort is 192.168.0.1 to network 0.0.0.0

     24.0.0.0/32 is subnetted, 1 subnets
R       24.182.143.0 [120/1] via 192.168.0.1, Ethernet0/0
     192.168.0.0/24 is variably subnetted, 2 subnets, 2 masks
C       192.168.0.0/24 is directly connected, Ethernet0/0
R       192.168.0.1/32 [120/1] via 192.168.0.1, Ethernet0/0
R*   0.0.0.0/0 [120/1] via 192.168.0.1, Ethernet0/0
Cisco2611#
```

Think It Over

Review your comprehension of the material in this chapter by answering these questions. Find out how you did in Appendix A.

11.1   On an Ethernet network, when a collision occurs, which of the following is the random collision timer for forced delays?

O Carrier Sense with Multiple Access

O Carrier Sense with Multiple Access and Collision Detection

O Back-off algorithm

11.2   Which of the following Ethernet topologies defines a structure where endpoints are connected to a common central switch or hub by direct links?

O Bus

O Star

O Point-to-Point

11.3   Which of the following Ethernet topologies defines a linear LAN where a station's transmissions are propagated and viewed by all stations?

O   Bus

O   Star

O   Point-to-Point

11.4   Which of the following Ethernet topologies defines a physical connection where communication passes from one station to another?

O   Bus

O   Star

O   Point-to-Point

11.5   Due to signal degradation, which segment is limited to fewer than 500 meters, with a maximum of 100 stations per segment of 1,024 stations total?

O   10Base5

O   10Base2

O   10BaseT

O   100BaseT

O   1000BaseCX

O   1000BaseSX

O   1000BaseLX

11.6   Due to signal degradation, which segment defines the cable between a station and a hub that is limited to fewer than 100 meters?

O   10Base5

O   10Base2

O   10BaseT

O   100BaseT

O   1000BaseCX

O   1000BaseSX

O   1000BaseLX

11.7   Due to signal degradation, which segment is limited to fewer than 185 meters, with a maximum of 30 stations per segment of 1,024 stations total?

O   10Base5

○ 10Base2

○ 10BaseT

○ 100BaseT

○ 1000BaseCX

○ 1000BaseSX

○ 1000BaseLX

11.8. Which segment operates at up to 316 meters, or 1,036 feet, in half-duplex, and in full-duplex mode up to 550 meters, or 1,804 feet?

○ 10Base5

○ 10Base2

○ 10BaseT

○ 100BaseT

○ 1000BaseCX

○ 1000BaseSX

○ 1000BaseLX

11.9. Which segment operates at up to 316 meters, or 1,036 feet, in half-duplex, and in full-duplex mode up to 5,000 meters, or 16,404 feet?

○ 10Base5

○ 10Base2

○ 10BaseT

○ 100BaseT

○ 1000BaseCX

○ 1000BaseSX

○ 1000BaseLX

11.10. Which of the following statements are true?

○ TCP provides unreliable packet delivery.

○ UDP provides unreliable packet delivery.

○ TCP is connectionless.

○ TCP is connection-oriented.

○ TCP and UDP operate at the Transport layer.

11.11 Which of the following are attributes of UDP?

○ Sliding window

○ Sequence/Acknowledgment numbers

○ HTTP

○ FTP

○ Telnet

○ No error checking and no sliding window

○ TFTP

11.12   Which of the following are attributes of TCP?

○ Sliding window

○ Sequence/Acknowledgment numbers

○ Video

○ FTP

○ HTTP

○ No error checking and no sliding window

○ TFTP

11.13   Which of the following EXEC command sequences best describes an IP address configuration on an interface?

○ Cisco2611(config)#interface ethernet 0/0
   Cisco2611(config-if)#ip address 192.168.0.2

○ Cisco2611(config)interface ethernet 0/0
   Cisco2611(config-if)ip address 192.168.0.2
   255.255.255.0

○ None of these

11.14   Which of the following IOS commands is used to display IP status for an interface?

○ show ip interface

○ show ip route

○ show ip traffic

○ None of these

11.15   Which of the following IOS commands is used to display the gateway of last resort?

○ show ip interface

○ show ip route

○ show ip traffic

○ None of these

11.16 Which of the following IOS commands is used to display ICMP statistics?

- ○ `show ip interface`
- ○ `show ip route`
- ○ `show ip traffic`
- ○ None of these

11.17 Select the IOS command that is used to display this extract:

```
Internet address is 192.168.0.4/24
Broadcast address is 255.255.255.255
Address determined by setup command
MTU is 1500 bytes
```

- ○ `show ip interface`
- ○ `show ip route`
- ○ `show ip traffic`
- ○ None of these

11.18 Select the IOS command that is used to display this extract:

```
UDP statistics:
  Rcvd: 10276 total, 0 checksum errors, 1451 no port
  Sent: 729 total, 0 forwarded broadcasts

TCP statistics:
  Rcvd: 79 total, 0 checksum errors, 0 no port
  Sent: 72 total
```

- ○ `show ip interface`
- ○ `show ip route`
- ○ `show ip traffic`
- ○ None of these

11.19 Which of the following Cisco encapsulation types is used for Ethernet_802.2?

- ○ Arpa
- ○ Sap
- ○ Snap
- ○ Novell ether
- ○ Token

11.20 Which of the following Cisco encapsulation types is used for Ethernet_802.3?

O Arpa

O Sap

O Snap

O Novell ether

O Token

11.21 Which of the following Cisco encapsulation types is used for Ethernet_SNAP?

O Arpa

O Sap

O Snap

O Novell ether

O Token

11.22 Which of the following EXEC command sequences best describes an IPX address configuration on an interface?

O `Cisco2611(config)#interface ethernet 0/0`
   `Cisco2611(config-if)#ipx network c8023 encapsulation novell-ether`

O `Cisco2611(config)#ipx routing`
   `Cisco2611(config)#ipx network c8023 encapsulation novell-ether`
   `Cisco2611(config)#ipx network c8022 encapsulation sap secondary`

O None of these

11.23 Which of the following is the maximum hop count metric for RIP?

O 1

O 5

O 10

O 15

11.24 Which of the following loop prevention mechanisms define poison reverse?

O Updates are not sent back out the interface from which they were received.

○ Updates are sent back out the interface from which they were received, but are advertised as unreachable.

○ Specifies a maximum hop count, whereby a packet can only traverse through so many interfaces.

○ When a link status has changed, this sets a waiting period before a router will advertise the potential faulty route.

○ When link topology changes, updates can be triggered to be advertised immediately.

11.25 Which of the following loop prevention mechanisms define split horizon?

○ Updates are not sent back out the interface from which they were received.

○ Updates are sent back out the interface from which they were received, but are advertised as unreachable.

○ Specifies a maximum hop count, whereby a packet can only traverse through so many interfaces

○ When a link status has changed, this sets a waiting period before a router will advertise the potential faulty route.

○ When link topology changes, updates can be triggered to be advertised immediately.

11.26 Which of the following loop prevention mechanisms define triggered updates?

○ Updates are not sent back out the interface from which they were received.

○ Updates are sent back out the interface from which they were received, but are advertised as unreachable.

○ Specifies a maximum hop count, whereby a packet can only traverse through so many interfaces.

○ When a link status has changed, this sets a waiting period before a router will advertise the potential faulty route.

○ When link topology changes, updates can be triggered to be advertised immediately.

11.27 Which of the following protocols, by default, sends updates every 90 seconds?

○ RIP

○ RIP v.2

○ IGRP

11.28 Which of the following protocols, by default, sends updates every 30 seconds?

○ RIP

○ RIP v.2

○ IGRP

11.29 Which of the following EXEC command sequences best describes an IGRP configuration?

○ `Cisco2611(config)#router igrp`
   `Cisco2611(config-router)#network 192.168.0.0`

○ `Cisco2611(config)#router igrp 1`
   `Cisco2611(config-router)#network 192.168.0.0`

○ None of these

11.30 Which of the following is the binary of 185?

○ 10111001

○ 10101001

○ 10110001

○ 10011001

11.31 Which of the following is the hex of 185?

○ b9

○ e0

○ b5

○ e2

WAN Internetworking

This chapter completes the discussion on Cisco fundamentals. In this coverage of wide area network (WAN) internetworking, you'll learn about WAN protocols—Frame Relay, Point-to-Point (PPP), and Integrated Services Digital Network (ISDN). You'll be introduced to Frame Relay terms and features; you'll learn the listing commands for configuring Frame Relay Local Management Interfaces (LMIs), maps, and subinterfaces, along with the listing commands for monitoring Frame Relay operation in the router, reviewing ISDN networking, and for identifying ISDN protocols, function groups, reference points, and channels; and you'll also become familiar with the PPP operations used to encapsulate WAN data on Cisco routers. We close out this chapter by addressing network security with access lists. You'll learn to configure standard and extended access lists to filter Internet Protocol/Internetwork Packet Exchange (IP/IPX) traffic and to monitor and verify selected access list operations on the router.

 Hands-on simulations of the information in this chapter can be found on the book's companion CD-ROM.

WAN Protocols

By now you know that communication media make up the infrastructure that connects stations into local area networks (LANs), LANs into WANs, and

WANs into internets. Now it's time to explore the wide area protocols that govern external communications. As just stated, these protocols are Frame Relay, PPP, and ISDN. Let's start with Frame Relay.

Frame Relay

This section provides an overview of the popular packet-switched communication medium called Frame Relay. This overview covers Frame Relay operation, devices, congestion control, the Local Management Interface (LMI), and frame formats.

Packet-switching technology, as it pertains to Frame Relay, gives multiple networks the capability to share a WAN medium and available bandwidth. This medium transmits variable-length packets at speeds up to 45 Mbps. Frame Relay generally costs less than point-to-point leased lines—leased lines involve a cost that is based on the distance between endpoints, whereas Frame Relay subscribers incur a cost based on desired bandwidth allocation. A Frame Relay subscriber will share a router, data service unit (DSU, a high-speed leased line modem), and backbone bandwidth with other subscribers, thereby reducing usage costs. If subscribers require dedicated bandwidth, called a *committed information rate* (CIR), they pay more to have guaranteed bandwidth during busy time slots.

Operation, Devices, Data-Link Connection Identifiers, and Virtual Circuits

Devices that participate in a Frame Relay WAN include data terminal equipment (DTE) and data circuit-terminating equipment (DCE). Customer-owned equipment such as routers and network stations are examples of DTE devices. Provider-owned equipment includes switching and clocking services, which fall under the DCE device category. Figure 12.1 illustrates an example of a Frame Relay WAN.

Frame Relay operates at the lower layers of the Open Systems Interconnection (OSI) model, specifically Layer 2 (Data Link), offering best-effort unreliable delivery of data at speeds from 56 Kbps to 45 Mbps. Data-link communication between devices is connected with an identifier and implemented as a Frame Relay *virtual circuit*. A virtual circuit is the logical connection between two DTE devices through a Frame Relay WAN. These circuits support bidirectional communication; the identifiers from one end to another are called *data-link connection identifiers* (DLCIs). Each frame that passes through a Frame Relay WAN contains the unique numbers that identify the owners of the virtual circuit to be routed to the proper destinations. Virtual circuits can pass through any number of DCE devices. As a result, there are many paths between a sending and receiving device over Frame Relay.

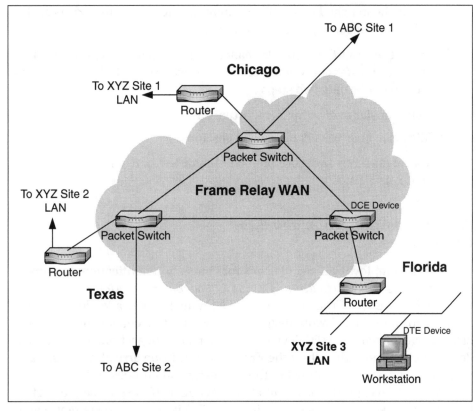

Figure 12.1 In a Frame Relay WAN, DTE devices are subscriber-owned and DCE devices are provider-owned.

 For the purposes of this overview, Figure 12.1 illustrates only three packet switches within the Frame Relay WAN. In practice, there may be 10 or 20 routers assimilating a multitude of potential courses from one end to another.

There are two types of virtual circuits in Frame Relay: *switched virtual circuits* (SVCs) and *permanent virtual circuits* (PVCs), defined as follows:

Switched Virtual Circuits. Periodic, temporary communication sessions for infrequent data transfers. A SVC connection requires four steps:

1. Call setup between DTE devices.

2. Data transfer over temporary virtual circuit.

3. Defined idle period before termination.

4. Switched virtual circuit termination.

SVCs can be matched up to ISDN communication sessions and, as such, use the same signaling protocols therein.

Permanent Virtual Circuits. Permanent communication sessions for frequent data transfers between DTE devices over Frame Relay. A PVC connection requires only two steps:

1. Data transfer over permanent virtual circuit.

2. Idle period between data transfer sessions.

PVCs are currently the more popular communication connections in Frame Relay WANs.

Congestion Notification and Error Checking

Frame Relay employs two mechanisms for congestion notification: *forward-explicit congestion notification* (FECN) and *backward-explicit congestion notification* (BECN). From a single bit in a Frame Relay header, FECN and BECN help control bandwidth degradation by reporting congestion areas. As data transfers from one DTE device to another, and congestion occurs, a DCE device such as a switch will set the FECN bit to 1. Upon arrival, the destination DTE device will be notified of the congestion and process this information to higher-level protocols to initiate flow control. If the data sent back to the originating sending device contains a BECN bit, notification is sent that a particular path through the network is congested.

During the data transfer process from source to destination, Frame Relay utilizes the common cyclic redundancy check (CRC) mechanism to verify data integrity, as explained in the Ethernet section of Chapter 11.

Local Management Interface

The main function of Frame Relay's LMI is to manage DLCIs. As DTE devices poll the network, LMI reports when a PVC is active or inactive. When a DTE device becomes active in a Frame Relay WAN, LMI determines which DLCIs available to the DTE device are active. LMI status messages between DTE and DCE devices provide the necessary synchronization for communication. LMI exchanges *keep alive messages* with the Frame Relay switch every 10 seconds, and every 60 seconds for a complete interface status update.

The LMI frame format consists of nine fields, defined in the following list:

Flag. Identifies the beginning of the frame.

LMI DLCI. Specifies that the frame is an LMI frame, rather than a standard Frame Relay frame.

Unnumbered Information Indicator (UII). Sets the poll bit to 0.

Protocol Discriminator (PD). Always includes a value, marking the frame as an LMI frame.

Call Reference. Contains zeros; not used at this time.

Message Type. Specifies the following message types:

- *Status-inquiry message.* Allows devices to request a status
- *Status message.* Supplies response to status-inquiry message

Variable Information Elements (VIE). Specifies two individual information elements:

- *IE identifier.* Identifies the information element (IE)
- *IE length.* Specifies the length of the IE

Frame Check Sequence (FCS). Verifies data integrity.

Flag. Specifies the end of the frame.

Frame Relay Frame Format

The following descriptions explain the standard Frame Relay frame format and the fields therein:

Flag. Specifies the beginning of the frame.

Address. Specifies the 10-bit DLCI value, 3-bit congestion control notification, and FECN and BECN bits.

Data. Contains encapsulated upper-layer data.

Frame Check Sequence (FCS). Verifies data integrity.

Flag. Specifies the end of the frame.

Configuring Frame Relay

Generally speaking, there are four configuration steps to learn when implementing Frame Relay, including serial interface encapsulation, LMI, map and subinterface:

1. *Encapsulation:* Frame Relay encapsulates upper-layer data from the DTE interface to the cloud. The interface command syntax is the following:

   ```
   Cisco2611(config-if)#encapsulation frame-relay (ietf)—to use
       RFC1490/RFC2427 encapsulation; otherwise Cisco is the default.
   ```

2. *LMI:* Frame Relay's local management interface is used for reporting when a PVC is active or inactive (as DTE devices poll the network). The command syntax is the following:

```
Cisco2611(config-if)#frame-relay lmi-type (cisco, ansi, or q933a)—
    cisco is the default, ansi, is Annex D defined by ANSI standard T1.617, and q933a is
    Annex A defined by Q933a.
```

3. *LMI Map:* Used to map the ends of the virtual circuits with the DLCIs. The interface command syntax is the following:

```
Cisco2611(config-if)#frame-relay map (protocol—see the following
    list) (protocol address) (DLCI—identifier between 16-1007, the
    receiving device would configure the other DLCI end)
```

You supply the network protocol from this list:

apollo	Apollo Domain
appletalk	AppleTalk
bridge	Bridging
bstun	Block Serial Tunnel
clns	ISO CLNS
decnet	DECnet
dlsw	Data Link Switching
ip	Internet Protocol
ipx	Novell IPX
rsrb	Remote Source-Route Bridging
stun	Serial Tunnel
vines	Banyan VINES
xns	Xerox Network Services

4. *(Optional) Subinterface.* Using subinterfaces enables multiple virtual circuits on a single serial interface, each with its own network features (i.e., one virtual circuit for IP and another for, say, IPX, etc.). The syntax to start our Frame Relay configuration with a subinterface is the following:

```
Cisco2611(config)#interface serial 0/0.1 (point-to-point or
    multipoint—to treat as a multipoint link). You can then map multiple
    virtual circuits with unique network features.
```

Let's now look at the complete configuration of both the sending and receiving routers as they apply to the illustration in Figure 12.2. Based on the four steps just enumerated, the Frame Relay router configurations for both Chicago and Florida devices would be the following:

For Chicago. Mapped with Florida's DLCI (201), using IP:

```
Cisco2611#config t
Cisco2611(config)#interface serial 0/1
```

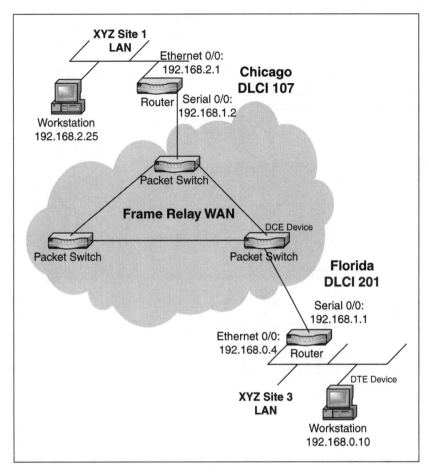

Figure 12.2   Frame Relay router configuration example network.

```
Cisco2611(config-if)#encapsulation frame-relay
Cisco2611(config-if)#frame-relay lmi-type cisco
Cisco2611(config-if)#frame-relay map ip 192.168.1.1 201
Cisco2611(config-if)#^Z
Cisco2611#
```

For Florida. Mapped with Chicago's DLCI (107), using IP:

```
Cisco2611#config t
Cisco2611(config)#interface serial 0/0
Cisco2611(config-if)#encapsulation frame-relay
Cisco2611(config-if)#frame-relay lmi-type cisco
Cisco2611(config-if)#frame-relay map ip 192.168.1.2 107
Cisco2611(config-if)#^Z
Cisco2611#
```

Florida's complete configuration could look like this:

```
Current configuration:
!
version 12.0
service config
service timestamps debug uptime
service timestamps log uptime
no service password-encryption
!
hostname Cisco2611
!
enable secret 5 $1$SQNi$S2EBRbGRX3m2mLv/A1qh00
enable password cisco
!
ip subnet-zero
!
interface Ethernet0/0
 ip address 192.168.0.3 255.255.255.0
 no ip directed-broadcast
no mop enabled
!
interface Serial0/0
 ip address 192.168.1.1 255.255.255.0
 no ip directed-broadcast
 encapsulation frame-relay
 frame-relay map ip 192.168.1.2 107
 frame-relay lmi-type cisco
!
interface Ethernet0/1
 no ip address
 no ip directed-broadcast
 shutdown
!
interface Serial0/1
 no ip address
 no ip directed-broadcast
 shutdown
!
router rip
 network 192.168.0.0
!
router igrp 1
 network 192.168.0.0
!
ip classless
no ip http server
!
dialer-list 1 protocol ip permit
dialer-list 1 protocol ipx permit
!
!
line con 0
```

```
 transport input none
line aux 0
line vty 0 4
 password vterminal
 login
!
no scheduler allocate
end
```

Monitoring Frame Relay

For our purposes here, there are four basic monitoring commands to use with Frame Relay: show interface, show frame-relay pvc, show frame-relay lmi, and show frame-relay traffic. They are defined as follows:

show interface. Used for displaying interface status and configuration. In regard to Frame Relay, this command will display the encapsulation type, LMI type, and traffic, as shown here:

 Boldface output corresponds to what information to look for in regard to the primary topic for each section.

```
Cisco2611#show interface serial 0/0

Serial0/0 is administratively down, line protocol is down
  Hardware is PowerQUICC Serial
  Internet address is 192.168.1.1/24
  MTU 1500 bytes, BW 1544 Kbit, DLY 20000 usec,
     reliability 255/255, txload 1/255, rxload 1/255
  Encapsulation FRAME-RELAY, loopback not set
  Keepalive set (10 sec)
  LMI enq sent  0, LMI stat recvd 0, LMI upd recvd 0, DTE LMI down
  LMI enq recvd 0, LMI stat sent  0, LMI upd sent  0
  LMI DLCI 1023  LMI type is CISCO  frame relay DTE
  FR SVC disabled, LAPF state down
  Broadcast queue 0/64, broadcasts sent/dropped 0/0, interface
      broadcasts 0
  Last input never, output never, output hang never
  Last clearing of "show interface" counters 00:14:12
  Input queue: 0/75/0 (size/max/drops); Total output drops: 0
  Queueing strategy: weighted fair
  Output queue: 0/1000/64/0 (size/max total/threshold/drops)
     Conversations  0/0/256 (active/max active/max total)
     Reserved Conversations 0/0 (allocated/max allocated)
  5 minute input rate 0 bits/sec, 0 packets/sec
  5 minute output rate 0 bits/sec, 0 packets/sec
     0 packets input, 0 bytes, 0 no buffer
```

```
             Received 0 broadcasts, 0 runts, 0 giants, 0 throttles
        0 input errors, 0 CRC, 0 frame, 0 overrun, 0 ignored, 0 abort
             0 packets output, 0 bytes, 0 underruns
             0 output errors, 0 collisions, 0 interface resets
             0 output buffer failures, 0 output buffers swapped out
             0 carrier transitions
             DCD=down   DSR=down   DTR=down   RTS=down   CTS=down
```

show `frame-relay` pvc. Used for displaying PVC statistics. This command will display any PVCs with associated DLCIs, as you can see here:

```
Cisco2611#show frame-relay pvc

PVC Statistics for interface Serial0/0 (Frame Relay DTE)

                Active      Inactive      Deleted      Static
  Local           0            1             0            0
  Switched        0            0             0            0
  Unused          0            0             0            0

DLCI = 107, DLCI USAGE = LOCAL, PVC STATUS = INACTIVE, INTERFACE =
Serial0/0

  input pkts 0          output pkts 0          in bytes 0
  out bytes 0           dropped pkts 0         in FECN pkts 0
  in BECN pkts 0        out FECN pkts 0        out BECN pkts 0
  in DE pkts 0          out DE pkts 0
  out bcast pkts 0       out bcast bytes 0
  pvc create time 00:16:48, last time pvc status changed 00:16:48
```

show `frame-relay` lmi— used for displaying LMI statistics:

```
Cisco2611#show frame-relay lmi

LMI Statistics for interface Serial0/0 (Frame Relay DTE) LMI TYPE =
CISCO
  Invalid Unnumbered info 0          Invalid Prot Disc 0
  Invalid dummy Call Ref 0           Invalid Msg Type 0
  Invalid Status Message 0           Invalid Lock Shift 0
  Invalid Information ID 0           Invalid Report IE Len 0
  Invalid Report Request 0          Invalid Keep IE Len 0
  Num Status Enq. Sent 0            Num Status msgs Rcvd 0
  Num Update Status Rcvd 0          Num Status Timeouts 0
```

show `frame-relay` `traffic`—used for displaying Frame Relay protocol statistics.

```
Cisco2611#show frame-relay traffic

Frame Relay statistics:
        ARP requests sent 0, ARP replies sent 0
        ARP request recvd 0, ARP replies recvd 0
```

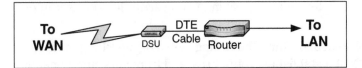

Figure 12.3 The T1 line is attached to a DSU, which is attached to a router via a DTE cable. The router is connected to a LAN switch or hub as it routes data between the LANs and WANs.

Point-to-Point Protocol

The PPP is an encapsulation protocol enabling the transportation of IP over serial or leased-line point-to-point links. PPP is compatible with any DTE/DCE interface, whether internal (integrated in a router) or external (attached to an external DSU). DTE is a device that acts as a data source or data destination that connects to a network through a DCE device, such as a DSU or modem. The DCE provides clocking signals and forwards traffic to the DTE. A DSU is a high-speed modem that adapts the DTE to a leased line, such as a T1, and provides signal timing, among other functions (see Figure 12.3). Through four steps, PPP supports methods of establishing, configuring, maintaining, and terminating communication sessions over a point-to-point connection.

PPP Operation

The PPP communication process is based on transmitting datagrams over a direct link. The PPP datagram delivery process can be broken down into three primary areas: datagram encapsulation, Link Control Protocol (LCP), and Network Control Protocol (NCP) initialization:

Datagram encapsulation. Datagram encapsulation during a PPP session is handled by the High-Level Data-link Control (HDLC) protocol. HDLC (the default encapsulation for Cisco routers) supports synchronous, half- and full-duplex transmission (see Chapter 11 for explanation of duplexing). The primary function of HDLC is to formulate the link between local and remote sites over a serial line.

Logical Link Protocol. As mentioned, in a four-step process, PPP supports establishing, configuring, maintaining, and terminating communication sessions using LCP. Here are the steps:

1. LCP opens a connection and negotiates configuration parameters through a configuration acknowledgment frame.

2. An optional link quality inspection takes place to determine sufficient resources for network protocol transmission.

3. NCP negotiates Network layer protocol configuration and transmissions.

4. LCP initiates a link termination, assuming no carrier loss or user intervention occurred.

Network Control Protocol. Initiated during step 3 of the PPP communication process, NCP establishes, configures, and transmits simultaneous network layer protocols.

Frame Structure

Six fields make up the PPP frame structure, as defined by the ISO HDLC standards:

Flag. A 1-byte field specifying the beginning or end of a frame.

Address. A 1-byte field containing the network broadcast address.

Control. A 1-byte field initiating a user data transmission in an unsequenced frame.

Protocol. A 2-byte field indicating the enclosed encapsulated protocol

Data. The datagram of the encapsulated protocol specified in the Protocol field.

Frame Check Sequence (FCS). A 2- to 4-byte field containing the FCS negotiation information.

Command Syntax

To configure PPP on a Cisco router, use the interface `encapsulation ppp` command:

```
Cisco2611#config t
Cisco2611(config)#interface serial 0/1
Cisco2611(config-if)#encapsulation ppp
Cisco2611(config-if)#^Z
Cisco2611#
```

Integrated Services Digital Network

ISDN is a digital version of switched analog communication. Digitization enables transmissions to include voice, data, graphics, video, and other services, whereas analog signals are carried over a single *channel* (a conduit through which information flows). In ISDN communication, a channel is a bidirectional or full-duplex time slot in a telephone company's facilitation equipment. In a nutshell, ISDN offers improved performance and bandwidth, voice and data transmissions, and speedier call placement.

Devices

ISDN communication transmits through a variety of devices, including:

Terminals. These come in type 1 (TE1) and type 2 (TE2). TE1s are specialized ISDN terminals (i.e., computers or ISDN telephones) that connect to an ISDN network via four-wire twisted-pair digital links. TE2s are non-ISDN terminals (i.e., standard telephones) that require terminal adapters for connectivity to ISDN networks.

Network termination devices. These devices come in type 1 (NT1) and type 2 (NT2). Basically, network termination devices connect TE1s and TE2s (just described) to conventional two-wire local-loop wiring used by a telephone company.

Reference Points

The reference point for defining ISDN devices include the following:

R   The reference point between non-ISDN equipment and TA

S   The reference point between user terminals and an NT2

T   The reference point between NT1 and NT2 devices

U   The reference point between NT1 devices and line termination equipment

Service Types

ISDN provides two types of services, *Basic Rate Interface* (BRI) and *Primary Rate Interface* (PRI). BRI consists of three channels, one D-channel and two B-channels, for transmission streaming. Under normal circumstances, the D-channel provides signal information for an ISDN interface. Operating at 16 Kbps, the D-channel typically includes excess bandwidth of approximately 9.6 Kbps to be used for additional data transfer.

The dual B-channels operate at 64 Kbps and are primarily used to carry data, voice, audio, and video signals. Basically, the relationship between the D-channel and B-channels is that the D-channel is used to transmit the message signals necessary for service requests on the B-channels. The total bandwidth available with BRI service is 144 Kbps (2×64 Kbps + 16 Kbps; see Figure 12.4).

In the United States, the PRI service type offers 23 B-channels and 1 D-channel, operating at 64 Kbps, totaling 1.54 Mbps available for transmission bandwidth.

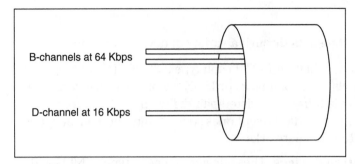

Figure 12.4 Basic Rate Interface (BRI) cable specifications.

Operation

ISDN operates at the Physical, Data Link, and Network layers of the OSI model:

Physical layer. ISDN Basic Rate Interfaces (BRI) and ISDN Primary Rate Interfaces (PRI).

Data Link layer. Link Access Procedure D channel (LAPD).

Network layer. User-to-user, circuit, and packet-switched connections.

Features of ISDN include the following:

Bandwidth-on-demand. Adds B-channel resources based on a load threshold.

PPP encapsulation. Adds access control and compression methods.

Dial-on-Demand Routing (DDR). Activates a call based on conditions and then drops the call once the link is no longer needed.

Command Syntax

In the Cisco world, ISDN offers WAN connectivity with PPP encapsulation, bandwidth-on-demand, and dial-on-demand (DDR) routing features. To configure an ISDN BRI interface on a Cisco router, simply specify the switch type and service profile IDs—like the phone number for each B-channel—all given to you by your call provider:

```
Cisco2611#config t
Cisco2611(config)#isdn switch-type basic-dms100
  Cisco2611(config)#interface bri0
Cisco2611(config-if)#isdn spid1 630123456
Cisco2611(config-if)#isdn spid2 630123457
Cisco2611(config-if)#encapsulation ppp
Cisco2611(config-if)#^Z
Cisco2611#
```

To get a listing of switch types in the preceding syntax, use the help command (?).

Network Security with Access Lists

At the top of the access router market, Cisco is a worldwide internetworking leader offering lines of modular, multiservice access platforms for small, medium, and large offices and Internet service providers (ISPs). These access products provide solutions for data, voice, video, dial-in access, virtual private networks (VPNs), and multiprotocol LAN-to-LAN routing. The continued growth of the Internet and the advances in technology have attracted external threats to core Internet access routers or any company with connectivity. To ensure that incoming and outgoing traffic (to/from the router) adheres to operating policies, internetworking administrators apply access control lists (ACLs). ACLs are really just a collection of *permit* and *deny* statements, applied to router traffic to allow/restrict packets, according to restrictions you apply. ACLs are enabled by the Cisco Internetworking Operating System (IOS) software to provide packet-filtering capabilities.

IP Access Lists

IP access lists come in two flavors, *standard* and *extended*. Two steps are required for each. The first step is the access list configuration; the second is to apply and activate the list. It is important to keep in mind two rules when working with access lists:

1. Access lists are examined in order from top to bottom. This means that for each packet the router intercepts for filtering, the router will compare the packet to each list line by line. When a match is made, the action takes place.

2. By default, there is an unseen implicit deny all at the end of each list. If and when a packet being compared to the access lists does not find a match, it is automatically discarded.

Standard

Standard access lists examine the source address of each packet and either permit or deny packets. When a packet is denied, the router simply discards it. The command syntax for creating standard access lists is the following:

```
Access-list (number) (permit or deny) (source address)
```

where:

> *number* is the standard IP access list; number can be between 1 and 99.
>
> *permit/deny* indicates whether to allow or discard the packet.
>
> *source address* is the IP address or network address.

You can use wildcard masking for the subnet mask here. Using a wildcard, you can choose to filter a single IP address or entire network. To implement the wildcard, input a 0 for each octet in the subnet mask, matching each octet in the address for those you want to match up; all ones will be discarded.

 Refer to Chapter 10, for a discussion on subnetting.

For example, the address 192.168.1.0 with wildcard mask 0.0.0.255 means that the first three octets, 192.168.1, must be matched, whereas the 255 (remember, in binary, 255 is all 1s: 11111111) means that the last octet is ignored—the router doesn't need to concern itself with any number here. If the first three octets match the source address, the router will perform the filtering. Again, if the first three do not match up here or with any other access list, the packet will be discarded automatically.

Alternatively, you can use the word host or any to specify a single host or any/all hosts, respectively.

The access-list command is configured during the privileged EXEC configuration mode, as shown here:

```
IP access-group (number) (in or out)
```

where:

> *number* is the corresponding standard IP access list, between 1 and 99.
>
> *in/out* specifies whether to filter incoming or outgoing traffic on a particular interface.

The access-group command is configured during the privileged EXEC configuration *interface* mode. Let's look at the complete configuration syntax:

```
Cisco2611#config t
Enter configuration commands, one per line.  End with CNTL/Z.
Cisco2611(config)#access-list 10 deny 192.168.1.55 0.0.0.0
Cisco2611(config)#access-list 10 permit 192.168.1.0 0.0.0.255
Cisco2611(config)#interface serial 0/0
Cisco2611(config-if)#ip access-group 10 in
Cisco2611(config-if)#^Z
Cisco2611#
```

In this example, we chose **10** for the list number (to specify a standard access list), **deny** to discard the matching packet with source address 192.168.1.55, **permit** to allow all other addresses from 192.168.1.0, and **in** to have the router inspect all incoming packets on this interface. The wildcard address 0.0.0.0 tells the router to match up all four octets (the entire IP address 192.168.1.55) and, if there's a match in the source address field of the packet, to discard the packet. The wildcard address 0.0.0.255 tells the router to match up the first three octets (192.168.1) and, if there's a match in the source address, to allow the packet.

Alternatively, in place of wildcard masking, we could change our deny command to read:

```
Cisco2611(config)#access-list 10 deny host 192.168.1.55
```

 All other packets will be denied. Remember rule 2; there is an implicit deny at the end of the access list.

Extended

Extended access lists examine more than just the source address of each packet to either permit or deny packets. They examine the *source address*, *destination address*, *protocol* (such as Transmission Control Protocol, or TCP, and User Datagram Protocol, or UDP), and *port* (such as File Transfer Protocol, or FTP). The command syntax for creating extended access lists is the following:

```
Access-list (number) (permit or deny) (protocol) (source address)
    (destination address) (port)
```

where:

> *number* is the extended IP access list, a number between 100 and 199.
>
> *permit or deny* indicates whether to allow or discard the packet.
>
> *protocol* is an IP protocol, from this list:

```
ahp       Authentication Header Protocol
eigrp     Cisco's EIGRP routing protocol
esp       Encapsulation Security Payload
gre       Cisco's GRE tunneling protocol
icmp      Internet Control Message Protocol
igmp      Internet Gateway Message Protocol
igrp      Cisco's routing protocol
ip        Any Internet Protocol
ipinip    IP in IP tunneling
```

```
nos       KA9Q NOS compatible IP over IP tunneling
ospf      OSPF routing protocol
pcp       Payload Compression Protocol
pim       Protocol Independent Multicast
tcp       Transmission Control Protocol
udp       User Datagram Protocol
```

source address is the IP or network address. (*Note*: As with standard access lists, you can use wildcard masking for the subnet mask here. Refer to the example in the preceding section to see how to use wildcard masking.)

destination address indicates the IP or network address. You can use wildcard masking for the subnet mask here:

```
any       Any destination host
eq        Match only packets on a given port number
gt        Match only packets with a greater port number
host      A single destination host
lt        Match only packets with a lower port number
neq       Match only packets not on a given port number
range     Match only packets in the range of port numbers
```

Alternatively, you can use the word host or any to specify a single host or any/all hosts, respectively.

port is the IP service port. It has two parts: Part 1 is the match command, from this list:

```
ack          Match on the ACK bit
eq           Match only packets on a given port number
established  Match established connections
fin          Match on the FIN bit
gt           Match only packets with a greater port number
log          Log matches against this entry
log-input    Log matches against this entry, including input interface
lt           Match only packets with a lower port number
neq          Match only packets not on a given port number
precedence   Match packets with given precedence value
psh          Match on the PSH bit
range        Match only packets in the range of port numbers
rst          Match on the RST bit
syn          Match on the SYN bit
time-range   Specify a time-range
tos          Match packets with given TOS value
urg          Match on the URG bit
```

Part 2 is the actual port, from this list:

```
<0-65535>    Port number
bgp          Border Gateway Protocol (179)
```

```
chargen        Character generator (19)
cmd            Remote commands (rcmd, 514)
daytime        Daytime (13)
discard        Discard (9)
domain         Domain Name Service (53)
echo           Echo (7)
exec           Exec (rsh, 512)
finger         Finger (79)
ftp            File Transfer Protocol (21)
ftp-data       FTP data connections (used infrequently, 20)
gopher         Gopher (70)
hostname       NIC hostname server (101)
ident          Ident Protocol (113)
irc            Internet Relay Chat (194)
klogin         Kerberos login (543)
kshell         Kerberos shell (544)
login          Login (rlogin, 513)
lpd            Printer service (515)
nntp           Network News Transport Protocol (119)
pim-auto-rp    PIM Auto-RP (496)
pop2           Post Office Protocol v2 (109)
pop3           Post Office Protocol v3 (110)
smtp           Simple Mail Transport Protocol (25)
sunrpc         Sun Remote Procedure Call (111)
syslog         Syslog (514)
tacacs         TAC Access Control System (49)
talk           Talk (517)
telnet         Telnet (23)
time           Time (37)
uucp           Unix-to-Unix Copy Program (540)
whois          Nicname (43)
www            World Wide Web (HTTP, 80)
```

The `access-list` command is configured during the privileged EXEC configuration mode:

```
IP access-group (number)(in or out)
```

> *number* is the corresponding standard IP access list number, between 100 and 199.

> *in or out* specifies whether to filter incoming or outgoing traffic on a particular interface.

The `access-group` command is configured during the privileged EXEC configuration *interface* mode. Let's look at the complete configuration syntax:

```
Cisco2611#config t
Enter configuration commands, one per line.  End with CNTL/Z.
Cisco2611(config)#access-list 115 permit tcp any host 192.168.1.121 eq ftp
Cisco2611(config)#access-list 115 permit ip any 192.168.1.0 0.0.0.255
```

```
Cisco2611(config)#interface serial 0/0
Cisco2611(config-if)#ip access-group 115 out
Cisco2611(config-if)#^Z
Cisco2611#
```

In this example, for the following access list,

```
Cisco2611(config)#access-list 115 permit tcp any host 192.168.1.121 eq ftp
```

we chose **115** for the list number (to specify an extended access list), **permit** to allow the matching packets using **TCP** from **any** internal source to access only **host 192.168.1.121**, using only (**eq**) the **FTP** service port.

In this example, for the following access list,

```
Cisco2611(config)#access-list 115 permit ip any 192.168.1.0 0.0.0.255
```

we chose **115** for the list number (to specify an extended access list), **permit** to allow the matching packets using any **IP** protocol from **any** internal source to access only machines on the remote network that match the first three octets, **192.168.1,** by using the wildcard mask of 0.0.0.255.

We applied the list to our outgoing (with **out**) Serial 0/0 interface:

```
Cisco2611(config-if)#ip access-group 115 out
```

 Again, all other packets will be denied, following rule 2.

IPX Access Lists

Like IP ACLs, IPX access lists come in two flavors, *standard* and *extended*, and are used to control IPX traffic. And note that the following same two rules apply when working with IPX access lists:

1. Access lists are examined in order from top to bottom. This means that for each packet the router intercepts for filtering, the router will compare the packet to each list line by line. When a match is made, the action takes place.

2. By default, there is an unseen implicit deny all at the end of each list. If and when a packet being compared to the access lists does not find a match, it is automatically discarded.

Standard

Standard IPX access lists examine both the source and destination address of each packet and either permit or deny them. When a packet is denied, the router simply discards it. The command syntax for creating standard access lists is the following:

```
Access-list (number) (permit or deny) (source network) (destination
    network)
```

where:

number is the standard IPX access list; number can be between 800 and 899.

permit or deny indicates whether to accept or reject the packet.

source network is the network the packet originated from.

destination network is the network the packet is predestined to reach.

```
IPX access-group (number) (in or out)
```

where:

number is the corresponding standard IPX access list number, between 800 and 899.

in or out specifies whether to filter incoming or outgoing traffic on a particular interface.

The access-group command is configured during the privileged EXEC configuration *interface* mode. Let's look at the complete configuration syntax example:

```
Cisco2611#config t
Enter configuration commands, one per line.  End with CNTL/Z.
Cisco2611(config)#access-list 800 permit 20 40
Cisco2611(config)#access-list 800 deny 10 40
Cisco2611(config)#interface ethernet 0/0
Cisco2611(config-if)#ipx access-group 800 out
Cisco2611(config-if)#^Z
Cisco2611#
```

In this example, for the following access list,

```
Cisco2611(config)#access-list 800 permit 20 40

Cisco2611(config-if)#ipx access-group 800 out
```

we chose **800** for the list number (to specify a standard IPX access list), **permit** to allow the matching packets from IPX network **20** to communicate with IPX network **40** going **out** Ethernet 0/0 router interface.

In this example, for the following access list,

```
Cisco2611(config)#access-list 800 deny 10 40

Cisco2611(config-if)#ipx access-group 800 out
```

again, we chose **800** for the list number (to specify a standard IPX access list), **deny** to discard the matching packets from IPX network **10** trying to communicate with IPX network **40** going **out** Ethernet 0/0 router interface.

Extended

Extended IPX access lists examine more than just the source address of each packet to either permit or deny transmission. They examine the *source address*, *destination address*, *protocol* (such as TCP and UDP), and *port* (such as FTP). The command syntax for creating extended access lists is the following:

```
Access-list (number) (permit or deny) (protocol type) (source) (source
    socket) (destination) (destination socket) (options)
```

where:

number is the extended IP access list; number can be between 900 and 999.

permit/deny indicates whether to allow or discard the packet.

protocol type is a protocol from this list:

```
<0-255>  Protocol type number (DECIMAL)
any      Any IPX protocol type
ncp      NetWare Core Protocol
netbios  IPX NetBIOS
rip      IPX Routing Information Protocol
sap      Service Advertising Protocol
spx      Sequenced Packet Exchange
```

source is an address, log, time-range, or network:

```
<0-FFFFFFFF>  Source net
N.H.H.H       Source net.host address
any           Any IPX net
log           Log matches against this entry
time-range    Specify a time-range
<cr>
```

source socket is the originated packet type, protocol type, or time-range:

```
<0-FFFFFFFF>  Source Socket HEXIDECIMAL
all           All sockets
```

```
cping         Cisco IPX ping
diagnostic    Diagnostic packet
eigrp         IPX Enhanced Interior Gateway Routing Protocol
log           Log matches against this entry
ncp           NetWare Core Protocol
netbios       IPX NetBIOS
nlsp          NetWare Link State Protocol
nping         Standard IPX ping
rip           IPX Routing Information Protocol
sap           Service Advertising Protocol
time-range    Specify a time-range
trace         Trace Route packet
<cr>
```

destination is a destination network, host address, log, or time-range:

```
<0-FFFFFFFF>  Destination net
N.H.H.H       Destination net.host address
any           Any IPX net
log           Log matches against this entry
time-range    Specify a time-range
<cr>
```

destination socket is the target packet type, protocol type, or time-range:

```
<0-FFFFFFFF>  Destination Socket HEXIDECIMAL
all           All sockets
cping         Cisco IPX ping
diagnostic    IPX Diagnostic packet
eigrp         IPX Enhanced Interior Gateway Routing Protocol
log           Log matches against this entry
ncp           NetWare Core Protocol
netbios       IPX NetBIOS
nlsp          NetWare Link State Protocol
nping         Standard IPX ping
rip           IPX Routing Information Protocol
sap           Service Advertising Protocol
time-range    Specify a time-range
trace         IPX Trace Route packet
<cr>
```

options are a time-range or log:

```
log         Log matches against this entry
time-range  Specify a time-range
<cr>
```

The `access-list` command is configured during the privileged EXEC configuration mode:

```
IP access-group (number) (in or out)
```

where:

> *number* is the corresponding standard IP access list number, between 900 and 999.

> *In or out* specifies whether to filter incoming or outgoing traffic on a particular interface.

The `access-group` command is configured during the privileged EXEC configuration *interface* mode. Let's look at the complete configuration syntax:

```
Cisco2611#config t
Enter configuration commands, one per line.  End with CNTL/Z.
Cisco2611(config)#access-list 900 permit any 10 all 30 all
Cisco2611(config)#interface ethernet 0/0
Cisco2611(config-if)#ip access-group 900 out
Cisco2611(config-if)#^Z
Cisco2611#
```

In this example, for the following access list,

```
Cisco2611(config)#access-list 900 permit any 10 all 30 all
Cisco2611(config)#interface ethernet 0/0
Cisco2611(config-if)#ip access-group 900 out
```

we chose **900** for the list number (to specify an extended IPX access list), **permit** to allow the matching packets using **any** IPX protocol type, from source IPX network **10** using any (**all**) source sockets, to communicate with destination IPX network **30**, using any (**all**) destination sockets—all going **out** the Ethernet 0/0 router interface.

A Word about IPX SAP Filters

Using the same methodology for IPX access lists, you can apply IPX Service Advertisement Protocol (SAP) filters to control advertisements. Actually, you're really controlling access to SAP devices. The command syntax for creating IPX SAP filters is the following:

```
Access-list (number) (permit or deny) (source) (service) (optional SAP
    server name)
```

where:

> *number* is the IPX access filter, a number between 1000 and 1099.

> *Permit or deny* indicates whether to allow or discard the packet.

> *source* is the originated network or host address:

```
-1           Any IPX net
<0-FFFFFFFF> Source net
N.H.H.H      Source net.host address
```

service is the SAP type code (see SAP types in Chapter 7) or host mask:

```
<0-FFFF>  Service type-code (0 matches all services)
N.H.H.H   Source net.host mask
<cr>
```

optional SAP server name is the server computer name:

```
WORD  A SAP server name
<cr>

IPX access-group (number) (in or out)
```

where:

number is the corresponding standard IPX access list number, between 800 and 899.

In or out specifies whether to filter incoming or outgoing traffic on a particular interface.

The `access-group` command is configured during the privileged EXEC configuration *interface* mode. Let's look at an example configuration:

```
Cisco2611#config t
Enter configuration commands, one per line.  End with CNTL/Z.
Cisco2611(config)#access-list 1000 deny -1 0
Cisco2611(config)#interface serial 0/0
Cisco2611(config-if)#ip access-group 1000 out
Cisco2611(config-if)#^Z
Cisco2611#
```

Here we chose **1000** for the list number (to specify an IPX SAP access list), **deny** to discard the matching packets from any internal IPX network (**-1**), matching all services (**0**), from going **out** the serial 0/0 router interface.

Monitoring Access Lists

To monitor access lists, you'll use these commands:

Show access-lists (interface). Displays all access lists applied to a specific interface.

Show IP access-list. Displays all IP access lists, as shown here:

```
Cisco2611#show ip access-lists
```

```
Standard IP access list 10
    deny    192.168.1.0
Extended IP access list 115
    permit tcp any any eq ftp
    permit ip any 192.168.1.0 0.0.0.255
Cisco2611#
```

Show IPX access-list. Displays all IPX access lists.

Show access-lists. Displays all access lists, as shown:

```
Cisco2611#show access-lists

IPX extended access list 900
    permit any 10 all 40 all
IPX sap access list 1000
    deny FFFFFFFF 0
Standard IP access list 10
    deny    192.168.1.0
Extended IP access list 115
    permit tcp any any eq ftp
    permit ip any 192.168.1.0 0.0.0.255
Cisco2611#
```

Show running-config. Verifies access lists in configuration

```
Cisco2611#show running-config

Current configuration:
!
version 12.0
service config
service timestamps debug uptime
service timestamps log uptime
no service password-encryption
!
hostname Cisco2611
!
enable secret 5 $1$SQNi$S2EBRbGRX3m2mLv/A1qh00
enable password cisco
!
ip subnet-zero
!
!
interface Ethernet0/0
 ip address 192.168.0.3 255.255.255.0
 no ip directed-broadcast
no mop enabled
!
interface Serial0/0
 ip address 192.168.1.1 255.255.255.0
 ip access-group 10 in
 no ip directed-broadcast
 encapsulation frame-relay
```

```
      shutdown
      frame-relay map ip 192.168.1.2 107
      frame-relay lmi-type cisco
     !
    interface Ethernet0/1
      no ip address
      no ip directed-broadcast
      shutdown
     !
    interface Serial0/1
      no ip address
      no ip directed-broadcast
      shutdown
     !
    router igrp 1
      network 192.168.0.0
     !
    ip classless
    no ip http server
     !
    access-list 10 deny    192.168.1.0
    access-list 115 permit tcp any any eq ftp
    access-list 115 permit ip any 192.168.1.0 0.0.0.255
    access-list 900 permit any 10 all 40 all
    access-list 1000 deny FFFFFFFF 0
    dialer-list 1 protocol ip permit
    dialer-list 1 protocol ipx permit
     !
     !
    line con 0
      transport input none
    line aux 0
    line vty 0 4
      password vterminal
      login
     !
    end
```

Think It Over

See how many of these questions you can answer correctly, to review the material in this chapter. Find out how well you did in Appendix A.

12.1. Which of the following is true about Frame Relay?

   O Data-link communication between devices is connected with an identifier

   O Has dual B-channels that operate at 64 Kbps

   O Operates using PVCs

   O Uses LAPD at the Data Link layer

12.2. Which of the following is a SVC connection step?

  ○ Call setup between DTE devices

  ○ Data transfer over temporary virtual circuit

  ○ Data transfer over permanent virtual circuit

  ○ Idle period between data transfer sessions

  ○ Defined idle period before termination

  ○ Switched virtual circuit termination

12.3. Which of the following is a PVC connection step?

  ○ Call setup between DTE devices

  ○ Data transfer over temporary virtual circuit

  ○ Data transfer over permanent virtual circuit

  ○ Idle period between data transfer sessions

  ○ Defined idle period before termination

  ○ Switched virtual circuit termination

12.4. ISDN subscribers who require dedicated bandwidth can get a committed information rate (CIR) to have guaranteed bandwidth during busy time slots.

  ○ True

  ○ False

12.5. As DTE devices poll the network, LMI reports when a PVC is active or inactive.

  ○ True

  ○ False

12.6. Which of the following is a Frame Relay LMI type?

  ○ Cisco

  ○ Ansi

  ○ Annex D

  ○ Annex A

  ○ DLCI

12.7. Which of the following commands is used for displaying Frame Relay protocol statistics?

  ○ `show interface`

  ○ `show frame-relay pvc`

○ `show frame-relay lmi`

○ `show frame-relay traffic`

12.8. Which of the following commands is used for displaying Frame Relay DLCIs?

○ `show interface`

○ `show frame-relay pvc`

○ `show frame-relay lmi`

○ `show frame-relay traffic`

12.9. Which of the following commands is used for displaying the Frame Relay encapsulation type?

○ `show interface`

○ `show frame-relay pvc`

○ `show frame-relay lmi`

○ `show frame-relay traffic`

12.10. Which is the default encapsulation type on Cisco routers?

○ PPP

○ Frame Relay

○ HDLC

○ LAPD

12.11. Which of these will negotiate Network layer protocol configuration and transmissions in PPP?

○ LCP

○ NCP

○ LAPD

12.12. What does the ISDN U reference point identify?

○ The reference point between non-ISDN equipment and TA

○ The reference point between user terminals and an NT2

○ The reference point between NT1 and NT2 devices

○ The reference point between NT1 devices and line termination equipment

12.13. What does the ISDN R reference point identify?

○ The reference point between non-ISDN equipment and TA

○ The reference point between user terminals and an NT2

○ The reference point between NT1 and NT2 devices

○ The reference point between NT1 devices and line termination equipment

12.14.   What does the ISDN S reference point identify?

○ The reference point between non-ISDN equipment and TA

○ The reference point between user terminals and an NT2

○ The reference point between NT1 and NT2 devices

○ The reference point between NT1 devices and line termination equipment

12.15.   Which of the following is a valid IPX extended access list?

○ `access-list 900 permit any 10 all 30 all`

○ `access-list 800 permit any 10 all 30 all`

○ `ipx access-list 900 permit any 10 all 30 all`

12.16.   Which of the following is a standard IPX access list that will allow the matching packets from IPX network 35 to communicate with IPX network 40?

○ `access-list 800 permit 35 40`

○ `ipx access-list 800 permit 35 40`

○ `access-list 800 permit 40 35`

○ `access-list 900 permit 35 40`

12.17.   Which of the following is a valid IP standard access list?

○ `access-list 100 deny 192.168.1.55 0.0.0.0`

○ `access-list 75 deny host 192.168.1.55`

○ `access-list 10 deny host 192.168.1.55`

12.18.   Which of the following is an extended IP access list that will allow the matching packets using the TCP protocol from any internal source to access only 192.168.1.50, using only the Telnet service port?

○ `access-list 100 permit tcp any host 192.168.1.50 eq telnet`

○ `access-list 99 permit tcp any host 192.168.1.50 eq 23`

○ `access-list 115 permit udp any host 192.168.1.50 eq telnet`

○ `access-list 50 permit tcp any host 192.168.1.50 any`

Appendix A

This appendix contains the answers to the *Think It Over* questions found in Chapters 2 through 12. For your convenience, all the questions and answers are repeated here, with the correct answers highlighted in boldface. In some cases, you also find explanatory notes that expand on the answer, to improve your comprehension of the material at hand.

Chapter 2: Installation and Basic Configuration

INSTALLING WINDOWS NT SERVER/WORKSTATION

2.1. Which Windows NT (WINNT) command is used to create new boot disks for a standard setup?

○ WINNT /B

● **WINNT /OX**

○ WINNT /U

○ WINNT /W

2.2. Which WINNT command is used to copy the boot files to your local drive and then uses your hard disk drive as if it were a boot disk?

● **WINNT /B**

○ WINNT /OX

○ WINNT /U

○ WINNT /W

2.3.   Which WINNT command is used to set up Windows NT from within Windows?

   ○ WINNT /B

   ○ WINNT /OX

   ○ WINNT /U

   ● **WINNT /W**

2.4.   Which WINNT command is used for an unattended setup on computers in which all the hardware components are standard and no user input is required for third party drivers, etc?

   ○ WINNT /B

   ○ WINNT /OX

   ● **WINNT /U**

   ○ WINNT /W

2.5.   If you were to install a single Windows NT server on a network with 50 concurrent connections, which licensing method would typically be most economical?

   ○ Per Seat

   ● **Per Server** [The Per Server mode is most economical in single-server, occasional, or specialty-use server solutions (with multiple concurrent connections.)]

2.6.   If you were to install a Windows NT server on a network with multiple NT servers, which licensing method would typically be most economical?

   ● **Per Seat** (The Per Seat mode is most economical in distributed computing environments where multiple servers within an organization provide services to clients, such as a company that uses Windows NT Server for file and print services.)

   ○ Per Server

2.7.   A PDC will retain a copy of the domain group database from the BDC.

   ○ True

   ● **False** (A BDC will retain a copy of the domain group database from the PDC. It can also provide user authentication to spread out the logon process load.)

2.8.   Why is it important not to overwrite a PDC?

   ● **Existing BDCs and/or users will not be able to communicate via the new SID.**

○ The BDC will have to be promoted to the PDC level.

○ The first server in a domain must act as the PDC.

2.9. A PDC can be configured for an existing domain.

○ True

● **False** (A PDC cannot be configured for an existing domain—a PDC creates the domain.)

2.10. Which NT server type is easy to move from domain to domain without reinstalling the operating system?

○ PDC

○ BDC

● **Stand-Alone**

BASIC WINDOWS NT CONFIGURATIONS

2.11. What is the connection called that is made between a network card, protocol(s), and the service(s) installed?

○ WINS

● **Binding**

○ DNS

○ DHCP

2.12. Subnetting is the process of obtaining an IP address class and expanding it to create a larger physical network.

○ True

● **False** (Subnetting is the process of dividing an assigned or derived address class into smaller, individual, but related, physical networks.)

2.13. Adding a protocol to be bound to an interface is a relatively simple process that you launch from the Protocols tab in the Network administration module found in the Control Panel.

● **True**

○ False

2.14. Out of the given 32 bits that make up IP addresses, match the default availability (for networks versus hosts), for the following blocks:

Class A (first octet between 0 and 127):

● **8 bits**

○ 16 bits

○ 24 bits

Class B (first octet between 128 and 191):

○ 8 bits

● **16 bits**

○ 24 bits

Class C (first octet between 192 and 223):

○ 8 bits

○ 16 bits

● **24 bits**

2.15. When a bit in a subnet mask octet is set to 1, it is an indication that it is being used.

● **True**

○ False

2.16. Which subnet mask would most likely be used to accommodate 12 subnets with 10 workstations each?

○ 255.255.255.192

○ 255.255.255.224

● **255.255.255.240**

○ 255.255.255.248

○ 255.255.255.252

2.17. Which subnet mask would most likely be used to accommodate 3 subnets with 25 workstations each?

○ 255.255.255.192

● **255.255.255.224**

○ 255.255.255.240

○ 255.255.255.248

○ 255.255.255.252

2.18. Which subnet mask would most likely be used to accommodate 20 subnets with 5 workstations each?

○ 255.255.255.192

○ 255.255.255.224

○ 255.255.255.240

● **255.255.255.248**

○ 255.255.255.252

2.19. Which of the following represents 6 bits in the subnet mask?

- ○ 255.255.255.192
- ○ 255.255.255.224
- ○ 255.255.255.240
- ○ 255.255.255.248
- ● **255.255.255.252**

2.20. Which of the following represents 3 bits in the subnet mask?

- ○ 255.255.255.192
- ● **255.255.255.224**
- ○ 255.255.255.240
- ○ 255.255.255.248
- ○ 255.255.255.252

Chapter 3: Subsequent Configuration and Administration

DESKTOP INTERFACE

3.1. On the Windows NT desktop, you can left- and right-mouse click to manipulate icons, create new folders and icons, install software, and modify the display properties, including background, screen saver, and overall appearance.

- ○ True
- ● **False** (You cannot install software using this technique.)

3.2. On the Windows NT desktop, you can jump between different open programs in forward sequence using which key combination?

- ● **Alt-Tab**
- ○ Shift-Alt-Tab
- ○ Ctrl-Esc

3.3. On the Windows NT desktop, you can jump between different open programs in forward sequence using which key combination?

- ○ Alt-Tab
- ● **Shift-Alt-Tab**
- ○ Ctrl-Esc

3.4. On the Windows NT desktop, the My Computer window displays which of the following?

○ A directory of all files within its hierarchy

● **A link to the Control Panel and Printers**

● **All available drives such as floppy, CD-ROM, and hard disk drive mappings**

3.5. Pertaining to the Windows NT Explorer, which of the following are true statements?

● **The Windows NT Explorer is a global file/folder management utility.**

● **Using this feature, you can quickly explore the system's entire contents and move, copy, view, rename, and delete files.**

● **You can customize views and map drives directly within the Explorer window.**

BASIC ADMINISTRATION

3.6. Which of the following best describes the Windows NT Control Panel?

● **The Control Panel houses programs used to change many of the computer's settings.**

○ The Control Panel lists a directory of all files within its hierarchy.

○ The Control Panel is used to enable and disable device configurations.

3.7. Which of the following sequences best describes using the Add/Remove Programs module from the Control Panel to remove a Windows NT Setup component?

● **Double click Add/Remove Programs in the Control Panel. From the Windows NT Setup tab, select the component you want to remove. To remove all parts of a component, clear its check box. To remove some parts of a component, highlight the component, then click Details. Clear the parts as needed, then click OK.**

○ Double-click Add/Remove Programs in the Control Panel. From the Windows NT Setup tab, select the component you want to remove. To remove all parts of a component, check its check box, then click OK.

○ Double click Add/Remove Programs in the Control Panel (refer to Figure 3.9). From the Install/Uninstall tab, click Uninstall. Follow the Windows prompt to insert a CD-ROM, floppy disk, or to identify a hard disk drive.

3.8. Changing the startup type of a Boot or System device may potentially do what?

○ Nothing

○ Reboot the system

● **Crash the system**

3.9. In the Device module from the Control Panel, if a device is essential to system operation, the Stop button will be unavailable.

● **True**

○ False

3.10. In the Licensing module from the Control Panel, the Per-Seat license agreement allows you a one-time, one-way option to change to Per-Server licensing mode later.

○ True

● **False** (The Per-Server license agreement allows you a one-time, one-way option to change to Per-Seat licensing mode later.)

3.11. Closing open shared resources from the Server module in the Control Panel may result in loss of data.

● **True**

○ False

3.12. Using the Server module under managing locks, stabilization, and sub-tree replication for the subdirectories, which best describes the process to temporarily stop exporting a subdirectory?

● **Click the subdirectory, then click Add Lock.**

○ Click the subdirectory, then click Remove Lock.

○ Click the subdirectory, then select the Entire Subtree check box.

3.13. As related to server and resource use, which of the following administrative alerts are generated by the system?

● **Security problems**

● **Access problems**

○ Drive mapping problems

● **User session problems**

○ Licensing problems

● **Server shutdown problems**

● **Printer problems**

3.14. When a server authenticates a logon request, and that user account has a logon script assigned, Windows NT locates the logon script by combining a local logon script path specified using the Server option in Control Panel with a filename as specified in User Manager.

- ● **True**
- ○ False

3.15. Any Windows computer can be set up as a replication export server.

- ○ True
- ● **False** (Only Windows NT Server computers can be set up as replication export servers.)

3.16. To configure service startup, you do not have to be logged on to a user account that has membership in the Administrators local group.

- ○ True
- ● **False** (To configure service startup, you must be logged on to a user account that has membership in the Administrators local group.)

Chapter 4: Administration Tools

USING THE ADMINISTRATIVE TOOLS STEP BY STEP

4.1 Which Windows NT file system supports permission security?

- ○ FAT
- ● **NTFS**

4.2. Two copies of the FAT are kept in case one is damaged.

- ● **True**
- ○ False

4.3. The NTFS is best used on partitions of less than 400 MB.

- ○ True
- ● **False** (Because of the amount of space overhead, NTFS should generally not be used on volumes smaller than 400 MB.)

4.4. Under Windows NT, hardware-based fault-tolerant mechanisms offer the same performance as the software-based ones in regard to RAID performance and reliability.

- ○ True

- **False** (Hardware-based fault-tolerant mechanisms under Windows NT offer much better RAID performance and reliability.)

4.5. Which RAID technique is being used when data is written to two identical disks simultaneously?

   ○ Level 0

   ● **Level 1** (This level provides *disk mirroring*, which is a technique whereby data is written to two identical disks simultaneously. If one of the disk drives goes down, the system can instantly switch to the other disk without any loss of data or interruption in service.)

   ○ Level 5

4.6. Which best describes RAID level 5?

   ○ Reserves one dedicated disk for error correction data, with good performance and some level of fault tolerance.

   ○ Provides data striping, which means blocks of each file are spread across multiple disks.

   ● **Provides byte-level data striping and error correction.**

4.7. A single hard disk drive always contains more than one volume.

   ○ True

   ● **False** [A single hard disk drive can contain more than one volume (via partitions); it's also possible for a single volume to contain or span multiple hard disk drives.]

4.8. In a volume set, a file is stored equally on each segment simultaneously.

   ○ True

   ● **False** (Files are stored sequentially; after the first segment is filled, the second segment is filled, then the third, and so on.)

4.9. In a stripe set, data is written equally to all segments in the set.

   ● **True**

   ○ False

4.10. In a stripe set with parity, if a physical hard drive becomes corrupt or fails, not all data in the stripe set will be lost.

   ● **True**

   ○ False

4.11.   What is the overhead space requirement for a mirror drive set?

  ○ 20 percent

  ○ 25 percent

  ○ 30 percent

  ● **50 percent** (Two 500-MB mirrored segments equaling 1,000 MB, or 1 GB, total space, allows for 500 MB of actual data storage and retrieval.)

4.12.   Using Event Viewer, when a log is archived, the sort order affects files that you save in text format or comma-delimited text format. The sort order does not affect event records you save in log-file format.

  ● **True**

  ○ False

4.13.   Which utility enables you to quickly install network client software by creating a network installation startup disk or an installation disk set?

  ○ Disk Administrator

  ○ Event Viewer

  ○ License Manager

  ● **Network Client Administrator**

  ○ Server Manager

  ○ System Policy Editor

  ○ User Manager for Domains

4.14.   To administer a domain and its servers using Server Manager, it is not necessary to be logged on to a user account that is a member of the Administrators, Domain Admins, or Server Operators group for that domain.

  ○ True

  ● **False** (You must be logged on to a user account that is a member of the Administrators, Domain Admins, or Server Operators group for that domain.)

4.15.   Which of the following is a true statement about domain management?

  ○ Global groups typically organize users by department, job, and/or security level and can be used only on the local system.

  ● **A local group is used only on the system from which it was created, unless it was created on a domain controller from which it would be propagated.**

○ Local groups are typically organized to access all domain resources and therefore are created by service.

4.16. In regard to managing security policies, the Account Policy controls how passwords must be used by all user accounts.

● **True**

○ False

4.17. In regard to managing security policies, the Audit Policy utility manages the rights granted to groups and user accounts.

○ True

● **False** (The Audit Policy is used to track selected user activities by auditing security events and storing the data in a security log.)

4.18 In regard to managing security policies, which policy is used to track selected user activities?

○ Account Policy

● **Audit Policy**

○ User Rights Policy

4.19. In regard to managing security policies, which policy defines maximum password age, minimum password age, whether a password history is maintained, and whether users must log on before changing their passwords?

● **Account Policy**

○ Audit Policy

○ User Rights Policy

Chapter 5: Advanced System Configurations: Networking and Optimization

5.1. When manually mapping a network drive by assigning a drive letter to a resource from your desktop or NT Explorer, which of the following would most accurately be an example of your input into the Path field?

○ //domain/computername/foldername (shared directory)

○ \ computername\ foldername (shared directory)

● **\\ computername\ foldername (shared directory)**

○ //computername\ foldername (shared directory)

5.2. When mapping a network drive from Network Neighborhood, to connect using a different user account on a different domain, which of the following would most accurately be an example of your input to the Connect as field?

○ /domain/user

○ //domain/user

● **domain\ user**

○ \ domain\ user

5.3. Which of the following best defines a print server?

● **A logical interface that governs user print jobs and schedules with physical printers**

○ A physical interface that governs user print jobs and schedules with logical printers

○ A physical interface that governs user print jobs and schedules with physical printers

○ A logical interface that governs user print jobs and schedules with logical printers

5.4. Which of the following best defines printer spooling?

○ A logical interface that governs user print jobs and schedules with physical printers

○ A single logical printer that sends the same job to many physical printers

● **The buffer that provides a waiting area until the specified printer is ready to print**

5.5. Which of the following best defines printer pooling?

○ A logical interface that governs user print jobs and schedules with physical printers

● **A single logical printer that sends the same job to many physical printers**

○ The buffer that provides a waiting area until the specified printer is ready to print

5.6. With the Add Printer Wizard you can install only a local printer to an NT server.

○ True

● **False** (With the Add Printer Wizard you can install a local or network-shared printer.)

5.7. When configuring a printing device, from which of the following configuration modules can you specify the amount of time to elapse before being notified that the printing device is not responding?

○ Add Port

● **Configure Port**

○ Port Properties

5.8. Which of the following user groups has full-control permission to modify printer settings by default?

● **Administrators**

● **Server Operators**

● **Print Operators**

● **Power Users**

5.9. Which of the following is used if your printer driver provides two-way dialog or reports setting and status information?

● **Bidirectional Support**

○ Printer Pooling

○ Printer Spooling

5.10. Which of the following list provides an overview of some of the things you can do with Windows NT Backup to protect data?

● **Back up and restore both local and remote files on the NTFS or FAT volumes from your own computer using an attached tape drive**

● **Select files for backing up or restoring by volume, directory, or individual filename, and view detailed file information, such as size or modification date**

● **Place multiple backup sets on a tape, and either append new backup sets or overwrite the whole tape with the new ones**

● **Span multiple tapes with both backup sets and files, because there is no file-size restriction**

● **Create a batch file to automate repeated backups of drives**

● **Control the destination drive and directory for a restore operation, and receive appropriate options for action you can take when a restore would overwrite a more recently created file**

5.11. To erase a tape that is causing a problem, which of the following would you type at the command prompt?

○ ntbackup /missingtape

● **ntbackup /nopoll**

○ ntbackup /erase

5.12. To specify that a tape is omitted from the backup set when the set spans several tapes, which of the following would you type at the command prompt?

● **ntbackup /missingtape**

○ ntbackup /nopoll

○ ntbackup /erase

5.13. Which of the following tape maintenance utilities will remove loose spots on the tape by fast-forwarding to the end of the tape and then rewinding?

○ Format Tape

● **Retension Tape**

○ Erase Tape

5.14. Under Windows NT, some of the program code and other information is kept in RAM, whereas other information is temporarily swapped to a file named what?

○ Paging File

○ Virtual memory File

● **Pagefile.sys**

5.15. Performance Monitor is a graphical tool for measuring the performance of your own computer or other computers on a network. On each computer, you can view which of the following behavior objects?

● **Processors**

● **Memory**

○ Logs

● **Cache**

● **Threads**

○ Alerts

● **Processes**

5.16. In regard to Performance Monitor, which of the following describes an object?

  ● **A standard mechanism for identifying and using a system resource**

  ● **Representations of individual processes, sections of shared memory, and physical devices**

  ○ A set of counters that provide information about network usage

Chapter 6: Advanced Service Configurations

6.1. Using dynamic addressing, a device can be assigned a different IP address each time it connects to the network.

  ● **True**

  ○ False

6.2. Configuring DHCP servers for a network provides which of the following benefits?

  ● **Simplifies network administration because the server keeps a real-time tally of assigned IP addresses.**

  ● **Allows the administrator to centrally specify global and subnet-specific TCP/IP parameters for the entire internetwork and define parameters for clients using reserved addresses.**

  ○ Uses a distributed database that contains information for each node currently available.

  ● **Does not require manual TCP/IP configuration for client computers. When a client computer moves between subnets, it is automatically reconfigured for TCP/IP when the computer is started.**

6.3. Most routers can't forward DHCP configuration requests, so DHCP servers are required on every subnet in the internetwork.

  ○ True

  ● **False** (Most routers can forward DHCP configuration requests, so DHCP servers are not required on every subnet in the internetwork.)

6.4. At the command prompt, which command can be used to start the DHCP Server service?

  ○ `net continue dhcp`

  ○ `net begin dhcp server`

● `net start dhcpserver`

○ `dhcpserver /start`

6.5. Which of the following best defines a DHCP scope?

● **A DHCP scope is a grouping of computers running the DHCP client service in a subnet. The scope is used to define parameters for each subnet.**

○ A DHCP scope contains lease duration values to be assigned to DHCP clients with dynamic addresses.

○ A DHCP scope contains address pools that make up the properties of subnet identifiers.

6.6. When a DHCP scope is deactivated, it does not acknowledge lease or renewal requests, so existing clients lose their leases at renewal time and reconfigure with another available DHCP server.

● **True**

○ False

6.7. To ensure that all clients migrate smoothly to a new scope, you should deactivate the old scope for at least half of the lease time or until all clients have been moved off the scope manually. To move a client manually, at the command prompt, which command can be used?

○ `ipconfig renew`

○ `net dhcpserver /renew`

● `ipconfig /renew`

○ `net dhcpserver /ipconfig renew`

6.8. If you are using a third-party DHCP server, be aware that Microsoft DHCP clients do not support option overlays. If your option set is too large, be sure that the settings used by Microsoft DHCP clients are included at the beginning of the option list. Microsoft DHCP clients do not read settings beyond which number of bytes?

● **The first 312 bytes**

○ The first 624 bytes

○ 936 bytes

6.9. A computer running the WINS server does not require a fixed IP address; it can be a DHCP client.

○ True

- **False** (A computer running the WINS server should be assigned a fixed IP address. The WINS server computer should not be a DHCP client.)

6.10. Using WINS servers can offer which of the following benefits on your internetwork?

- **Dynamic database maintenance to support computer name registration and name resolution. Although WINS provides dynamic name services, it offers a NetBIOS namespace, making it much more flexible than DNS for name resolution.**

- **Centralized management of the computer name database and the database replication policies, thereby alleviating the need for managing LMHOSTS files.**

- ○ Dramatic increase of IP broadcast traffic in LAN Manager internetworks.

- **Clients running Windows NT and Windows for Workgroups on a Windows NT Server network can browse domains on the far side of a router without a local domain controller being present on the other side of the router.**

- ○ A nonscaleable design, making it a good choice for name resolution only for very large internetworks.

6.11. At the command prompt, which of the following commands can be used to start the WINS service manager?

- **`start winsadmn`**
- **`start winsadmn 192.168.0.2`**
- **`start winsadmn mywinsserver`**
- ○ `net start wins`

6.12. At the command prompt, which of the following commands can be used to start the WINS server service?

- ○ `start winsadmn`
- ○ `start winsadmn 192.168.0.2`
- ○ `start winsadmn mywinsserver`
- **`net start wins`**

6.13. When configuring multiple WINS servers to increase the availability and to balance the load among servers, which of the following is an obligatory step?

- **Each WINS server must be configured with another as its replication partner.**

    ○ Each WINS server must also be configured as its own replication partner.

    ● **For each WINS server, you must configure threshold intervals for triggering database replication, based on a specific time, a time period, or a certain number of new records.**

6.14. Which of the following is the file in which database update operations are saved?

    ● **JET.LOG**

    ○ LMHOSTS

    ○ SYSTEM.MDB

    ○ WINS.MDB

    ○ WINSTMP.MDB

6.15. Which of the following files is used by WINS for holding information about the structure of its database?

    ○ JET.LOG

    ○ LMHOSTS

    ● **SYSTEM.MDB**

    ○ WINS.MDB

    ○ WINSTMP.MDB

6.16. Which of the following files is the WINS database file?

    ○ JET.LOG

    ○ LMHOSTS

    ○ SYSTEM.MDB

    ● **WINS.MDB**

    ○ WINSTMP.MDB

6.17. Which of the following files remains in the \\ WINS folder after a crash?

    ○ JET.LOG

    ○ LMHOSTS

    ○ SYSTEM.MDB

    ○ WINS.MDB

    ● **WINSTMP.MDB**

6.18. You should always compact the WINS database whenever it approaches what size?

  ○ 10 MB

  ○ 20 MB

  ● **30 MB**

  ○ 60 MB

6.19. On the server side, RAS can be configured to support modem pools with up to how many ports?

  ○ 4

  ○ 64

  ○ 128

  ● **256**

6.20. RAS supports which of the following network communication protocols?

  ● **TCP/IP**

  ● **IPX**

  ○ NetBIOS

  ● **NetBEUI**

  ○ PPTP

  ○ PPP

6.21. Remote access connections can be established over which of the following?

  ● **Public telephone lines**

  ● **X.25 networks**

  ● **ISDN networks**

  ● **PPTP connections**

6.22. Which of the following authentication method uses a cleartext process?

  ○ MS-CHAP

  ○ SPAP

  ● **PAP**

6.23. Which of the following authentication methods is the most secure protocol supported by RAS?

● **MS-CHAP**

○ SPAP

○ PAP

6.24. Which of the following authentication methods is an implementation for Shiva remote client software support?

○ MS-CHAP

● **SPAP**

○ PAP

6.25. Browsing for users and their permissions over a remote connection takes a long time. Which of the following processes is used to turn browsing off by default?

● **On the Options menu, click Low Speed Connection.**

○ Select Remote Access Service from the Network Service list and click OK to turn browsing off.

○ On the Options menu, click Configure and select the check box to turn browsing off.

○ On the Server menu, click Stop Remote Access Service.

Chapter 7: Advanced Gateway Configurations

7.1. DNS is a gateway service to the Internet that translates domain names into IP addresses.

● **True**

○ False

7.2. The records in the DNS directory are split into files called what?

○ DNS records

○ DNS record types

● **DNS zones**

○ DNS servers

7.3. Which of the following best describes the function of a DNS server that is authoritative for some zone?

● **Performs a caching function for all other DNS information**

○ Consists of DNS data, DNS servers, and Internet protocols for providing data from the servers

○ Maps an alphabetic domain name into an IP address, and forwards users to view Web sites

7.4. Which of the following, by default, consists of three reverse lookup zones that are associated with each DNS server?

● **0.In-addr.arpa**

● **127.In-addr.arpa**

○ Zone.In-addr.arpa

● **255.In-addr.arpa**

7.5. What is the name of the domain that is at the root of the DNS namespace section whose resource records will be managed in the resulting zone file?

● **Zone name**

○ Primary zone

○ Host name

7.6. A new subdomain will work with WINS Lookup.

○ True

● **False** (A new subdomain will not work with WINS Lookup. WINS Lookup will only resolve names that are direct descendants—that, is, children—of the zone root domain.)

7.7. Which of the following is a connectionless datagram protocol and, as such, is similar to unreliable datagram delivery offered by the Internet Protocol?

○ ARP

○ SPX

● **IPX**

○ SAP

7.8. Which of the following is a method by which network resources, such as file servers, advertise their addresses and the services they provide?

○ ARP

○ SPX

○ IPX

● **SAP**

7.9. Which of the following is a packet that is broadcast to all hosts attached to a physical network?

● **ARP**

○ SPX

○ IPX

○ SAP

7.10. Which of the following is the most common NetWare transport protocol?

○ ARP

● **SPX**

○ IPX

○ SAP

7.11. A SAP packet can contain service messages for up to how many servers?

○ 1

○ 3

○ 5

● **7**

7.12. Which of the following is a distributed database that maintains information about every resource on the network and access to such?

● **NDS**

○ NWLINK

○ Bindery

○ Tree

7.13. With Windows NT you can create gateways to both NDS and bindery resources.

● **True**

○ False

7.14. If NWLink detects no network traffic or any frames of type 802.2, to what does it set the frame type?

○ Auto

○ 802.3

● **802.2**

7.15. Access to NetWare is subject to trustee rights for which of the following?

● **Gateway user account**

● **NTGATEWAY group**

○ Admin group

7.16   To redirect the H drive to the directory \ data\ mydata of the SERVER volume on a server called NetWare411 using UNC naming syntax, what syntax would you use from the command prompt?

○ `net use H: \\SERVER\netware411\data\mydata`

● `net use H: \\netware411\SERVER\data\mydata`

○ `net use \\netware411\SERVER\data\mydata H:`

7.17. To connect as user *jchirillo* with the password *tigertools* to the directory \ data\ mydata within the SERVER volume on a server called NetWare411 using the H drive, what syntax would you use from the command prompt?

○ `net use /user:jchirillo tigertools\\netware411`
   `\SERVER\data\mydata H:`

● `net use H: \\netware411\server\data\mydata`
   `/user:jchirillo tigertools`

○ `net use H: \\SERVER\netware411\data\mydata`
   `/user:jchirillo tigertools`

7.18. IIS includes which of the following components?

● **Internet services: WWW, FTP, and Gopher**

● **Internet Service Manager**

● **Key manager**

● **A tool for installing Secure Sockets Layer (SSL) keys**

7.19. What must you do if you want to provide access to databases through the Microsoft Internet Information Server?

● **Set up the ODBC drivers and data sources using the ODBC applet in the Windows NT Control Panel**

○ Close all applications and services that use ODBC

○ Configure the WWW service to have Log on locally rights in Windows NT Server User Manager for Domains, then set up the ODBC drivers and data sources

7.20. Which of the following password authentication types is often used in conjunction with Secure Sockets Layer (SSL) to ensure that usernames and passwords are encrypted before transmission?

● **Basic**

○ Windows NT Challenge/Response

○ Clear Text

7.21. Which of the following password authentication types automatically encrypts usernames and passwords?

○ Basic

● **Windows NT Challenge/Response**

○ Clear Text

7.22. In regard to the Universal Naming Convention (UNC), if you specify a username and password to connect to a network drive, all Internet Information Server access to that directory will use that user name and password.

● **True**

○ False

Chapter 9: Win 2K Networking Services Configuration

9.1. Which of the following is a domain located in the namespace tree directly beneath another domain name?

○ Parent domain

● **Child domain**

○ Domain tree

○ Forest

9.2. Which of the following is the hierarchical tree structure that is used to index domain names?

○ Parent domain

○ Child domain

● **Domain tree**

○ Forest

9.3. Which of the following is a set of one or more trees that do not form a contiguous namespace?

○ Parent domain

○ Child domain

○ Domain tree

● **Forest**

9.4. Each security and distribution group has a scope that identifies the extent to which the group is applied in domain tree or forest. Which of the three different scopes can have as its members groups and accounts from any Windows 2000 domain in the domain tree or forest and can be granted permissions in any domain in the domain tree or forest?

● **Universal**

○ Global

○ Domain local

9.5. Each security and distribution group has a scope that identifies the extent to which the group is applied in the domain tree or forest. Which of the three different scopes can have as its members groups and accounts from a Windows 2000 or Windows NT domain and can be used to grant permissions only within a domain?

○ Universal

○ Global

● **Domain local**

9.6. Each security and distribution group has a scope that identifies the extent to which the group is applied in the domain tree or forest. Which of the three different scopes can have as its members groups and accounts only from the domain in which the group is defined and can be granted permissions in any domain in the forest?

○ Universal

● **Global**

○ Domain local

9.7. Groups in native-mode domains or distribution groups in mixed-mode domains have their membership determined as which of the following for groups with universal scope?

- ● **They can have as their members: user accounts, computer accounts, other groups with universal scope, and groups with global scope from any domain.**

- ○ They can have as their members: user accounts from the same domain and other groups with global scope from the same domain.

- ○ They can have as their members: user accounts, groups with universal scope, and groups with global scope, all from any domain. They can also have as members other groups with domain local scope from within the same domain.

9.8. Groups in native-mode domains or distribution groups in mixed-mode domains have their membership determined as which of the following for groups with global scope?

- ○ They can have as their members: user accounts, computer accounts, other groups with universal scope, and groups with global scope from any domain.

- ● **They can have as their members: user accounts from the same domain and other groups with global scope from the same domain.**

- ○ They can have as their members: user accounts, groups with universal scope, and groups with global scope, all from any domain. They can also have as members other groups with domain local scope from within the same domain.

9.9. Groups in native-mode domains or distribution groups in mixed-mode domains have their membership determined as which of the following for groups with domain local scope?

- ○ They can have as their members: user accounts, computer accounts, other groups with universal scope, and groups with global scope from any domain.

- ○ They can have as their members: user accounts from the same domain and other groups with global scope from the same domain.

- ● **They can have as their members: user accounts, groups with universal scope, and groups with global scope, all from any domain. They can also have as members other groups with domain local scope from within the same domain.**

9.10.   Explicit trusts create trust relationships to domains outside the forest.

○ True

● **False** (They are trust relationships that you create yourself, as opposed to trusts created automatically during installation of a domain controller.)

9.11.   Shortcut trusts are two-way transitive trusts that enable you to shorten the path in a complex forest.

● **True**

○ False

9.12.   Which of the following terms represents a limited sequence of IP addresses within a scope, excluded from DHCP service offerings?

○ Scope

○ Superscope

● **Exclusion range**

○ Reservation

○ Option types

○ Options class

9.13.   Which of the following terms represents a way for the server to further manage option types provided to clients?

○ Scope

○ Superscope

○ Exclusion range

○ Reservation

○ Option types

● **Options class**

9.14.   Which of the following terms represents a permanent address lease assignment by the DHCP server?

○ Scope

○ Superscope

○ Exclusion range

● **Reservation**

○ Option types

○ Options class

9.15. Which of the following terms represents an administrative grouping of scopes that can be used to support multiple logical IP subnets on the same physical subnet?

○ Scope

● **Superscope**

○ Exclusion range

○ Reservation

○ Option types

○ Options class

9.16. Which of the following terms represents a way for the server to further manage option types provided to clients?

○ Scope

○ Superscope

○ Exclusion range

○ Reservation

● **Option types**

○ Options class

9.17. Which of the following terms represents the full consecutive range of possible IP addresses for a network?

● **Scope**

○ Superscope

○ Exclusion range

○ Reservation

○ Option types

○ Options class

9.18. A superscope can have scopes added to it either during or after its creation.

● **True**

○ False

9.19. Which of the following DHCP options are applied for all scopes defined at a DHCP server?

● **Server options**

○ Scope options

○ Class options

○ Client options

9.20. Which of the following DHCP options are applied only to clients that are identified as members of a specified user or vendor class when obtaining a lease?

○ Server options

○ Scope options

● **Class options**

○ Client options

9.21. Which of the following DHCP options are applied specifically to all clients that obtain a lease within a particular scope?

○ Server options

● **Scope options**

○ Class options

○ Client options

9.22. To manage and troubleshoot DNS servers and clients, which of the following best describes the Nslookup command?

● **This command is used to perform query testing of the DNS domain namespace.**

○ This utility is useful in scripting batch files to help automate routine DNS management tasks or to perform simple unattended setup and configuration of new DNS servers on a network.

○ This command is used to view and modify IP configuration details used by the computer.

9.23. To manage and troubleshoot DNS servers and clients, which of the following best describes the Ipconfig command?

○ This command is used to perform query testing of the DNS domain namespace.

○ This utility is useful in scripting batch files to help automate routine DNS management tasks or to perform simple unattended setup and configuration of new DNS servers on a network.

● **This command is used to view and modify IP configuration details used by the computer.**

9.24. A zone transfer might occur during which of the following scenarios?

- **When the refresh interval expires for the zone**
- **When a secondary server is notified of zone changes by its master server**
- **When the DNS Server service is started at a secondary server for the zone**
- **When the DNS console is used at a secondary server for the zone to manually initiate a transfer from its master server**

Chapter 10: Cisco Router Fundamentals

10.1. Which of the following OSI model layers is responsible for encoding, decoding, compression, and encryption?

- ○ Application
- ● **Presentation**
- ○ Session
- ○ Transport
- ○ Network
- ○ Data Link
- ○ Physical

10.2. Which of the following OSI model layers is responsible for framing packets with a MAC address?

- ○ Application
- ○ Presentation
- ○ Session
- ○ Transport
- ○ Network
- ● **Data Link**
- ○ Physical

10.3. Which of the following OSI model layers is responsible for reliable, connection-oriented communication between nodes?

○ Application

○ Presentation

○ Session

● **Transport**

○ Network

○ Data Link

○ Physical

10.4. Which of the following OSI model layers is responsible for bringing networking to the application and for performing application synchronization?

● **Application**

○ Presentation

○ Session

○ Transport

○ Network

○ Data Link

○ Physical

10.5. Which of the following OSI model layers is responsible for routing protocols and logical network addressing?

○ Application

○ Presentation

○ Session

○ Transport

● **Network**

○ Data Link

○ Physical

10.6. Which of the following OSI model layers is responsible for data coordination between nodes and Novell Service Access Points (SAPs)?

O Application

O Presentation

● **Session**

O Transport

O Network

O Data Link

O Physical

10.7. Which of the following can be best described as the primary information units in the Internet?

● **Datagrams**

O Packets

O Frames

10.8. Which of the following can be best described as a logical grouping of information, which includes a header containing control information and, usually, user data?

O Datagrams

● **Packets**

O Frames

10.9. When datagrams traveling in frames cross network types with different specified size limits, routers must sometimes divide the datagram to accommodate a smaller MTU. This defines which of the following processes?

O Encapsulation

● **Fragmentation**

O Segmentation

10.10. At which of the following layers is data converted to segments??

O Application

O Presentation

○ Session

● **Transport**

○ Network

○ Data Link

○ Physical

10.11. At which of the following layers are segments converted to packets/datagrams?

○ Application

○ Presentation

○ Session

○ Transport

● **Network**

○ Data Link

○ Physical

10.12. At which of the following layers is user information converted to data?

○ Application

● **Presentation**

○ Session

○ Transport

○ Network

○ Data Link

○ Physical

10.13. At which of the following layers are frames converted to bits?

○ Application

○ Presentation

○ Session

○ Transport

○ Network

○ Data Link

● **Physical**

10.14. At which of the following layers are packets/datagrams converted to frames?

○ Application

○ Presentation

○ Session

○ Transport

○ Network

● **Data Link**

○ Physical

10.15. Which of the following describes a connection-oriented service?

○ Unreliable, best-effort delivery of data

● **Reliable delivery of data**

● **A three-way handshake, whose purpose is to synchronize the sequence number and acknowledgment numbers of both sides of the connection, while exchanging TCP window sizes**

10.16. Which of the following describes a connectionless service?

● **Unreliable, best-effort delivery of data**

○ Reliable delivery of data

○ A three-way handshake, whose purpose is to synchronize the sequence number and acknowledgment numbers of both sides of the connection, while exchanging TCP window sizes

10.17. A network address is 32 bits in length.

● **True**

○ False

10.18. A data link address can be defined as a logical, dynamic, virtual address.

○ True

● **False** (The data link address is the hardware or MAC address.)

10.19. The default availability (for networks versus hosts) for a Class B address block is which of the following?

○ 8 bits

● **16 bits**

○ 24 bits

10.20. Given 206.0.139.81 255.255.255.224, what is the network address?

● **205.0.125.64**

To calculate the network address for this host, let's map out the host octet (81) and the subnet-masked octet (224) by starting from the left, or largest, number:

```
(81)
Bits:      1    1    1
Value:    128  64   32   16   8    4    2    1
-------------------------------------------------
                64 + 16 + 1                   = 81


(.224)
Bits:      1    1    1
Value:    128  64   32   16   8    4    2    1
-------------------------------------------------
          128 + 64 + 32                       = 224
```

Now we can perform a mathematic "logical AND" to obtain the network address of this host (the value 64 is the only common bit):

```
(81)
Bits:      1    1    1
Value:    128  64   32   16   8    4    2    1

(224)
Bits:      1    1    1
Value:    128  64   32   16   8    4    2    1
-------------------------------------------------
                64                            = 64
```

We simply put the 1s together horizontally and record the common value (205.0.125.64).

○ 205.0.125.128

○ 205.0.125.32

10.21. Given IPX address 48F30106.00A024F9173B, which is the node number?

○ 48F30106.00A024F9173B

○ 48F30106

● **00A024F9173B**

10.22. Which of the following are advantages of LAN segmentation?

● **Separate collision domains**

● **Less congestion**

● **Individual broadcast domains**

10.23. Of the switching types, which of the following methods represents when the switch does not wait for the packet to be completely received or checks the CRC?

○ Store-and-forward

● **Cut-through**

○ Fragment-free

10.24. Of the switching types, which of the following methods represents when the switch waits for the collision window (64 bytes) to pass before forwarding?

○ Store-and-forward

○ Cut-through

● **Fragment-free**

10.25. Which of the following router elements stores the original IOS, bootstrap startup program, and hardware tests?

● **ROM**

○ Flash

○ NVRAM

○ RAM/DRAM

10.26. Which of the following router elements stores the running configuration, routing tables, caching, and buffering?

○ ROM

○ Flash

○ NVRAM

● **RAM/DRAM**

10.27. Which of the following router elements stores the startup configuration?

○ ROM

○ Flash

● **NVRAM**

○ RAM/DRAM

10.28. The EXEC privileged mode can be entered by taking which of the following actions?

○ Logging in

● **Typing `enable` at the command prompt**

○ Typing `config t` at the command prompt

○ Telnetting with the virtual terminal session

10.29. Typing which of the following EXEC commands will display the NVRAM contents?

○ `show running-config`, at the privileged mode command prompt

● **`show startup-config`, at the privileged mode command prompt**

○ `show running-config`, at the user mode command prompt

○ `show flash`, at the user mode command prompt

10.30. Typing which of the following EXEC commands will display the RAM contents?

● **`show running-config`, at the privileged mode command prompt**

○ `show startup-config`, at the privileged mode command prompt

○ `show running-config`, at the user mode command prompt

○ `show flash`, at the user mode command prompt

10.31. Which of the following keyboard sequence editing features will exit configuration mode?

○ Crtl-A

○ Crtl-E

○ Crtl-F

○ Crtl-B

● **Crtl-Z**

○ Crtl-P

○ Crtl-N

○ Tab

○ Esc-B

○ Esc-F

10.32. Which of the following keyboard sequence editing features will recall the previous command?

○ Crtl-A

○ Crtl-E

○ Crtl-F

○ Crtl-B

○ Crtl-Z

● **Crtl-P**

○ Crtl-N

○ Tab

○ Esc-B

○ Esc-F

10.33. Which of the following keyboard sequence editing features will complete the command entry?

○ Crtl-A

○ Crtl-E

○ Crtl-F

○ Crtl-B

○ Crtl-Z

○ Crtl-P

○ Crtl-N

● **Tab**

○ Esc-B

○ Esc-F

10.34. Which of the following keyboard sequence editing features will move the cursor to the beginning of the command line?

● **Crtl-A**

○ Crtl-E

○ Crtl-F

○ Crtl-B

- ○ Crtl-Z
- ○ Crtl-P
- ○ Crtl-N
- ○ Tab
- ○ Esc-B
- ○ Esc-F

10.35. Which of the following EXEC commands will save the current configuration in RAM to NVRAM?

- ○ `configure memory`
- ○ `copy tftp running-config`
- ● **`copy running-config startup-config`**
- ○ `show running-config`
- ○ `copy running-config tftp`
- ○ `show startup-config`
- ○ `erase startup-config`

10.36. Which of the following EXEC commands will display the configuration in NVRAM?

- ○ `configure memory`
- ○ `copy tftp running-config`
- ○ `copy running-config startup-config`
- ○ `show running-config`
- ○ `copy running-config tftp`
- ● **`show startup-config`**
- ○ `erase startup-config`

10.37. Which of the following EXEC commands will load the configuration from NVRAM?

- ● **`configure memory`**
- ○ `copy tftp running-config`
- ○ `copy running-config startup-config`
- ○ `show running-config`
- ○ `copy running-config tftp`
- ○ `show startup-config`
- ○ `erase startup-config`

10.38.   Which of the following EXEC commands will display the startup configuration?

   ○ `configure memory`

   ○ `copy tftp running-config`

   ○ `copy running-config startup-config`

   ○ `show running-config`

   ○ `copy running-config tftp`

   ○ **`show startup-config`**

   ○ `erase startup-config`

10.39.   Which of the following EXEC commands sequences will change the virtual terminal password?

   ● `2611(config)#line vty 0 4`
     `2611(config-line)#login`
     `2611(config-line)#password xxx`

   ○ `2611(config)#line console 0`
     `2611(config-line)#login`
     `2611(config-line)#password xxx`

   ○ `2611(config)#enable password xxx`
     `2611(config)#^Z`
     `2611#`

Chapter 11: LAN Internetworking

11.1.   On an Ethernet network, when a collision occurs, which of the following is the random collision timer for forced delays?

   ○ Carrier Sense with Multiple Access

   ○ Carrier Sense with Multiple Access and Collision Detection

   ● **Back-off algorithm**

11.2.   Which of the following Ethernet topologies defines a structure where endpoints are connected to a common central switch or hub by direct links?

   ○ Bus

   ● **Star**

   ○ Point-to-Point

11.3. Which of the following Ethernet topologies defines a linear LAN where a station's transmissions are propagated and viewed by all stations?

● **Bus**

○ Star

○ Point-to-Point

11.4. Which of the following Ethernet topologies defines a physical connection where communication passes from one station to another?

○ Bus

○ Star

● **Point-to-Point**

11.5. Due to signal degradation, which segment is limited to fewer than 500 meters, with a maximum of 100 stations per segment of 1,024 stations total?

● **10Base5**

○ 10Base2

○ 10BaseT

○ 100BaseT

○ 1000BaseCX

○ 1000BaseSX

○ 1000BaseLX

11.6. Due to signal degradation, which segment defines the cable between a station and a hub that is limited to fewer than 100 meters?

○ 10Base5

○ 10Base2

● **10BaseT**

○ 100BaseT

○ 1000BaseCX

○ 1000BaseSX

○ 1000BaseLX

11.7. Due to signal degradation, which segment is limited to fewer than 185 meters, with a maximum of 30 stations per segment of 1,024 stations total?

○ 10Base5

● **10Base2**

     ○ 10BaseT

     ○ 100BaseT

     ○ 1000BaseCX

     ○ 1000BaseSX

     ○ 1000BaseLX

11.8.   Which segment operates at up to 316 meters, or 1,036 feet, in half-duplex, and in full-duplex mode up to 550 meters, or 1,804 feet?

     ○ 10Base5

     ○ 10Base2

     ○ 10BaseT

     ○ 100BaseT

     ○ 1000BaseCX

     ● **1000BaseSX**

     ○ 1000BaseLX

11.9.   Which segment operates at up to 316 meters, or 1,036 feet, in half-duplex, and in full-duplex mode up to 5,000 meters, or 16,404 feet?

     ○ 10Base5

     ○ 10Base2

     ○ 10BaseT

     ○ 100BaseT

     ○ 1000BaseCX

     ○ 1000BaseSX

     ● **1000BaseLX**

11.10. Which of the following statements are true?

     ○ TCP provides unreliable packet delivery.

     ● **UDP provides unreliable packet delivery.**

     ○ TCP is connectionless.

     ● **TCP is connection-oriented.**

     ● **TCP and UDP operate at the Transport layer.**

11.11. Which of the following are attributes of UDP?

     ○ Sliding window

     ○ Sequence/Acknowledgment numbers

     ○ HTTP

● **FTP**

○ Telnet

● **No error checking and no sliding window**

● **TFTP**

11.12. Which of the following are attributes of TCP?

● **Sliding window**

● **Sequence/Acknowledgment numbers**

○ Video

● **FTP**

● **HTTP**

○ No error checking and no sliding window

○ TFTP

11.13. Which of the following EXEC command sequences best describes an IP address configuration on an interface?

○ `Cisco2611(config)#interface ethernet 0/0`
  `Cisco2611(config-if)#ip address 192.168.0.2`

○ `Cisco2611(config)interface ethernet 0/0`
  `Cisco2611(config-if)ip address 192.168.0.2 255.255.255.0`

● **None of these.** (The correct syntax (in privileged mode) would be:
  `Cisco2611(config)#interface ethernet 0/0`
  `Cisco2611(config-if)#ip address 192.168.0.2 255.255.255.0)`

11.14. Which of the following IOS commands is used to display IP status for an interface?

● `show ip interface`

○ `show ip route`

○ `show ip traffic`

○ None of these

11.15. Which of the following IOS commands is used to display the gateway of last resort?

○ `show ip interface`

● `show ip route`

○ `show ip traffic`

○ None of these

11.16. Which of the following IOS commands is used to display ICMP statistics?

○ show ip interface

○ show ip route

● **show ip traffic**

○ None of these

11.17. Select the IOS command that is used to display this extract:

```
Internet address is 192.168.0.4/24
Broadcast address is 255.255.255.255
Address determined by setup command
MTU is 1500 bytes
```

● **show ip interface**

○ show ip route

○ show ip traffic

○ None of these

11.18. Select the IOS command that is used to display this extract:

```
UDP statistics:
   Rcvd: 10276 total, 0 checksum errors, 1451 no port
   Sent: 729 total, 0 forwarded broadcasts

TCP statistics:
   Rcvd: 79 total, 0 checksum errors, 0 no port
   Sent: 72 total
```

○ show ip interface

○ show ip route

● **show ip traffic**

○ None of these

11.19. Which of the following Cisco encapsulation types is used for Ethernet_802.2?

○ Arpa

● **Sap**

○ Snap

○ Novell ether

○ Token

11.20. Which of the following Cisco encapsulation types is used for Ethernet_802.3?

    ○ Arpa

    ○ Sap

    ○ Snap

    ● **Novell ether**

    ○ Token

11.21. Which of the following Cisco encapsulation types is used for Ethernet_SNAP?

    ○ Arpa

    ○ Sap

    ● **Snap**

    ○ Novell ether

    ○ Token

11.22. Which of the following EXEC command sequences best describes an IPX address configuration on an interface?

    ●
```
Cisco2611(config)#interface ethernet 0/0
Cisco2611(config-if)#ipx network c8023 encapsulation novell-
ether
```

    ○
```
Cisco2611(config)#ipx routing
Cisco2611(config)#ipx network c8023 encapsulation novell-ether
     Cisco2611(config)#ipx network c8022 encapsulation sap
         secondary
```

    ○ None of these

11.23. Which of the following is the maximum hop count metric for RIP?

    ○ 1

    ○ 5

    ○ 10

    ● **15**

11.24. Which of the following loop prevention mechanisms define poison reverse?

    ○ Updates are not sent back out the interface from which they were received.

    ● **Updates are sent back out the interface from which they were received but are advertised as unreachable.**

○ Specifies a maximum hop count, whereby a packet can only traverse through so many interfaces.

○ When a link status has changed, this sets a waiting period before a router will advertise the potential faulty route.

○ When link topology changes, updates can be triggered to be advertised immediately.

11.25. Which of the following loop prevention mechanisms define split horizon?

● **Updates are not sent back out the interface from which they were received.**

○ Updates are sent back out the interface from which they were received but are advertised as unreachable.

○ Specifies a maximum hop count, whereby a packet can only traverse through so many interfaces.

○ When a link status has changed, this sets a waiting period before a router will advertise the potential faulty route.

○ When link topology changes, updates can be triggered to be advertised immediately.

11.26. Which of the following loop prevention mechanisms define triggered updates?

○ Updates are not sent back out the interface from which they were received.

○ Updates are sent back out the interface from which they were received but are advertised as unreachable.

○ Specifies a maximum hop count, whereby a packet can only traverse through so many interfaces.

○ When a link status has changed, this sets a waiting period before a router will advertise the potential faulty route.

● **When link topology changes, updates can be triggered to be advertised immediately.**

11.27. Which of the following protocols, by default, sends updates every 90 seconds?

○ RIP

○ RIP v.2

● **IGRP**

11.28. Which of the following protocols, by default, sends updates every 30 seconds?

- ● **RIP**
- ● **RIP v.2**
- ○ IGRP

11.29. Which of the following EXEC command sequences best describes an IGRP configuration?

- ○ `Cisco2611(config)#router igrp`
  `Cisco2611(config-router)#network 192.168.0.0`

- ● `Cisco2611(config)#router igrp 1`
  `Cisco2611(config-router)#network 192.168.0.0`

- ○ None of these

11.30. Which of the following is the binary of 185?

- ● **10111001**
- ○ 10101001
- ○ 10110001
- ○ 10011001

11.31. Which of the following is the hex of 185?

- ● **b9**
- ○ e0
- ○ b5
- ○ e2

Chapter 12: WAN Internetworking

12.1. Which of the following is true about Frame Relay?

- ● **Data-link communication between devices is connected with an identifier.**
- ○ Has dual B-channels that operate at 64 Kbps.
- ● **Operates using PVCs.**
- ○ Uses LAPD at the Data Link layer.

12.2. Which of the following is a SVC connection step?

- ● **Call setup between DTE devices**
- ● **Data transfer over temporary virtual circuit**
- ○ Data transfer over permanent virtual circuit
- ○ Idle period between data transfer sessions
- ● **Defined idle period before termination**
- ● **Switched virtual circuit termination**

12.3. Which of the following is a PVC connection step?

- ○ Call setup between DTE devices
- ○ Data transfer over temporary virtual circuit
- ● **Data transfer over permanent virtual circuit**
- ● **Idle period between data transfer sessions**
- ○ Defined idle period before termination
- ○ Switched virtual circuit termination

12.4. ISDN subscribers who require dedicated bandwidth can get a committed information rate (CIR) to have guaranteed bandwidth during busy time slots.

- ○ True
- ● **False** (This is true for Frame Relay subscribers, not ISDN.)

12.5. As DTE devices poll the network, LMI reports when a PVC is active or inactive.

- ● **True**
- ○ False

12.6. Which of the following is a Frame Relay LMI type?

- ● **Cisco**
- ● **Ansi**
- ● **Annex D**
- ● **Annex A**
- ○ DLCI

12.7 Which of the following commands is used for displaying Frame Relay protocol statistics?

- ○ `show interface`
- ○ `show frame-relay pvc`

○ show frame-relay lmi

● **show frame-relay traffic**

12.8. Which of the following commands is used for displaying Frame Relay DLCIs?

○ show interface

● **show frame-relay pvc**

○ show frame-relay lmi

○ show frame-relay traffic

12.9. Which of the following commands is used for displaying the Frame Relay encapsulation type?

● **show interface**

○ show frame-relay pvc

○ show frame-relay lmi

○ show frame-relay traffic

12.10. Which is the default encapsulation type on Cisco routers?

○ PPP

○ Frame Relay

● **HDLC**

○ LAPD

12.11. Which of these will negotiate Network layer protocol configuration and transmissions in PPP?

○ LCP

● **NCP**

○ LAPD

12.12. What does the ISDN U reference point identify?

○ The reference point between non-ISDN equipment and TA

○ The reference point between user terminals and an NT2

○ The reference point between NT1 and NT2 devices

● **The reference point between NT1 devices and line termination equipment**

12.13. What does the ISDN R reference point identify?

● **The reference point between non-ISDN equipment and TA**

○ The reference point between user terminals and an NT2

○ The reference point between NT1 and NT2 devices

○ The reference point between NT1 devices and line termination
equipment

12.14. What does the ISDN S reference point identify?

○ The reference point between non-ISDN equipment and TA

● **The reference point between user terminals and an NT2**

○ The reference point between NT1 and NT2 devices

○ The reference point between NT1 devices and line termination
equipment

12.15 Which of the following is a valid IPX extended access list?

● `access-list 900 permit any 10 all 30 all`

○ `access-list 800 permit any 10 all 30 all`

○ `ipx access-list 900 permit any 10 all 30 all`

12.16. Which of the following is a standard IPX access list that will allow the
matching packets from IPX network 35 to communicate with IPX network 40?

● `access-list 800 permit 35 40`

○ `ipx access-list 800 permit 35 40`

○ `access-list 800 permit 40 35`

○ `access-list 900 permit 35 40`

12.17. Which of the following is a valid IP standard access list?

○ `access-list 100 deny 192.168.1.55 0.0.0.0`

○ `access-list 75 deny host 192.168.1.55`

● `access-list 10 deny host 192.168.1.55`

12.18. Which of the following is an extended IP access list that will allow the
matching packets using the TCP protocol from any internal source to
access only 192.168.1.50, using only the Telnet service port?

● `access-list 100 permit tcp any host 192.168.1.50`
`eq telnet`

○ `access-list 99 permit tcp any host 192.168.1.50`
`eq 23`

○ `access-list 115 permit udp any host 192.168.1.50`
`eq telnet`

○ `access-list 50 permit tcp any host 192.168.1.50`
`any`

Appendix B

This appendix contains additional internetworking exam questions that have been contributed by the Web community to my Web site, www.TigerTools.net. Testing your proficiency with these questions will give you additional help in preparing for the Cisco Certified Network Associate and Professional certifications. The answers are in Appendix C. Good luck!

B.1. Select the two functions for the Logical Link Control (LLC) layer.

O To enable upper layers of the OSI model to gain independence from local area network (LAN) media access

O To allow service access point (SAP) interface sublayers to access upper-layer functions

O To provide data representation and code formatting

O To establish, maintain, and manage sessions between applications

B.2. There are seven layers to the Open Systems Interconnection (OSI) model. What functions are the responsibilities of the physical layer?

O Activate the physical link between systems

O Maintain the physical link between systems

O Segment and reassemble data into a data stream

O Determine the best way to move data from one place to another

B.3. Which statements are true about setting passwords on Cisco routers?

O Passwords are case-sensitive.

O Passwords are not case-sensitive.

O Passwords can be set on the individual interfaces and the privileged EXEC mode.

O Passwords can only be set from within the privileged EXEC mode.

B.4.   Which of the following best defines standards?

○ A set of rules or procedures that are widely used and/or officially specified

○ A connection of computers, printers, and other devices for purposes of communication

○ A set of rules that govern how computer workstations exchange information

○ A device connected to a computer to provide auxiliary functions

B.5.   In what order do most routers search for boot system commands?

○ First they look to NVRAM, then to Flash memory, and finally to a network alternative.

○ First they look to Flash, then to NVRAM, and finally to a network alternative.

○ First they look to the network, then to Flash memory, and finally to NVRAM.

○ First they look to the network, then to NVRAM, then to Flash.

B.6.   You are reviewing a consultant's design for your 10Base2, thin Ethernet network. The following distances are outlined:

Host A to Host B is 190 meters.
Host B to Host C is 160 meters.
Host C to Host D is 300 meters.

Which distances are too far according to the specification?

○ Host A to Host B

○ Host B to Host C

○ Host C to Host D

○ No answer is correct

B.7.   As described by the OSI model, how does data move across a network?

○ Directly from each layer at one computer to the corresponding layers at another computer

○ Through wires connecting each layer from computer to computer

○ Down through the layers at one computer and up through the layers in the other

○ Through layers in wires between computers

B.8. Which command will show you how the router is loading the software image?

O `show version`

O `show interfaces`

O `show controllers`

O `show bootstrap`

B.9. As a system administrator, you need to set a password on incoming Telnet sessions. Which command would you use?

O `line vty 0 4`

O `line console 0`

O `enable password`

O `enable telnet vty 0 4`

B.10. Which of the following describes the host layers of the OSI model?

O Control the physical delivery of messages over the network

O Make up the lower layers in the OSI model

O Contain data that is more like 1s and 0s than like human language

O Provide for accurate delivery of data between computers

B.11. Which best defines the function of the lower (media) layers of the OSI model?

O Provide for the accurate delivery of data between computers

O Convert data into the 1s and 0s that a computer understands

O Receive data from peripheral devices

O Control the physical delivery of messages over the network

B.12. Which layer of the OSI model provides connectivity and path selection between two end systems where routing occurs?

O Physical

O Data Link

O Network

O Transport

B.13. What analogy might be used to describe encapsulation?

O Like a blueprint for building a car

O Like sending a package through the mail

O Like building a fence around your backyard

O Like driving a car to the store to buy groceries

B.14. Cisco Discovery Protocol (CDP) can discover any directly connected routers. On which OSI model layer does it work?

○ Data Link

○ Physical

○ Network

○ Session

○ Presentation

B.15. Which network layer protocol is used to map the MAC address to the network address?

○ ARP

○ DNS

○ WINS

○ TCP/IP

B.16. Which three activities need to happen before data can be transferred in a connection-oriented session?

○ Synchronization

○ Connection negotiation

○ Acknowledgment

○ Presentation

○ Sectoring

B.17. Which statements are true about a MAC address?

○ It is often called a BIA, for burned-in-address.

○ It is made up of 12 hexadecimal bits.

○ It is made up of 24 hexadecimal bits.

○ 000.0c12.3456 is an example of a MAC address.

○ The first six hexadecimal digits are known as the Organizational Unique Identifier (OUI).

B.18. You have typed in *enable password Cisco* at the global configuration prompt. What did this command accomplish?

○ It set "Cisco" as the password to the privileged EXEC mode.

○ It set "Cisco" as the password for any incoming Telnet sessions.

○ It set "Cisco" as the password for the console terminal.

○ It set "Cisco" as the password for all access.

B.19. Which of the following best defines encapsulation?

O Segmenting data so it will flow uninterrupted through the network

O Compressing data so it will move faster

O Moving data in groups so it will stay together

O Wrapping data in a particular protocol header

B.20. Which layer of the OSI model establishes, manages, and terminates sessions between applications and manages data exchange between Presentation layer entities?

O Transport

O Session

O Presentation

O Application

B.21. You are reviewing a consultant's design for your 10Base5, thick Ethernet network. The following distances are outlined:

Host A to Host B is 190 meters.
Host B to Host C is 160 meters.
Host C to Host D is 300 meters.
Host D to Host E is 600 meters.

Which distances are too far according to the specification?

O Host A to Host B

O Host B to Host C

O Host C to Host D

O Host D to Host E

B.22. What will the show flash command tell you about the router?

O Total amount of memory

O Available memory

O Name of system image file

O Available interfaces

O IOS version

B.23. Routers can be configured using several sources. Which of the following sources can be used?

O Console port

O Virtual terminals

O TFTP server

O Floppy disk

B.24. The IEEE subdivided the Data Link layer to provide for environments that need connectionless or connection-oriented services. What are the two layers called?

O MAC

O LLC

O Physical

O Session

O IP

B.25. Which OSI model layer enables different applications to share a connection by adding extra bits that give the message type, originating program, and protocols used?

O Transport

O Presentation

O Application

O Session

O Network

B.26. Which is the best definition of encapsulation?

O Each layer of the OSI model uses encapsulation to put the protocol data unit (PDU) from the upper layer into its Data field. It adds header and trailer information that is available to its counterpart on the system that will receive it.

O Data always needs to be tunneled to its destination; therefore, encapsulation must be used.

O Each layer of the OSI model uses compression to put the PDU from the upper layer into its Data field. It adds header and trailer information that is available to its counterpart on the system that will receive it.

O Each layer of the OSI model uses encryption to put the PDU from the upper layer into its Data field. It adds header and trailer information that is available to its counterpart on the system that will receive it.

B.27. Select the Data Link protocols.

O Dial-on-Demand

O SDLC

O PPP

O V.24

B.28.   Which layer of the OSI model identifies and establishes the availability of intended communication partners, synchronizes cooperating applications, and establishes agreement on procedures for error recovery and control of data integrity?

○ Transport

○ Session

○ Presentation

○ Application

B. 29.   How do you cause a router to enter Setup mode?

○ Type "`setup`" at the `Router#` prompt.

○ If the router is new or if NVRAM is corrupted, the router will automatically enter Setup mode.

○ The router is always in Setup mode.

○ You can't force the router to enter Setup mode.

B.30.   Put the following fields into order for an Ethernet frame. (*Note*: Not all of the fields belong to the Ethernet frame.)

FCS
Type
Data
Preamble
SA
DA
Length
802.2 Header and Data

○ Preamble, DA, SA, Type, Data, FCS

○ Preamble, DA, SA, Length, 802.2 Header and Data, FCS

○ Preamble, SA, DA, Length, Type, Data, FCS

○ Preamble, DA, SA, Type, 802.2 Header and Data, FCS

B.31.   Which of the following is a responsibility of the Session layer?

○ PICT, TIFF, and JPEG formats

○ SQL

○ NFS

○ RPC

○ ASP

B.32. Select the true statements.

    ○ The Data Link layer is concerned with frames, whereas the Physical layer is concerned with bits, signals, and clocking.

    ○ The Physical layer is concerned with frames, whereas the Data Link layer is concerned with bits, signals, and clocking.

    ○ EIA/TIA-232 standardizes a physical connection to voice-grade access.

    ○ EIA/TIA-232 standardizes a physical connection to data-grade access.

B.33. The physical media that support which of the following can connect CDP devices?

    ○ SNAP

    ○ TCP/IP

    ○ Novell IPX

    ○ AppleTalk

B.34. Which layer of the OSI model ensures that information sent by the Application layer of one system will be readable by the Application layer of another system, is concerned with the data structures used by programs, and negotiates data transfer syntax for the Application layer?

    ○ Transport

    ○ Session

    ○ Presentation

    ○ Application

B. 35. Once data transfer is initiated between two hosts, congestion can occur. What are two reasons for congestion?

    ○ A high-speed computer might be able to generate traffic faster than the network can transfer it.

    ○ When datagrams arrive at a host or gateway too quickly to process, they are stored in memory temporarily. The host or gateway can fill its memory so that it can accept no more datagrams.

    ○ Different applications can saturate the bandwidth with larger segments than the network can handle.

    ○ Some applications are written with less reliability than others.

B.36. You need to provide backup methods for your Cisco router so that it will always look to your tftp server for boot system options. The following show the router prompts and commands. Which selection will cause the router to boot from the tftp server?

O Method 1:
```
Router#configure terminal
Router(config)#boot system tftp test.exe 172.16.13.111
[Ctrl-Z]
Router#copy running-config startup-config
```

O Method 2:
```
Router#configure terminal
Router(config)#boot system flash c2500-js-1
[Ctrl-Z]
Router#copy running-config startup-config
```

O Method 3:
```
Router#configure terminal
Router(config)#boot system rom
[Ctrl-Z]
Router#copy running-config startup-config
```

O Method 4:
```
Router#configure terminal
Router(config)#boot system test.exe 172.16.13.111
[Ctrl-Z]
Router#copy running-config startup-config
```

B.37. How do you find out information about other CDP devices that are connected to you?

O Type show cdp neighbors at the Router# prompt.

O Type show cdp devices at the Router# prompt.

O Type show cdp at the Router# prompt.

O Type show cdp neighbors at the Router(config)# prompt.

B.38. Which of the following best describes the purpose of the Physical layer?

O Defines the electrical, mechanical, procedural, and functional specifications for activating, maintaining, and deactivating the link between end systems

O Provides reliable transit of data across a physical link

O Provides connectivity and path selection between two end systems

O Establishes, manages, and terminates sessions between applications, and manages data exchange between Presentation layer entities

B.39.   The Data Link layer provides which network functions?

O Physical transmission across the medium

O Error notification

O Network topology

O Flow control

O Device addressing

B.40.   You are working with graphic translations. Which layer of the OSI model is responsible for code formatting and conversion and graphic standards?

O Presentation

O Session

O Transport

O Network

B.41.   Which layer of the OSI model is concerned with physical addressing, network topology, line discipline, error notification, ordered delivery of frames, and flow control?

O Physical

O Data Link

O Transport

O Network

B.42.   At the console terminal, you type:

```
Router#show interface serial 1
```

You receive the following as part of the output:

```
Serial1 is up, line protocol is down
```

What could cause this? Select all that apply.

O There are no keep alives.

O There is no clock rate.

O There is a wrong connector.

O In a back-to-back connection, the other end of the connection is administratively down.

O The cable is disconnected.

B.43.   You need to disable CDP on your router. How would you do this?

O Type no cdp run at the Router(config)# prompt.

O Type no cdp run at the Router(config-if)# prompt.

○ Type no cdp enable at the Router(config)# prompt.

○ Type no cdp run at the Router(config)# prompt.

B.44. You need to disable CDP on a specific router interface. How would you do this?

○ Type no cdp run at the Router(config)# prompt.

○ Type no cdp run at the Router(config-if)# prompt.

○ Type no cdp enable at the Router(config)# prompt.

○ Type no cdp run at the Router(config)# prompt.

B.45. Which high-speed Ethernet option has a MAC layer that is not compatible with the 802.3 MAC layer?

○ 100VG-AnyLAN

○ 100BaseFX

○ 100BaseT4

○ 100BaseTX

B.46. What is the purpose of a MAC address in a network environment?

○ MAC addresses will help the Application layer to provide needed network services.

○ MAC addresses are used to implement security procedures.

○ MAC addresses are implemented in non-Frame Relay networks only.

○ MAC addresses are used to locate specific ports in the network.

○ MAC addresses provide modulation access control.

B.47. A Cisco router uses which letter to indicate an Ethernet interface?

○ E

○ S

○ Et

○ St

B.48. A Cisco router provides many editing shortcuts. Which shortcut would you use to move to the beginning of a line?

○ Ctrl-A

○ Ctrl-E

○ Esc-B

○ Ctrl-F

B. 49. Which layer of the OSI model is responsible for reliable network communication between end nodes and provides mechanisms for the establishment, maintenance, and termination of virtual circuits; transport fault detection and recovery; and information flow control?

○ Physical

○ Data Link

○ Network

○ Transport

B.50. Which statements are true about the Network layer of the OSI model?

○ Manages device addressing

○ Tracks the location of devices on the network

○ Determines the best way to move data from one place to another

○ Segments and reassembles data into a data stream

○ Handles error notification control

B.51. A user is downloading data from an online service (a bulletin board system, BBS) through a dial-in connection. After the download, the file will not execute because some of the data became corrupted. On which layer of the OSI model did the corruption get overlooked?

○ Data Link

○ Physical

○ Network

○ Application

B.52. You are a network administrator investigating some data transmission problems. On running a network monitor, you determine that some TCP segments have not been formatted correctly. Which layer of the OSI model is responsible for the formation of segments?

○ Transport

○ Network

○ Data Link

○ Physical

○ Session

B.53. You are working in a word processing program that is run from the file server. Your data comes back to you in an unintelligible form. Which layer of the OSI model would you investigate?

   O Presentation

   O Application

   O Session

   O Network

   O Data Link

B.54. You need to retrieve a file from the file server for your word processing application. Which layer of the OSI model is responsible for this function?

   O Application

   O Presentation

   O Session

   O Transport

   O Data Link

B.55. Which of the following accurately describes the OSI model?

   O A conceptual framework that specifies how information travels through networks

   O A model that describes how data makes its way from one application program to another through a network

   O A conceptual framework that specifies which network functions occur at each layer

   O All of the above

B.56. Which of these applications are internetworking applications?

   O Electronic Data Interchange

   O World Wide Web with browsers

   O Email gateways

   O Eudora

   O Simple Network Management Protocol (SNMP)

B.57. Which field in the LLC header points to a memory buffer on the receiving station?

   O DSAP

   O SSAP

○ CTRL

○ OUI

○ Ether Type

B.58. Which is the IEEE specification for Token Ring?

○ 802.5

○ 802.3

○ 802.4

○ 802.10

B.59. An MSAU (multistation access unit) can connect up to how many Token Ring stations?

○ 8

○ 14

○ 20

○ 28

B.60. What is the Transport layer of the OSI model responsible for?

○ Segmenting and reassembling data into a data stream

○ Error notification, network topology, and flow control

○ Device addressing

○ Establishment, maintenance, and management of sessions between applications

○ Activating and maintaining the physical link between systems

B.61. What are data packets?

○ Logically grouped units of information

○ Transmission devices

○ Auxiliary function provided by peripherals

○ Virtual circuits

B.62. CDP, by default, is set to discard CDP packets from other routers after 180 seconds. You have a network that has frequent changes to the router configuration files. What should you do to have the routers update more quickly?

○ Configure the CDP hold time to be less than that on the CDP timer

○ Configure the CDP hold time to be more than that on the CDP timer

○ Configure the CDP hold time to equal that on the CDP timer

○ Type no CDP holdtime

B.63. You have decreased the CDP time to 30 seconds. What impact will this have on your network?

○ Router updates will be quicker.

○ Bandwidth usage will increase.

○ Bandwidth usage will decrease.

○ Router updates will be slower.

B.64. What is the correct prompt and command to configure the CDP timer?

○ cdp timer [seconds] at the Router# prompt

○ cdp timer [seconds] at the Router(config)# prompt

○ cdp holdtime [seconds] at the Router# prompt

○ cdp timer [seconds] at the Router(config-if)# prompt

B.65. When Host A on the same subnet needs the address of another host, Host B, it broadcasts a request that is answered by Host B, which provides its own MAC address. What happens when the two hosts are separated into two separate subnets by a router?

○ The router replies to Host A with the MAC address of Host B.

○ The router listens for the broadcast and returns its own address. The first host then sends data to the router, which sends it on to the second host.

○ The router forwards the broadcast on to the second subnet so that Host B can answer the request itself.

B.66. A user calls you saying that he or she can't connect to the network. When you investigate, all other users in the caller's office are connecting. You suspect that there is a problem with the NIC or the cable running to the wall. At which layer of the OSI model is the problem occurring?

○ Physical

○ Data Link

○ Network

○ Transport

○ Session

B.67. As a network system administrator, you are installing a new router. The first two tasks that you want to do are to configure a name for the router and to add a message that will greet other administrators when they log on. The name of the router is ABC1, and the message is "Only authorized users can use this system!" Which two commands would you use?

O `hostname ABC1`

O `name router ABC1`

O `router ABC1`

O `banner motd # Only authorized users can use this system! #`

O `banner message # Only authorized users can use this system! #`

B.68. Which Ethernet standard is usually connected to a hub?

O 10BaseT

O 10Base2

O 10Base5

O 10Base1

B.69. You have enabled password encryption with the `service password-encryption` command. You now need to disable it. Which command do you use?

O `no service password-encryption`

O `no service password`

O `no service password encryption`

O `no password`

B.70. You have loaded all of your configuration files on to your router. When you restart the router, the configuration is not what you had planned. What could have caused this problem?

O Insufficient flash memory on the router.

O Inadequate processor speeds on the network server.

O Inadequate bandwidth on the network.

O You switched off and on the wrong router.

Appendix C

This appendix contains the answers to the questions found in Appendix B.

B.1. Select the two functions for the Logical Link Control (LLC) layer.

- **To enable upper layers of the OSI model to gain independence from local area network (LAN) media access**
- **To allow service access point (SAP) interface sublayers to access upper-layer functions**
- ○ To provide data representation and code formatting
- ○ To establish, maintain, and manage sessions between applications

B.2. There are seven layers to the Open Systems Interconnection (OSI) model. What functions are the responsibilities of the physical layer?

- **Activate the physical link between systems**
- **Maintain the physical link between systems**
- ○ Segment and reassemble data into a data stream
- ○ Determine the best way to move data from one place to another

B.3. Which statements are true about setting passwords on Cisco routers?

- **Passwords are case-sensitive.**
- ○ Passwords are not case-sensitive.
- ○ Passwords can be set on the individual interfaces and the privileged EXEC mode.
- ○ Passwords can only be set from within the privileged EXEC mode.

B.4. Which of the following best defines standards?

● **A set of rules or procedures that are widely used and/or officially specified**

○ A connection of computers, printers, and other devices for purposes of communication

○ A set of rules that govern how computer workstations exchange information

○ A device connected to a computer to provide auxiliary functions

B.5. In what order do most routers search for boot system commands?

● **First they look to NVRAM, then to Flash memory, and finally to a network alternative.**

○ First they look to Flash, then to NVRAM, and finally to a network alternative.

○ First they look to the network, then to Flash memory, and finally to NVRAM.

○ First they look to the network, then to NVRAM, then to Flash.

B.6. You are reviewing a consultant's design for your 10Base2, thin Ethernet network. The following distances are outlined:

Host A to Host B is 190 meters.

Host B to Host C is 160 meters.

Host C to Host D is 300 meters.

Which distances are too far according to the specification?

● **Host A to Host B**

○ Host B to Host C

● **Host C to Host D**

○ No answer is correct

B.7. As described by the OSI model, how does data move across a network?

○ Directly from each layer at one computer to the corresponding layers at another computer

○ Through wires connecting each layer from computer to computer

● **Down through the layers at one computer and up through the layers in the other**

○ Through layers in wires between computers

B.8. Which command will show you how the router is loading the software image?

● `show version`

○ `show interfaces`

○ `show controllers`

○ `show bootstrap`

B.9. As a system administrator, you need to set a password on incoming Telnet sessions. Which command would you use?

● `line vty 0 4`

○ `line console 0`

○ `enable password`

○ `enable telnet vty 0 4`

B.10. Which of the following describes the host layers of the OSI model?

○ Control the physical delivery of messages over the network

○ Make up the lower layers in the OSI model

○ Contain data that is more like 1s and 0s than like human language

● **Provide for accurate delivery of data between computers**

B.11. Which best defines the function of the lower (media) layers of the OSI model?

○ Provide for the accurate delivery of data between computers

○ Convert data into the 1s and 0s that a computer understands

○ Receive data from peripheral devices

● **Control the physical delivery of messages over the network**

B.12. Which layer of the OSI model provides connectivity and path selection between two end systems where routing occurs?

○ Physical

○ Data Link

● **Network**

○ Transport

B.13. What analogy might be used to describe encapsulation?

○ Like a blueprint for building a car

● **Like sending a package through the mail**

○ Like building a fence around your backyard

○ Like driving a car to the store to buy groceries

B.14. Cisco Discovery Protocol (CDP) can discover any directly connected routers. On which OSI model layer does it work?

● **Data Link**

○ Physical

○ Network

○ Session

○ Presentation

B.15. Which network layer protocol is used to map the MAC address to the network address?

● **ARP**

○ DNS

○ WINS

○ TCP/IP

B.16. Which three activities need to happen before data can be transferred in a connection-oriented session?

● **Synchronization**

● **Connection negotiation**

● **Acknowledgment**

○ Presentation

○ Sectoring

B.17. Which statements are true about a MAC address?

○ It is often called a BIA, for burned-in-address.

○ It is made up of 12 hexadecimal bits.

○ It is made up of 24 hexadecimal bits.

○ 000.0c12.3456 is an example of a MAC address.

● **The first six hexadecimal digits are known as the Organizational Unique Identifier (OUI).**

B.18. You have typed in *enable password Cisco* at the global configuration prompt. What did this command accomplish?

● **It set "Cisco" as the password to the privileged EXEC mode.**

○ It set "Cisco" as the password for any incoming Telnet sessions.

○ It set "Cisco" as the password for the console terminal.

○ It set "Cisco" as the password for all access.

B.19. Which of the following best defines encapsulation?

   ○ Segmenting data so it will flow uninterrupted through the network

   ○ Compressing data so it will move faster

   ○ Moving data in groups so it will stay together

   ● **Wrapping data in a particular protocol header**

B.20. Which layer of the OSI model establishes, manages, and terminates sessions between applications and manages data exchange between Presentation layer entities?

   ○ Transport

   ● **Session**

   ○ Presentation

   ○ Application

B.21. You are reviewing a consultant's design for your 10Base5, thick Ethernet network. The following distances are outlined:

   Host A to Host B is 190 meters.
   Host B to Host C is 160 meters.
   Host C to Host D is 300 meters.
   Host D to Host E is 600 meters.

   Which distances are too far according to the specification?

   ○ Host A to Host B

   ○ Host B to Host C

   ○ Host C to Host D

   ● **Host D to Host E**

B.22. What will the show flash command tell you about the router?

   ● **Total amount of memory**

   ● **Available memory**

   ● **Name of system image file**

   ○ Available interfaces

   ○ IOS version

B.23. Routers can be configured using several sources. Which of the following sources can be used?

   ● **Console port**

   ● **Virtual terminals**

   ● **TFTP server**

   ○ Floppy disk

B.24. The IEEE subdivided the Data Link layer to provide for environments that need connectionless or connection-oriented services. What are the two layers called?

- ● **MAC**
- ● **LLC**
- ○ Physical
- ○ Session
- ○ IP

B.25. Which OSI model layer enables different applications to share a connection by adding extra bits that give the message type, originating program, and protocols used?

- ● **Transport**
- ○ Presentation
- ○ Application
- ○ Session
- ○ Network

B.26. Which is the best definition of encapsulation?

- ● **Each layer of the OSI model uses encapsulation to put the protocol data unit (PDU) from the upper layer into its Data field. It adds header and trailer information that is available to its counterpart on the system that will receive it.**
- ○ Data always needs to be tunneled to its destination; therefore, encapsulation must be used.
- ○ Each layer of the OSI model uses compression to put the PDU from the upper layer into its Data field. It adds header and trailer information that is available to its counterpart on the system that will receive it.
- ○ Each layer of the OSI model uses encryption to put the PDU from the upper layer into its Data field. It adds header and trailer information that is available to its counterpart on the system that will receive it.

B.27. Select the Data Link protocols.

- ● **Dial-on-Demand**
- ● **SDLC**
- ● **PPP**
- ○ V.24

B.28. Which layer of the OSI model identifies and establishes the availability of intended communication partners, synchronizes cooperating applications, and establishes agreement on procedures for error recovery and control of data integrity?

O Transport

O Session

O Presentation

● **Application**

B. 29. How do you cause a router to enter Setup mode?

● **Type "setup" at the Router# prompt.**

● **If the router is new or if NVRAM is corrupted, the router will automatically enter Setup mode.**

O The router is always in Setup mode.

O You can't force the router to enter Setup mode.

B.30. Put the following fields into order for an Ethernet frame. (*Note:* Not all of the fields belong to the Ethernet frame.)

>   FCS
>   Type
>   Data
>   Preamble
>   SA
>   DA
>   Length
>   802.2 Header and Data

● **Preamble, DA, SA, Type, Data, FCS**

O Preamble, DA, SA, Length, 802.2 Header and Data, FCS

O Preamble, SA, DA, Length, Type, Data, FCS

O Preamble, DA, SA, Type, 802.2 Header and Data, FCS

B.31. Which of the following is a responsibility of the Session layer?

O PICT, TIFF, and JPEG formats

● **SQL**

● **NFS**

● **RPC**

● **ASP**

B.32. Select the true statements.

● **The Data Link layer is concerned with frames, whereas the Physical layer is concerned with bits, signals, and clocking.**

○ The Physical layer is concerned with frames, whereas the Data Link layer is concerned with bits, signals, and clocking.

● **EIA/TIA-232 standardizes a physical connection to voice-grade access.**

○ EIA/TIA-232 standardizes a physical connection to data-grade access.

B.33. The physical media that support which of the following can connect CDP devices?

● **SNAP**

○ TCP/IP

○ Novell IPX

○ AppleTalk

B.34. Which layer of the OSI model ensures that information sent by the Application layer of one system will be readable by the Application layer of another system, is concerned with the data structures used by programs, and negotiates data transfer syntax for the Application layer?

○ Transport

○ Session

● **Presentation**

○ Application

B. 35. Once data transfer is initiated between two hosts, congestion can occur. What are two reasons for congestion?

● **A high-speed computer might be able to generate traffic faster than the network can transfer it.**

● **When datagrams arrive at a host or gateway too quickly to process, they are stored in memory temporarily. The host or gateway can fill its memory so that it can accept no more datagrams.**

○ Different applications can saturate the bandwidth with larger segments than the network can handle.

○ Some applications are written with less reliability than others.

B.36. You need to provide backup methods for your Cisco router so that it will always look to your tftp server for boot system options. The following show the router prompts and commands. Which selection will cause the router to boot from the tftp server?

● **Method 1:**

```
Router#configure terminal
Router(config)#boot system tftp test.exe 172.16.13.111
[Ctrl-Z]
Router#copy running-config startup-config
```

○ Method 2:

```
Router#configure terminal
Router(config)#boot system flash c2500-js-1
[Ctrl-Z]
Router#copy running-config startup-config
```

○ Method 3:

```
Router#configure terminal
Router(config)#boot system rom
[Ctrl-Z]
Router#copy running-config startup-config
```

○ Method 4:

```
Router#configure terminal
Router(config)#boot system test.exe 172.16.13.111
[Ctrl-Z]
Router#copy running-config startup-config
```

B.37. How do you find out information about other CDP devices that are connected to you?

● **Type show cdp neighbors at the Router# prompt.**

○ Type show cdp devices at the Router# prompt.

○ Type show cdp at the Router# prompt.

○ Type show cdp neighbors at the Router(config)# prompt.

B.38. Which of the following best describes the purpose of the Physical layer?

● **Defines the electrical, mechanical, procedural, and functional specifications for activating, maintaining, and deactivating the link between end systems**

○ Provides reliable transit of data across a physical link

○ Provides connectivity and path selection between two end systems

○ Establishes, manages, and terminates sessions between applications, and manages data exchange between Presentation layer entities

B.39. The Data Link layer provides which network functions?

- ● **Physical transmission across the medium**
- ● **Error notification**
- ● **Network topology**
- ● **Flow control**
- ○ Device addressing

B.40. You are working with graphic translations. Which layer of the OSI model is responsible for code formatting and conversion and graphic standards?

- ● **Presentation**
- ○ Session
- ○ Transport
- ○ Network

B.41. Which layer of the OSI model is concerned with physical addressing, network topology, line discipline, error notification, ordered delivery of frames, and flow control?

- ○ Physical
- ● **Data Link**
- ○ Transport
- ○ Network

B.42. At the console terminal, you type:

```
Router#show interface serial 1
```

You receive the following as part of the output:

```
Serial1 is up, line protocol is down
```

What could cause this? Select all that apply.

- ● **There are no keep alives.**
- ● **There is no clock rate.**
- ● **There is a wrong connector.**
- ● **In a back-to-back connection, the other end of the connection is administratively down.**
- ○ The cable is disconnected.

B.43. You need to disable CDP on your router. How would you do this?

- ● **Type no cdp run at the Router(config)# prompt.**
- ○ Type no cdp run at the Router(config-if)# prompt.

○ Type no cdp enable at the Router(config)# prompt.

○ Type no cdp run at the Router(config)# prompt.

B.44. You need to disable CDP on a specific router interface. How would you do this?

○ Type no cdp run at the Router(config)# prompt.

○ Type no cdp run at the Router(config-if)# prompt.

● **Type no cdp enable at the Router(config)# prompt.**

○ Type no cdp run at the Router(config)# prompt.

B.45. Which high-speed Ethernet option has a MAC layer that is not compatible with the 802.3 MAC layer?

● **100VG-AnyLAN**

○ 100BaseFX

○ 100BaseT4

○ 100BaseTX

B.46. What is the purpose of a MAC address in a network environment?

○ MAC addresses will help the Application layer to provide needed network services.

○ MAC addresses are used to implement security procedures.

○ MAC addresses are implemented in non-Frame Relay networks only.

● **MAC addresses are used to locate specific ports in the network.**

○ MAC addresses provide modulation access control.

B.47. A Cisco router uses which letter to indicate an Ethernet interface?

● **E**

○ S

○ Et

○ St

B.48. A Cisco router provides many editing shortcuts. Which shortcut would you use to move to the beginning of a line?

● **Ctrl-A**

○ Ctrl-E

○ Esc-B

○ Ctrl-F

B. 49. Which layer of the OSI model is responsible for reliable network communication between end nodes and provides mechanisms for the establishment, maintenance, and termination of virtual circuits; transport fault detection and recovery; and information flow control?

○ Physical

○ Data Link

○ Network

● **Transport**

B.50. Which statements are true about the Network layer of the OSI model?

● **Manages device addressing**

● **Tracks the location of devices on the network**

● **Determines the best way to move data from one place to another**

○ Segments and reassembles data into a data stream

○ Handles error notification control

B.51. A user is downloading data from an online service (a bulletin board system, BBS) through a dial-in connection. After the download, the file will not execute because some of the data became corrupted. On which layer of the OSI model did the corruption get overlooked?

● **Data Link**

○ Physical

○ Network

○ Application

B.52. You are a network administrator investigating some data transmission problems. On running a network monitor, you determine that some TCP segments have not been formatted correctly. Which layer of the OSI model is responsible for the formation of segments?

● **Transport**

○ Network

○ Data Link

○ Physical

○ Session

B.53. You are working in a word processing program that is run from the file server. Your data comes back to you in an unintelligible form. Which layer of the OSI model would you investigate?

○ Presentation

● **Application**

○ Session

○ Network

○ Data Link

B.54. You need to retrieve a file from the file server for your word processing application. Which layer of the OSI model is responsible for this function?

● **Application**

○ Presentation

○ Session

○ Transport

○ Data Link

B.55. Which of the following accurately describes the OSI model?

○ A conceptual framework that specifies how information travels through networks

○ A model that describes how data makes its way from one application program to another through a network

○ A conceptual framework that specifies which network functions occur at each layer

● **All of the above**

B.56. Which of these applications are internetworking applications?

● **Electronic Data Interchange**

● **World Wide Web with browsers**

● **Email gateways**

○ Eudora

○ Simple Network Management Protocol (SNMP)

B.57. Which field in the LLC header points to a memory buffer on the receiving station?

● **DSAP**

○ SSAP

○ CTRL

○ OUI

○ Ether Type

B.58. Which is the IEEE specification for Token Ring?

● **802.5**

○ 802.3

○ 802.4

○ 802.10

B.59. An MSAU (multistation access unit) can connect up to how many Token Ring stations?

● **8**

○ 14

○ 20

○ 28

B.60. What is the Transport layer of the OSI model responsible for?

● **Segmenting and reassembling data into a data stream**

○ Error notification, network topology, and flow control

○ Device addressing

○ Establishment, maintenance, and management of sessions between applications

○ Activating and maintaining the physical link between systems

B.61. What are data packets?

● **Logically grouped units of information**

○ Transmission devices

○ Auxiliary function provided by peripherals

○ Virtual circuits

B.62. CDP, by default, is set to discard CDP packets from other routers after 180 seconds. You have a network that has frequent changes to the router configuration files. What should you do to have the routers update more quickly?

● **Configure the CDP hold time to be less than that on the CDP timer**

○ Configure the CDP hold time to be more than that on the CDP timer

○ Configure the CDP hold time to equal that on the CDP timer

○ Type no CDP holdtime

B.63. You have decreased the CDP time to 30 seconds. What impact will this have on your network?

● **Router updates will be quicker.**

● **Bandwidth usage will increase.**

○ Bandwidth usage will decrease.

○ Router updates will be slower.

B.64. What is the correct prompt and command to configure the CDP timer?

○ cdp timer [seconds] at the Router# prompt

○ cdp timer [seconds] at the Router(config)# prompt

○ cdp holdtime [seconds] at the Router# prompt

● **cdp timer [seconds] at the Router(config-if)# prompt**

B.65. When Host A on the same subnet needs the address of another host, Host B, it broadcasts a request that is answered by Host B, which provides its own MAC address. What happens when the two hosts are separated into two separate subnets by a router?

○ The router replies to Host A with the MAC address of Host B.

● **The router listens for the broadcast and returns its own address. The first host then sends data to the router, which sends it on to the second host.**

○ The router forwards the broadcast on to the second subnet so that Host B can answer the request itself.

B.66. A user calls you saying that he or she can't connect to the network. When you investigate, all other users in the caller's office are connecting. You suspect that there is a problem with the NIC or the cable running to the wall. At which layer of the OSI model is the problem occurring?

● **Physical**

○ Data Link

○ Network

○ Transport

○ Session

B.67.   As a network system administrator, you are installing a new router. The first two tasks that you want to do are to configure a name for the router and to add a message that will greet other administrators when they log on. The name of the router is ABC1, and the message is "Only authorized users can use this system!" Which two commands would you use?

● `hostname ABC1`

○ `name router ABC1`

○ `router ABC1`

● `banner motd # Only authorized users can use this system! #`

○ `banner message # Only authorized users can use this system! #`

B.68.   Which Ethernet standard is usually connected to a hub?

● **10BaseT**

○ 10Base2

○ 10Base5

○ 10Base1

B.69.   You have enabled password encryption with the `service password-encryption` command. You now need to disable it. Which command do you use?

● `no service password-encryption`

○ `no service password`

○ `no service password encryption`

○ `no password`

B.70.   You have loaded all of your configuration files on to your router. When you restart the router, the configuration is not what you had planned. What could have caused this problem?

● **Insufficient flash memory on the router.**

○ Inadequate processor speeds on the network server.

○ Inadequate bandwidth on the network.

○ You switched off and on the wrong router.

References

Callon, R., RFC2185, "Routing Aspects of IPv6 Transition," September 1997.

Carpenter, B., RFC1671, "IPng: White Paper on Transition and Other Considerations," August 1994.

Carpenter, B., RFC2529, "Transmission of IPv6 over IPv4 Domains without Explicit Tunnels," March 1999.

Clark, K., and K. Hamilton, "Cisco LAN Switching," Indianapolis, IN: Cisco Press, 1999

Deering, S., RFC2460, "Internet Protocol, Version 6 (IPv6) Specification," December 1998.

Gilligan, R., RFC1933, "Transition Mechanisms for IPv6 Hosts and Routers," April 1996.

Hiden, Robert, "History of the IPng Effort," www.huygens.org/~dillema/ietf/doc/history.html, referred October 15,1999.

Hinden, R., RFC1517-RFC1519, "Classless Inter-Domain Routing," September 1993.

Information Sciences Institute, RFC791, "Internet Protocol," September 1981.

Internet Engineering Task Force (IETF), IPSec Working Group, www.ietf.org/html.charters/ipsec-charter.html, IETF.

Internet Software Consortium, www.isc.org/ds/WWW-9907/report.html, referred November 22, 1999.

Kent, S., RFC2402, "IP Authentication Header," November 1998.

Kent, S., RFC2406, "IP Encapsulating Security Payload," November 1998.

Lewis, C., "Cisco TCP/IP Routing Professional Reference," New York: Mc-Graw-Hill, 1997.

Narten, T., RFC2461, "Neighbor Discovery in IPv6," December 1998.

Postel, J., RFC801, "NCP/TCP Transition Plan," November 1981.

Postel, J., RFC 768, "User Datagram Protocol, STD 6," USC/Information Sciences Institute, August 1980.

Postel, J., ed., RFC 793, "Transmission Control Protocol—DARPA—Internet Program Protocol Specification," STD 7, USC/Information Sciences Institute, September 1981.

"Problem Areas for the IP Security Protocol," in *Proceedings of the Sixth Usenix UNIX Security Symposium*, 1996.

Spafford, G., and S. Garfinkel, *Practical UNIX and Internet Security*, 2nd Edition, Sebastopol, CA: O'Reilly & Associates, 1996.

Spafford, G., and S. Garfinkel, *Web Security & Commerce*, Sebastopol, CA: O'Reilly & Associates, 1997.

Index